International Commercial Agreements

INTERNATIONAL COMMERCIAL AGREEMENTS
An Edinburgh Law Guide

Michala Meiselles

EDINBURGH
University Press

To Hanna Levi-Meiselles (1947–2006): you inspired and inspire

© Michala Meiselles, 2013

Edinburgh University Press Ltd
22 George Square, Edinburgh EH8 9LF
www.euppublishing.com

Typeset in 10/12pt Ehrhardt MT Pro by
Servis Filmsetting Ltd, Stockport, Cheshire, and
printed and bound in Great Britain by
CPI Group (UK) Ltd, Croydon CR0 4YY

A CIP record for this book is available from the British Library

ISBN 978 0 7486 7903 4 (hardback)
ISBN 978 0 7486 7904 1 (paperback)
ISBN 978 0 7486 7905 8 (webready PDF)
ISBN 978 0 7486 7906 5 (epub)

The right of Michala Meiselles to be identified as author of this work has been asserted in accordance with the Copyright, Designs and Patents Act 1988.

Contents

Acknowledgements	x
Table of Cases	xi
Table of Statutes	xiv
Preface	xix
Guide to the Book	xxi

1 Planning an International Commercial Agreement — 1
Contents — 1
Overview — 1
Glossary — 1
   I   Form of international commercial agreements — 3
   II   Subject matter of the contract — 4
   III   Parties contracting — 4
   IV   Trade barriers — 5
   V   Implied terms — 8
   VI   Adaption of the contract — 10
   VII   Renegotiation of terms — 11
   VIII   Dispute resolution — 12
   IX   Researching local law — 18
   X   Available entry strategies — 25
Summary — 27
Useful links — 27
Further reading — 27
Notes — 28

2 Drafting an International Commercial Agreement — 35
Contents — 35
Overview — 35
Glossary — 35
   I   Freedom of contract — 36
   II   Legality — 37
   III   International instruments — 37
   IV   Dispute resolution — 37
   V   Choice of law in international agreements — 39

VI	Requirements relating to the form of the contract		43
VII	Missing or vague terms		43
VIII	Defined terms		43
IX	Language of contract		44
X	Checklist of provisions		46
XI	Structure		47
XII	Front of the contract		48
XIII	Body of the contract		53
XIV	Boilerplate clauses		55
XV	Back of the contract		60
Summary			63
Useful links			63
Further reading			63
Notes			63

3 International Sales Agreements — 68

Contents — 68
Overview — 68
Glossary — 68

I	The law applicable to a sales agreement	69
II	International law applicable to international sales of goods	70
III	English law governing international sales of goods	70
IV	Trade terms	75
V	Incoterms®	75
VI	Trade terms under English law	76
VII	Checklist of provisions	82
VIII	Front of the contract	83
IX	Body of the contract	83
X	Boilerplate clauses	102
XI	Back of the contract	102

Summary — 103
Useful links — 103
Further reading — 103
Notes — 104

4 International Distribution Agreements — 112

Contents — 112
Overview — 112
Glossary — 113

I	Vertical integration	113
II	The set-up in a distribution relationship	115
III	Strategies when working with a distributor	116
IV	The relationship between principal and distributor	118
V	Choosing between a traditional buyer and a distributor	119
VI	Choosing between an agent and a distributor	120

VII	The law governing international distribution agreements	124
VIII	Choice of law under European Union law	127
IX	European competition law and the treatment of distribution and agency agreements	128
X	Motivations and concerns of the distributor	130
XI	Motivations and concerns of the principal	131
XII	Distribution agreement and sales agreement	134
XIII	Checklist of provisions	134
XIV	Front of the contract	135
XV	Body of the contract	136
XVI	Boilerplate clauses	154
XVII	Back of the contract	154
Summary		155
Useful links		155
Further reading		155
Notes		156

5 International Agency Agreements — 164

Contents		164
Overview		164
Glossary		165
I	Agency arrangements – when and why?	166
II	Fundamentals of agency law	166
III	Common types of agency relationship	167
IV	The sources of law governing the agency relationship	168
V	Governing law under European Union law	169
VI	Formation of the agency agreement	170
VII	Creation of an agency relationship	171
VIII	Consequences of agency	173
IX	Termination of the agency agreement	175
X	Liability of the principal to the third party	175
XI	Disclosed and undisclosed agency	179
XII	Civil law contrasted with common law	180
XIII	General concerns of the parties	180
XIV	Agency agreements under EU law	184
XV	Agency law and international instruments	187
XVI	Checklist of provisions	191
XVII	Front of the contract	192
XVIII	Body of the contract	193
XIX	Boilerplate clauses and back of the contract	215
Summary		216
Useful links		217
Further reading		217
Notes		218

6	International Licensing Agreements		230
	Contents		230
	Overview		230
	Glossary		231
	I	Intellectual property defined	231
	II	Intellectual property law defined	232
	III	The role of intellectual property law	232
	IV	The role of intellectual property	232
	V	The concerns of the different actors	232
	VI	Characteristics of intellectual property rights	233
	VII	Main categories of intellectual property rights	233
	VIII	The role of international licensing agreements	237
	IX	The role of licensing	238
	X	General format of a licensing agreement	238
	XI	Main categories of international licensing agreements	239
	XII	Licensing a patent	239
	XIII	Licensing a trade mark	240
	XIV	Licensing a copyright	241
	XV	Technology transfer agreement	241
	XVI	Franchising	241
	XVII	The principal's benefits under a licensing agreement	246
	XVIII	The licensee's benefits under a licensing agreement	246
	XIX	General concerns of the parties	247
	XX	Governing law under European Union law	251
	XXI	Checklist of provisions	252
	XXII	Front of the contract	253
	XXIII	Body of the contract	254
	XXIV	Boilerplate clauses	272
	XXV	Back of the contract	272
	Summary		273
	Useful links		273
	Further reading		273
	Notes		274
7	International Instruments Governing International Commercial Agreements		282
	Contents		282
	Overview		282
	Glossary		282
	I	Introduction	283
	II	The UNIDROIT Principles and the Principles of European Contract Law (PECL)	286
	III	United Nations Convention on Contracts for the International Sale of Goods 1980 (CISG)	293

IV	Draft Common Frame of Reference (DCFR) and Common European Sales Law (CESL)	299
Summary		301
Useful links		301
Further reading		301
Notes		302
Index		312

Acknowledgements

I would like to thank:

My anchors . . .
Mr Damien Beal
My father, Dr E. Meiselles
My mother, Mrs D. Meiselles
My brothers and sister

And my sails . . .
Mrs Angela Jane Mortimer Ginger
Mr Doron Meiselles

I would also like to thank my editors, Mr John Watson and Ms Jenny Daly, for their continuing encouragement and sterling guidance and Mr Jonathan Wadman for his copy-editing and hard work.

Table of Cases

WTO
Japan-Taxes on Alcoholic Beverages, AB-1996-2, Report of the Appellate Body, 4 October 1996, WT/DS8/AB/R, WT/DS10/AB/R, WT/DS11/AB/R, 96-3951 .... 29n

European Union
CEPSA Estaciones de Servicio SA v. LV Tobar e Hijos SL, Case C-279/06 [2008] ECR I-668 .... 161n
Confederación Española de Empresarios de Estaciones de Servicio v. CEPSA, Case C-217/05 [2006] ECR I-11987 .... 161n
Consten & Grundig v. Commission, Cases 56/64 and 58/64, [1966] ECR 299; [1966] CMLR 418 .... 160n
Daimler Chrysler AG v. Commission, Case T-325/01 [2005] ECR II-3319 .... 161n
Georgios Kontorgeorgas v. Kartonpak AE, Case C-104/95 [1996] ECR I-6643 .... 228n
Ingmar GB Ltd v. Eaton Leonard Technologies Inc., Case C-381/98 [2000] ECR I-9305 .... 228n
Metro SB-Großmärkte GmbH & Co. KG v. Commission, Case 26/76 [1977] ECR 1875 .... 163n
Parker Pen Ltd v. Commission, Case T-77/92 [1994] ECR II-549 .... 161n
Pronuptia de Paris GmbH v. Pronuptia de Paris Irmgard Schillgallis, Case 161/84 [1986] ECR 353 .... 163n
Société Technique Mininère v. Maschinenbau Ulm GmbH, Case 56/65 [1966] ECR 235 (English) 161n
Viho Europe BV v. Commission, Case C-73/95 P [1996] ECR I-5457; [1997] 4 CMLR 419 .... 160n

National Cases
France
CLOUT Case No. 482 (Cour de Cassation, 5 January 1999) 309n
Traction Levage SA v. Drahtseilerei, Cour d'appel Paris, 6 November 2001 43
Germany
CLOUT Case No. 169 (OLG Düsseldorf, 11 July 1996) 162n
Switzerland
CLOUT Case No. 196 (Handelsgericht Zurich, 26 April 1995) 309n

United Kingdom

Aluminium Industrie Vaassen BV v. Romalpa Aluminium Ltd [1976] 1 WLR 676..219n
AMB Imballaggi Plastici Srl v. Pacflex Ltd [1999] 2 All ER 249 ....222n
Berger & Co. Inc. v. Gill & Duffus SA [1984] AC 382.....................................109n
Biggerstaff v. Rowatt's Wharf Ltd [1896] 2 Ch 93 ....220n
Boston Deep Sea Fishing and Ice Co. Ltd v. Farnham (Inspector of Taxes) [1957] 3 All ER 204...221n
Byrne & Co. v. Van Tienhoven & Co. (1880) 5 CPD 344.................................305n
Davies v. McLean (1873) 21 WR 264..108n
Decro-Wall International SA v. Practitioners in Marketing Ltd [1971] 2 All ER 216, [1971] 1 WLR 361, 162n...307n
Firth v. Staines [1897] 2 QB 70 ....221n
Frape v. Emreco International Ltd [2002] SLT 271 ....228n
Freeman & Lockyer v. Buckhurst Park Properties (Mangal) Ltd [1964] 2 QB 480 ....172–3, 218n
Gardner v. Akeroyd [1952] 2 QB 743 ....220n
Hely-Hutchinson v. Brayhead Ltd [1968] 1 QB 549 ....220n
Henthorn v. Fraser [1892] 2 Ch. 27..305n
Johnson v. Taylor Bros. & Co. Ltd [1920] AC 144.................................... 79, 109n
Keighley, Maxsted & Co. v. Durant [1901] AC 240..219n
L. Schuler AG v. Wickman Machine Tool Sales Ltd [1974] AC 235......................117
Manbré Saccharine Co. Ltd v. Corn Products Co. Ltd [1919] 1 KB 198 ....109n
Martin-Baker Aircraft Co. Ltd v. Canadian Flight Equipment Ltd [1955] 2 QB 556...162n
Mercantile International Group plc v. Chuan Soon Huat Industrial Group Ltd [2002] 1 All ER (Comm) 788 ....223n
Oystertec Plc's Patent [2003] RPC 29...221n
Panorama Developments (Guilford) Ltd v. Fidelis Furnishing Fabrics Ltd [1971] 2 QB 711 ....219n, 220n
Parks v. Esso Petroleum Company Ltd (1999) Trl Rep 232 ....223n
Plant Engineers (Sales) Ltd v. Davies (1969) 113 Sol Jo 484 ....221n
Pyrene Co. Ltd v. Scindia Steam Navigation Co. Ltd [1954] 2 QB 402, [1954] 2 All ER 158 ....108n
Read v. J. Lyons Co. Ltd [1947] AC 156; [1946] 2 All ER 471, HL......................33n
Ross T. Smyth and Co. Ltd v. Bailey, Son & Co. Ltd [1940] 3 All ER 60...........109n
Sanders Bros v. Maclean & Co. (1883) LR 11 QBD 327....................................110n
Sport International Bussum BV v. Hi Tec Sports Ltd (No. 1) [1988] RPC 329 ...161n
T. D. Bailey, Son & Co. v. Ross T. Smyth & Co. Ltd (1940) 56 TLR 825 ....108n
Tigana Ltd v. Decoro Ltd [2003] EWHC 23 QBD..228n
Wilson v. Tunman (1843) 6 Man. & G. 236..221n
Wimble, Sons & Co. Ltd v. Rosenberg & Sons [1913] 3 KB 743 ....76–7, 108n

United States

A. Gay Jenson Farms Co. v. Cargill Inc. 309 NW 2d 285 (Minn. 1981).............159n
Aaron E. Levine & Co v. Calkraft Paper Co., 429F. Supp. 1039 (ED Mich. 1976)... 157n, 158n, 278n

Arnott v. American Oil Co. Ltd, 609 F.2d 873, 1979-2 Trade Cases P 62, 967 (8th Cir. (SD) Oct 24, 1979) (NO. 79-1150) 279n
Asante Technologies Inc. v. PMC-Sierra, Inc. 164 F. Supp. 2d 1142 .. 43, 308n, 309n
Blanchard Importing & Distrib. Co. v. Charles Gilman & Son, Inc. 353 F 2d 400 (1st Cir. 1965), cert. denied, 383 US 968, 86 S.Ct. 1273, 16 L.ED.2d 308 (1966) (US).. 275n
Florida Lime & Avocado Growers, Inc. v. Paul, 373 US 132, 83 S.Ct. 1210 (1963) 279n
Georgia Pacific Corporation v. United States Plywood Corp. 318 F Supp 1116 (SDNY 1970) 1970.. 280n
Greenman v. Yuba Power Products, Inc. 377 P 2d 897..33n
Hines v. Davidowitz, 312 US 52 (1941) 279n
Honda Motor Co. v. Oberg 512 US 415 (1980) 32n
Keebler Co. v. Rovira Biscuit Corp., 624 F.2d 366 (1st Cir. 1980)...................... 275n
Larkin v. McCabe, 211 Minn. 11, 299 NW 649 (1941)..................................... 159n
Mariniello v. *Shell Oil Co.,* 511 F.2d 853 (1975) 250
O'Gilvie et al, Minors v. United States 519 US 79 (1996)................................... 32n
Palsgraf v. Long Island Raildroad Co. 248 N.Y. 339, 162 N.E. 99 (N.Y. 1928)....32n
Puget Sound National Bank v. Washington Department of Revenue 868 P2d 127 (Wash 1994).. 67n
Rockwell Graphic Systems, Inc. v. DEV Industries, Inc. 925 F 2d 174 (7th Cir. 1991)... 274n
Rubinger v. International Telephone & Telegraph Corp., 310F. 2d 552 (2d Cir. 1962), cert. Denied 375 US 820 (1962) 157n, 278n
Salinger v. Random House Inc. 811 F.2d Cir. 1987... 275n

Table of Statutes

International Conventions
1886 Berne Convention (Berne Convention for the Protection of Literary and Artistic Works).....................235
1921 Hague Rules (International Convention for the Unification of Certain Rules of Law relating to Bills of Lading) 109n
1924 Brussels Convention (ibid.)...109n
1964 Hague Convention on the Formation of Contracts for the International Sale of Goods 105n, 284
1964 Hague Convention on the International Sale of Goods 1, 105n, 284
1968 Hague-Visby Rules (Hague Rules as Amended by the Brussels Protocol 1968) 109n, 110n
1974 UNCITRAL Convention on the Limitation Period in the International Sale of Goods 286, 303n
1978 Hague Convention on the Law applicable to Agency 187, 188
1980 CISG (United Nations Convention on Contracts for the International Sale of Goods)..................... 284, 286
    Article 1...............................309n
    Article 1(1)..............................104n
    Article 2...............................308n

Article 3......................................65n
Article 3(2)....................... 294, 308n
Article 4....................................308n
Article 6............. 43, 64n, 65n, 109n, 111n, 287, 293, 309n, 310n
Article 10(a)...............................309
Article 11......................28n, 65n, 296
Article 12.........296, 304n, 309n, 310n
Article 14....................................294
Article 14(1)..............................309n
Articles 14–17............................294
Articles 14–24............................294
Article 15(1)..............................309n
Article 15(2)..............................309n
Article 16..................................309n
Article 17..................................309n
Article 18..................................309n
Articles 18–22............................294
Article 19(2)..............................309n
Article 19(3)...............................296
Article 22..................................309n
Article 23......................... 294, 309n
Article 24....................................294
Article 25..................................310n
Article 26..................................310n
Article 28..................................311n
Article 29(1)..............................310n
Articles 30–34............................310n
Article 33......................................90
Article 35.......... 9, 109n, 111n, 162n, 310n
Article 35(1)..............................310n
Article 35(2)..............................310n
Article 35(3)..............................310n
Articles 35–37............................310n

Article 37	310n, 311n
Article 38	310n
Article 38(1)	310n
Article 39	310n
Article 39(1)	310n
Article 41	310n
Article 42	310n
Article 43	310n
Article 43(1)	310n
Article 46	310n, 311n
Article 47	311n
Article 48	310n, 311n
Article 49	310n
Article 49(1)	310n
Article 50	310n, 311n
Articles 53–60	310n
Article 55	30n, 310n
Article 62	310n, 311n
Article 63	310n, 311n
Article 64	310n
Articles 66–70	9
Article 67(1)	30n, 109n
Article 67(2)	109n
Article 68	30n, 109n
Article 69	109n
Article 71	311n
Article 71(3)	311n
Articles 71–73	310n, 311n
Article 74	310n
Articles 74–76	310n
Article 77	311n
Article 78	310n
Article 81(1)	310n
1983 Geneva Convention on Agency in the International Sale of Goods	187, 188
1983 UNCITRAL Uniform Rules on Contract Clauses for an Agreed Sum Due upon Failure of Performance	286, 303n
1985 UNCITRAL Model Law on International Commercial Arbitration with amendments as adopted in 2006	16
Article 11(3)	31n
Article 12(1)	31n
Article 17D	31n
Article 17H	31n
Article 17L	31n
Article 18	31n
Articles 18–27	31n
Article 19	31n
Article 20	31n
Article 22	31n
Article 23	31n
Article 24	31n
Article 26	31n
Article 28	31n
Articles 28–33	31n
Article 30	31n
Article 31	31n
Article 32	31n
Article 34	31n
Article 35	31n, 32n
Article 36	31n, 32n
1996 UNCITRAL Model Law on Electronic Commerce	286
1997 OECD Convention on Bribery (OECD Convention on Combating Bribery of Foreign Public Officials in International Business Transactions)	181
2001 UNCITRAL Model Law on Electronic Signatures	286

European Union
Treaties
TFEU (Treaty on the Functioning of the European Union)

Article 101	128–30
Article 101(1)	113, 128–30
Article 101(2)	129, 161n
Article 101(3)	129–30

Convention
80/934/EEC (Convention on the law applicable to contractual obligations opened for signature in

Rome on 19 June 1980)
(Rome Convention 1980) 41,
104n, 127, 251–2
Regulations
  2790/1999 on Vertical
    Agreements (Commission
    Regulation (EC) No
    2790/1999 of 22
    December 1999 on the
    application of Article
    81(3) of the Treaty to
    categories of vertical
    agreements and concerted
    practices) 130
  1/2003 on the Implementation
    of Competition Rules
    (Council Regulation
    (EC) No 1/2003 on the
    implementation of the
    rules of competition laid
    down in Articles 81 and
    82 of the Treaty)
    Article 1.1 .... 161n
    Article 1.2 .... 161n
  593/2008/EC (Regulation
    (EC) No 593/2008 of the
    European Parliament and
    of the Council of 17 June
    2008 on the law applicable
    to contractual obligations)
    (Rome I Regulation) 41,
69, 127, 169, 251–2
    Article 3.1 .... 41, 127, 169, 252
    Article 3.2 .... 41, 127, 169, 252
    Article 4 .... 41, 127, 169, 252
    Article 4.1 .... 42, 127, 169, 252
    Article 4.2 .... 42, 127, 169, 252
    Article 4.3 .... 42, 127, 169, 252
    Article 4.4 .... 42, 127, 169, 252
    Article 19 .... 42, 127, 169, 252
    Article 22.1 .... 280n
  330/2010 on Vertical
    Agreements (Commission
    Regulation (EU) No
    330/2010 of 20 April
    2010 on the application
of Article 101(3) of
the Treaty on the
Functioning of the
European Union to
categories of vertical
agreements and concerted
practices) 130
    Article 1 .... 160n
    Article 10 161
Directives
  85/374/EEC on Product
    Liability (Council
    Directive 85/374/EEC
    of 25 July 1985 on the
    approximation of the
    laws, regulations and
    administrative provisions
    of the Member States
    concerning liability
    for defective products)
    (Product Liability
    Directive) 23
    Article 1 .... 33–4n, 34n
    Article 2 .... 34n
    Article 4 .... 34n
    Article 5 .... 34n
    Article 6 .... 34n
    Article 7 .... 34n
    Article 9 .... 34n
    Article 19 .... 34n
  85/577/EEC on Doorstep
    Selling (Council Directive
    85/577/EEC of 20
    December 1985 to protect
    the consumer in respect of
    contracts negotiated away
    from business premises) 64n
  86/653/EEC on Commercial
    Agents (Council Directive
    86/653/EEC of 18
    December 1986 on the
    coordination of the laws
    of the Member States
    relating to self-employed
    commercial agents) 124,
157n, 184, 203–15

TABLE OF STATUTES

Article 1(2) 222n, 223n
Article 1(3) 223n
Article 2(1) 223n
Article 2(2) 223n
Article 3 .... 226n
Article 3(1) 223n
Article 3(2) 223n, 226n
Article 4 .... 227n
Article 4(1) 223n, 227n
Article 4(2) 223n, 227n, 228n
Article 4(3) 223n, 227n
Articles 5–9 .... 227n
Article 6(1) 227n
Article 6(2) 227n
Article 7 .... 227n
Article 7(1) 228n
Article 7(2) 228n
Article 8 .... 227n, 228n
Article 9 .... 228n
Article 10(2) 208, 228n
Article 10(3) 208, 228n
Article 10(4) 228n
Article 11(1) 227n
Article 11(2) 228n
Article 11(3) 228n
Article 12(1) 227n
Article 12(2) 227n
Article 12(3) 227n
Article 13 176
Article 13(1) 223n
Article 13(2) 223n
Article 14 196
Article 15 196
Article 16 .... 228n
Article 17 213
Article 17(1) 228n
Article 17(4) 228n
Article 17(5) 228n
Article 18 .... 228n
Article 20(4) 226n
Commission Decisions
  Commission Decision of 26
    April 2010 Setting Up
    the Expert Group on
    a Common Frame of
    Reference in the Area
    of European Contract
    Law (2010:233/EU OJ
    L105/109) 300
  Preamble 311n
  Article 5 .... 311n

National Legislation
United Kingdom
  Bribery Act 2010 181–2
    §6 .... 221n
    §7(1) 182, 221n
    §7(5) 221n
    §9 .... 222n
  Computers Software
    Amendments Act 1985 .... 276n
  Consumer Protection Act 1987 23
    §1 .... 34n
  Consumer Safety Act 1978 .... 34n
  Consumer Safety
    (Amendment) Act 1986 .... 34n
  Copyright Act 1956 .... 276n
  Copyrights, Designs & Patents
    Act 1988 .... 236, 274n
    §2 .... 276n
    §§3–8 .... 276n
    §12(2) 276n
    §16 .... 276n
    §16(2) 276n
    §90 .... 276n
    §92 .... 276n
  Crown Agents Act 1979 186
  Explosives Act 1875
    §31 .... 34n
    §80 .... 34n
  Fabrics (Misdescriptions) Act
    1913 .... 34n
  Factors Act 1889
    §1(1) 219n
    §2 .... 219n
  Gambling Act 2005 .... 28n
  Gaming Act 1845
    §18 .... 28n
  Health and Safety at Work etc.
    Act 1974 .... 34n
  Mental Capacity Act 2005
    §2 .... 29n

Patents Act 1977	234
§1	274n
§1(2)	234
§1(3)	234
§1(5)	275n
Patents Act 2004	274n
Sales of Goods Act 1893	
§32(3)	77
Sales of Goods Act 1979	71
§1(1)	105n
§12	71, 73
§§12–15	73, 105n
§13	72, 107n
§14	72
§§16–26	105n
§20	78, 81
§26	105n
§§27–37	105n
§§38–48	105n
§§48A–48F	106n
§§49–54	106n
§55(1)	106n
§61	71
§64(2)	105n
Statute of Anne 1709	235
§1	275n
Supply of Goods and Services Act 1982	
§2	74
Trade Description Act 1972	34n
Trade Marks Act 1994	275n
§1(1)	275n
§14(1)	275n
§§14–21	275n
§24(1)	275n
§24(2)	275n
§24(3)	275n
Unfair Contract Terms 1977	71, 106n
§1	74
§1(3)	107n
§2(1)	107n
§2(3)	107n
§§2–7	73, 74
§3	74
§3(1)	107n
§4	74
§6(1)	107n
§6(3)	107n
§6(4)	106n
§7	107n
§11	73
§12	106n
§§16–21	74
§26(1)	107n
§26(2)	107n
§27(1)	107n
§31(2)	106n
Schedule 2	73
Uniform Laws on International Sales Act 1967	70
United States	
Constitution	
Article 1.8	276n
Article 6.2	250, 309n
Computers Software Protection Act 1980	276n
Copyright Act 1976	276n
Uniform Commercial Code	
§2-201	28n
§2-302	31n, 58
§2-303	30n, 109n
§2-305	30n
§2-309(1)	30n
§2-309(2)	30n
§2-314	30n
§2-315	30n
US Code Title 17	
§102	276n
§102.3	276n
§104	276n
§201(d)(2)	275n
§202m	275n
US Code Title 35	234
§101	275n
§103	275n
§1127	275n

Preface

This book presents an excellent guide to the complex world of international commercial agreements. Clear and concise, it is a key reference tool for business managers, lawyers and students. It addresses the essential issues that need to be dealt with, when negotiating, planning and writing international commercial agreements.

Contracts fulfil several functions. They spell out the rights and obligations of each of the parties to the contract, and manage any potential risks arising out of the contractual relationship, whilst at the same time supplying a contingency plan for each party in the event that the contractual relationship breaks down. This is true whether a contract is concluded between parties – individuals as well as firms – at the national level or the international level.

At the national level, classic contracts include those between employer and employee, between husband and wife, between bank and customer and between doctor and patient. At the international level, different types of contract are concluded depending on the role of each party in the relationship as well as the subject matter of the contract itself. Such contracts include sales agreements, supply agreements, agency agreements, distribution agreements and licensing agreements, to name a few.

As a risk management device, a contract addresses all potential risks involved in a relationship (commercial or otherwise). A contract also has a pre-emptive role, as it supplies a strategy for the parties if events do not proceed as planned. The contract will include provisions that aim to help the parties salvage their relationship in such an eventuality and, if the worst comes to the worst, it will also include provisions that address the rights and obligations of the parties on termination.

When negotiating the terms of a contract, the parties should be aware of all the issues that need to be addressed in the contract. The provisions of the contract should address each of these issues in turn. Obviously no contract is perfect but the parties should aim for perfection.

This book will look at the issues that should be taken into account when a business located in one country is contracting with one located in another country. It will explore the framework within which international commercial agreements are concluded and within which commercial entities operate at the international level.

After a general review of the key concerns that need to be addressed when entering into an international contractual arrangement, specific commercial agreements commonly used by businesses contracting in the international context will be reviewed (sales contracts, distribution agreements, agency agreements and licensing agreements). In relation to each such agreement, the book will consider the separate concerns of each contracting party, exploring the ways in which these respective concerns can be addressed using the provisions of the contract. For the purposes of this book, an 'international commercial agreement' is taken to mean an agreement entered into by business entities in different countries. Accordingly, this book will not look at transactions between sovereign agencies.

M.K.M.

Nomenclature

The terms *firm*, *entity* and *business* are used interchangeably to refer inter alia to corporations or companies, as well as partnerships and sole traders.

Principal is used throughout the precedents to denote the principal in an agency arrangement, a manufacturer or producer in a distribution arrangement and a licensor in a licensing arrangement.

Clause and *provision* are used interchangeably to refer to the terms in the contract.

Final words

The author has dealt with common issues and has tried to bring to the attention of the reader key problems that regularly arise in the context of international contracts. It is important to always ensure that a contract covers all risks and rights relevant to the particular transaction and to seek the advice of a lawyer when drafting or reviewing a contract.

Guide to the Book

This book contains a range of features which make it user friendly and accessible. This section shows you how these features operate.

Overview

At the start of each chapter, an overview will appear. This overview flags the main concepts dealt with in the chapter, whilst serving as a signpost for the reader by denoting to the reader what he can expect to learn by reviewing the chapter.

An example of a chapter overview

> **Overview**
>
> This chapter will examine the issues that must be considered and addressed when planning an international commercial agreement. By the end of this chapter, you will understand:

Sample clauses

Sample clauses are flagged using a shaded background. This is intended to help the reader find the clause, examine its wording and read about its purpose.

An example of a sample clause

> **SALE AGREEMENT**
>
> This sale agreement is dated 12 November 2009 and is between JONES STORAGE LTD, an English company ('<u>Jones</u>'), and IVES INC., a New York corporation ('<u>Ives</u>').

Summary of chapter

At the end of each chapter, a summary will appear. This summary helps bring together all the main points explored in the chapter, providing the reader with a quick reference tool.

An example of a chapter summary

Summary

This chapter has explained the main concerns associated with international contracts. Firstly...

Glossary

A glossary of key definitions will be provided at the start of each chapter. Terms defined are highlighted in the text in bold lettering.

Useful links

A list of links to useful websites will appear at the end of each chapter.

Further reading

A list of useful articles and books will appear at the end of each chapter.

1
Planning an International Commercial Agreement

Contents

Overview 1
Glossary 1
I Form of international commercial agreements 3
II Subject matter of the contract 4
III Parties contracting 4
IV Trade barriers 5
V Implied terms 8
VI Adaption of the contract 10
VII Renegotiation of terms 11
VIII Dispute resolution 12
IX Researching local law 18
X Available entry strategies 25
Summary 27
Useful links 27
Further reading 27
Notes 28

Overview

This chapter will examine certain matters that are relevant when considering the contractual process in the international business context. Firstly, it will examine the general issues that should be considered and addressed when planning an international commercial agreement. Secondly, it will make reference to the question of dispute resolution. Finally, it will consider the different strategies that a business entity may opt for when looking to expand operations abroad.

By the end of this chapter the reader will have a better understanding of

- the main concerns associated with international contracts;
- the impact of tariff and non-tariff barriers;
- the importance of planning for potential disputes;
- the key characteristics of mediation, conciliation, arbitration and litigation;
- the importance of researching the law in the target market; and
- the structures available to an entity looking to expand its operations abroad.

Glossary

Ad valorem duty A duty fixed as a percentage of the value of the goods.
Alternative dispute resolution clause See **out-of-court settlement clause**.
Bilateral trade agreements Trade agreements entered into by two countries.
Choice of court clause (also known as **choice of jurisdiction clause** or **choice of forum clause**) A contractual term that specifies in which court the party looking to

pursue the matter will need to commence a legal action.

Choice of forum clause See **choice of court clause**.

Choice of jurisdiction clause See **choice of court clause**.

Choice of law clause A contractual term specifying the body of law (the law of which jurisdiction) that the final arbiter will use in order to deal with the dispute between the contracting parties.

Claimant See **plaintiff**.

Class action A procedural device available in certain **jurisdictions** that permits one or more **representatives** to bring or defend a case on behalf of a larger group.

Common Customs Tariff A tariff applying to the importation of goods across the external borders of the European Union.

Compensatory damages Damages awarded to a person in acknowledgment of their loss, suffering or injury.

Country of export The country in which goods or services originate.

Country of importation The country to which goods or services are heading.

Customs duty See **tariff**.

Damages A monetary sum imposed by the law for the breach of a duty or violation of a right.

Defendant The party against whom an action is brought by the **plaintiff**.

Drafting a contract Setting out the terms of a contract.

Enforcement proceedings Court proceedings to enforce a judgment.

Export barriers Impediments affecting the export of goods or services.

Extra-judicial party A party that operates outside the judicial framework.

Flexible price term A contractual term that allows the price of goods to be varied upwards or downwards.

Force majeure clause A clause in a contract allowing the parties contracting to be excused from performing contractual obligations when an unanticipated event occurs.

Import barriers Impediments to the entrance or sale of imported goods or services.

Intentional tort Intentional behaviour resulting in the commission of a wrong.

Jurisdiction The official power that a court requires to adjudicate in a case.

Mixed charges A duty consisting of an **ad valorem duty** coupled with a **specific duty**.

Multilateral trade agreements Trade agreements entered into by several countries.

Negligence Non-intentional breach of a duty of care resulting in the commission of a wrong.

Non-tariff barriers Trade barriers other than **tariff** barriers.

Open price term A contract that leaves price open.

Out-of-court settlement clause (also known as an **alternative dispute resolution clause** or **ADR clause**) A contractual term that addresses dispute resolution with the aid of a third party but without the involvement of the courts.

Plaintiff (or **claimant** in English law) The party bringing a legal action.

Punitive damages Damages awarded in addition to **compensatory damages** in certain situations when the conduct of the **defendant** is found to be particularly harmful.

Quantitative restrictions (also known as QRs) Barriers that limit the quantity of a good being imported or exported.

Severance clause A term in the contract that allows for the removal of a clause that is rendered invalid, leaving the remainder of the contract intact.

Specific duty A duty linked to the number of units imported or the weight or volume of goods imported.

Strict liability Liability for a specific wrong imposed on a **defendant** irrespective of fault on his part.

Tariff (also referred to as a **customs duty**) A tax levied on goods by the **country of importation** at the time of import and/or because of their importation.

Tort A wrong recognised in law.

Tortfeasor The party that commits a wrong.

Void contract A contract that is void is automatically no contract at all. The contract is therefore treated as if it had never been made. Accordingly it can have no effect.[1]

Voidable contract A contract that remains valid until the party who has the right to complain takes steps to set it aside. If the party in question chooses not to set the contract aside then it will be valid and the usual consequences of a contract will flow from it.[2]

1 Form of international commercial agreements

Though agreements concluded orally may be deemed valid,[3] it is advisable to ensure that a contract is written and signed by the parties involved or at the very least that its terms are recorded in writing. This will ensure clarity in the relationship between the parties and prevent any potential for uncertainty if questions arise later between the parties in the context of their commercial relationship. What is more evidentially speaking a written record of the terms agreed by the parties will also be important if at a later date there is a dispute between the parties contracting as to what was agreed upon between them which ends up before a court, arbitration body or tribunal.

A written contract or record of the terms is particularly important bearing in mind the added complexities associated with international transactions, such as problems with transit, late delivery, political turmoil, strikes, currency fluctuations, the possibility of expropriation, the risk of **tariff** increases and changes to **non-tariff barriers**. A well-negotiated contract will go a long way towards tackling such concerns, ensuring as far as possible that the parties overcome their problems so that they can remain in their commercial relationship with each other, benefiting both parties as well as their respective stakeholders (those parties affected by the contract, such as employees and suppliers, to name a few).

International commercial agreements will involve legal concerns which are not necessarily associated with national contracts. Such concerns should be addressed when each party is preparing to negotiate the agreement. At the negotiation and in the final agreement that is drawn up and signed by the parties these concerns should be addressed in detail, in order to pre-empt possible future difficulties.

Formation of international commercial agreements

Where the parties intend to contract and the purpose is legal, a contract is likely to be formed through offer and acceptance on the proviso that the parties contracting have the necessary legal capacity to contract.

In Anglo-American law, once the acceptance becomes effective a contract is made and the contracting parties are bound to fulfil their respective obligations under the contract.

> **Box 1.1 An example of offer and acceptance**
> If a seller writes to the proposed buyer: 'I will sell you a crate of 50 bottles of Châteauneuf du Pape (vintage 1999) for €1000' and the buyer replies by saying 'I accept these terms', a contract will be concluded between the parties.

Difficulties arise in a number of situations when the contract involves some illegality or one of the parties lacks capacity[4].

II Subject matter of the contract

The subject matter of a contract can pose a problem when contracting. Though many countries allow the sale of most goods and the supply of most services and will uphold such contracts, the subject matter of the contract may affect the enforceability of the contract. The subject matter of a contract will be illegal if the contract involves goods or services the sale or supply of which (respectively) is illegal in countries where the parties are based or where these goods are to be delivered or services supplied. For example, the supply and sale of alcoholic beverages is illegal in certain countries.

In English law as a general rule the courts will not enforce illegal contracts.[5] Illegality could ensue in a number of situations under English law where the subject matter of a contract is illegal,[6] the contract is expressly prohibited by statute[7] or the contract entails some element that is deemed illegal as a result of public policy considerations[8]. In English law, a contract to commit a criminal offence is illegal whilst a contract envisaging the commission of a civil wrong (for example a contract involving the commission of a tort) will be tainted by illegality.

III Parties contracting

Before drafting a contract it is important to establish which parties are actually contracting. Parties to contract may be individuals, corporations (or companies), partnerships or governments.

Corporations contracting

If a corporation is contracting it is important to establish who will be representing the corporation and to determine whether or not they have the requisite authority to contract.[9] A person may have general authority to contract on behalf of the corporation. In the alternative, an individual may only have limited authority to enter into specific contracts; such authority could depend on the sums involved in the contract or on the subject matter of the contract.

When dealing with an individual who purportedly represents a corporation it is important to establish whether he or she has the authority of the corporation to contract. Such authority is usually awarded by the board of directors or by the constitution of the corporation[10]. A director will usually have the authority of the board of directors to contract but it is still worthwhile checking that the person is listed as a director and if so to verify the extent of his or her authority.

Dealing with an agent

If an agent is acting, once again the question of authority is central. Before contracting with an agent, it is important firstly to verify that the agent is in fact an agent for the principal (an authorised agent) and secondly to clarify the scope of their authority.[11]

Capacity[12]

In English law, the following parties may lack the capacity to contract: a minor, those with diminished decision-making powers and those under the influence of drugs or alcohol.

A minor under English law is a person under eighteen years of age. A contract concluded with a minor is not **void** although the minor will not usually be bound by the contract. Certain contracts concluded with minors are binding on the minor unless repudiated by him or her before he or she reaches the age of eighteen or within a reasonable time of reaching the age of eighteen. Such contracts can therefore be regarded as **voidable** rather than void.

Under English law,[13] a person may lack capacity if at the time of contracting he or she is either permanently or temporarily unable to make decisions[14]. A contract is voidable when it is concluded by an intoxicated person or by a person whose understanding and awareness are otherwise impaired at the time of contracting.[15]

IV Trade barriers[16]

Trade barriers can be divided into two categories. **Import barriers** are used as impediments to the entrance or sale of imported goods or services whilst **export barriers** affect the export of goods or services. When making trade and investment decisions a firm will need to consider not only the laws and regulations of the **country of export** (the country from which the goods are exported) and the **country of importation** (the country to which the goods are heading) but also those of the countries through which the goods are passing.

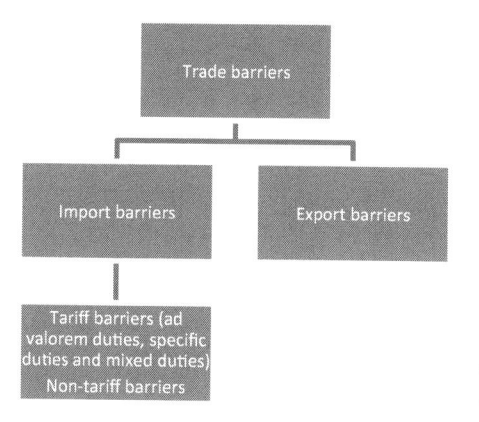

Whilst nations have accepted that their mutual interests can be served by encouraging freer trade or even completely free trade in goods and services, trade barriers in the form of import and export barriers still exist as they fulfil a number of national needs.[17] A nation may use import barriers for the generation of revenue (revenue is generated through, amongst other mechanisms, licensing fees, taxes and charges levied on imports) and the creation and in turn the preservation of jobs in domestic industry. Alternatively, a nation may employ barriers to imported goods and services to protect domestic industry against competition; to retaliate against the trade policies of another nation; to implement foreign policy (for example the imposition of a prohibition on imports from a country in violation of international norms); to implement national economic policies (by preserving reserves of foreign currency for instance); to protect emerging industries at the national level (infant industries); to ensure self-sufficiency of domestic industry for strategic reasons; to protect natural resources and the environment (a ban on the import of tuna caught using nets that are not dolphin friendly for example); and to protect health and safety of people, plants and animals (a ban on the import of disease-carrying fruit for example).

Import barriers

The main barriers to market access of goods are **tariff** barriers and **non-tariff barriers**.

Tariff barriers to trade in goods

A **tariff**, also referred to as a customs duty, is the most common device used to regulate imports of goods. A tariff is a tax levied on goods by the country of importation at the time of import and/or because of their importation. Tariffs are either specific, ad valorem or mixed. **Ad valorem duties** are calculated on the basis of the value of the good in question. **Specific duties** are linked to weight or volume, or to the number of units imported (the duty to be charged per unit is specified), whilst **mixed charges** consist of an ad valorem duty coupled with a specific duty. Ad valorem duties are more common than specific duties and mixed charges.

Countries that are members of the World Trade Organization (WTO) have agreed to certain obligations in exchange for the benefits that they derive and expect to derive as members of the WTO.[18] In exchange for these benefits members of the WTO have agreed to exercise their sovereignty according to the commitments they have made in the WTO Agreement. In this vein members of the WTO agree to

1. adhere to certain tariff commitments that they have agreed upon;[19] and
2. adhere to regulations governing the use of non-tariff barriers.

Subject to certain strict exceptions, a member of the WTO must apply the agreed tariff rate on goods being imported. These agreed tariff commitments are published so that all interested parties are privy to them, enhancing visibility, liberalising trade and encouraging competition.[20]

Box 1.2 World Trade Organization: history and objectives[21]

History
In 1947, a group of countries entered into the General Agreement on Tariffs and Trade (GATT 1947),[22] which entered into force on 1 January 1948. The WTO was established on 1 January 1995 and was created by the Uruguay Round negotiations that took place between 1986 and 1994. It is headquartered in Geneva. The WTO replaced GATT as an international forum but the updated GATT still exists as the WTO's umbrella treaty for trade in goods.

Objectives
The countries that entered into the Agreement Establishing the World Trade Organization[23] are committed to reducing tariff barriers and other barriers to trade as well as to the elimination of discrimination in international trade.[24]

The **Common Customs Tariff**[25] applies to the import of goods across the external borders of the European Union. The tariff is common to all European Union member states.[26]

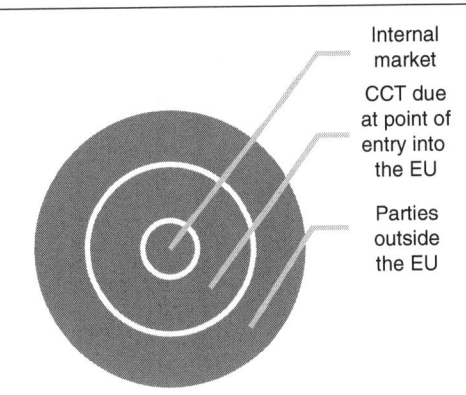

Internal market

CCT due at point of entry into the EU

Parties outside the EU

Non-tariff barriers to trade in goods

Generally less transparent than tariff barriers, **non-tariff barriers** encompass all other impediments to trade affecting the free flow of goods across frontiers and fall into two categories, namely **quantitative restrictions** and other non-tariff barriers.

Quantitative restrictions (also known as QRs)
These are barriers that limit the quantity of a good being imported or exported.

Box 1.3 Examples of quantitative restrictions

There are different types of quantitative restrictions.

Prohibition (or ban)
Such measures are absolute or conditional (effectively these measures are applicable in situations where certain conditions specified are not met).

Quota
A quota indicates the quantity that may be imported or exported. Quotas may be applied to imports and exports and are based on either value, quantity of goods (weight or number of units) or percentage share of the domestic market for the particular good.

Quotas are imposed by the importing country on goods of a particular kind coming from all countries, from a group of specific countries or only from one country.

Other non-tariff barriers
In addition to tariff barriers and quantitative restrictions, trade in goods is also adversely affected by other non-tariff barriers. This residual category of measures comprises all other barriers that restrict the access of goods to a given market. These measures make it comparatively more expensive or troublesome to import goods. Such barriers include laws, practices and administrative regulations which limit or discourage the sale or purchase of a foreign good in the target market. Such measures are typically employed in order to protect domestic industry from foreign competition.

Box 1.4 Examples of other non-tariff barriers

- Government procurement policies that encourage government departments, governmental bodies or public agencies to buy goods and services from domestic suppliers
- Sanitary measures
- Customs formalities and procedures
- Technical regulations and standards (including safety standards, electrical standards and environmental standards, for example a requirement that a car imported be fitted with an anti-pollution device).

In view of the tariff and non-tariff barriers that exist it may be worthwhile considering an operation that involves production of the goods in the target market itself (into which the goods would otherwise be imported).

In this context, the foreign entity has several options open to it. Firstly, it could contract with an existing entity in the target market, which would then assume responsibility for local production of the goods, occasionally using the intellectual property rights licensed to it by the foreign entity. Secondly, the foreign entity could set up a branch or subsidiary in the target market. Thirdly, it could enter into a joint venture with a local entity. Alternatively, the foreign entity could either merge with or buy a local entity, in turn taking charge of the facilities of the local entity in order to produce the goods.

Export controls

When making trade decisions, a business will also need to be aware of controls imposed by the country of export which limit or even in extreme circumstances forbid the shipment of products to another country. Such controls are likely to be in place to serve various political, economic and cultural interests. Examples include measures forbidding, limiting or controlling shipments of goods such as cultural artefacts, ivory, endangered species, local currency, foreign currency, arms, nuclear material and defence equipment, as well as oil, minerals, food and water (when these are in short supply).

Trade liberalisation[27]

Governments have cooperated in a bid to reduce tariffs to agreed levels and control the manner in which non-tariff barriers are used, ensuring increased trade between countries, economic development, improved competition and an enhanced standard of living. International trade in goods and (more recently) in services has been transformed since 1947, at first by the GATT 1947 (updated during the Uruguay Round, 1986–94) and later by the GATS (General Agreement on Trade in Services). The updated GATT and GATS are amongst the various agreements administered by the World Trade Organization.

Other international agreements have also been concluded that liberalise trade. Such agreements are known as **bilateral trade agreements** if concluded by two countries or **multilateral or regional trade agreements** if concluded by more than two countries. They govern trade in goods and/or services and the protection of intellectual property rights, with the aim of liberalising trade between the participating countries. NAFTA (The North American Free Trade Agreement) is an example of a regional trade agreement.

V Implied terms[28]

In many contracts, although the main provisions are contained in express terms, from time to time the contracting parties will not necessarily articulate all the principal obligations and rights that ensue under the contract or will not provide for every potential contingency that could arise in their dealings. Terms may be left out either intentionally or due to an oversight by the contracting parties. In such circumstances terms may be read into the contract pursuant to the law governing the contract. Such terms are referred to as **implied terms**.

In contracts governed by the contract principles formulated by the International Institute for the Unification of Private Law (the UNIDROIT Principles), these principles will incorporate terms when the parties have failed to determine the quality of performance,[29] the price,[30] the time of performance,[31] the order of performance,[32] the place of performance[33] and the currency of payment.[34] In contracts governed by the Principles of European Contract Law (PECL), these principles will incorporate terms when the parties have failed to determine the price,[35] the quality of performance,[36] the place of performance of a contractual obligation,[37] the time of performance[38] and the currency of payment.[39]

V IMPLIED TERMS

In contracts governed by the United Nations Convention on Contracts for the International Sale of Goods (CISG), where the parties fail to determine the allocation of risk between the seller and buyer, then as the governing law the CISG will incorporate terms governing allocation of risk.[40] Allocation of risk pursuant to the CISG is reviewed below.

Box 1.5 Allocation of risk under the CISG

If a contract is governed by the CISG and the parties to the contract have not determined the allocation of risk, the court will give effect to Articles 66 to 70 of the CISG.

If the contract of sale involves carriage of the goods and the seller is not obliged to hand the goods over at a particular place, the risk will pass to the buyer when the goods are handed over to the first carrier for transmission to the buyer in accordance with the provisions of the contract concluded between the parties.[41]

If the seller is obliged to hand the goods over to a carrier at a particular place, then the risk will not pass to the buyer until such a time as the goods are handed over to the carrier at that place.[42]

Where goods are sold in transit then the risk in relation to the goods so sold will pass to the buyer from the time of the conclusion of the contract.[43]

Where they are not excluded or varied by the parties contracting, certain warranties will be implied into the contract by the law governing the contract.[44] In the case of a contract governed by the CISG, then as the governing law the CISG will incorporate terms governing the warranties extended by the seller to the buyer. Warranties implied pursuant to the CISG are reviewed below.

Box 1.6 Implied warranties under the CISG

If the contract is governed by the CISG and the parties to the contract have neither excluded nor modified the warranties, the court will give effect to Article 35 of the CISG, which states that the seller must deliver goods of the quantity, quality and description set out in the contract which are contained or packaged in the manner stipulated by the contract and unless the parties have agreed otherwise, the goods will not be conform with the contract unless they

1. are fit for the purpose for which goods of the same description would ordinarily be used;
2. are fit for any particular purpose expressly or impliedly made known to the seller at the time of the conclusion of the contract;
3. possess the qualities of the goods which the seller has held out to the buyer as a sample; and
4. are contained or packaged in the manner usual for such goods or, where there is no such manner, in a manner adequate to preserve and protect the goods.

Other provisions are available pursuant to the national law of different countries.[45]

Planning for dispute resolution[46]

During the negotiation phase, when the contracting parties are negotiating the terms of their deal, it is wise for them to give due consideration to certain practical considerations, such as how they plan to make future decisions regarding their working relationship, how they plan to address unforeseen events, how they wish to communicate and resolve disputes and how and if they wish to include a provision permitting renegotiation. When provision is made for such eventualities, the agreement drawn up will help foster efficient sharing of information, lower the costs of complex adaption and permit rapid exploitation of unexpected opportunities without the parties having to monitor and enforce compliance with the contract.[47] With this in mind, the parties may make provision in the contract inter alia for consultation, adaption and renegotiation.

Consultation[48]

When making provision for consultations in their agreement, certain considerations should be borne in mind by the contracting parties, namely

- how often they wish to consult with each other;
- the extent of such consultations (what information will be discussed at such consultations);
- the format of such consultations (will a consultation be formal or informal; will it be reactive, in response to a difficulty encountered, or proactive); and
- the format of the agenda for such consultations (will an agenda for the consultations be drawn up; if so, will it be drawn up with the agreement of the other contracting party or parties; and so on).

VI Adaption of the contract[49]

Many contracts will include provisions permitting the contract and the relationship of the parties to be adjusted and adapted to changes in circumstances without provoking a breach or forcing the parties into some kind of formal dispute resolution. Effectively the parties to the contract are able to use these provisions where a change in circumstances occurs thereby averting a breach and removing the need for formal dispute resolution. Several such provisions are reviewed below, namely **force majeure clauses**, **flexible price terms, severance clauses** and modification clauses.

Force majeure clause

A **force majeure clause** will enable the parties to be excused from their performance of contractual obligations when an unanticipated event or events occurs. Such events will be specified by the parties in the contract. If the event persists, the contract will probably include a provision that allows the parties to convene for good faith discussions in order to find a solution that will enable them to remain in the contractual relationship.

Flexible price term

A **flexible price term** will allow the price of products to be varied upwards or downwards in order to reflect and adjust to changes in market conditions. Alternatively, a flexible price term may make reference to an industry-recognised index of prices. Such a practice is common in the construction industry, for example, where reference is made to the index of prices for steel.

> **Box 1.7 Flexible price terms**
> By way of an example, a business that uses oil derivatives in the production of its products is likely to insist that the price of its products be allowed to fluctuate upwards and downwards in order to reflect changes in the price of oil. In such circumstances to ensure certainty, which is especially important for budgeting purposes, the business using the oil derivatives may also choose to include an upper cap as well as a lower cap in the provision addressing pricing. So if and when the price approaches either of the caps, the parties meet for good faith discussions in order to find a solution that will enable both parties to adapt to the change in circumstances.

Open price term

Even when the contract does not include a term that sets price, if the parties so intend they will be treated as having concluded a contract for sale with a so-called **open price term**.

Open price terms are permitted under the CISG, the UNIDROIT Principles and PECL. In the event that the price is left open, the UNIDROIT Principles will incorporate a term determining the price,[50] as will PECL[51] and the CISG[52]. A similar test is used by all three instruments for the determination of price. In effect, where no determination regarding price is made by the contracting parties, then the price to be charged will be the generally charged price, at the time that the contract was made, for such performance in comparable circumstances in the trade concerned.[53]

In the United States, open price terms are permitted and in such a situation the price will be deemed to be the reasonable price at the time of delivery.[54]

Severance clause[55]

A **severance clause** in the contract will permit the removal of a clause that is rendered invalid, unenforceable or illegal, for example by reason of a change in law, leaving the remainder of the contract intact. Similarly the law governing a contract may allow a court as a matter of law to enforce the rest of the contract without the unconscionable clause or limit the application of any unconscionable clause so as to avoid an unconscionable result.[56]

Modification clause[57]

In the event that there is a change in circumstances, the contract may make provision in a modification clause for modification of terms.

VII Renegotiation of terms[58]

If the contract cannot be modified to accommodate for a change in circumstances, the process of renegotiation may permit the parties contracting to renegotiate the contract or certain provisions within it. A renegotiation will simply allow for a dialogue or discussion between the contracting parties where a disagreement arises. Such a renegotiation will have as its goal the resolution of the disagreement by means of mutual consent.

A contract, especially one intended by the parties contracting to be long term, will often include a provision that requires the parties to renegotiate, proactively or reactively, if difficulties arise, so that the parties are able to attempt to resolve disputes in an amicable manner. By means of a successful renegotiation, the contracting parties may find a mutually acceptable solution to their difficulties and may redraft the provisions of the contract to reflect the results of their renegotiation. A renegotiation will mean that the contracting parties will not need to resort to a more formal dispute resolution mechanism or, in the worst-case scenario, bring their contractual relationship to an end.

Renegotiation offers several key advantages to the contracting parties when compared to the alternative forms of dispute resolution. Firstly, a renegotiation is usually far more cost effective and expedient than the alternatives (such as arbitration or litigation). Secondly, in a renegotiation resolution is neither coerced nor imposed by an external entity, which is likely to mean that the parties contracting will be more open to the agreement that they have reached together and as such more likely to implement it. Thirdly, a renegotiation can be undertaken whilst the contract continues to be performed.

A renegotiation provision may be general in scope or more targeted. A renegotiation provision that is general in scope may permit either of the contracting parties to convene a meeting to renegotiate the contractual provisions if a change of circumstances arises affecting the ability of the party in question to perform its contractual obligations. Such a meeting is commonly referred to as a bona fide meeting (in other words a good faith meeting). A renegotiation provision that is more targeted in scope may permit renegotiation of specific contractual provisions if certain circumstances arise. For example in a contract in which the price of the goods is permitted to fluctuate, reference may also be made to an upper and/or lower cap and a provision may be included permitting renegotiation of pricing terms if the price approaches either cap.

A renegotiation may be proactive as well as reactive. A reactive renegotiation is a renegotiation that is undertaken in response to a request by at least one of the contracting parties. The facility for a proactive renegotiation may be included as a standard template provision (a boilerplate term) within the provisions of a contract.[59]

In certain contracts, it is worthwhile considering the inclusion of provisions that permit the contracting parties to meet at regular intervals for the purpose of reviewing their circumstances and, if necessary, informally discussing possible revisions to the contractual terms that reflect their present position. Such a provision is particularly pertinent in long-term contracts under which the parties are contractually engaged either indefinitely (indefinite term agreements) or for a long period of time (sometimes several decades). A contract concluded in 1970, for example, is likely to require regular revisions to ensure that it is adapted to contemporary conditions generally and to the dynamics of each party to the contract specifically. Examples of the types of change that will need to be reflected in the provisions of the contract include changes in the corporate structures of the contracting parties and changes in the details of the contracting parties, including names and addresses.

VIII Dispute resolution[60]

The arrangements made by the parties in the contract with regards to the resolution of disputes between them are particularly important in international commercial agreements for a number of reasons. Firstly, at least two possible legal systems are usually involved in such agreements. More legal systems may be involved if the contract involves elements connected to other countries. Secondly, the fact the parties are based in different countries means that the physical distance between them may hinder resolution through renegotiation. Furthermore, possible cultural differences will also affect the manner in which dispute resolution is handled.

When planning, negotiating, drafting and agreeing on the terms of an agreement the contracting parties should consider the procedure (or procedures, in certain circumstances) that they will employ in the event that a dispute arises between them under the contract. Once the procedure or procedures are agreed upon between the parties, their determination should be reflected in the terms of the contract. Using such terms, the parties are able to lay down the groundwork for addressing potential disputes pre-emptively.

Box 1.8 Dispute resolution in international commercial agreements and the considerations of the contracting parties

A number of issues should be borne in mind in the context of dispute resolution, as the parties negotiate, draft and conclude their international commercial agreement.

Firstly, will they make provision for interparty meetings of a regular or ad hoc nature in order to address interpretative differences and to renegotiate the terms of their contract in a bid to accommodate existing and emerging changes in circumstances?

Secondly, will they allow for potentialities in the provisions of their contract, in order to ensure that their contract is dynamic and flexible, adaptable to changes as the contractual relationship evolves?

Thirdly, in the event that adaption and renegotiation fail, will they make provision for the resolution of disputes without litigating, by either attempting to resolve their differences alone (with or without the help of their lawyers) or with the aid of a neutral, extra-judicial third party (operating outside the judicial framework and otherwise known as out-of-court settlement, alternative dispute resolution or ADR)? In the event that the parties contracting decide to pursue this option, it would be prudent for them to also determine whether there will be a right to appeal the decision of the third party.

Fourthly, if the matter does proceed to court, consideration should be given to the following questions:

- In which court will the party looking to pursue the matter commence a legal action? The contractual provision addressing this question is called the choice of court clause where a court is involved, or a choice of jurisdiction clause or the choice of forum clause where either a court or indeed an arbitration body is involved.
- Which law will the court (or arbitrator) be using in order to address the dispute? The contractual provision addressing this question is called the choice of law clause.
- Finally, if and when a judgment is made or a settlement is arrived at by the parties, where will the judgment or settlement need to be enforced? If for example one of the contracting parties is based in the United States and the other in England and the judgment awarded to the US-based party by a court based in the state of New York needs to be executed against property located in England and belonging to the English party, then the separate questions of recognition and enforceability of a foreign judgment arise. Here the English courts will need to first recognise the foreign judgment awarded by the court in the state of New York and then to allow it to be enforced against the property of the English party.

These considerations mirror the different stages in the process of judicial resolution of international disputes.

The devices used in international dispute resolution include mediation, conciliation, arbitration and litigation. All the methods used to resolve disputes save litigation require the consent of both parties to the dispute. The advantages and disadvantages associated with each method should be considered when planning, negotiating and writing this section of the contract. In this context, it is wise to bear in mind certain factors when making a choice of mechanism, namely time, expense, expertise, finality, right of appeal, degree of control and level of privacy. Litigation is usually not only time consuming (due to the waiting lists, court timetable and litigation procedure) but is more of a public affair so that brand image, share price and corporate reputation can be adversely affected, whilst trade secrets and confidential information may be revealed, damaging the commercial stability of an operation.

When looking to resolve a dispute, the parties may first consider attempting an **out-of-court settlement** with or without the assistance of their respective lawyers. At first, the parties are likely to try to resolve matters between them by means of discussion, especially when a long-term relationship is at stake. If such negotiations prove futile they may decide to resort to arbitration or even mediation in an attempt to resolve their differences. Only when all other attempts to resolve the matter fail are the parties likely to take the matter to court.

Alternative dispute resolution

Various forms of **alternative dispute resolution** exist, including but not limited to mediation, conciliation and arbitration.

Mediation

Mediation is typically a voluntary, non-binding, private conciliation process, by means of which the parties themselves reach an agreement with the help of a third party (the mediator). The final decision rests with the parties themselves. The parties will usually also reserve the right in law to resort to arbitration or litigation.

Mediation has certain advantages: it is conciliatory, fairly informal (commercial mediation can be conducted using formal rules), expedient and private. In terms of disadvantages, more complex mediations can take a great deal of time and most involve the expense of hiring the mediator.

Conciliation

Conciliation is a process by which a person or a panel (of several people) helps the parties to the dispute in their attempt to reach an amicable settlement.[61] In disputes involving several different parties (multiparty disputes), as well as interests and issues that are complex and multilateral, conciliation may be a suitable way of resolving certain issues disputed, if not the dispute itself.

A good example of a situation where conciliation may be employed in order to avoid complex and thus drawn-out litigation is insolvency. In such a scenario, conciliation may be useful in addressing the competing needs and conflicting interests of the different classes of creditors and the different creditors themselves, as well as the debtors, in turn making it easier for the parties to find common ground on many of the issues disputed. These different and competing interests and needs will likely draw out an attempt to resolve the matters by negotiation (between the parties themselves, with or without the help of the insolvency practitioner or lawyers) or adjudication. In such a situation, perhaps with the help of a third party who is appointed to help the parties discuss the various solutions available and to make suggestions, it will be easier to find a solution or, at the very least, to narrow down the number of conflicting interparty issues.

Conciliation is distinct from the process of negotiation between the parties, as instead of attempting to handle the dispute alone, the parties approach the conciliator, as an independent third party, to assist them in resolution of their dispute. In contrast with the process of arbitration, where the parties entrust resolution of the dispute and the outcome of the dispute to an arbitral tribunal that imposes a binding decision on the parties, the conciliator, in response to an approach by the parties, provides independent and impartial assistance to the parties, in a bid to help them resolve their dispute themselves. This process also differs from arbitration in that the parties retain full control over the process and the outcome.

Arbitration[62]

Arbitration is the submission for determination of the disputed matter to a neutral third party for resolution by agreement of the parties. The third party may be a person or panel selected by the parties or by means of a process set down by the parties or by law where the parties fail to do so. Arbitration clauses are popular in many international commercial agreements.

There are several advantages associated with arbitration. Relative to litigation, the arbitration process is generally faster. Importantly the process is private, so that the fact that the matter is being arbitrated upon is confidential as is any final settlement or arbitral order made. This helps protect the parties' reputation, share price (especially where the shares are publicly traded), goodwill and brand image. Also, the parties are free to select the arbitrating body. Each body has its own procedures, rules of evidence and fees. Both parties are likely to agree on an arbitration body considered to be neutral in its affiliation. What is more, the arbitrators appointed will possess an expertise necessary to consider and resolve the dispute. Where a dispute arises involving the quality of specialised commodities (chemical compounds or pharmaceutical products for example) or services (construction and so on), it is essential that the parties arbitrating the dispute are able to understand the issues at hand. Long-term contracts lend themselves to arbitration: the parties involved will prefer to resort to arbitration over litigation, so that they can resolve their dispute as amicably as possible, salvaging their relationship.

The disadvantages associated with arbitration include expense (the arbitrator's fees are relatively high when compared with standard court fees) and the fact that there may be no right, or at the very least a limited right, of appeal.

Arbitration clauses usually include the name of the body that will arbitrate on the matter. On occasion the clause will include a note of which procedural rules govern the arbitration body and which law the arbitration body should apply to resolve the dispute at hand. Supplementary clauses accompanying the arbitration clause will include an indication of how the costs of and associated with the arbitration (including arbitrator's expenses and legal fees) will be dealt with. Costs may for example be the joint responsibility of the parties or the responsibility of the losing party.

An arbitration is quasi-judicial with the arbitrator replacing the judge. It is usually as formal as litigation, as the procedural rules laid down by the arbitration body will need to be followed by the parties. Each party will probably need to be legally represented, which will entail additional expenditure. Each party will need to submit evidence (occasionally the arbitrator or panel of arbitrators will ask the parties to provide further information or additional documentation). The parties may be questioned at the hearing (by the arbitrator, the panel and/or the lawyers representing the parties).

Each arbitration body has its own set of procedural rules. Many states have formulated their national rules on arbitration using the model rules set out by the United Nations Commission on International Trade Law (UNCITRAL).[63] The following section provides an overview of these model rules.

Composition
The parties are allowed to agree on the number of arbitrators on the panel. If they fail to do so, the number of arbitrators shall be three.[64] Moreover, the parties are free to decide on the procedure for the appointment of arbitrators. In default of an agreement, each party is permitted to appoint one arbitrator. The two appointed arbitrators will then appoint the third arbitrator.[65] A person appointed as an arbitrator must disclose any circumstance which could comprise his impartiality or independence.[66]

The tribunal has the power to grant an interim measure (a temporary order made pending a final decision) in response to a request by one of the parties.[67] Such a measure may include a request that a party preserve the assets out of which the subsequent award may be satisfied, or that a party preserve evidence relevant to resolution of the dispute. It may be modified, suspended or terminated on a party's application or the tribunal's own initiative.[68] Subject to limited exceptions (proper notice was not given to the party affected, one of the parties lacked capacity or the act was ultra vires to the arbitration agreement),[69] the interim measure shall be recognised as binding and, unless otherwise provided by the arbitral tribunal, enforced upon application to the competent court, irrespective of the country in which it was issued.[70]

Conduct of the arbitral tribunal[71]
The parties are treated equally and each has the opportunity to present its case[72]. The parties can agree the procedure for the tribunal, the location where the arbitration will take place and the language or languages to be used during the arbitration.[73] If no agreement can be reached, the tribunal itself will have the discretion to set its own procedural rules as well as the place of arbitration.[74]

Unless otherwise agreed, the applicant shall set out the facts supporting his claim, the points at issue and the remedy sought, and the respondent shall state his defence in respect of these particulars[75]. Each party retains the right to modify the particulars of their case, unless the parties have otherwise agreed and subject to the right of the tribunal to refuse the amendment due to the delay it may cause.[76]

Hearing[77]
Subject to an agreement to the contrary, the tribunal can decide either to hold oral hearings for the presentation of evidence or to base the proceedings on documents and other materials.[78] If the parties have agreed that no hearings shall be held, the tribunal may decide to hold such hearings in response to a request by one of the parties.[79] Sufficient advance notice of any hearing and of any meeting of the arbitral tribunal for the purposes of inspection of goods, other property or documents must be provided to the parties.[80]

Expert evidence[81]

Subject to a contrary agreement by the parties, the tribunal may appoint one or more experts to report on specific issues that the tribunal must decide upon and may order that a party provide the expert with evidence and information. Moreover, at the discretion of the tribunal or in response to a request by one of the parties, the expert shall, after delivery of his report, participate in the hearing so that the parties have an opportunity to put questions to the expert.[82]

Making an award and termination of the proceedings[83]

The tribunal will reach its decision based on the law selected by the parties in the contract to resolve disputes. Where the parties have not made such a selection, the tribunal will resort to the law determined by the conflict of laws rules which it considers applicable.[84]

Where the tribunal includes more than one arbitrator, decisions will be made by a majority of all its members, subject to a contrary decision by the parties[85].

If during the arbitral proceedings, the parties settle the dispute, the tribunal will put a stop to the proceedings and, at the request of the parties subject to the tribunal's right to object, record the settlement in the form of an arbitral award on agreed terms.[86] The final award will be written and signed by the arbitrator or arbitrators[87] and will bring the arbitral proceedings to an end[88].

Recourse against an award[89]

Within a three-month period starting with the date the award was made, a party can apply to court to set aside the award, so long as it can provide the necessary proof to demonstrate that one of the parties to the arbitration was under some incapacity; or the agreement was not valid under the law governing the agreement; or the party in question was not given notice of the appointment of the arbitrator or the arbitration proceedings, or was unable to present its case; or the court finds that the award was counter to public policy of the state; or the subject matter of the dispute was not capable of settlement by arbitration.[90]

Recognition and enforcement of an arbitral award[91]

An award made by an arbitral body will be recognised as binding and its enforcement will ensue,[92] irrespective of the country where the award was made, on the application of a party to the arbitration to a competent court,[93] subject only to limited restrictions.[94]

Litigation

At the international level there is no court or tribunal that has the **jurisdiction** to handle disputes between commercial entities. For this reason commercial disputes of an international character will typically be dealt with in national courts. In an international commercial dispute the adjudicating court may be based in the country of one of the contracting parties or in a third country with a perceived reputation for fairness and neutrality.

The parties are not obliged in most jurisdictions to exhaust out-of-court modes of resolution. In those jurisdictions where the parties do have an obligation to attempt to resolve the matter out of court before litigation commences, the court will stay the case until the parties have done so. Nevertheless, litigation is usually a last resort after the parties have exhausted all other options. Often it spells out the end of the commercial relationship between the parties. Where the parties aspire to resolve the issue or issues between them, so that they are able to continue their commercial relationship, then they are better off trying to use mediation or conciliation. If this option fails, the parties will resort to either arbitration or litigation.

Litigation has certain advantages. It is generally final so once a decision is made, unless there is some valid ground for appeal, that decision is conclusive and the losing party must comply with the court ruling. If the losing party fails to do so the winning party has the option of reapplying to the court to get the judgment it has obtained enforced against the losing party (**enforcement proceedings**).

Contractual terms governing litigation
When a contract is negotiated between two business entities located in separate countries, they should consider which court or tribunal will have the power to resolve those disputes that may arise between them. In addition, they should agree on the law applicable for the purpose of resolving such disputes.

It is important when choosing the law applicable to consider the position of the law chosen. In effect, does it favour one of the parties over the other or does it treat both on an equal footing? The parties should bear in mind that resolution of issues may differ depending on the law that they have chosen as applicable to their contract.

The problem litigating an international commercial dispute is that in default of a **choice of court clause** in the contract, there will be a race to issue in a forum perceived as favourable to the litigant (known as forum shopping). Forum shopping increases uncertainty and results in even more friction between the parties, reducing the prospect of an amicable settlement out of court.

IX Researching local law

When planning and drafting an international commercial agreement due regard needs to be given to a large number of issues in order to ensure that the agreement has legal force and is lawful and sound. A detailed examination of all these matters is beyond the scope of this book, but a review of some of these issues will be made to ensure a comprehensive overview of the essential components of an international agreement.[95]

Each business entity should research the market into which it is planning to export its goods, or in which it is looking to supply its services, or in which it is looking to contract with a local entity be it as an agent, a distributor, a licensee or a partner. When exporting, a business entity should examine the target market not only to find out what consumer preferences are in that market, but also to determine any local law that is applicable to the sale of the goods it is producing and looking to export into this market.

A business that plans to recruit a local agent, distributor or licensee should consider addressing the issue of responsibility for compliance with the local laws that affect the supply of the goods in question on the target market. Furthermore, when using a local agent, distributor or licensee, the foreign business entity should consider any applicable law that regulates these commercial relationships. The specific provisions that will be required in such contracts will be explored in Chapters 4, 5 and 6. The areas of law applicable to the sale of goods and the supply of services will include amongst others **tort**, product liability and criminal law. In the event that the foreign business entity plans to set up a permanent operation in the target market, either alone or in partnership with a local business entity, it will increase its exposure to local law.

A foreign business entity should address not only the legal regulations applicable in its country of origin but also any laws that affect its foreign operation. In the context of its foreign operation, the business entity should give due consideration to employment law, immigration law, tax law, competition law, corporate law and environmental law, amongst others.

Whilst this book cannot offer an overview of the law in each country, some brief and useful indicators are reviewed below.

Tort[96]

Tort obligations are owed by one party to another, such obligations embody norms of conduct that arise outside the contract.[97] Tort law permits one party to whom an obligation is owed to bring and pursue a remedy on his behalf where a breach of the relevant norm infringing his interests has arisen, to the extent that it is recognised in law as an infringement.[98] Generally in tort law, where a recognised infringement that results in injury to a person as well as to property and the economic interests of the person has occurred, the person to whom the obligation which has been breached is owed will be permitted to bring and pursue a remedy against the party that committed the wrong. The party that commits the wrong is referred to as the **tortfeasor**. Various categories of tort exist in English law including negligent invasions of personal interests, property interests and economic interests; intentional invasions of personal interests and property interests (including the torts of trespass to the person and trespass to land, as well as wrongful interference with goods); and torts involving strict or stricter liability (such as product liability).

When a tort has been committed the injured party or parties (where several parties are injured) or their personal representatives (where the injured party is unable to bring a claim – for example, where the injured party has died) may bring a claim against the tortfeasor or tortfeasors (when more than one party is responsible for the wrong).[99] In the event that the wrong results in the death of a party, the estate of that party may pursue the claim.[100] Where the party for some reason lacks capacity, by virtue of age or mental ability for instance, then another party may be given permission to pursue a claim on behalf of the injured party. For example this could happen when a child is injured and the parent is permitted to bring an action on behalf of the injured child.

Unless the case involves **strict liability**, the party or parties bringing and pursuing the claim (the **plaintiff** or in English law the **claimant**)[101] will have the responsibility of proving liability on the part of the party allegedly responsible for the wrong (the **defendant** or, where there are several parties, the **defendants**).[102] Beyond liability, the plaintiff is typically responsible for demonstrating a causal link between the wrong and the injury sustained (causation) and for proving the extent of his loss (quantum).[103]

If an **out-of-court settlement** fails, then the injured party will probably need to take the matter before a court of law possessing the power to adjudicate on the case (**jurisdiction**). The injured party may do so alone or as part of a **class action**.[104] Where a court action is commenced by the plaintiff, the defendant will have the option of either admitting the plaintiff's claim or pursuing a defence in relation to the entirety of the plaintiff's case or one or more of its components (such as liability, quantum, causation and foreseeability).[105] Just like the plaintiff, the defendant will need to adduce evidence in support of his defence.

The forms of evidence produced will depend primarily on the nature of the claim. The evidence adduced by the plaintiff and the defendant may take a variety of forms including witness evidence, site reports, inspection reports and expert evidence. Expert reports such as medical and physiological reports may be commissioned to comment on any injuries sustained by the plaintiff, where they were allegedly sustained as a result of the wrong committed by the defendant. Such reports are likely to comment not only on the extent of the injuries but also on the likelihood that the wrong led to the injuries themselves. Engineering reports and site reports may be used where for example the wrong involved a plant (manufacturing site, mine and so on) or vehicle (train, plane, car, ship and so on).

Any judgment rendered by the judges or arbitral award granted by the arbitrators must be capable of enforcement.

The plaintiff's objective is typically the recovery of **damages**.[106] Two categories of damages exist: **compensatory damages** and **punitive damages**. Punitive damages may also be available in certain legal systems against the defendant or defendants.[107]

Recovery of compensation is typically limited by the rules of remoteness.[108] The plaintiff is obliged at all times to keep his losses down (duty of mitigation). The defendant may attempt to argue for a reduction in the level of compensatory damages due or the exclusion of a claim by the plaintiff.[109] If the court agrees with the defendant, the plaintiff's claim may be reduced or barred altogether. Consider an employee, who fails to wear the protective equipment provided by his employer, sustaining an injury that could have been minimised or avoided completely. In such a scenario, the defendant is probably going to demand that the claim of the plaintiff be reduced to take account of the negligence of the plaintiff himself.

Torts and the crossover between tort and crime/contract[110]

Whereas civil law is primarily concerned with the rights and duties of individuals amongst themselves, criminal law defines duties which a person owes to society. Criminal law aims to protect the interest of the public at large (or the state) whereas the primary function of tort is to protect the interests of individuals. In criminal law, the wrong is of such a serious nature (amounting to a violation of a public duty) that the appropriate level of government steps in to punish the offender, deterring others from repeating this wrong.

Certain types of conduct simultaneously constitute both a crime and a tort. A thief who steals a watch commits in English law both a crime (theft) and a tort (conversion). When a person intentionally strikes another during a fight, in English law, the person will have committed a tort (battery) and crime (battery). If the crime is such that it results in physical harm to an identifiable person, that person may also sue the tortfeasor in tort. If a driver goes through a red light causing the death of another, the state may prosecute the driver for dangerous driving and manslaughter, whilst the representatives of the deceased and his dependants have the option of suing the tortfeasor (the offending driver) in tort.

It is also true that one set of circumstances may give rise to a claim in both tort and contract. A lawyer who negligently advises a client may be sued in contract and tort (in the tort of **negligence**). A surgeon who negligently treats a patient may be found to have breached an obligation in contract law (to take reasonable care) and to have committed a tortious act by invasion of a tort-protected interest (the interest in freedom from physical harm) for which an action in negligence will lie.

Apart from the formal distinction between a duty in contract and one in tort, there is a substantial difference in the respective aims of the two. The contractual duty is said to result from the agreement between the parties whilst the duty in tort is one created by law independently of the consent of the parties. The purpose of a contract is always to protect the same interest, namely the interest in the performance of the promises by the other contracting party or parties, whilst the interests of tort are more diverse.

New legal issues have emerged in the field of tort due to developments in technology and innovations involving cyberspace. Interception of emails, the use of another person's identity and the making of false statements about another, using the internet, are all examples of contemporary torts.

Types of tort

There are three types of tort in English law:

1. **intentional tort** to a person or property
2. **negligence**
3. **strict liability**.

Intentional torts[111]
Two types of **intentional tort** exist, that involving the person and that involving property. Intentional torts to the person comprise acts of the defendant which directly and either intentionally or negligently[112]

1. cause some physical contact with the person of the plaintiff without the consent of the latter (battery);
2. cause the plaintiff to immediately apprehend some contact with his person (assault); or
3. result in the total confinement of the plaintiff within an area delimited by the defendant in a situation where the plaintiff has not agreed to this confinement (false imprisonment).

Other torts to another affected by the defendant will include the intentional act of intruding into the private affairs of another (invasion of privacy) and making an untrue statement about another to a third party, either verbally (slander) or in writing (libel).

Intentional torts involving property belonging to another person comprise those acts of the defendant which either intentionally or negligently interfere with goods owned by another without the permission of the latter. The act of displacing property belonging to another, taking possession of property belonging to another or touching property belonging to another are examples of intentional torts involving the property of another, as are the following scenarios: the act of staying on land belonging to another or entering that land without permission from the owner (trespass on land); the making of false statements to a third party about another's product or service (product disparagement); attempting to interfere with the execution of a contract (wrongful interference with contracts).

The tort of negligence[113]
Negligence arises in situations where someone is exercising less care than they would be expected to exercise in a given situation, bearing in mind the standard of care a reasonable person would employ in the same situation. To succeed against a defendant, a plaintiff needs to show that the defendant or defendants (when several parties are allegedly responsible) owed a duty of care to the plaintiff, which has been breached and which has resulted in injury to the plaintiff. Foreseeability and causation must also be proven by the plaintiff if he is to succeed against the defendant.

Box 1.9 Scenarios which may give rise to claims in negligence

A loose tile falls off a roof on to a passer-by or a person that enters the property. In such a situation the facts may lead to a claim in negligence as the owner of the property is deemed in law to have a duty to take care of his property so that its condition does not cause hazards to visitors to the property or passers-by.

Businesses have a duty to keep their premises in order, so that visitors and workers are not injured by foreseeable hazards. A customer in a restaurant who falls down a flight of stairs due to a defect in one of the stairs may have a viable claim in negligence. Similarly, a customer or employee of a shop who slips on spilt liquid may claim against the shop owners.

Strict liability[114]

Due to public policy considerations liability may be imposed on a defendant for a specific wrong irrespective of fault on his part.[115] Such liability is referred to as **strict liability**. In such a situation, it is irrelevant whether the defendant who committed the act did so intentionally or negligently.

Absolute standard of liability is imposed by law for public policy reasons, in order to guarantee protection in exceptional situations that the legislature and courts have deemed necessitate a high degree of protection. For this reason, few defences are available in these situations.

Product liability[116]

Products dominate our lives even though most of us do not necessarily reflect on the degree to which our day-to-day existence is built upon, controlled by and lived through them.[117] Product liability refers to the liability for injury, death and/or damage to property that arises during the course of using or consuming a product. When a party is injured by a defective product or his property is damaged as a result of the said product, he may rely on three optional courses of action against either the producer or seller of the said product:[118] negligence, breach of contract and/or strict liability. In contrast with other jurisdictions that have approached product liability by way of contract law obligations, the United States has opted for a tort law approach to product liability which is rooted in the duty not to injure the user of a product.[119]

Strict liability in product cases basically means that negligence on the part of the producer or seller of the defective product need not be proven by the injured party.[120] An advantage associated with a claim based on strict liability, from the perspective of the plaintiff, is the fact that no contractual relation is required between the defendant and the injured party in order for the injured party to pursue an action against the defendant. So if for example a gift causes injury to the recipient, the recipient of the gift may sue the owner of the shop where the gift was purchased even though the recipient of the gift had no contract with the shop owner. The injured party will only need to demonstrate that the defendant sold the product in a defective or dangerous condition and that the defect resulted in his injury. The courts have promoted the doctrine of strict liability as a way of protecting the consumer, who is perceived as being powerless to protect himself, by making sure that the producer is made responsible for improving the quality of its goods, whilst at the same time deterring it from producing and selling unsafe goods.

Potential claims commonly arise from product defects, either in manufacturing or in design. A manufacturing defect is a fault that appears during the manufacturing process (a failure to meet design specifications). Such a defect will not typically appear in other products off the production line. A design defect can result from an inadequate design or poor choice of materials. Such a defect will render the product dangerous to users.

Strict liability in the context of product liability

Strict liability arises in the context of product liability in the European Union[121] and invariably in the United Kingdom as consequence of its membership of the EU.[122] Strict liability can be found in US law.[123] A defendant will be held liable in strict liability if the plaintiff shows

- an injury to his person or to his property;
- that the injury was caused by a defect in the product which made the product unreasonably dangerous (typically a product is dangerous if its characteristics do not meet the consumer's expectations); and
- that the defect must have existed at the time the product left the hands of the defendant and did not substantially change along the way.[124]

Strict liability will permit the injured party to recover **damages** even if the seller has exercised all possible care in the manufacture and sale of the product. Negligent conduct on the part of the manufacturer or seller is not requisite as it is the presence of the defect itself that is the basis for liability.

Strict liability in relation to defective products that cause injury to the buyer, the user, a bystander or their respective property may extend to all parties in the chain of distribution, including producer, distributor, wholesaler and retailer. Nowadays, many jurisdictions impose strict liability on the various links in the chain of distribution so that the injured party is entitled to recover compensation against these parties without having to demonstrate that the defendant in question was negligent or otherwise at fault. Under EU law, by way of an example, the parties liable for damage caused by a defect in a product include

- all the producers involved in the production process including the manufacturer of the finished product and the component parts, the producer of any raw material as well as any person who by putting his name or trade mark or other distinguishing feature on the product presents himself as its producer;
- each supplier of the product if the producer cannot be identified unless the supplier informs the injured person within a reasonable time of the identity of the producer or the person who supplied him with the product; and
- the importer of the product into the EU.[125]

Product liability under EU law[126]

The 1985 Directive required member states in the EU to implement the provisions of the directive within a period of three years from its date of notification.[127] The UK for its part implemented the 1985 Directive by means of Part I of the Consumer Protection Act 1987 (CPA),[128] which came into force on 1 March 1988.[129]

Pursuant to EU law, a producer is liable for damage caused by a defect in his product[130] and a product is deemed to be defective when it does not provide the safety which a person is entitled to expect.[131] Where two or more parties are liable for the same damage, they are liable jointly and severally.[132] In this context, a claim may be pursued for damage caused by death or personal injury as well as damage to or destruction of property.[133] Under the 1985 Directive as amended by the 1999 Directive, a product is defined as meaning all movables even if incorporated into another movable or into an immovable[134] and is deemed to include electricity.[135]

The injured party is required to prove the damage, the defect and the causal relationship between the defect and the damage.[136] The liability of the producer under the directives in relation to the injured person may not be limited or excluded by means of a contractual provision limiting the liability of the producer or exempting him from liability.[137] Under EU law, a producer will escape liability if, inter alia, he did not put the product into circulation or he did not manufacture the product for sale or in the course of his business, or if the state of scientific and technical knowledge at the time that the product was put into circulation was not such as to allow the defect to be discovered (the state of the art defence, otherwise referred to as the development risk defence), or if the defect probably did not exist at the time that the product was put into circulation.[138]

Warning on goods
A product must carry adequate warnings of the risks associated with normal use as well as being accompanied by a set of instructions for safe use. Whilst an adequate warning may protect a manufacturer where the product is properly designed and manufactured, an adequate warning will not shield the manufacturer where the product is defectively designed or manufactured.

Liability of third parties for damages of others

An employer may be potentially liable not only to his employees (for failure to exercise reasonable care in the provision of a safe working environment for example) but also for torts committed by his employees, during the course of their employment or in connection with their employment. An employer may therefore be sued for accidents caused by his employees during office hours for example.

Successor liability

Businesses that purchase ongoing concerns could potentially find themselves liable not only for contracts of the former owner but also for his claims in tort. Successor liability may arise for example where an injury to an employee has been sustained over the course of a number of years or decades, during which time the factory in which the employee works has been owned by a succession of firms. This is the case with industrial diseases claims such as vibrating white finger and claims involving deafness or loss of hearing. In such a situation, the co-defendants if deemed liable will be required to apportion the claim of the plaintiff (the employee) between them.

Crime[139]

From the point of view of a business, beyond the traditional crimes that involve injury to a person or property or the use or threat of force (such as theft and arson), other crimes exist that do not necessarily involve force or violence or indeed direct injury to person or property (for example bribery). Whilst liability under criminal law will be borne by the party responsible for the criminal act itself (such as an employee, manager or consultant), it can also be borne by the officers and directors of a corporation who failed to prevent the commission of the crime or who incited the employee to commit the crime, and even by the corporation itself.

Tax

It is impossible to generalise about the tax systems found in the various countries of the world; however, some brief observations may prove useful in this context. Most countries have a system of taxation aimed at generating revenue for the state, typically using sales taxes (also known as value added taxes, and levied on the sale of most goods and the supply of the majority of services), capital gains taxes (levied on the profit generated by the sale of assets) and income taxes (levied on the income generated by corporations, businesses and individuals). A business that runs a foreign operation or has foreign investments must consider the tax regime in its own country as well as the tax regime in the foreign market in which it has interests. Such a business must obtain specialised tax advice on the subject.

X Available entry strategies[140]

Export markets, traditionally the sole province of large multinational businesses, are now being explored by small to medium-sized business entities.[141] This expansion of business interests has been helped along by a number of factors, including modern technology, the liberalisation of foreign markets, developments in transportation, access to the internet and the availability of easily accessible information about investment opportunities in different markets worldwide.

An entity will look to establish new markets and diversify existing markets for a number of reasons, which may include a desire to diversify investments, to expand market share, to increase a revenue stream and to remain competitive. Moreover, such an entity may opt to expand beyond its home market in order to hedge against periodic domestic instability.[142]

A number of entry structures are available to an entity that is looking to develop a foreign market for its goods and/or services. They can be divided into two main categories, namely contractual arrangements for entry into a given market (distribution, licensing, franchising and so on) or equity structures allowing entry into a given market (representative office, foreign branch, foreign subsidiary and so on).[143] In the context of contractual arrangements, typically the entity will select from one or more of the following entry structures:

- exporting goods manufactured in the country of origin directly to the end customer
- working with an agent in the target market who is responsible for sourcing customers and on occasion for concluding contracts and supplying the contracted goods to the customers[144]
- using the services of a confirming house in the foreign market
- distributing products through an affiliated entity that is distinct from the manufacturer
- licensing a foreign firm to use process or product technology to manufacture goods and/or supply services.[145]

In the context of equity structures, the entity will typically employ one or both of these:

- Establishing a branch office staffed by personnel recruited locally and personnel originating from the head office or one of the other offices of the foreign firm. The branch will either operate alone or in cooperation with other parties charged with the given market (be it the agent, distributor or licensee affiliated to the foreign firm). The branch may be responsible for providing a service to the local customers

(for example an after-sales service), for organising promotional activities on the given market and for assisting and overseeing the efforts of an agent or distributor operating on the given market.
- Setting up a subsidiary in the given market which will assume responsibility for certain operations on that market either alone or in cooperation with other parties charged with the market. This structure will permit the entity to retain control over the operation and to maximise its return, but will also involve substantial manpower, risk and outlay. Such operations may include sales, marketing and/or production.

A seller wishing to promote sales abroad will be greatly advantaged if it retains the services of a representative to promote its interests in the target market. In the alternative, the seller may decide either to enter into a licensing agreement with an existing firm in the target market or to create a more permanent presence in the target market, by opening a branch, entering into a joint venture with a local entity or several local entities, setting up a local corporation incorporated in the target market, or merging with or acquiring a local business concern. Indeed, the entity might eventually generate greater profits from producing its goods in or within the vicinity of the target market. Should such an entity produce goods in the target market it will certainly avoid many if not all of the overheads associated with export and import operations, as well as the risks and costs associated with the transportation of goods to the target market. Local production of goods or provision of services will also ensure that such goods or services are adapted to local trends and conform to local law.

By engaging a foreign party to take on the manufacturing or merchandising, an entity is able to avoid many of the risks and legal concerns that are associated with capital investment abroad. For example, by granting a licence to an existing entity based in the target market, the principal (in this case acting as a licensor) will be relying on the entity to which the licence is granted (the licensee) to use the intellectual property rights (IPRs) owned by the principal when producing the goods. The licensee will in turn be responsible for the bulk of the investment and the risk.

When an entity first establishes a presence abroad, it becomes subject to regulation in the country that it is looking to penetrate. As the presence of the foreign entity in the host country becomes more permanent (for example progressing from a representative office to a locally incorporated subsidiary) the level of host country regulation intensifies. An entity that builds a factory in a foreign country will become subject to national law and on occasion relevant regional law (this will be relevant when setting up in one of the member states of the European Union for example). As such it will be governed inter alia by employment law, environmental law, health and safety law, product liability law, tax law, technology transfer laws and laws governing the appropriate level of foreign ownership of businesses as well as competition law.

Investment abroad will not only involve a more substantial capital outlay and increased legal entanglement, but will entail exposure to political forces and local policy. In contrast with international commercial law and international trade law, in which substantial harmonisation has already taken place as a result of the efforts of UNCITRAL, the WTO and the EU institutions, the laws governing foreign investment are peculiarly reflective of local culture, politics and attitudes. Moreover, these rules are constantly evolving.

Summary

This chapter has explained the main concerns associated with international contracts.

Firstly, it looked at the importance of form and the process of contract formation, as well as the importance of subject matter. Secondly, it examined the impact of tariff and non-tariff barriers and their importance when deciding if and how to contract. Thirdly, it considered the importance of planning for potential disputes (here we looked at the need to include provisions providing for adaption and renegotiation and if all fails, provisions providing for alternative dispute resolution and litigation). Fourthly, it highlighted the importance of researching the law in the target market, focusing on questions of liability in tort, crime and tax law. Finally, it reviewed the different entry strategies that a business entity can opt for when it is looking to develop a foreign market. Typically such an entity will have a choice between different strategies including

- sale directly to a customer;
- appointment of an agent;
- appointment of a distributor;
- licensing of the intellectual property belonging to the entity; and
- foreign production of goods or supply of services by the entity.

Useful links

http://eur-lex.europa.eu/LexUriServ/LexUriServ.do?uri=CELEX:31985L0374:en:HTML (Council Directive 85/374/EEC)

http://www.uncitral.org/uncitral/en/uncitral_texts/sale_goods.html (full text of the CISG)

http://www.wto.org (World Trade Organization)

Further reading

Barnard, Catherine (2007), *The Substantive Law of the EU: The Four Freedoms*, 2nd ed., Oxford University Press.

Brazier, Margaret (1988), *Street on Torts*, 8th ed., Butterworths.

Dignam, Alan and Lowry, John (2006), *Company Law*, 4th ed., Oxford University Press.

Elliott, Catherine and Quinn, Frances (2008), *Criminal Law*, 7th ed., Pearson Longman.

Folsom, Ralph, Gordon, Michael, Spanogle, John and Fitzgerald, Peter (2009), *Folsom, Gordon, Spanogle and Fitzgerald's International Business Transactions: A Problem-oriented Coursebook*, West Group.

Howells, Geraint and Weatherill, Stephen (2005), *Consumer Protection Law*, 2nd ed., Ashgate.

Matsushita, Mitsuo, Schoenbaum, Thomas J. and Mavroidis, Petros C. (2006), *The World Trade Organization: Law, Practice and Policy*, 2nd ed., Oxford University Press.

Murphy, John and Witting, Christian (2012), *Street on Torts*, 13th ed., Oxford University Press.

Pettet, Ben (2005), Company Law, 2nd ed., Pearson Education.

Poole, Jill (2008), *Textbook on Contract Law*, Oxford University Press.
Schulze, Reiner, Schulte-Nölke, Hans and Jones, Jackie (2002), *A Casebook on European Consumer Law*, Hart.
Slapper, Gary and Kelly, David (2010), *The English Legal System*, 11th ed., Routledge.
Van den Bossche, Peter (2005), *The Law and Policy of the World Trade Organization: Text, Cases and Materials*, Cambridge University Press.
Whittaker, Simon (2005), *Liability for Products: English Law, French Law, and European Harmonization*, Oxford University Press.
Wild, Charles and Weinstein, Stuart (2010), *Smith and Keenan's English Law: Text and Cases*, Pearson Education.

Notes

1. Poole, Jill (2008), *Textbook on Contract Law*, Oxford University Press, 21.
2. Ibid., 21–2.
3. United Nations Convention on Contracts for the International Sale of Goods 1980 (CISG) available at http://www.uncitral.org/uncitral/en/uncitral_texts/sale_goods.html (last accessed 17th July 2012). The CISG has rejected the formalistic approach adopted by the statute of frauds in the United States. Pursuant to the Uniform Commercial Code §2-201 (1995) used in the various states in the United States, a contract for the sale of goods for the price of $500 or more is not enforceable unless there is some writing sufficient to indicate that a contract for sale has been concluded and signed by the party or by his authorised agent against whom enforcement is sought. In contrast, the CISG adopts a practical approach by stating that a contract for the sale of goods need not be concluded in writing or evidenced in writing and is not subject to any requirement as to form (Article 11 CISG).
4. Illegality and capacity to contract under English law are addressed in Poole (2008), Chapter 16.
5. Illegality and its effect on contracts under English law is reviewed in Poole (2008), Chapter 16.
6. Under English law, §18 Gaming Act 1845 provided that gambling contracts were null and void so that there could be no action in the courts pertaining to the recovery of winnings. The Gambling Act 2005 reverses §18 Gaming Act 1845. Gambling contracts under English law are reviewed in Poole (2008: 628).
7. Statutory illegality under English law is reviewed in Poole (2008: 627–8).
8. The impact of public policy on the legality of contracts in English law is reviewed in Poole (2008: 629–30).
9. Relations with third parties on behalf of a company under English law are reviewed in Pettet, Ben (2005), *Company Law*, 2nd ed., Pearson Education, Chapter 7. Pre-incorporation contracts and the role and liability of the promoters under English law are reviewed in Dignam, Alan and Lowry, John (2006), *Company Law*, 4th ed., Oxford University Press, Chapter 4.
10. Organisation of functions in a company and corporate powers under English law are reviewed in Pettet (2005), Chapter 6.

11. Agency and the authority of agents will be addressed later on in this book.
12. Capacity to contract under English law is addressed in Poole (2008), Chapter 16.
13. Mental impairment and the capacity to contract under English law are reviewed in Poole (2008: 646–7).
14. §2 Mental Capacity Act 2005.
15. The position of intoxicated persons and those whose understanding and awareness are impaired under English law are reviewed in Poole (2008: 647).
16. Trade barriers are reviewed in van den Bossche, Peter (2005), *The Law and Policy of the World Trade Organization: Text, Cases and Materials*, Cambridge University Press, Chapter 5, and Matsushita, Mitsuo, Schoenbaum, Thomas J. and Mavroidis, Petros C. (2006), *The World Trade Organization: Law, Practice and Policy*, 2nd ed., Oxford University Press, Chapter 8.
17. The topic of trade liberalisation versus protectionism is reviewed in van den Bossche (2005), Chapter 1.
18. Paragraph 32, Japan-Taxes on Alcoholic Beverages, AB-1996-2, Report of the Appellate Body, 4 October 1996, WT/DS8/AB/R, WT/DS10/AB/R, WT/DS11/AB/R, 96-3951 reads: 'The WTO Agreement is a treaty – the international equivalent of a contract. It is self-evident that in an exercise of their sovereignty, and in pursuit of their own respective national interests, the Members of the WTO have made a bargain. In exchange for the benefits they expect to derive as Members of the WTO, they have agreed to exercise their sovereignty according to the commitments they have made in the WTO Agreement.'
19. Tariff concessions and schedules of concessions are reviewed in van den Bossche (2005: 398–425).
20. Tariff data is available at http://www.wto.org/english/res_e/statis_e/statis_e.htm (last accessed 14 January 2013).
21. The origins of the WTO and its mandate, composition, institutional structure and decision-making procedure are reviewed in van den Bossche (2005), Chapter 2 and Matsushita et al. (2006), Chapter 1.
22. The General Agreement on Tariffs and Trade 1947 is available at http://www.wto.org/english/docs_e/legal_e/gatt47_01_e.htm (last accessed 14 January 2013).
23. The Agreement Establishing the World Trade Organization is available at https://www.wto./english/docs_e/legal_e/04-wto.pdf (last accessed 14 January 2013).
24. See the preamble to the Agreement Establishing the World Trade Organization.
25. The online customs tariff database for the European Union is available at http://ec.europa.eu/taxation_customs/customs/customs_duties/tariff_aspects/customs_tariff/index_en.htm (last accessed 14 January 2013).
26. The topic of the external economic relations of the EU is reviewed in Barnard, Catherine (2007), *The Substantive Law of the EU: The Four Freedoms*, 2nd ed., Oxford University Press, Chapter 10.
27. Trade liberalisation is reviewed in van den Bossche (2005), Chapter 1.
28. This topic is discussed in more detail in Chapter 7.
29. Article 5.1.6 UNIDROIT Principles.
30. Article 5.1.7 UNIDROIT Principles.

31. Article 6.1.1 UNIDROIT Principles.
32. Article 6.1.4 UNIDROIT Principles.
33. Article 6.1.6 UNIDROIT Principles.
34. Article 6.1.10 UNIDROIT Principles.
35. Article 6:104 PECL.
36. Article 6:108 PECL.
37. Article 7:101 PECL.
38. Article 7:102(3) PECL.
39. Article 7:108 PECL.
40. In the US, §2-303 UCC.
41. Article 67(1) CISG.
42. Ibid.
43. Article 68 CISG.
44. In the US, §§2-314, 2-315 UCC.
45. Where the parties fail to specify the place for delivery of the goods, §2-309(1) UCC. Where the parties fail to determine the time for shipment or delivery of goods, §2-309(1) UCC. Where the parties fail to define a term, §2-309 (2) UCC.
46. Fortgang, Ron S., Lax, David A. and Sebenius, James (2008), 'Negotiating the Spirit of the Deal', *Harvard Business Review OnPoint*, Summer 2008, 86.
47. Fortgang et al. 2008: 92.
48. Fortgang et al. 2008: 93.
49. Adaptation is mentioned in Fox, William F. Jr (1992), *International Commercial Agreements: A Primer on Drafting, Negotiating and Resolving Disputes*, Kluwer Law and Taxation, 83.
50. Article 5.1.7 UNIDROIT Principles.
51. Article 6:104 PECL.
52. Article 55 CISG.
53. Article 5.1.7 UNIDROIT Principles refers to the price generally charged at the time of the conclusion of the contract for such performance in comparable circumstances in the trade concerned as the standard for determination of pricing. Article 55 CISG refers to the price 'generally charged at the time of the conclusion of the contract for such goods sold under comparable circumstances in the trade concerned' as the standard for determination of pricing. Article 6:104 PECL indicates that where the contract does not fix the price and no method for determining price is included in the contract, then the parties are treated as having agreed on a reasonable price. Pursuant to PECL, reasonableness is determined by reference to 'what persons acting in good faith and in the same situation as the parties would consider to be reasonable. In particular, in assessing what is reasonable the nature and purpose of the contract, the circumstances of the case, and the usages and practices of the trades or professions involved should be taken into account.' (Article 1:302 PECL).
54. §2-305 UCC.
55. Severance clauses are reviewed in Chapter 2.
56. In the US, §2-302 UCC.
57. Modification clauses are reviewed in Chapter 2.

58. Renegotiation is mentioned in Fox (1992: 84). In Fortgang et al. (2008: 92), consideration is given to using re-evaluation and renegotiation. In Ertel, Danny (2008), 'Getting past Yes: Negotiating as if Implementation Mattered', *Harvard Business Review OnPoint*, Summer 2008, consideration is given to the idea of bargaining using an implementation mind-set in order to set the stage for a long-term relationship.
59. Reviewed in Chapter 2.
60. Dispute resolution is reviewed in Murray, Carole, Holloway, David and Timson-Hunt, Daren (2007), *Schmitthoff's Export Trade: The Law and Practice of International Trade*, 11th ed., Sweet & Maxwell, Chapters 21–4.
61. *Guide to Enactment and Use of the UNCITRAL Model Law on International Commercial Conciliation* (2002), United Nations, Article 1(3), Para. 5.0.
62. Arbitration is reviewed in Murray et al. (2007), Chapter 23.
63. *UNCITRAL Model Law on International Commercial Arbitration 1985 with Amendments as Adopted in 2006* (2008), United Nations.
64. Ibid., Article 12.
65. Ibid., Article 11(3).
66. Ibid., Article 12(1).
67. Ibid., Article 17D.
68. Ibid., Article 17D.
69. Ibid., Article 17I.
70. Ibid., Article 17H.
71. Ibid., Articles 18–27.
72. Ibid., Article 18.
73. Ibid., Articles 19, 20, 22.
74. Ibid., Articles 19, 20, 22.
75. Ibid., Article 23.
76. Ibid., Article 23.
77. Ibid., Article 24.
78. Ibid., Article 24.
79. Ibid., Article 24.
80. Ibid., Article 24.
81. Ibid., Article 26.
82. Ibid., Article 26.
83. Ibid., Articles 28–33.
84. Ibid., Article 28.
85. Ibid., Article 28.
86. Ibid., Article 30.
87. Ibid., Article 31.
88. Ibid., Article 32.
89. Ibid., Article 34.
90. Ibid., Article 34.
91. Ibid., Articles 35, 36.
92. Reflecting the rules found in the 1958 Convention on the Recognition and Enforcement of Foreign Arbital Awards, also known as the New York Convention.

93. *UNCITRAL Model Law on International Commercial Arbitration 1985 with Amendments as Adopted in 2006* (2008), Article 35.
94. Ibid., Article 36.
95. The rules governing international contracts for the sale of goods are reviewed in Chapter 7.
96. English law on torts is reviewed in Murphy, John and Witting, Christian (2012), *Street on Torts*, 13th ed., Oxford University Press.
97. Definition provided in Murphy and Witting (2012: 3).
98. Definition provided ibid.
99. The principles of compensation for personal injury and other losses under English tort law are reviewed in Murphy and Witting (2012), Chapter 27.
100. Capacity and parties in English tort law are reviewed in Murphy and Witting (2012), Chapter 25.
101. Whilst a plaintiff is known as a claimant in English law, where reference is made in this book to the 'claimant' the term is regarded as encompassing both claimants and plaintiffs.
102. Strict or stricter liability in English tort law is reviewed in Murphy and Witting (2012), Chapters 15–19. Negligent invasions of interests in the person, property interests and economic interests under English law are reviewed in Murphy and Witting (2012), Chapters 2–7.
103. Duty of care, breach of duty of care, causation and remoteness in English tort law are reviewed in Murphy and Witting (2012), Chapters 2–5.
104. Class actions are permitted in certain jurisdictions. In the US, for example, they are permitted by Rule 23 of the Federal Rules of Civil Procedure, available at http://www.law.cornell.edu/rules/frcp/rule_23 (last accessed 15 January 2013).
105. Defences in English tort law are reviewed in Murphy and Witting (2012) as follows: Chapter 6 reviews defences to claims in negligence, Chapter 11 defences to intentional torts, Chapter 16, §6 defences to nuisance claims, Chapter 19, §6 defences to breaches of statutory duties, Chapter 21 defences to defamation, and Chapter 22, §3 defences to misuse of private information.
106. The principles of compensation for personal injury and other losses under English tort law are reviewed in Murphy and Witting (2012), Chapter 27.
107. Such punitive damages are permitted in the US. See in this regard the judgments in the US cases of *Honda Motor Co.* v. *Oberg* 512 US 415 (1980) and *O'Gilvie et al, Minors* v. *United States* 519 US 79 (1996).
108. See the judgment in the US case of *Palsgraf* v. *Long Island Railroad Co.* 248 NY 339, 162 NE 99.
109. Contributory negligence, voluntary assumption of risk, limitation and exclusion of liability under English law are reviewed in Murphy and Witting (2012), Chapter 6.
110. The crossover between tort and other branches of common law (contract and crime) in English law is reviewed in Murphy and Witting (2012), Chapter 1.
111. Intentional invasions of personal and property interests are reviewed in Murphy and Witting (2012) Chapters 8–11; interference with economic and intellectual property interests are reviewed in Murphy and Witting (2012),

Chapters 12–14; interests in reputation are reviewed in Murphy and Witting (2012), Chapters 20 and 21; and misuse of private information is reviewed in Murphy and Witting (2012), Chapter 22 (all with respect to English law).
112. Brazier, Margaret (1988), *Street on Torts*, 8th ed., Butterworths, 21 (definition of battery), 25 (definition of assault); 27–8 (definition of false imprisonment).
113. Negligent invasions of personal, property and economic interests under English law are reviewed in Murphy and Witting (2012), Chapters 2–7.
114. Torts involving strict and stricter liability in English law are reviewed in Murphy and Witting (2012),: Chapters 15–19.
115. Strict liability is regarded as an ambiguous term – see *Lord Macmillan, Read v. J. Lyons & Co. Ltd* [1947] AC 156, 171, [1946] 2 All ER 471, HL. The definition of strict liability varies from tort to tort (Brazier 1988: 290).
116. Product liability in general is reviewed in the following articles: Orban, Frank (1978), 'Products Liability: A Comparative Restatement – Foreign National Law and the EEC Directive', *Georgia Journal of International and Comparative Law* 8, 342, 344–5; Boger, William (1983), 'The Harmonization of European Products Liability Law', *Fordham International Law Journal* 7:1, 1; Owen, David (1990), 'Products Liability: Principles of Justice for the 21st Century', *Pace Law Review* 11, 63; Owen, David (1991), 'Products Liability: Principles of Justice', *Anglo-American Law Review* 20, 238.
117. Owen 1991: 239.
118. Boger 1983: 1.
119. Ibid.
120. Orban 1978: note 2 at 345.
121. The EU has adopted two directives addressing the issue of liability for defective products, namely Council Directive 85/374/EEC of 25 July 1985 on the Approximation of the Laws, Regulations and Administrative Provisions of the Member States Concerning Liability for Defective Products (the 1985 Directive, available at http://eur-lex.europa.eu/LexUriServ/LexUriServ.do?uri=CELEX:31985L0374:en:HTML (last accessed 15 January 2013)) and Directive 1999/34/EC of the European Parliament and of the Council of 10 May 1999, Amending the 1985 Directive (the 1999 Directive, available at http://eur-lex.europa.eu/LexUriServ/LexUriServ.do?uri=OJ:L:1999:141:0020:0021:EN:PDF (last accessed 15 January 2013)).
122. In the United Kingdom, the 1985 Directive was enacted as the Consumer Protection Act 1987, available at http://www.legislation.gov.uk/ukpga/1987/43 (last accessed 15 January 2013).
123. The concept of strict liability in US law is discussed in the case of *Greenman v. Yuba Power Products Inc.*, 377 P2d 897 and is incorporated in §402A Restatement (Second) of Torts (as amended by Restatement (3rd) of Torts adopted by several states).
124. Article 1, 1985 Directive states: 'Producer shall be liable for damage caused by a defect in his product.' Article 6(1), 1985 Directive reads: 'A product is defective when it does not provide the safety which a person is entitled to expect taking all circumstances into account, including: a) presentation of the product; b) the use to which it could reasonably be expected that the product

would be put; c) the time when the product was put into circulation.' §402A Restatement (Second) of Torts reads: 'One who sells any product in a defective condition unreasonably dangerous to the user or consumer or to his property is subject to liability for physical harm thereby caused to the ultimate user or consumer, or to his property if

>The seller is engaged in the business of selling such a product, and It is expected and does reach the user or consumer without substantial change in the condition in which it was sold.'

125. Article 3, 1985 Directive.
126. Product liability under EU law is reviewed in Howells, Geraint and Weatherill, Stephen (2005), *Consumer Protection Law*, 2nd ed., Ashgate.
127. Article 19, 1985 Directive.
128. The full title of the CPA is 'An Act to make provision with respect to the liability of persons for damage caused by defective products; to consolidate with amendments the Consumer Safety Act 1978 and the Consumer Safety (Amendment) Act 1986; to make provision with respect to the giving of price indications; to amend Part I of the Health and Safety at Work etc. Act 1974 and sections 31 and 80 of the Explosives Act 1875; to repeal the Trade Descriptions Act 1972 and the Fabrics (Misdescription) Act 1913; and for connected purposes'.
129. §1 CPA states: 'This part shall have the effect for the purpose of making such provision as is necessary to comply with the product liability Directive and shall be construed accordingly.'
130. Article 1, 1985 Directive.
131. Article 6, 1985 Directive.
132. Article 5, 1985 Directive.
133. Article 9, 1985 Directive.
134. Article 2, 1985 Directive as amended by the 1999 Directive.
135. Article 2, 1985 Directive.
136. Article 4, 1985 Directive.
137. Article 12, 1985 Directive.
138. Article 7, 1985 Directive.
139. Criminal law in England is reviewed in Elliott, Catherine and Quinn, Frances, (2008), *Criminal Law*, 7th ed., Pearson Longman.
140. These different entry structures are reviewed in Berwind, Michael, (1983), 'Strategies for Entering Foreign Markets', *Hastings International and Comparative Law Review* 7, 293; Handel, Stephen (1992), 'Entering International Markets: An Experimental Guide', *Currents* 1:2, 23; Yelpaala, Kojo (1994), 'Strategy and Planning in Global Product Distribution: Beyond the Distribution Contract', *Law and Policy in International Business* 25:3, 839; Moosa, Imad (2002), *Foreign Direct Investment: Theory, Evidence and Practice*, Palgrave.
141. Handel 1992: 23.
142. Ibid.
143. Berwind 1983: 293–302.
144. More in Chapter 5.
145. More in Chapter 6.

2

Drafting an International Commercial Agreement[1]

Contents

Overview 35
Glossary 35
I Freedom of contract 36
II Legality 37
III International instruments 37
IV Dispute resolution 37
V Choice of law in international agreements 39
VI Requirements relating to the form of the contract 43
VII Missing or vague terms 43
VIII Defined terms 43
IX Language of contract 44
X Checklist of provisions 46
XI Structure 47
XII Front of the contract 48
XIII Body of the contract 53
XIV Boilerplate clauses 55
XV Back of the contract 60
Summary 63
Useful links 63
Further reading 63
Notes 63

Overview

This chapter looks at the key considerations for the parties entering into an international contract and sets out the main provisions that such contracts should include, discussing the purpose and wording of each provision.

By the end of this chapter the reader will have a better understanding of

- the considerations that should be borne in mind when entering into an international contract;
- which provisions should be included in international commercial agreements and the importance of each provision; and
- the wording of such provisions.

Glossary

Alphabetical-numeration system System of numeration that uses sequential lettering.
Arbiter The party empowered to determine the issue or issues disputed, whether this is a judge, an arbitrator or another.
Assignee The party to whom rights or obligations under the contract are assigned. The assignee assumes all the legal rights and obligations of the **assignor**.
Assignment Transfer of rights or obligations under a contract to a party who is not a contracting party.
Assignor The contracting party who assigns his rights or obligations under a contract.

Boilerplate clauses Standard contractual terms which are routinely included in many contracts.
Common noun A noun that names general things.
Conflict of laws rules (also known as **rules of private international law**) Rules that are used to determine the law applicable to a matter.
Defined terms Set terms used throughout a contract.
Freedom of contract The notion that persons (natural or artificial) are free to choose whether or not they wish to enter into a given contract and to determine the terms of their contract.
Hybrid choice of law clause Clauses that combine two or more bodies of law in the same choice of law clause.
Legalese Legal terminology.
Merger clause, entire agreement clause, zipper clause or integration clause A contractual term which states that the contract contains all the terms agreed upon by the contracting parties.
Multiple-numeration system System of numeration that employs sequential numbering.
Notarisation In certain jurisdictions, the signing of the contract needs to be notarised, which effectively means that a notary public is required to certify the vaility of a signature on the contract.
Recitals Situated after the title and before the body of the contract, these set out the background information that the parties consider relevant to the body of the contract.
Rules of private international law See **conflict of laws rules**.
Severance clause Contractual term that permits the removal of a clause rendered invalid for whatever reason.
Term or Term of the agreement Duration of the agreement.

1 Freedom of contract[2]

This chapter starts off with a review of the key considerations that the parties entering into an international contract should bear in mind when formulating the terms of their contract and follows on with a look at the language and structure of such a contract. Further matters pertaining to the planning stages are reviewed in Chapter 1.

When negotiating dealings between each other, parties are generally free not only to determine the requirements for the formation of their contract but also to shape the contract itself as they wish.[3] As such they may determine firstly whether or not to contract, how the contract will be formed and then to agree on the contents of the contract itself. This right, known as the **freedom of contract**, is a cornerstone of Anglo-Saxon law. Freedom of contract is not, however, an absolute freedom, as constraints will usually exist in national law defining in certain situations the terms of the contract and in others the manner in which the contract may be formed.[4] Such rules may invalidate certain agreements or permit their invalidation; or, in the alternative, they may result in the incorporation of terms into an existing contract (implied terms).[5]

Invalidation of a contract may occur when the contract concluded contravenes public order, public morality or the law itself. The law may also invalidate a contract where there is some flaw in the procedure. This may occur if it turns out that one of the contracting parties did not have the prerequisite capacity to contract, perhaps lacking the necessary power of judgement at the moment in time when the contract was concluded. Invalidation may be an option when a consumer is induced to contract away from the business premises of the trader in circumstances where it is the trader that initiates the negotiation of the contract and the consumer is unprepared for the negotiations or did not expect such negotiations. This could occur for example on the doorstep of the consumer's home or at his workplace, when he did not anticipate the visit of the trader. In such a situation, the law (an instance of which can be found in the European Union)[6] may intervene to protect the consumer, who did not have the opportunity to compare the quality and price of the offer made by the trader or who was induced to enter into a bad deal, by extending him a period of reflection. This period of reflection is known as the cooling-off period.

Certain terms implied into contracts by operation of the law may be excluded by agreement of the parties. For example, the United Nations Convention on Contracts for the International Sale of Goods (CISG) extends the contracting parties the discretion to exclude the application of the convention or derogate from or vary the effect of any of its provisions.[7]

II Legality[8]

It is important for the parties contracting to verify that the contract is valid under the law of the country selected by the parties to govern the contract. Obviously the laws of different countries vary; it is essential therefore to confirm the position with a legal professional familiar with the law of the country governing the contract.

III International instruments[9]

Several attempts have been made at the level of international law to formulate a uniform body of rules governing international contracts. Such attempts have taken the form of binding and non-binding instruments. Many binding conventions have been brought into being through the work of the United Nations Commission on International Trade Law (UNCITRAL), and prominent amongst these conventions is the CISG. Non-binding instruments include the UNIDROIT Principles,[10] the Principles of European Contract Law (PECL)[11] as well as the instruments produced by the International Chamber of Commerce (including the International Commercial Terms, known simply as the Incoterms®). Due to the importance of the CISG to international sales agreements, including distribution agreements, this instrument and its applicability will be reviewed in a separate chapter.

IV Dispute resolution[12]

If a problem arises the contracting party that encounters it will typically make contact with the other contracting party in an attempt to resolve it. Such discussions may take place with or without the assistance of the legal counsel for the contracting parties. If the problem is one of late delivery, the contracting parties may agree on later delivery coupled with compensation. If the problem is one of late payment, the contracting parties may agree on payment at a later date of the lump sum plus interest and compensatory damages. In those situations where the contracting parties are unable to agree on a suitable solution then either both parties or the aggrieved party will need to look to the provisions of the contract in order to ascertain the manner agreed upon for the resolution of disputes.

Alternative dispute resolution[13]

In this context, the parties may have incorporated out-of-court provisions in their contract (also known as alternative dispute resolution provisions or ADR provisions). If no ADR provisions are included in the contract the contracting parties may still decide to opt for out-of-court resolution of the dispute between them (see below for a sample ADR clause).

Court proceedings[14]

Where ADR is not an option, the contracting parties will need to check to see if they have included in the contract a provision stating which forum (court, arbitral body and so on) will have the power to hear the dispute. Such a provision, which is known as a choice of forum clause, a choice of jurisdiction clause or a choice of court clause, will predetermine the court with jurisdiction over the case and the contracting parties (a sample jurisdiction clause is included below).[15] The contracting parties may opt in such a provision for a specific court ('the High Court of Justice in London') or the courts of a certain jurisdiction ('the courts of England').

Once it has been established which jurisdiction is the competent jurisdiction the contracting parties will need to verify which law they have stipulated in their contract as the law to be used by the named forum or court to resolve the dispute between them.[16] This matter will be determined in the choice of law clause agreed upon by the parties.[17]

Pre-empting potential disputes

When drafting a contract it is wise to think about and to include terms that make provision for situations where a dispute arises under the contract. In this context the contracting parties should bear in mind a number of different issues, some of which are listed below.

Firstly, the contracting parties should decide whether they will hold regular or ad hoc meetings of an informal nature to address any interpretative differences that (may) arise between them.

Secondly, each contracting party should consider where the other contracting party has property against which it can enforce any (potential) judgment handed down by the **arbiter**. Where a judgment is handed down by a forum (a court, tribunal and so on) outside the jurisdiction where the property in question is located, the judgment, which will be treated as a foreign judgment, will need to be recognised before it can be enforced against the property in question.

Thirdly, each contracting party should consider the law proposed either by them or by the other contracting party as the law governing the contract. In this context, it would be advisable for each party to decide with the help of its lawyers whether the proposed law governing the contract provides it with the best protection possible or whether the law proposed in fact favours the other party over it.

Fourthly, the contracting parties should decide whether or not they will attempt to resolve potential disputes between them with the help of a third neutral extra-judicial party without taking the matter to court (in other words, ADR). If they do so, they should then consider agreeing on the following:

1. the form of ADR they will use (arbitration, mediation, conciliation and so on)
2. the ADR body they will opt for
3. the rules of procedure the ADR body will use
4. the law the ADR body will use
5. the costs of the ADR and how these will be borne
6. the right to appeal the decision made by the ADR body.

In this context it is worthwhile noting that the body selected will use the law chosen by the contracting parties as the law governing the contract.

Fifthly, if the matter does proceed to a court, the contracting parties should consider which court will be used to resolve the dispute at hand, which law the court in question will use to resolve the dispute and finally where any potential judgment handed down by the court will need to be enforced.

These different questions reflect the different stages in the process of judicial resolution of international disputes, namely jurisdiction, choice of law and recognition and enforcement of judgments (respectively).

Box 2.1 Dispute resolution and the considerations of the contracting parties

When planning international commercial agreements, the contracting parties should consider including the following provisions in their agreement:
- informal meetings – ad hoc or regular – to address 'interpretative differences' and matters that require renegotiation[18]
- ADR provisions
- jurisdiction clause
- choice of law clause.

V Choice of law in international agreements[19]

The parties contracting will typically select the law that will govern the contract concluded between them. In the event that they do not do so (for example the contract is made verbally and the parties overlook this clause, or for some reason this clause is left out of the written agreement between the parties) **conflict of laws rules**[20] will be used by the body with jurisdiction to hear the case in order to determine the law applicable to the contract.

Express choice of the contracting parties

Domestic contracts

When two businesses in England draft a contract they will usually elect to have the contract and disputes arising under the contract dealt with using English law, which will in turn involve the application of certain instruments of European Union law.[21]

Contracts between businesses based in different countries within the EU

In a contract between businesses based and/or operating in different member states of the European Union, the parties contracting may decide to opt for national law or international law as their governing law. So for example where a French buyer contracts with an English seller, the parties may select a body of national law to govern their contract (such as English law, French law or a body of law perceived to be neutral by both parties such as German law), or a body of international law. In the latter case the parties may decide to opt for the CISG, the PECL and/or the Draft Common Frame of Reference (DCFR)[22] as the governing law in their contract.

In such international sales agreements, the parties may elect to use more than one body of law to govern their contract (due for example to limitations in the scope of the body of international law). As such they may decide for example to use the CISG to govern those aspects of the transaction covered by the CISG and the PECL to effectively govern those aspects of the transaction not covered by the CISG.

Contracts between businesses where at least one is based outside the EU

In a contract concluded between businesses based and/or operating outside the European Union, or between a business based and/or operating outside the EU and one based and/or operating within the EU, several bodies of governing law are available to the contracting parties. The contracting parties may select a body of national law to govern their contract. As such they may opt for one that they perceive as a neutral choice. For example, in negotiations between a business based in Japan and a business based in England the parties may decide to use the law of Switzerland as the governing law. Alternatively, the contracting parties may select a body of international law to govern their contract. As such they may decide to opt for the CISG, the UNIDROIT Principles[23] and/or the PECL as the governing law in their contract.

In international sales agreements, the parties may elect to use more than one body of law to govern their contract (due for example to limitations in the scope of the body of international law). As such they may decide to use the CISG to govern those aspects of the transaction covered by the CISG and the UNIDROIT Principles or the PECL to effectively govern those aspects of the transaction not covered by the CISG.

Hybrid choice of law clauses

Due to the fact that the CISG is limited in its scope of application and in its coverage of issues, the contracting parties should give due consideration to two possibilities. Firstly, due consideration should be given to the use of **hybrid choice of law clauses** (which combine two or more bodies of law in the same choice of law clause). A hybrid choice of law clause could involve for example the application of the UNIDROIT Principles, the PECL, the DCFR or national law, alongside the CISG. Secondly, in certain circumstances, due consideration should be given to the possibility of concluding separate contracts, where each contract addresses a different and distinct subject matter.

Mixed contracts[24]

The CISG applies to international contracts involving the sale of goods as well as to contracts involving the sale of goods and the supply of services (mixed contracts) where the former is the predominant component in the contract.

Where a mixed contract is involved the contracting parties will have two options available to them. Firstly, they may elect to use a hybrid choice of law clause, so that the CISG covers the aspects of the relationship that fall within its scope of application, whereas other matters (not within the scope of application of the CISG) can be governed by a separate body of law. Secondly, and as an alternative to the first option described above, the contracting parties may elect to conclude separate contracts. As such, where the mixed contract involves the sale of goods and the supply of services, the contracting parties may choose to separate out the different components so that the contract involving the sale of goods is governed by the CISG and the contract for the supply of services is governed by some other body of law (such as the UNIDROIT Principles, the PECL, the DCFR or a body of national law).

Restrictions on scope[25]

The CISG is limited in terms of the matters that it addresses as differences of opinion during the drafting process regarding the substance of the rules governing some particularly contentious topics led to their omission. Where the contracting parties elect to use the CISG, due consideration should be given to the possibility of including a hybrid choice of law clause in the contract to address those issues that are not covered by the CISG. Such a hybrid choice of law clause could involve the application of the UNIDROIT Principles, the PECL, the DCFR or national law alongside the CISG.

The use of national law in the choice of law clause

It is also worthwhile bearing in mind that national law does not necessarily address all the concerns of international contracting parties, whereas instruments such as the UNIDROIT Principles, the PECL, the DCFR and the CISG have been drafted with the specific concerns of international contracting parties in mind.

Conflict of laws rules[26]

If the parties have not chosen the law that will govern their relationship, the law applicable to the contract will be determined by the final arbiter using **conflict of laws rules**. If one or more of the contracting parties is based and/or operating in a member state of the European Union, the arbiter will apply the provisions of Rome I in order to determine the law applicable to the contract.[27] In international contracts the arbiter will usually apply national conflict of laws rules in order to determine the law applicable to the contract at hand.

In international contracts involving the sale of goods, the arbiter may use the CISG if it is applicable. If the CISG is not applicable the arbiter will probably use national law to resolve the dispute before it, though on occasion the arbiter will resort to the UNIDROIT Principles and the PECL.[28]

Conflict of laws rules under European Union law

In the European Union contracts are governed by the provisions of Rome I. Rome I governs all contracts concluded after 17 December 2009. Contracts concluded either before or on 17 December 2009 are governed by the Convention on the Law Applicable to Contractual Obligations opened for signature in Rome on 19 June 1980 (the Rome Convention),[29] the predecessor to Rome I. Rome I and the Rome Convention both apply to contractual obligations in situations where there is a choice between the laws of different countries.[30] They both contain rules that define the law applicable to a contract and those rules are mandatory in application.

Freedom to choose the governing law
Whilst the contracting parties are free to choose the law applicable to the contract between them,[31] if they do not do so Rome I will intercede to make the selection for them in accordance with the rules set out in Article 4.

Article 3.1 of Rome I permits the parties contracting to choose the law governing their contract. The parties may choose the law applicable to the whole of their contract or alternatively to just part of it.[32] Furthermore, Article 3.2 permits the parties contracting to modify by agreement the law governing the contract. Any such selection must be made expressly or clearly demonstrated by the terms of the contract or the circumstances of the case.[33]

Wherever possible, it is advisable for the contracting parties to expressly identify the law that they have chosen to govern the contract concluded between them. This will ensure certainty and clarity in their relation and will ward against any potential litigation that could later ensue on this very question.

In the absence of a choice by the parties

Article 4.1 of Rome I sets out specific choice of law rules for particular categories of cases. Where Article 4.1 does not supply a conclusive choice of law then the general rule articulated in Article 4.2 applies. Further general displacement rules – included in Articles 4.3 and 4.4 – are intended to introduce flexibility in those situations where the application of one of the specific choice of law rules does not produce the appropriate result.

Pursuant to Article 4.1, in circumstances where the law applicable to the contract has not been chosen in line with Article 3, the law governing the contract will be determined using the following rules:

1. A contract for the sale of goods shall be governed by the law of the country where the seller has his habitual residence.
2. A contract for the provision of services shall be governed by the law of the country where the service provider has his habitual residence.
3. A franchise contract shall be governed by the law of the country where the franchisee has his habitual residence.
4. A distribution contract shall be governed by the law of the country where the distributor has his habitual residence.

'Habitual residence' is defined by Article 19 of Rome I as follows:

- For companies and other bodies (corporate or unincorporated), habitual residence will be the place of central administration.
- For a natural person acting in the course of a business activity, habitual residence will be his principal place of business.
- For a contract concluded in the course of the operations of a branch, agency or any other establishment, or if, under the contract, performance is the responsibility of such a branch, agency or establishment, the place where the branch, agency or any other establishment is located shall be treated as the place of habitual residence.

For the purposes of determining the habitual residence, the relevant point in time is the time of the conclusion of the contract.

Excluding the CISG[34]

If the parties entering into an international sales agreement do not want the CISG to apply to their contractual relationship then it is sensible for them to ensure that the agreement clearly states that the CISG is excluded. Such a move is permitted by the provisions of the CISG.[35] The fact that the parties elect to use the contract law of a particular state or country will not by itself be sufficient to exclude the CISG, as the following extracts demonstrate.

In applying the CISG the courts have held that the CISG will apply absent proof of a common intention of the parties to exclude the CISG. An intention to opt out must be clearly evinced and such an intention must be shared by the contracting parties.

Box 2.2 Sample cases illustrating the need to evince clear intent to opt out of the CISG

In the United States case of *Asante Technologies, Inc. v. PMC-Sierra, Inc.*[36] the district court held that 'the particular choice of law provisions in the "Terms and Conditions" of both Parties are inadequate to effectuate an opt out of the CISG. Although selection of a particular choice of law ... could amount to implied exclusion of the CISG, the choice of law clauses at issue here do not evince a clear intent to opt out of the CISG.'

In the French case of *Traction Levage SA v. Drahtseilerei*[37] the appellate court emphasised that 'a unilateral note in the buyer's commercial documents stating that any dispute would be governed by French law was found not to constitute adequate proof. Such a note did not demonstrate that the two Parties intended to exercise the option set out in Article 6 of the Convention.'

For this reason it is wise for the parties contracting to state within the body of the contract itself, in the choice of law clauses, words to the effect that they have chosen to exclude the CISG. A sample clause that could result in an opt-out from the CISG is given below:

This agreement shall be governed by and interpreted in accordance with the laws of N—— giving no effect to the United Nations Convention on Contracts for the International Sale of Goods 1980.

VI Requirements relating to the form of the contract

If the parties select the CISG as the law governing their contract it is worthwhile bearing in mind that under the CISG a contract can be verbal: there is no requirement that the terms be written.[38] Moreover, the CISG does not impose any major formalities to be complied with in order for the contract to be valid.[39]

VII Missing or vague terms

In the event that certain contractual terms are left out of the contract, through oversight or lack of agreement between the parties contracting, or the terms of the contract themselves are unclear then the court with jurisdiction will fill in any such gaps in the contract or unravel any such unclear terms using the law governing the contract. With this in mind and in a bid to avoid confusion and minimise the risk of unnecessary litigation with the associated costs and loss of time, the contracting parties should make sure that their rights and obligations are defined as clearly and completely as possible within the terms of the contract. In addition, the parties should make sure that they plan for every possible contingency that could arise in their dealings when formulating and negotiating terms of the contract.

VIII Defined terms[40]

There are a number of advantages associated with the use of **defined terms**.[41] Firstly, defined terms will make it easier to read the contract as their use will remove the need for repetition of a definition throughout the contract. Secondly, defined terms will also ensure uniformity as the term defined will mean the same thing throughout the contract.

When terms are defined they are defined either in a dedicated section of the contract (in the definitions clause) or within the text of the contract itself.[42] In the following extract, the term 'Trade Marks' is defined within the text of the contract itself, whilst the terms 'Principal', 'Distributor', 'Territory' and 'Goods' will have been defined in a separate section of the contract. The defined term is usually a noun ('property', 'lease', 'patent') but may also be a verb ('lease', 'sell', 'buy').[43]

A definition can be inclusive or exclusive. A inclusive definition sets out what is included within the defined term. A exclusive definition states what is not included within its scope.[44] A definition can also be open or closed. An open definition allows for the inclusion of unstated items that are not previously mentioned. A closed definition is one to which nothing further can be added. A closed definition is therefore as stated.

Defined terms are typically flagged within the text of the contract with initial capital letters. In the extract below 'Principal', 'Distributor', 'Territory' and 'Goods' are all defined terms.[45] When a term is defined it may also be highlighted by being underlined and/or placed within quotation marks. In the following extract the term being defined – 'Trade Marks' – is flagged with both underlining and quotation marks.

> The Principal authorises the Distributor to use its trade marks and service marks ('Trade Marks') in the Territory on or in relation to the Goods for the purposes only of exercising its rights and performing its obligations under this agreement.

IX Language of contract[46]

When writing a contract it is sensible for the parties to remain consistent and employ plain language. The following review provides a non-exhaustive list of guidelines to help parties draft the terms of their contract. Whilst these guidelines are applicable to international contracts they are also equally relevant when drafting a domestic contract.

The importance of remaining consistent

When a certain format is selected within a contract it is wise to ensure that that format is used in a consistent manner throughout the body of the contract as well as in other contracts.

Employing plain English

Wherever possible it is helpful to use plain English within the body of a contract, although occasionally the use of legal terminology (**legalese**) is unavoidable as certain legal terms cannot be replaced.[47] The use of plain English will help prevent vagueness and will ease the understanding of terms in the contract for lawyers and non-lawyers alike.

Language of performance[48]

When employing the language of performance within a contract it is worthwhile bearing in mind certain guidelines. Wherever possible active language should be employed within the contract and such language should be set out in the present tense.

Employing the present tense[49]

Wherever possible the terms of the contract should incorporate verbs that are conjugated in the present tense. By employing the present tense of the verb resulting sentences are clearer.

Box 2.3 Sentences employing the present tense of the verb

It is better to state **Jack Marshall grants a lease to Manchester Storage** (this sentence uses the verb 'grant' in its present tense) than **Jack Marshall will grant a lease to Manchester Storage** (this sentence uses the future tense of the verb)

Employing the active voice[50]

A sentence is active when the subject of the sentence does something to the object. In the alternative, a sentence is passive when something is done to the subject by the object. Sentences employing the active voice are generally clearer than those employing the passive voice.

Box 2.4 Sentences employing the active and passive voice

It is better to state **Dan carried the bucket to the top of the hill** or **The Buyer shall pay the Seller the contract price on 1 February 2009** (these sentences use the active voice) than **The bucket was carried to the top of the hill by Dan** or **The contract price shall be paid by the Buyer to the Seller on 1 February 2009** (these sentences use the passive voice).

Language of obligation[51]

Language of obligation is used to denote the obligations of the contracting party or parties.

Employing 'shall' to indicate obligation[52]

The word 'shall' is employed within a sentence to denote that someone is bound to execute an act or not to execute an act as the case may be.

Box 2.5 Sentences using 'shall' to indicate obligation

It is better to state **Jack Marshall shall lease Manchester Storage the Property** (in this sentence 'shall' indicates that Jack Marshall is bound to lease Manchester Storage the Property) or **Jack Marshall shall not assign the Lease** (in this sentence 'shall not' indicates that **Jack Marshall is obliged not to assign the Lease**) than **Manchester Storage is bound to lease the Property**, **Manchester Storage undertakes to lease the Property from Jack Marshall** or **Manchester Storage covenants and agrees to lease the Property from Jack Marshall**

Employing 'will' rather than 'shall'[53]

'Will' is used to indicate a future time rather than an obligation.

Language of discretion[54]

Language of discretion indicates that a party has a choice. As such the party concerned has the option of either executing a given act or not.

Employing 'may' to convey discretion[55]

'May' can be employed in the active voice to indicate that a party has discretion to do something or has authority to do something.

Box 2.6 Sentence using 'may' to convey discretion

The Licensor may refuse any assignment by the Licensee of its Intellectual Property Rights (in this sentence the licensor retains discretion regarding assignment by the licensee)

Employing 'may' to indicate limited discretion or possibility[56]

'May' can also be employed to indicate that a party has limited discretion to do something or to indicate the possibility of something occurring.

Box 2.7 Sentences using 'may' to indicate limited discretion or possibility

A situation where 'may' is used to convey limited discretion: **Jack Marshall may sell only unit 23 of the Property** (in this sentence Jack Marshall has limited discretion).

A situation where 'may' is used to convey possibility: **Jack Marshall may pay for legal services provided to Manchester Storage** (in this sentence there is a possibility that Jack Marshall will pay for the legal services provided)

Language of prohibition[57]

Language of prohibition is used to outline that which the parties to the contract are not permitted to do. In this context it is preferable to employ the phrases 'shall not' and 'must not', as opposed to the phrase 'may not'.

Employing 'shall not' or 'must not' rather than 'may not'[58]

Whilst 'shall not' and 'must not' denote a duty not to do something, 'may not' is not as clear cut, as the following example demonstrates.

Box 2.8 Sentences using 'shall not' or 'must not' rather than 'may not'

It is better to state **Manchester Storage shall not assign its right under the Lease** or **Manchester Storage must not assign its rights** than **Manchester Storage may not assign its rights** (in this sentence 'may not assign' could indicate either that Manchester Storage is authorised not to assign its rights or that it is not authorised to assign its rights).

X Checklist of provisions

The following checklist gives the provisions that should be considered by the parties contracting in the context of a simple international sales or distribution agreement. This agreement is intended for

XI STRUCTURE

use in international transactions between commercial parties. Separate checklists are provided for international agency agreements and international licensing agreements.[59]

Not all the provisions in the checklists are mandatory. However, when planning, negotiating and finalising the terms of the contract it is sensible for each party contracting to consider each of these provisions in turn before deciding whether or not to use it.

Box 2.9 Checklist of provisions

Preface to the contract
✓ Cover sheet
✓ Table of contents (optional in longer contracts)
✓ Index of defined terms

Front of the contract (see section XII)
✓ Title
✓ Introductory clause (type of agreement, date of agreement, parties to agreement)
✓ Recitals

Body of the contract (see section XIII)[60]

Boilerplate clauses (see section XIV)
✓ Assignment clause
✓ Merger clause
✓ Modifications clause
✓ Severance clause
✓ Notice clause
✓ Representation clause
✓ Dispute resolution (informal discussions, renegotiation, adaption, ADR, choice of jurisdiction, choice of law)
✓ Language clause

Back of the contract (see section XV)
✓ Concluding clause
✓ Signature blocks
✓ Attachment (exhibits and schedules)

XI Structure[61]

Box 2.10 Overall structure of contract
- Cover sheet
- Table of contents (in longer contracts; optional)
- Index of defined terms
- Front of the contract
- Body of the contract
- Back of the contract

The body of the contract will be preceded by the front of the contract and will be followed by the back of the contract. The body of the contract will contain the key provisions governing the relationship between the contracting parties.

Cover sheet

The cover sheet contains a concise version of the introductory clause.

Table of contents

If the contract is long, a table of contents should be included after the cover sheet (thereby ensuring that the first page of the contract is not the table of contents), listing page numbers (for articles and sections) and all attachments.

Index of defined terms

An index of defined terms lists the defined terms in alphabetical order, noting the page of the contract at which the definition of the term is found. If such an index is used it should be placed immediately after the table of contents.

XII Front of the contract[62]

Box 2.11 Overall structure of front of the contract
- Title
- Introductory clause
- Recitals

The body of the contract will be preceded by the title, the introductory clause and the recitals. The following extract is taken from a sales agreement and includes a title and introductory clause but no **recitals**.

> *Sale agreement*
> This sale agreement is dated 12 November 2009 and is between MANCHESTER STORAGE LTD, an English company ('MANCHESTER'), and BOLTON HAULAGE INC., a New York corporation ('BOLTON HAULAGE').

The extract above incorporates

1. a title:

> *Sale agreement*

2. an introductory clause:

> This sale agreement is dated 12 November 2009 and is between MANCHESTER STORAGE LTD, an English company ('MANCHESTER'), and BOLTON HAULAGE INC., a New York corporation ('BOLTON HAULAGE')

No recitals are included in this extract.[63]

XII FRONT OF THE CONTRACT

Title

The title, placed at the top centre of the first page, denotes the kind of agreement involved.[64] Such a title should be concise and should typically include the word 'agreement' or 'contract' within it.

Introductory clause[65]

The introductory clause comes after the title and states in the following order:

1. the type of agreement involved
2. the date of the agreement
3. the parties to the agreement.

Type of agreement[66]

Sale agreement
This **sale agreement** is dated 12 November 2009 and is between MANCHESTER STORAGE LTD, an English company ('MANCHESTER'), and BOLTON HAULAGE INC., a New York corporation ('BOLTON HAULAGE').

Here the wording used in the title is replicated using lower case and is preceded by the word 'This'. Initial capitals are employed here (for example Sale Agreement) if the agreement referred to is defined in the definition clause (a defined term).

Verb[67]

Sale agreement
This sale agreement is **dated** 12 November 2009 and is between MANCHESTER STORAGE LTD, an English company ('MANCHESTER'), and BOLTON HAULAGE INC., a New York corporation ('BOLTON HAULAGE').

Like any sentence the introductory clause will require a verb. 'Dated' is probably the simplest option and is clearer than 'made', 'concluded' or 'entered into'.

Date of agreement[68]

Sale agreement
This sale agreement is dated **12 November 2009** and is between MANCHESTER STORAGE LTD, an English company ('MANCHESTER'), and BOLTON HAULAGE INC., a New York corporation ('BOLTON HAULAGE').

The date in the introductory clause is the date on which the contract becomes effective unless the contract states otherwise. This date is important not only because it pinpoints the date on which the obligations and rights of the parties contracting commence but also because it is used to determine the duration of the agreement (also referred to as the term of the agreement) as well as the times for payment and delivery.

The contracting parties should take care to ensure that the date in the introductory clause corresponds with the date or dates noted throughout the contract; as such the date in the provision addressing the term of the agreement and if appropriate setting the initial period should be identical to the date in the introductory clause.[69]

When it is likely to take some time to get the contract signed it is sensible for the parties to leave the date out of the introductory clause. In such a situation the parties should date their signatures when signing the contract whilst at the same time making sure that reference is made within the terms of the contract to the fact that the contract will become effective only when the last party signs the contract.

Format of date[70]

When noting dates (for the example delivery and payment dates) in a contract it is a good idea to avoid a shorthand format as this can cause confusion due to different dating protocols. For example, '11/12/09' could be read as November 12 2009 or 11 December 2009. Instead it is sensible for the parties to note such dates in full.

Box 2.12 Format for dating

It is best for the parties to consider employing one of the following formats:

24 November 2009 (rather than 24/11/09) or November 24 2009 (rather than 11/24/09).

The parties to the agreement

Sale agreement

This sale agreement is dated 12 November 2009 and is between **MANCHESTER STORAGE LTD**, an English company ('**MANCHESTER**'), and **BOLTON HAULAGE INC.**, a New York corporation ('**BOLTON HAULAGE**').

An agreement is binding on the parties who sign it. It is important therefore that the parties contracting are clearly identified within the agreement. For this reason each party should be identified by its full name in the introductory clause.

Where the contracting party is a legal entity[71]

In the introductory clause each entity should be identified by the name under which it is registered. To help them stand out, it is worthwhile using capital letters for these names. Reference should also be made within the introductory clause to the following:

1. the type of entity involved (partnership, limited liability company and so on)
2. the designation of the form of entity ('Ltd', 'plc', 'GmbH', 'Inc.' and so on)
3. the jurisdiction of organisation (brevity is important here so 'English company' should be used rather the longer version

'a company incorporated under English law')

4. an indication of whether the entity is an affiliate of another entity.

Consider this sample extract:

MANCHESTER STORAGE LTD, an English company and a wholly owned subsidiary of Manchester Storage and Transport plc. ("<u>MANCHESTER</u>")

It incorporates

1. the type of entity involved (a company);
2. the designation of the form of the entity ('Ltd');
3. the jurisdiction of the organisation (England); and
4. a mention of the fact that the entity is an affiliate of another ('a wholly owned subsidiary of Manchester Storage and Transport plc').

What is more, in order to highlight the name of the contracting party it is presented in capital letters ('MANCHESTER STORAGE LTD').

The following information should be noted elsewhere in the contract:

- The addresses of the contracting parties. They should be noted in the notice provision. In a situation where a contracting party has more than one address the address given should be that of the registered office or the principal place of business.
- Details of an authorised representative. These should be noted in the representation clause.

Questions as to whether the party representing the entity has authority should be resolved well before the contract is drawn up.[72]

The names of the parties[73]

If a party's name is to be used in a shortened form in the contract it is important to include this shortened form in the introductory clause, after the jurisdiction reference and the indication of affiliation. In the extract above the shortened form of the party's name – 'MANCHESTER' – appears in the introductory clause, after the jurisdiction reference ('English') and the indication of affiliation ('a wholly owned subsidiary of Manchester Storage and Transport plc'). The shortened form should be included in parentheses after the full name of the party.

A **defined term** should appear in quotation marks and underlined for emphasis. Since the party's name in the extract above is also a defined term it appears in quotation marks and is underlined ('"<u>MANCHESTER</u>"'). It is worthwhile noting that there is no need to use any introductory text in the parentheses such as 'hereinafter' or 'hereinafter referred to'.

Where the contract involves a corporation whose name includes two or more words, it is advisable to opt for one or two words from its name. For example Manchester Storage and Transport plc could be referred to as MANCHESTER or MANCHESTER STORAGE.

To avoid confusion it is worthwhile using no more than one defined term. As such, one should avoid the following format:

> Manchester Storage and Transport plc referred to as MANCHESTER or THE COMPANY or MANCHESTER STORAGE.

Where the contract refers to an individual, the defined term should use the individual's surname:

> JACK JACOB MARSHALL, an English solicitor ('MARSHALL').

Where the contract refers to two or more individuals who share the same surname, then first names should be used:

> JACK JACOB MARSHALL, an English solicitor ('JACK MARSHALL') and JENNY FREDA MARSHALL, an English barrister ('JENNY MARSHALL').

The name used as the defined term for the party should be based on the name of the party.[74] It is important to avoid **common nouns** wherever possible (nouns that name general things – for example, whilst 'country' is a common noun, 'Ireland' is a proper noun), unless the contract is of a kind that traditionally employs common-noun defined terms (credit agreements are examples of such contracts) or the identity of one of the parties is unknown.

The defined term 'this Agreement'

Even though it is commonplace to create the defined term 'this Agreement' in the introductory clause, it is not essential as the presence of the demonstrative 'this' in the phrase 'this Agreement' removes the need for a defined term. For the same reason, the initial letter of 'agreement' does not need to appear in capitals.[75]

Recitals

Most contracts of any length or complexity will contain a number of recitals. **Recitals** are optional and simple commercial agreements do not necessarily need to include them.

Recitals are situated after the title and before the body of the contract and set out the background information that the parties consider relevant to the body of the contract. The arbiter will use such recitals to determine the intention of the parties contracting. The use of recitals can prove useful in a number of situations:[76] firstly, when certain terms in the contract are left vague and the arbiter needs to establish what the parties intended; and secondly, when certain terms are omitted completely from the contract and the arbiter is left to fill in the gap or gaps.

There are different categories of recitals, each category fulfilling a different function. The categories are as follows:[77]

1. Context recitals. They list the circumstances that led the parties to contract. Such recitals typically describe the business of one or more of the parties.
2. Purpose recitals. They indicate what the parties intend to achieve by contracting.

3. Simultaneous transaction recitals. They describe other agreements concluded at the same time as the agreement containing the recitals.
4. The lead-in recital. It serves to introduce the body of the contract by indicating that the parties agree to what follows rather than providing the background information.

Headings (such as 'WITNESSETH', 'RECITALS', 'BACKGROUND') and lead-ins (such as 'WHEREAS', 'NOW', 'THEREFORE') can be avoided, as it will be clear from the information provided and the placement of these provisions in the contract that the provisions function as recitals.[78] Conventional paragraph structure with complete sentences should be used in recitals, and clauses ending in semicolons should be avoided. Consider this sample recital:

> The Manufacturer agrees to appoint the Distributor as its exclusive distributor for resale in the Territory of the Products on the terms set out in this agreement.

XIII Body of the contract

Between the recitals and the back of the contract is the body of the contract. The body of the contract incorporates the provisions that the parties have agreed upon.

Division of text in the body of the contract[79]

> **Box 2.13 Division of text in body of the contract**
> • Articles
> • Sections
> • Subsections
> • Enumerated clauses

The body of the contract will typically be divided into sections (in longer contracts sections can be grouped together into articles), subsections and enumerated clauses, making it easier to read and allowing for cross-referencing.

Articles and sections[80]

Articles are numbered sequentially (1, 2, 3 and so on) and contain all the provisions relating to a particular topic. Sections within these articles should be numbered using the **multiple-numeration system** (so that the sections contained within Article 1 would be numbered 1.1, 1.2, 1.3 and so on). If the contract is not divided into articles, but only into sections, then the sections will be numbered 1, 2, 3 and so on.

Subsections[81]

Sections may be divided into enumerated subsections. When this is done it is for one of two reasons: either to break up an otherwise lengthy section, or to bring together within a subsection all the information on a specific aspect of a topic (i.e. the subject matter of the section in question).

Subsections may be designated using one of two systems of numeration:

- the **alphabetical-numeration system** (a, b, c and so on)
- the **multiple-numeration system** (1.1, 1.2, 1.3 and so on).

The former may be simpler for the reader to follow.

The following extract contains all the necessary information on the reasons for the termination of a contract. The information is grouped together in a section headed Grounds for Termination. This section is in turn divided into subsections grouping together all the information on the specific aspects of the subject matter of the section, namely the grounds for termination.

Option A: alphabetical-numeration system
7. Grounds for termination
a. Either Party shall be allowed to terminate this agreement by giving the other Party no less than —— written notice if:
1. That other Party commits any material breach of any of the provisions of this agreement and, in the case of a breach capable of remedy, fails to remedy such a breach within —— after receipt of written notice, setting out the particulars of the breach and requiring the breach to be rectified.
2. A receiver is appointed over any of the property or assets of the other Party.
3. That other Party enters into a voluntary arrangement with its creditors or becomes the subject of an administration order.
4. That other Party goes into liquidation.
5. Anything analogous to any of the aforementioned under the law of any jurisdiction occurs in relation to that other Party.
6. That other Party ceases, or threatens to cease, to carry on business.
7. There is at any time a material change in the management, ownership or control of the other Party.
8. That other Party is substantially prevented from performing its obligations under the agreement.
9. That other Party assigns or attempts to assign the agreement without prior authorisation.

b. Any waiver by either Party of a breach of any provision of this agreement shall not constitute a waiver of any consequent breach of the same or any other provision thereof.
c. Any termination of this agreement shall be without prejudice to any rights or remedies of either Party in respect of the breach concerned (if any) or any other breach.

Option B: Multiple-numeration system
7. Grounds for termination
7.1. Either Party shall be allowed to terminate this agreement by giving the other Party no less than —— written notice if:
7.1.1. That other Party commits any material breach of any of the provisions of this agreement and, in the case of a breach capable of remedy, fails to remedy such a breach within —— after receipt of written notice, setting out the particulars of the breach and requiring the breach to be rectified.
7.1.2. A receiver is appointed over any of the property or assets of the other Party.
7.1.3. That other Party enters into a voluntary arrangement with its creditors or becomes the subject of an administration order.
7.1.4. That other Party goes into liquidation.
7.1.5. Anything analogous to any of the aforementioned under the law of any jurisdiction occurs in relation to that other Party.

7.1.6. That other Party ceases, or threatens to cease, to carry on business.
7.1.7. There is at any time a material change in the management, ownership or control of the other Party.
7.1.8. That other Party is substantially prevented from performing its obligations under the agreement.
7.1.9. That other Party assigns or attempts to assign the agreement without prior authorisation.

7.2. Any waiver by either Party of a breach of any provision of this agreement shall not constitute a waiver of any consequent breach of the same or any other provision thereof.
7.3. Any termination of this agreement shall be without prejudice to any rights or remedies of either Party in respect of the breach concerned (if any) or any other breach.

Definitions clause

The definitions clause lists the key terms and phrases in the contract, determining in turn the scope of each and every key provision in the contract. For this reason, it is sensible to take care when negotiating the definitions in this clause and then again when reviewing this clause in the draft contract.

XIV Boilerplate clauses[82]

Boilerplate clauses are standard contractual terms that are routinely included in many contracts.

Box 2.14 Types of boilerplate clause

1. Assignment clause
2. Merger clause
3. Modification clause
4. Severance clause
5. Language clause
6. Notice clause
7. Execution in counterparts
8. Jurisdiction clause
9. Choice of law clause
10. Alternative dispute resolution clause (including informal discussions, renegotiation and adaption)

Assignment clause

The contracting parties acquire rights in the contract as well as undertaking certain obligations under the contract. An **assignment** will occur when there is a transfer of rights or obligations acquired in the contract to a party who is not a contracting party.[83] The contracting party who is transferring his rights or obligations under the contract is the **assignor**. The party to whom rights or obligations are transferred under the contract is called the **assignee**. Generally on assignment, the assignee will obtain all the rights of the assignor under the contract unless the agreement states otherwise[84].

An assignment is likely to occur in a number of situations. Firstly, when one of the contracting parties decides to sell his business as a going concern he may want to sell the rights under the contract to the party to whom he is selling his business. In such a situation the contracting party who is selling his business will need to transfer (or assign) the rights that he has under the contract to the party acquiring his business. Secondly, one of the contracting parties may be looking to raise capital and in order to do so needs to assign the agreement as security for a loan. In such a situation the assignee may be a bank or financial institution. Thirdly, an assignment can occur if there is a merger or takeover involving the business of the contracting party.

Where one of the contracting parties assigns its rights to another, the remaining party or parties (if more than two parties have contracted) may wish to reassess their options. This is especially so when there is a sale of the business to another as the remaining contracting party (or parties) will be left with a new and unknown business partner.

Box 2.15 Scenario where an assignment may occur

Assignment of a distribution agreement

In a distribution agreement if the principal decides to sell his business to another, part of the goodwill of the principal's business will include the assignment of the agreements he has, amongst them the said distribution agreement, to the buyer of his business.

The distributor will accordingly find himself after the sale contracted to an unknown party, namely the buyer of the manufacturing business. In such a situation, the distributor will probably become concerned about the ability of the new principal to adhere to the (existing) terms of the contract. As such the distributor will probably want to assess his future options.

The contracting parties may either opt for an outright ban on assignments (see option C below) or limit the right to assign (see options A and B below). Care should be taken when including an outright prohibition on assignments (option C) as such a clause if challenged may be held to be unreasonable and therefore unenforceable by the arbiter. As an alternative, the contracting parties may choose to protect their respective positions by either requiring prior written consent before assignment (option A) or limiting the right to assign (option B). Typically options A and B will benefit both parties to the contract, though one party may be able to secure itself a unilateral benefit to the exclusion of the other contracting party or parties (consider option C in this context).

Obviously where a one-off transaction is involved, an assignment clause is unlikely to be of any importance. However, in a long-term relationship the contracting parties may wish to secure the right to assign the agreement to another.

Option A

Neither Party, without the written consent of the other, shall assign, transfer, mortgage, charge, dispose or delegate any of its rights, duties or interests under this agreement.

Neither Party shall unreasonably withhold consent.

This clause stipulates that without written permission, rights and duties under the agreement are personal to the contracting parties and as such non-transferable.

Option B

1. Neither Party, without the written consent of the other, shall assign, transfer, mortgage, charge, dispose or delegate any of its rights, duties or interests under this agreement. 2. The ⎯⎯ may withhold consent if: The ⎯⎯ is in default of any of its duties under this agreement; The proposed assignee cannot perform the remaining obligations of the ⎯⎯ under this agreement;	The proposed assignee does not agree to perform all of the remaining duties of the ⎯⎯ under this agreement; or The proposed assignee fails to meet the standards set by the ⎯⎯ for the new ⎯⎯. Such standards are the standards in place at the time that the consent is sought.

Using this option one party is able to limit the right of the other party to assign (clause 1) by refusing to furnish the requisite consent needed to assign. What is more, this clause permits the party or parties contracting to retain the right to deny assignment in specific circumstances (clause 2).

Option C

1. This agreement is personal to ⎯⎯. 2. Only ⎯⎯ has the right to assign all or	some of its rights, duties or interests under this agreement.

Merger clause

This agreement expresses the full intent of the Parties to this agreement in relation to the subject matter of this agreement. This agreement sets forth the entire agree-	ment of the Parties and supersedes all previous agreements and understandings between the Parties whether made in writing or verbally.

Many commercial agreements include a clause indicating that the contract contains all the terms agreed upon by the contracting parties and that these cannot be contradicted or supplemented by any extrinsic evidence.[85] Such clauses are commonly referred to as **merger clauses**, **entire agreement clauses**, **zipper clauses** or **integration clauses**.[86] They are used by parties contracting to ensure the clarity of their obligations and rights under the contract and to protect themselves against any attempt by the other contracting party to argue that new terms were agreed upon by the parties in correspondence, conversations and so on. In the event that the contracting parties wish to add or modify the agreement they will have the option of doing so using a written and signed instrument (see **modification clause** below).

In the absence of a merger clause, extrinsic evidence supplementing or contradicting a written contract may be admissible.

Modification clause

> This agreement may only be varied by a written instrument signed by the Parties to this agreement or their duly authorised representatives.

To avoid uncertainty about modifications to the agreement, it is sensible to insist that modifications are written and signed by authorised representatives for the contracting parties.

Severance clause

> If any provision of this agreement is, becomes or is deemed to be invalid, illegal or unenforceable in any respect or is abrogated or materially modified by the action of a competent authority, either:
> Such a provision shall be deemed amended to comply with the applicable laws so as to be valid and enforceable; or
> If the provision cannot be so amended, without substantially changing the intentions of the Parties, it shall be removed and the rest of this agreement shall remain in full force and effect.

A **severance clause** in the contract will permit the removal or amendment of a provision that is rendered invalid, illegal or unenforceable for whatever reason,[87] for example by reason of a change in the law governing the contract. A severance clause (such as the one used above) either permits the amendment of the offending provision so that it complies with the appicable laws or allows the offending provision to be cut out of the contract whilst leaving the remainder of the contract intact.[88]

Similarly the law governing the contract may be capable of removing certain clauses from the contract. Under US law an unconscionable clause may be removed from the body of a contract. In US Law, Section 2-302 of the Uniform Commercial Code (UCC[89]) states that

> if the court as a matter of law finds . . . any clause of the contract to have been unconscionable at the time it was made the court may enforce the remainder of the contract without the unconscionable clause, or it may so limit the application of any unconscionable clause as to avoid any unconscionable result.

Language Clause

> The English text of this agreement is the only authentic text.

International contracts should have a choice of language clause to avoid disputes arising out of any language and translation problems. Such a clause may designate an official language by which the contract will be interpreted in the event of disagreement. In the sample clause reproduced above the English text of the agreement has been selected as the authentic text. Obviously if the agreement is written in another language, this clause should be modified to indicate the language of the agreement.

The UNIDROIT Principles address the issue of linguistic discrepancies. According to Article 4.7 of UNIDROIT,

> where a contract is drawn up in two or more language versions which are equally authoritative there is, in case of discrepancy between the versions, a preference for the interpretation according to a version in which the contract was originally drawn up.

Notice clause[90]

> Every notice required or allowed under this agreement shall be written and shall be delivered or sent by prepaid first class airmail to the addresses provided in this agreement or to any other addresses specified by the Parties in a notice hereunder. Such notices shall be treated as given:
> a. When delivered; or
> b. —— days after mailing by first class airmail, whichever is the earlier.

Execution in counterparts

> This agreement may be executed in any number of counterparts, each of which when executed and delivered shall constitute an original of this agreement, but all the counterparts shall together constitute the same agreement.

This clause allows the contract to be executed using counterparts where the parties cannot be in the same place for signature of the contract.[91] The counterpart functions as a duplicate original of the contract that the contracting parties can sign at separate times.[92]

Jurisdiction clause

> The Parties to this agreement shall submit to the jurisdiction of —— for the purposes of resolving any dispute and/or enforcing any claim arising under this agreement.

Choice of law clause

> *Option A*
> The agreement shall be governed by and interpreted in accordance with the laws of ——.
>
> *Option B*
> This agreement shall be governed by and interpreted in accordance with the laws of —— giving no effect to the 1980 United Nations Convention on Contracts for the International Sale of Goods (CISG).

The choice of law clause indicates the law that will govern any dispute relating to the contract. In the absence of such a clause, conflict of laws rules will be used to determine the law governing the contract.[93] Any such selection should be determined by whether the body of law selected is well developed and predictable and is hostile or friendly to the contracting parties.[94] Option A is a simple choice of law clause whereas option B is the clause that contracting parties in international sales agreements should use in order to ensure that the CISG is not applied by the arbiter.

ADR clause

The Parties shall settle any dispute arising out of this agreement or relating to this agreement, any breach, termination or invalidity of this agreement, using [*arbitration, mediation and so on*] in accordance with the rules of [*selected body*] as at present in force.
a. The authority shall be [*name of institution or person*];
b. The number of [*arbitrators, mediators and so on*] shall be [*insert agreed number*];
c. The place of [*arbitration, mediation*] shall be [*insert town or country*];
d. The language(s) to be used in the arbitral proceedings shall be [*list language(s)*];
e. The body shall apply the law selected by the Parties in [*cross-reference to choice of law clause here*]

XV Back of the contract

The back of the contract, which comes at the end of the contract after the body of the contract, consists of the concluding clause, signature blocks and where appropriate attachments.

Box 2.16 Structure of the back of the contract
- Concluding clause
- Signature blocks
- Attachments (exhibits and schedules)

Concluding clause

The signature blocks at the end of the contract are occasionally introduced by a clause (the concluding clause) stating for example that 'each Party acknowledges that it has read and understood the terms of this agreement, and accordingly signs below'.[95] Since the concluding clause often repeats that which is already known, it is often dispensed with. However, where such a clause is employed it serves to ease the otherwise abrupt transition between the body of the contract and the signature blocks.[96] In the event that each signature needs to be dated then the concluding clause may be omitted or else it may state that 'each Party is signing the agreement on the date noted alongside the signature of each Party'.[97]

Signature blocks[98]

The signature blocks either stand alone or are introduced by a concluding clause. Each contracting party will have a separate signature block, consisting of the name of the contracting party coupled with a signature line. Signature blocks are usually aligned one above the other along the right hand side of the page (see extract below). In the alternative in order to save space the signature blocks may be placed alongside each other. If signature of the agreement has to be witnessed then a signature block will be included for the witness or witnesses.

XV BACK OF THE CONTRACT

Signature block when the contracting party is a legal entity[99]

Where the contracting party is a legal entity then the name of the entity should appear in capital letters above the signature line. In the sample clause below, the names of the contracting parties (Manchester Storage Ltd and Bolton Haulage Inc.), which are both entities, are spelt out in capital letters above each signature line. Where the signatory for a legal entity is also a legal entity (for example the signatory may be a corporation) then the signature block will include within it a further signature block. In the sample clause below, the signatory for Manchester Storage Ltd is Manchester Storage and Transport plc, therefore within the signature block for Manchester Storage Ltd a further signature block has been included for Manchester Storage and Transport plc.

The word 'by' situated alongside the signature line is included for the purpose of indicating that the person signing does not do so in his or her personal capacity, but rather on behalf of the contracting entity. The name and title of the person signing should be denoted beneath the signature line in lower case letters with initial capitals. In the extract below, the name (James Coulson) and title (CEO) of the person signing on behalf of Bolton Haulage Inc. are noted below the signature line and introduced by the word 'by'.

In order to save time and where known the name and title of the person signing on behalf of the contracting legal entity may be entered into the contract.

Each Party acknowledges that it has read and understood the terms of this agreement and accordingly signs below. MANCHESTER STORAGE LTD By: Manchester Storage and Transport plc, its manager By: _____	Name: Title: BOLTON HAULAGE INC. By: _____ Name: James Coulson Title: CEO

Signature block when the contracting party is an individual[100]

Where the contracting party is an individual then his or her name should be noted under the signature line in capital letters to distinguish it from the name of the signatory signing on behalf of the legal entity. In a bid to prevent any risk of confusion it is wise to also add the phrase 'signing in his or her own capacity' after the name of the person signing. In the sample below, Jack Marshall is an individual and therefore his name is noted under his signature line in capital letters, in order to distinguish it from the name of the signatory signing on behalf of Manchester Storage Ltd.

The Parties are signing this agreement on the date noted in the introductory clause MANCHESTER STORAGE LTD By: Manchester Storage and Transport plc, its manager By: _____	Name: Title: _____ JACK MARSHALL signing in his own capacity

Witnessing and notarising

Commercial agreements do not usually need witnessing except when required by law. In those situations where the signing of the agreement does not need to be witnessed then the witness signature lines can be dispensed with.

A signatory is not usually required to have his or her signature **notarised** unless once again this is required by law or where one of the contracting parties requests this.[101] Where notarisation is required then a notary public will need to certify the validity of a signature on the contract. Notarisation may be requested by one of the contracting parties in order to ensure that there is no risk that anyone will question whether or when the person signed the contract.

Attachments[102]

Often documents are attached to the back of the contract. Such documents are referred to interchangeably as attachments, annexes or appendices. There are two main types of attachment: an exhibit and a schedule. References to exhibits and schedules are highlighted (in the contract) by ensuring they are always underlined (Exhibit A or Schedule B).

Exhibits are identified using sequential lettering or numbering. Numbers and letters are assigned sequentially to exhibits based on the order in which they appear in the text of the contract (1, 2, 3 and so on or A, B, C and so on). Schedules can either be identified using sequential lettering or numbering or else by linking to the sections in the contract to which they relate (for example, if a schedule relates to Section 3.3 then it would become Schedule 3.3). If more than one schedule relates to a section it is advisable to identify them using sequential lettering or numbering.

Exhibit[103]

An exhibit is a document that is independent of the contract itself. It may be a document that already exists before the signing of the contract or it may be one that will become effective after the signing of the contract. A contract may for example have annexed to it a lease of one of the contracting parties (that already existed) or the contract may refer to a further (and ancillary) contract to be concluded between the contracting parties at some point in time after the signing of the main contract.

As an exhibit is by definition attached to the contract the contracting parties can dispense with phrases such as 'attached as' and 'hereto', as it is unnecessary to state the obvious. As such the contracting parties should consider simply referring to 'Exhibit A' rather than using phrases such as 'attached as Exhibit A hereto'. The exhibit designation is clearly noted either in the top centre or top right-hand corner of the first page of each exhibit.

Schedule[104]

Schedules contain materials that form part of the contract but have been displaced to the section after the signature blocks. There are a number of reasons for doing this: firstly to save on space; secondly to allow for separate collation of materials; thirdly to protect the confidentiality of proprietary information (schedules are rarely attached to the contract when the latter is filed externally).

Summary

In this chapter we examined a number of key issues material to the planning, drafting and conclusion phases in the contracting process. Firstly, in the context of the planning stage of the contracting process, we considered the concepts of freedom of contract and illegality, reviewed some of the international instruments available to parties contracting transnationally and examined dispute resolution in the context of international commercial agreements. Secondly, in the context of the planning and drafting stages of the contracting process, we considered choice of law in international commercial agreements, requirements as to the form of the contract, the treatment of missing or vague terms, the role and wording of defined terms, introductory clauses, recitals, boilerplate clauses, signature blocks, exhibits and schedules. Thirdly, in the context of the drafting stage of the contracting process, we reviewed the general structure of a commercial agreement, the division of text in the body of the contract and the language of the contract.

Useful links

http://www.iccwbo.org (International Chamber of Commerce)

http://www.jus.uio.no/lm/eu.contract.principles.parts.1.to.3.2002 (Principles of European Contract Law)

http://www.uncitral.org (United Nations Commission on International Trade Law, otherwise known as UNCITRAL)

http://www.unidroit.org/english/principles/contracts/principles2010/blackletter2010-english.pdf (UNIDROIT Principles of International Commercial Contracts).

Further reading

Adams, Kenneth (2007), *A Manual of Style of Contract Drafting*, 2nd ed., American Bar Association.
Poole, Jill (2008), *Textbook on Contract Law*, Oxford University Press.
Shippey, Karla C. (1999), *A Short Course in International Contracts: Drafting the International Sales Contract for Attorneys and Non-attorneys*, World Trade Press.
Stark, Tina L. (ed.) (2003), *Negotiating and Drafting Contract Boilerplate*, ALM.
Stark, Tina L. (2007), *Drafting Contracts: How and Why Lawyers Do What They Do*, Aspen.

Notes

1. An excellent guide to the drafting of contracts is provided by Adams, Kenneth (2007), *A Manual of Style of Contract Drafting*, 2nd ed., American Bar Association. Further reading on the subject can be found in Stark, Tina L. (2007), *Drafting Contracts: How and Why Lawyers Do What They Do*, Aspen.

2. Williston, Samuel (1921), 'Freedom of Contract', *Cornell Law Quarterly* 6:4, 365; Kessler, Friedrich (1943), 'Contracts of Adhesion: Some Thoughts about Freedom of Contract', *Columbia Law Review* 43, 629; Kessler, Friedrich and Fine, Edith (1964), 'Culpa in Contrahendo, Bargaining in Good Faith, and Freedom of Contract: A Comparative Study', *Harvard Law Review* 77:3, 401; Pettit, Mark (1999), 'Freedom, Freedom of Contract, and the "Rise and Fall"', *Boston University Law Review* 79, 263; Movsesian, Mark (2002), 'Two Cheers for Freedom of Contract', *Cardozo Law Review* 23:4, 1529; Poole, Jill (2008), *Textbook on Contract Law*, Oxford University Press, 12.
3. Williston 1921: 367–8.
4. For example, certain contracts will need to be written. For a review of formality requirements, see Poole 2008: 176–87.
5. Poole 2008: 229–40. Implied terms are reviewed in Chapter 1.
6. Council Directive 85/577/EEC of 20 December to Protect the Consumer in Respect of Contracts Negotiated Away from Business Premises, available at http://eur-lex.europa.eu/LexUriServ/LexUriServ.do?uri=CELEX: 31985L00477:EN:HTML (last accessed 15 January 2013).
7. Article 6 CISG. A review of case law, legislation and writings on this article is available at http://cisgw3.law.pace.edu/cisg/text/e-text-06.html (last accessed 15 January 2013).
8. The question of legality is reviewed in Chapter 1.
9. Certain international instruments are reviewed in Chapter 7.
10. The International Institute for the Unification of Private Law is responsible for the UNIDROIT Principles of International Commercial Contracts. The latest version of the principles, from 2010, is available at http://www.unidroit.org/english/principles/contracts/principles2010/blackletter2010-english.pdf (last accessed 15 January 2013).
11. Available at http://www.jus.uio.no/lm/eu.contract.principles. parts.1.to.3.2002/ (last accessed 15 January 2013).
12. Dispute resolution is reviewed in Chapter 1.
13. Alternative dispute resolution is reviewed in Chapter 1.
14. Court proceedings are reviewed in Chapter 1.
15. These matters are reviewed in Chapter 1.
16. This topic is reviewed in Chapter 1.
17. This topic is reviewed in Chapter 1.
18. These matters are reviewed in Chapter 1.
19. See Murray, Carole, Holloway, David and Timson-Hunt, Daren (2007), *Schmitthoff's Export Trade: The Law and Practice of International Trade*, 11th ed., Sweet & Maxwell, Chapter 21.
20. See below.
21. Hartley, T. C., (2010), *The Foundations of European Union Law: An Introduction to the Constitutional and Administrative Law of the European Union*, 7th ed., Oxford University Press, Chapter 7, and Fairhurst, John, (2010), *The Law of the European Union*, 7th ed., Longman, Chapter 2 address the sources of EU law.

22. The CISG, the PECL and the DCFR are reviewed in Chapter 7. The DCFR is available at http://ec.europa.eu/justice/policies/civil/docs/dcfr_outline_edition_en.pdf (last accessed 15 January 2013).
23. The UNIDROIT Principles are reviewed in Chapter 7.
24. Article 3, CISG. The CISG and its scope of application are reviewed in Chapter 7, in the section entitled 'Matters dealt with by the CISG and issues excluded'.
25. This topic is reviewed in Chapter 7, in the section entitled 'Matters dealt with by the CISG and issues excluded'.
26. For English and European law see McClean, David and Beevers, Kisch (2005), *Morris: The Conflict of Laws*, 6th ed., Sweet & Maxwell, Chapters 1, 13; for US law see Scoles, Eugene F., Hay, Peter, Borchers, Patrick J. and Symeonides, Symeon C. (2004), *Conflict of Laws*, 4th ed., Thomson West. See also Ferrari, Franco and Leible, Stefan (eds) (2009), *Rome I Regulation: The Law Applicable to Contractual Obligations in Europe*, Sellier European Law Publishers; Murray et al. (2007), Chapter 21.
27. The full title of Rome I is Regulation (EC) No 593/2008 of the European Parliament and the Council of 17 June 2008 on the Law Applicable to Contractual Obligations. It is available at http://eur-lex.europa.eu/LexUriServ/LexUriServ.do?uri=OJ:L:2008:177:0006:0006:en:PDF (last accessed 21 January 2013).
28. This topic is reviewed in Chapter 7.
29. 80/934/EEC: Convention on the Law Applicable to Contractual Obligations Opened for Signature in Rome on 19 June 1980, available at http://eur-lex.europa.eu/LexUriServ/LexUriServ.do?uri=CELEX:41980A0934:EN:HTML (last accessed 21 January 2013).
30. Where states have several territorial units each of which has its own rules of law in relation to contractual obligations then each territorial unit will be treated as a country for the purposes of identifying the law applicable under Rome I (Article 22.1 Rome I).
31. Article 3 Rome I.
32. Article 3(1) Rome I.
33. Ibid.
34. This topic is reviewed in Chapter 7.
35. Article 6 CISG.
36. *Asante Technologies, Inc. v. PMC-Sierra, Inc.*, US Federal District Court [California], 27 July 2001, available at http://cisgw3.law.pace.edu/cases/010727u1.html (last accessed 16 January 2013).
37. *Traction Levage SA v. Drako Drahtseilerei Gustav Kocks GmbH*, Cour d'appel Paris, 6 November 2001, available at http://cisgw3.law.pace.edu/cases/011106f1.html (last accessed 16 January 2013).
38. Article 11 CISG states: 'A contract of sale need not be concluded in or evidenced by writing and is not subject to any other requirement as to form. It may be proved by any means, including witnesses.'
39. Article 11 CISG.
40. Adams 2007, Chapters 2, 6; Stark 2007, Chapters 5, 7.

41. Adams 2007: 73; Stark 2007: 73.
42. Adams 2007: 8–11, 77, 80–1; Stark 2007: 76–7.
43. Adams 2007: 73–4.
44. Adams 2007: 75–6.
45. Adams 2007: 73–4.
46. Adams 2007, Chapter 3; Stark 2007, Chapters 12, 13, 18, 20, 21.
47. Stark 2007: 201.
48. Adams 2007: 20–1.
49. Ibid.
50. Ibid.
51. Adams 2007: 22–5.
52. Ibid.
53. Adams 2007: 23, 29.
54. Adams 2007: 31–6.
55. Adams 2007: 31.
56. Adams 2007: 32.
57. Adams 2007: 36–7.
58. Adams 2007: 36.
59. Checklists for international agency agreements and international licensing agreements are provided in Chapters 5 and 6 respectively.
60. Each agreement will include a different list of provisions in the body of the agreement. These will be reviewed separately in the following chapters.
61. Adams 2007, Chapters 2, 4, 5; Stark 2007, Chapters 5, 6, 17.
62. Adams 2007, Chapter 2; Stark 2007, Chapters 5–7.
63. See below for more on recitals.
64. Adams 2007: 3.
65. Adams 2007: 3–11.
66. Adams 2007: 4.
67. Adams 2007: 4–5.
68. Ibid.
69. The provision addressing the term of the agreement and the initial period is reviewed in Chapter 4.
70. Adams 2007: 5.
71. Adams 2007: 7.
72. This matter is reviewed in Chapter 1.
73. Adams 2007: 7.
74. Adams 2007: 8.
75. Adams 2007: 11.
76. Stark 2007: 61.
77. Adams 2007: 11–13.
78. Adams 2007: 14.
79. Adams 2007: 51–62.
80. Adams 2007: 51.
81. Adams 2007: 54, 56.
82. Stark 2007, Chapter 16.
83. Stark 2007: 168.

84. *Puget Sound National Bank* v. *Washington Department of Revenue* 868 P2d 127 (Wash 1994).
85. Stark 2007: 178.
86. Ibid.
87. Stark 2007: 176.
88. Stark 2007: 177.
89. Formulated as model law by the National Conference of Commissioners on Uniform State Laws as well as by the American Law Institute, the UCC is effective in some form in nearly all the US jurisdictions.
90. Stark 2007: 175–6.
91. Stark 2007: 179.
92. Ibid.
93. Stark 2007: 173.
94. Ibid.
95. Adams 2007: 63.
96. Ibid.
97. Ibid.
98. Stark 2007, Chapter 17.
99. Adams 2007: 66.
100. Adams 2007: 67.
101. Ibid.
102. Adams 2007: 68.
103. Ibid.
104. Adams 2007: 69.

3

International Sales Agreements

Contents

Overview 68
Glossary 68
I The law applicable to a sales agreement 69
II International law applicable to international sales of goods 70
III English law governing international sales of goods 70
IV Trade terms 75
V Incoterms® 75
VI Trade terms under English law 76
VII Checklist of provisions 82
VIII Front of the contract 83
IX Body of the contract 83
X Boilerplate clauses 102
XI Back of the contract 102
Summary 103
Useful links 103
Further reading 103
Notes 104

Overview

This chapter explores the following topics:
- the law applicable to a sales agreement
- international and English law applicable to international sales of goods
- trade terms generally and Incoterms® specifically.

It also examines the main provisions that an international sales agreement should include, discussing the purpose and wording of each provision.

By the end of the chapter the reader will have a better understanding of
- the law governing international sales of goods;
- the role of trade terms and the manner in which these trade terms operate;
- which provisions should be included in international sales agreements;
- the purpose of each provision; and
- the proposed wording of each provision.

Glossary

Bearer bill of lading A negotiable bearer document that can be transferred from one party to another by mere delivery of the document.

Bill of lading An instrument issued by the ocean carrier to the shipper.

Conflict of laws rules (also known as **rules of private international law**)[1] Rules used by the arbiter in order to determine the law applicable to a dispute.

Documents against payment An arrangement by which the seller agrees to deliver a **bill of lading** to a bank situated in the country of the buyer, in turn enabling the buyer to confirm that the goods have in fact been shipped.

Emblement Annual crops grown through human labour.

Implied terms Terms incorporated into a contract by operation of the law.

Irrevocable letter of credit A letter of credit which may be changed or cancelled but only with the agreement of the parties.

Letter of credit An instrument issued by a bank or other institution in response to an application by an account party. It obliges the issuer to pay the beneficiary a sum of money if the beneficiary complies with the conditions stipulated by the account party.

Non-conforming goods Goods that fail to meet warranties (express or implied).

Order bill of lading A bill of lading that is transferable.

Personal chattel An item that can be touched and moved. For example a table, a chair or a car.

Revocable letter of credit A letter of credit that can be changed or cancelled at any time without prior notice to the beneficiary.

Rules of private international law See conflict of laws rules.

Shipping terms Contractual terms setting out the respective responsibilities of the seller and buyer in relation to the transport arrangements and costs, inter alia freight, export and import licences, port charges and insurance.

Straight bill of lading A bill of lading that names the consignee of the cargo.

Thing in action Right which can be enforced in court.

I The law applicable to a sales agreement[2]

The law governing the contract will be selected either by the contracting parties (in their choice of law clause) or, in the event that the parties have not made such a selection, by the **conflict of laws rules**. Conflict of laws rules (also known as the **rules of private international law**) are the rules used by the arbiter in order to determine the law applicable to a dispute. They are used when the parties have failed to select the law governing their contract and the contract and the relationship between the parties to the contract involves the law of two or more jurisdictions.

The conflict of laws rules are part of national law and will typically differ from one jurisdiction to another. Effectively this will mean that the result is likely to differ depending on the conflict of laws rules applied to the case. In other words, the choice of law determined pursuant to the conflict of laws rules of country A will probably differ from the choice of law determined under the conflict of laws rules of country B.

Moves have been made at the international level to harmonise conflict of laws rules. Examples of such harmonising efforts can be found in the European Union where attempts been made to unify the conflict of laws rules of the different member states in a number of fields of law. To this end, in the field of contract law, the regulation known as Rome I has been introduced[3].

> **Box 3.1 The law applicable to the agreement illustrated**
>
> If the international parties contracting decide that their contract is to be governed by the law of France then the contract in question and any issues or disputes arising under the contract will be addressed using the law of France. This same contract will probably also be governed by any international instruments that form part of the national law governing the contract (in this case, the law of France) – for example the United Nations Convention on Contracts for the International Sale of Goods (CISG), since France has adopted the CISG.[4]

In order to ensure certainty it is sensible for the parties concluding an international contract to select the law governing their contract within the terms of the contract itself, namely in their choice of law clause.

II International law applicable to international sales of goods[5]

Beyond national law, efforts have been made at the international level to create some uniform rules to govern international trade generally and different aspects associated with international trade specifically. Many of these initiatives originate from intergovernmental organisations and international agencies including the United Nationals Commission on International Trade Law (UNCITRAL) and the International Chamber of Commerce (ICC).

Several attempts have been made at the international level to formulate a body of rules that can be used in the context of commercial contracts of an international nature. Such attempts take the form of binding instruments as well as non-binding ones. An example of a binding instrument is the CISG, brought about through the efforts of UNCITRAL. Illustrations of non-binding instruments include the PECL and UNIDROIT as well as the instruments issued by the ICC such as the Incoterms® and the model contracts (for sales, distribution and agency).[6]

At the European level a number of directives have been introduced addressing trade in goods and services.

III English law governing international sales of goods[7]

International sales agreements are governed by certain international instruments that address sales agreements in the general sense (such as the CISG)[8] as well as by certain other international instruments that address specific aspects inherent in international sales transactions[9]. The United Kingdom is a party to two conventions governing international transactions involving the sale of goods.[10] Both of these conventions have been implemented into English law by the Uniform Laws on International Sales Act 1967 (the Uniform Laws).[11] The United Kingdom has not ratified the CISG. Whilst contracting parties are permitted to incorporate the Uniform Laws into their contract if they so wish, this is not commonly done.[12] For this reason, most international sales contracts[13] that are governed by English law are governed by national law.

Perhaps one of the striking features of English law is the overall absence of a dedicated body of law governing international sales agreements.[14] In England an international sales agreement will be governed by the general law governing sales as set out in English law of contract, statute (including the Sale of Goods Act 1979)[15] and the case law interpreting the provisions of the statute.[16] All in all the parties to an international contract that is governed by English law are subject to less restriction than parties to a domestic contract, since the Unfair Contract Terms Act 1977[17] does not apply to international supply contracts.[18]

Sale of Goods Act 1979[19]

The Sale of Goods Act 1979, which consolidates the original Sale of Goods Act 1893 and other later enactments, came into force on 1 January 1980[20] and is applicable in England and Wales, Scotland and Northern Ireland. The Sale of Goods Act 1979 (the 1979 Act) has been subject to successive revisions since its enactment in 1980.

The 1979 Act, which applies to contracts for the sale of goods made on or after (but not before) 1 January 1894,[21] governs

1. the formation of the contract;[22]
2. the effects of the contract;[23]
3. the performance of the contract;[24]
4. the rights of the unpaid seller;[25]
5. the additional rights of the buyer in consumer cases;[26] and
6. actions for breach of the contract.[27]

Contracts for the supply of services are excluded from the scope of the 1979 Act.

Key terms used throughout the 1979 Act are defined in Section 61 of this Act. According to this section a buyer is defined as a person who buys or agrees to buy goods, whilst a seller is defined as a person who sells or agrees to sell goods. According to this section a business is deemed to include a profession and activities of public entities (government departments, local authorities and public authorities) and a sale includes a bargain and sale as well as a sale and delivery.

The term 'goods', which is widely defined within the 1979 Act (as amended), includes all **personal chattels** other than **things in action** and money, and in Scotland all corporeal moveables except money.[28] In particular the term 'goods' includes **emblements** (annual crops grown through human labour), industrial growing crops, and things attached to or forming part of the land which are agreed to be severed before sale or under the contract of sale as well as an undivided share in goods.[29]

The 1979 Act as amended addresses amongst other issues the seller's right to sell,[30] the sale of goods by description[31] and the quality of the goods and their fitness for purpose.[32] Terms are incorporated into contracts for the sale of goods by virtue of the provisions in the 1979 Act (as amended). Terms so incorporated are referred to as **implied terms** since they are inferred into the contract.

Seller's right to sell[33]

Pursuant to Section 12 of the 1979 Act (as amended), in a contract for the sale of goods there is an implied term on the part of the party selling that in the case of a sale he has the right to sell the goods.[34] As such it is also an implied term in the contract for the sale of the goods that the goods are and will be free, until the time when property is to pass, from any charge or encumbrance not disclosed or made known to the buyer before the contract and that the buyer will be able to enjoy quiet possession of the goods, except in so far as it may be disturbed by the owner or other person entitled to the benefit of any **charge** or **encumbrance** that is disclosed to the buyer or made known to him.[35]

Sale of goods by description[36]

Pursuant to Section 13 of the 1979 Act (as amended), it is an implied term in a contract for the sale of goods by description that the goods will correspond with the description.[37] Where the sale of goods is by means of a sample as well as by description it will not be sufficient if the bulk of the goods corresponds with the sample if the goods themselves do not also correspond with the description.[38]

Quality of the goods and their fitness for purpose[39]

Pursuant to Section 14 of the 1979 Act (as amended), where the seller is selling goods in the course of business there is an implied term in the contract for the sale of goods that the goods so supplied are of a satisfactory quality.[40] This term implied does not extend to any matter making the quality of goods unsatisfactory

1. which is specifically drawn to the attention of the buyer before the contract is made, or
2. where the buyer examines the goods before the contract is made, which that examination of the goods ought to have revealed, or
3. where there is a contract for a sale by sample, which would have been apparent from a reasonable examination of the sample.[41]

Section 14 of the 1979 Act (as amended) will apply to a sale made by

1. a seller to the buyer, and
2. a person who in the course of business is acting as an agent for another, unless the latter is not selling in the course of a business and either the buyer knows this or reasonable steps are taken to bring this fact to the buyer's notice before the contract is made.[42]

Goods are of a satisfactory quality under the 1979 Act (as amended) when they meet the standard that a reasonable person would regard as satisfactory bearing in mind the description of the goods, their price (if relevant) and all other relevant circumstances.[43] In this context, the following factors (amongst others) will be pertinent to the question of the quality of the goods:

1. their state and condition
2. aspects of their quality such as their fitness for all the purposes for which goods of the same kind are commonly supplied
3. their appearance and finish
4. the absence of minor defects
5. their safety and durability.[44]

In circumstances where the seller sells the goods in the course of a business and the buyer makes known to the seller either expressly or by implication any particular purpose for which the goods are being bought, there is an implied term in the contract for the sale of goods that the goods so supplied are reasonably fit for that purpose.[45] The same is true whether or not the purpose so made known is a purpose for which such goods are commonly supplied.[46]

Terms incorporated by law into the contract for the sale of goods may be excluded.[47] Subject to the Unfair Contract Terms Act 1977, any right, duty or liability which arises under a contract for the sale of goods by implication of law may be 'negatived or varied' in one of several ways:

1. by express agreement of the parties
2. by the course of dealing between the parties

3. by such usage as binds both parties to the contract.[48]

An express term will not have the effect of negating an implied term implied by this Act unless it is inconsistent with the implied term.[49]

Unfair contract terms under English law

The Unfair Contract Terms Act 1977[50] (1977 Act) came into force on 1 February 1978[51] and is applicable in England and Wales, Northern Ireland and Scotland.[52] Nothing in the Act applies to contracts made before 1 February 1978.[53]

Part I 1977 Act (applicable in England and Wales and Northern Ireland)

Part I of the 1977 Act must be read subject to the Part III of the Act and Sections 2, 3, 4 and 7 must be considered subject to the exceptions made by Schedule 1.

A number of the provisions in Part I apply to business-to-consumer transactions (known as B-to-C transactions), where one of the parties is dealing as a consumer whilst the other is dealing in the course of business.[54] Since the focus of this book is on business-to-business transactions (B-to-B transactions) this review is tailored accordingly.

In contract and tort Sections 2–7 of the 1977 Act apply[55] only to liability for the breach of obligations or duties resulting from things done or to be done by a person in the course of a business, whether the business is the person's own or belongs to another (in other words business liability).[56] A person is not permitted to exclude his liability for death or personal injury resulting from negligence using either a contractual term or a notice supplied to persons generally or to particular persons.[57] In this context the agreement of a person to the contractual term or notice purporting to exclude or limit liability or their awareness of the same is not of itself to be taken as indicating the voluntary acceptance of any risk by the person in question.[58]

A breaching party cannot by reference to any contract term exclude or limit any liability that he may have in relation to the breach; or claim to be entitled to render contractual performance substantially different from that which was reasonably expected of him or in respect of the whole or any part of his contractual obligation to render no performance at all, except in so far as the contract term satisfies the requirement of reasonableness.[59] This section applies as between contracting parties where one of them deals as a consumer or on the other party's written standard terms of business.[60]

The exclusion or limitation of liability for breach of obligations arising from Section 12 of the Sale of Goods Act 1979 (the seller's right to sell) is not permitted by reference to any contractual term.[61] In contrast, the exclusion or limitation of liability for breach of obligations arising out of Sections 13–15 of the 1979 Act (as amended)[62] is allowed if certain conditions are fulfilled.[63] Such liability must be excluded or limited

1. by reference to a term of the contract, as against a person who is not dealing as a consumer (a person dealing in a business or professional capacity for example); and
2. only so long as the contractual term satisfies the requirement of reasonableness (elaborated upon by Section 11 and Schedule 2 of the 1977 Act).[64]

As against a person dealing as a non-consumer, liability for breach of an obligation arising by implication of law can be excluded or limited with reference to a term of the contract only if the term in question satisfies the requirement of reasonableness. In contrast, liability for a breach of obligations arising out of Section 2 of the Supply of Goods and Services Act 1982 (implied terms relating to title for the transfer of property in the goods) cannot be excluded or limited by reference to any such clause.[65]

To the extent that Part I of the 1977 Act prevents the exclusion or restriction of any liability, it also prevents

1. making liability or its enforcement subject to restrictive or onerous conditions; and
2. exclusion or restriction of any right or remedy in relation to liability.[66]

The key terms in Part I of the Act are defined in Section 1 (negligence) and Section 14 (the remaining terms). 'Business' is defined as including a profession as well as the activities of a public entity (be it a government department or a local or public authority). 'Goods' has the same definition under the 1977 Act as it does under the Sale of Goods Act 1979. 'Personal injury' under the 1977 Act is defined as including any disease as well as any impairment of physical or mental condition. 'Negligence' is defined by Section 1 of the 1977 Act as a breach of

1. any obligation to take reasonable care or exercise reasonable skill in the performance of the contract resulting from the express or implied terms of a contract; or
2. any common law duty to take reasonable care or exercise reasonable skill.

Part III 1977 Act (applicable to the whole of the UK)

International supply agreements are subject to a special regime under the 1977 Act. Firstly, limits imposed by the 1977 Act on the manner and extent to which a person may exclude or limit his liability using a contract term do not apply to liability arising under an international supply agreement.[67] Secondly, the terms of such agreements will not be subject to any requirement of reasonableness (pursuant to Sections 3 and 4 of the 1977 Act).[68]

An agreement must fulfil three prerequisites in order to be classed as an international supply agreement:

1. It must be an agreement for the sale of goods or one under which or as a result of which possession or ownership of goods is transferred.
2. It must have been concluded between parties whose places of business (or if the parties have no places of business their habitual residence/s) are in the territories of different states.[69]
3. Either
   a. the goods constituting the subject matter of the agreement are at the time of conclusion of the contract in the course of carriage from the territory of one State to the territory of another State; or
   b. the acts constituting offer and acceptance have been carried out in the territories of different States; or
   c. the contract provides for the goods to be delivered to the territory of a State other than the State in which the acts of offer and acceptance were performed.[70]

Where the law governing the contract selected by the contracting parties is the law of any part of the United Kingdom then the following sections of the 1977 Act will not operate as part of the law applicable to the contract:[71] Sections 2–7 (applicable in England, Wales and Northern Ireland)[72] or Sections 16–21 (applicable in Scotland).

IV Trade terms[73]

Parties to a contract are free to determine the trade terms that will govern the rights and obligations of each party vis-à-vis transportation of the goods (**shipping terms**) as well as the **transfer of risk** in the goods between the parties. The **risk transfer point** determines the point at which risk transfers from the seller to the buyer.

Over the years certain standard trade terms have evolved through international commercial practice. These standard terms can be selected by the parties in the contract between them. Where the parties fail to define their trade terms and the contract is governed by English law, the rights and obligations of each party in relation to transportation and the transfer of risk will be determined by English common law.

In English law, certain standard trade terms are so widely used by the industry that the rights and obligations attached to each term have been recognised by the English courts.[74]

V Incoterms®

The most commonly used set of trade terms in international trade are the trade terms drafted by the ICC, namely the Incoterms®.[75] These terms are intended to reflect international commercial practice[76] and as such these terms are regularly updated by the ICC in order to mirror developments in international commercial practice.[77]

Based on an assessment of international commercial usage the Incoterms®, which were originally introduced in 1936, have been successively revised, in 1957, 1967, 1976, 1980, 1990, 2000 and most recently in 2010. Whilst these terms are primarily intended for international trade they are also available for use in domestic trade, notably in large countries (such as the US) where long distances are involved in transportation of goods from seller to buyer.[78] Incoterms® stipulate the responsibilities of the contracting parties for transport arrangements and costs, addressing inter alia export and import formalities, insurance cover, freight and transport expenses. These terms also stipulate the point in time when risk and title pass from seller to buyer. When an Incoterm® is selected the contracting parties should avoid amending or supplementing the underlying terms of the selected Incoterm® as this could cause unexpected discrepancies.

The most recent revision to the Incoterms® resulted from the need to make it clear how the 2000 terms were to be used in practice and to enhance the use of these terms in the US, where the 1941 definitions of trade terms were removed from the UCC.[79] Incoterms® 2010 are divided into two groups: Group 1, consisting of EXW, FCA, CPT, CIP, DAT, DAP and DDP,[80] are trade terms for all modes of transportation; and Group 2, consisting of FAS, FOB, CFR and CIF,[81] are trade terms for sea and inland waterway transport.

In order to keep the Incoterms® up to date, the ICC in its 2010 version of the Incoterms® has made a number of changes. Firstly it has listed the trade terms available for all modes of transportation first. Secondly it has introduced two new trade terms, namely DAT and DAP.[82] Thirdly they have removed DES (Delivered ex ship) and DEQ (Delivered on quay), these terms being logically superfluous since DAP and DAT may be used instead.[83] Finally they have changed the risk transfer point under FOB, CFR and CIF due to the longstanding problems associated with using the rail of the ship as the risk transfer point.[84]

VI Trade terms under English law[85]

Having recognised mercantile practice, the legal parameters of most standard contracts are now well recognised by the English courts. As a result the rights and obligations of the parties will be clearly defined both commercially and legally.[86] A review of certain key trade terms recognised in English law is provided below. The terms chosen for this review are 'ex works' (EXW), 'free on board' (FOB) and 'cost, insurance and freight' (CIF).

Ex-works contracts (EXW) under English law

Under EXW contracts the seller is obliged to ensure that the contract goods are made ready for collection by the buyer. As such the seller is responsible for making sure that the goods which are made available are conforming goods, in so far as they meet the express and implied terms of the contract. What is more, the seller is responsible for ensuring that the contract goods are suitably packaged and are ready for collection by the buyer or his agent. The seller will also need to furnish an invoice for the goods and any other documentation agreed upon by the parties, such as certification of conformity.[87] The location of the pick-up point must been transmitted by the seller to the buyer or his agent in time.[88]

For his part, the buyer is responsible firstly for collecting the contract goods when these are made available by the seller either himself or using the services of an agent and secondly for paying for these goods.[89] Moreover, the buyer or his agent will also need to make all the necessary arrangements to transport the goods from the point of collection to their final destination. Accordingly the buyer or his agent will need to assume responsibility for organising such transportation, taking charge inter alia of transportation arrangements and costs, loading charges, export and import formalities, insurance and storage of the goods.

Free on board (FOB) contracts under English law

Under a FOB contract the seller will assume far more responsibility than he does under an EXW contract. Generally under a FOB contract, the seller is obliged to place the goods on board the ship named by the buyer at an agreed port of shipment and at an agreed time.[90] Thereafter, the seller is expected to notify the buyer that the goods have been loaded. Under a FOB contract all the arrangements (and the charges associated with such arrangements) up to and including delivery of the goods on board the ship are the responsibility of the seller, whilst all the arrangements (and charges associated with these arrangements) from that point onwards are the responsibility of the buyer.

As will be seen later there are variants on the FOB contract. The general features of a classic FOB contract are defined in the English case of *Wimble, Sons & Co. Ltd* v. *Rosenberg & Sons* [1913].[91]

Box 3.2 Parties' responsibilities and the risk transfer point under a classic FOB contract

Wimble, Sons & Co. Ltd v. Rosenberg & Sons [1913]
The brokers of De Winter, an Antwerp-based business (plaintiffs in this case),[92] entered into a contract with the buyers (the defendants in this case) dated 27 June 1912 for the sale of 200 bags of rice 'f.o.b. Antwerp to be shipped as required by buyers, cash against bills of

VI TRADE TERMS UNDER ENGLISH LAW

> lading'. The parties agreed that the brokers should be treated as the actual sellers.
>
> On 9 August 1912 the buyers sent the brokers instructions to ship the rice to Odessa and to pay freight, leaving the brokers to select the ship. On the same day the brokers asked De Winter to ship the rice on the first steamer to Odessa on account of the buyers and to pay the freight. The rice was shipped on 24 August and the ship set sail the following day. The ship became stranded and was a total loss. On 29 August the buyers received advice of shipment from the brokers. The buyers had not insured the rice as it was not their custom to insure until receipt of notice of the particular ship on which the goods were loaded. The buyers refused to pay and the brokers brought an action for the price of the rice and the freight paid by the brokers on the buyers' account.
>
> On an appeal to the Court of Appeal against the decision of the judge of the first instance court (Bailhache J) both Vaughan Williams and Buckley LJJ ruled that Section 32(3) of the Sale of Goods Act 1893 applies to a FOB contract.[93] This section states that 'unless otherwise agreed, where goods are sent by the seller to the buyer by a route involving sea transit, under circumstances in which it is usual to insure, the seller must give such notice to the buyer as may enable him to insure them during their sea transit, and, if the seller fails to do so, the goods shall be deemed to be at his risk during such sea transit'.[94] On the facts Buckley LJ held (Vaughan Williams LJ dissenting) that prior to shipment the buyers had all the information that they required in order to insure the goods, as the brokers were not obliged to give the buyers notice of the shipment on a specific ship. According to Buckley LJ the seller is obliged pursuant to Section 32(3) to give the buyer such notice as to enable the buyer to insure the goods. The wording in Section 32(3) is satisfied according to Buckley LJ in one of two scenarios: firstly when the buyer has knowledge of all the facts that he needs to know in order to insure the goods, and secondly if such notice as has been given to the buyer completes his knowledge of the facts so that he is able to insure the goods.
>
> Vaughan Williams LJ held that the contract of sale did not provide the information that the buyers needed in order to insure the goods during transit and that the knowledge of the buyer (actual, inferred or assumed) which would enable the buyer to insure did not alleviate the seller of his obligation under the Sale of Goods Act 1893 to give notice to the buyer as may enable the buyer to insure the goods during transit. Unless excluded by the agreement of the parties, the obligation on the seller was to furnish notice to the buyer with the details required to enable the buyer to take out marine insurance for the goods bought.[95]

Under the classic FOB contract, the seller is not only responsible for supplying conforming goods that are suitably packaged but also for arranging and paying for

1. transportation of the goods to the ship on which the goods are to be loaded;
2. export formalities (export licences and so on);
3. loading of the goods on to the ship named by the buyer at an agreed port of shipment at an agreed time; and
4. notification of the buyer that the goods have been loaded on board the named ship.

Under the classic FOB contract, the buyer will be responsible for paying for the goods, for arranging the carriage itself and for arranging and paying for

1. marine insurance;

2. unloading of goods at the port of destination;
3. import formalities (import licences, customs and so on); and
4. transport from the destination port.

Notwithstanding the key obligations reviewed in the 1913 case above the parties contracting will often choose to modify their respective duties under a FOB contract.[96] For this reason Devlin J referred to an FOB contract as a flexible instrument.[97] In order to determine the responsibilities of the parties under the contract it is important to consider the terms of the contract in detail.

Box 3.3 FOB as a flexible instrument

Devlin J isolated three different scenarios that could arise where a FOB contract is used by the parties:[98]

1. The classic FOB contract,[99] under which the buyer is responsible for nominating the ship and the seller is responsible for loading the goods on board for the buyer and procuring a **bill of lading** in terms usual in the trade. In this scenario the seller is a party to the contract of carriage at least until he takes out the bill of lading in the name of the buyer.
2. The seller is asked to make additional arrangements under the contract. For example, as in a CIF contract, the seller may be obliged in the contract to load the goods on board the ship, take a bill of lading out in his own name[100] and forward the bill of lading to the buyer in return for payment.
3. Commonly used when freight has to be paid in advance, the buyer appoints a forwarding agent of his own at the port of loading not only to book space on a ship but also to procure the bill of lading. In such a scenario the seller discharges his duty by putting the goods on board the ship, getting the receipt of the mate and handing this receipt over to the forwarding agent of the buyer in order to enable him to obtain the bill of lading.

Risk transfer point under a FOB contract

Section 20 of the Sale of Goods Act 1979 states that unless it is otherwise agreed upon by the parties the goods will remain at the risk of the seller until such a time as the property in these goods is transferred by the seller to the buyer. In addition this section states that once the property in the goods is transferred to the buyer the goods will be at the risk of the buyer irrespective of whether delivery of the goods has taken place. In line with this section, the risk will generally pass with property. Accordingly the risk will pass from the seller to the buyer when the goods cross the rail of the ship.

The FOB clause is commonly used to calculate the price of the goods sold even when another trade term is agreed upon by the parties. Export licensing authorities (including UK customs) commonly calculate the export value of goods using FOB.[101]

Cost insurance freight (CIF) contracts under English law

In use since at least the middle of the nineteenth century and initially known as CF&I, CIF was fairly prominent during the 1940s,[102] leading the noted appeal judge Lord Wright to remark that a large number of transactions in value amounting to untold sums are carried out every year using CIF contracts.[103]

Where the seller has access to first-class shipping and insurance facilities the buyer will likely opt for CIF. Under CIF contracts, the price charged by the seller will include cost, insurance and freight and when fixing the sale price the seller will take these three components into account, inserting an occasional margin in relation to each component. Professor Karl Llewellyn praises CIF for its clarity and logic as he states that the sequence of actions by the seller are neatly matched by those of the buyer: the seller arranges, ships and transmits the batch of documents to the buyer; the buyer for his part honours the draft when the documents are presented.[104]

In the absence of any specific provision under a CIF contract the seller is obliged to do the following:[105]

1. to draw up an invoice for the goods sold;
2. to ship at the port of shipment goods matching the description set out in the contract (the seller is responsible for arranging and paying for the carriage of the goods to the port of shipment and for executing export formalities);[106]
3. to procure a contract of affreightment under which the goods will be delivered at the destination agreed upon by the parties in the contract (the seller will usually be responsible for arranging and paying for the loading of the goods on board the ship);
4. to arrange insurance for the buyer's benefit on terms that are customary in the trade; and
5. with all reasonable dispatch to send forward and tender to the buyer the shipping documentation (namely the invoice, bill of lading and insurance policy).

Where the seller fails to ship the goods he will be in breach of his agreement.[107] Equally a failure to tender the shipping documents will also be a breach of the seller's agreement.[108]

Box 3.4 A failure to ship under CIF

Johnson v. Taylor Bros & Co. Ltd [1920]
Taylor Bros & Co. Ltd, a company carrying on its business in England, was the plaintiff and respondent in the appeal (T) whilst Axel Axelson Johnson, who carried on business in Sweden under the style of A. Johnson & Co., was the defendant and appellant in the appeal (J).

J agreed to supply T with Swedish pig iron between 1908 and 1920 inclusive. The contract between the parties was a sale of goods agreement based on CIF terms. T attempted to recover damages under the contract from J based on an alleged breach of the contract by J (the original contract, dated 23 May 1908, was supplemented by a contract dated 5 and 6 January 1914).

The issue of the appeal was whether the court should exercise its discretion in allowing an application by T to serve a writ for breach of contract out of jurisdiction, thus permitting T to serve the writ on J in Sweden. Lord Atkinson remarked[109] that in this case the seller failed to ship the goods in breach of his agreement and by doing so made the creation and tender of the shipping documents impossible. Concluding, Lord Atkinson stated[110] that the court should refuse to exercise its discretion to allow the application of T to serve a writ out of the jurisdiction since the real cause of action (the failure to ship) took place outside the jurisdiction and the trivial consequence of that breach (the failure to tender the shipping documents) should not constitute the basis for issuing proceedings in England against this foreign entity.

Delivery of the bill of lading under CIF contracts

Under a CIF contract delivery of the bill of lading to the buyer is regarded as the symbolic delivery to the buyer of the goods purchased.[111] As such a CIF contract is treated by the English courts as a contract for the sale of the documents representing the contract goods rather than a contract for the sale of goods.[112] This feature is important in international commerce since it facilitates the transfer of title from the seller to the buyer whilst the goods are in transit. From the stance of the buyer this feature enables him to acquire the right to dispose of the goods whilst these are still in transit, whilst from the point of view of the seller this feature permits him to obtain payment as against the documents.

The buyer is likely to want to acquire the right to dispose of the goods at the earliest possible opportunity so that he can sell the goods on or secure an advance from the bank on the goods.[113] The seller for his part will want to part with the risk for the goods at the earliest available opportunity. However, he will also want to ensure that he is paid the purchase price. The objectives of both parties are met by ensuring that the buyer (or the bank nominated in the contract) makes payment in the manner agreed upon against delivery of the documents representing the goods.[114] In consequence, the buyer obtains the documents representing the goods, enabling him to resell these goods or secure an advance from the bank on the goods, whilst the seller receives payment and transfers the risk to the buyer.

The essential characteristic of the CIF contract when compared with an ordinary contract for the sale of goods rests in the fact that performance of the bargain is achieved by the delivery of the documents representing the goods and not by the actual physical delivery of the goods themselves by the seller.[115] It is the documents representing the goods that give the right to require that the goods be delivered or the possible right that if for some reason these goods are lost or damaged, the value of the goods can be recovered from either the ship owners or the insurers.[116] For the same reason, there may be situations where the buyer will need to pay the full price for delivery of the document even though he will receive nothing out of them and even though no property in the goods will ever pass to him as buyer. Such a situation could arise when for example the goods are lost as a result of a peril that is not covered under an insurance policy.[117]

Where the documents conform to the contract, the buyer is obliged to accept the said documents. If he fails to do so, he will be deemed to be in breach of the contract. This is the case even if the goods that the documents represent do not conform with the contract, on their arrival.[118]

There are several advantages associated with a CIF contract from buyer's point of view. Firstly, using the bill of lading the buyer can trade in the goods or pledge them to a bank in return for an advance whilst they are still in transit.[119] Secondly, since the cost of the arrangements for which the seller is responsible is included within the contract price, the buyer does not need to be concerned about the risk of fluctuation in freight charges and thus in the contract price.[120]

Transfer of risk under CIF contracts

Aside from representing the symbolic delivery of the goods, delivery of the bill of lading also effectively places the goods at the risk of the buyer and entitles the seller to payment of the purchase price.[121] As a general rule, under a CIF contract the seller will typically tender shipping documents only against payment of the price less any freight costs the buyer is obliged to pay for.[122] In case of loss of the goods, the valid tender of documents by the seller to the buyer protects the interest of the seller and the buyer in the goods. Accordingly the value of the goods can be recovered from either the ship owners or the insurers.[123]

Section 20 of the Sale of Goods Act 1979 states that unless it is otherwise agreed upon by the parties, the goods will remain at the risk of the seller until such a time as the property in the said goods is transferred by the seller to the buyer. It goes on to state that once the property in the goods is transferred to the buyer, the goods will be at the risk of the buyer irrespective of whether delivery of the goods has taken place or not.

As an exception to the general rule in Section 20, under CIF contracts the goods are deemed to be at the risk of the buyer from the time of shipment even though property only passes when the documents are tendered by the seller to the buyer. From the buyer's point of view, although the risk will pass at the time of shipment he will have the benefit of an insurance policy as well as a contract of carriage, enabling him to claim under one or the other in relation to any loss or damage sustained from the time of shipment.[124]

Where no trade terms are selected

If the parties have not agreed on trade terms, the arbiter will decide which trade terms will apply based on the law applicable to the contract. In contracts governed by the CISG, where the parties fail to determine trade terms, reference will be made to the provisions of the CISG in a bid to determine the responsibilities of the parties contracting and the point in time at which the risk passes from seller to buyer. Where (in contracts governed by the CISG) the parties fail to determine the allocation of risk between the seller and buyer, then as the governing law the CISG will incorporate terms governing allocation of risk.[125] Allocation of risk pursuant to the CISG is reviewed below.

Box 3.5 Allocation of risk under the CISG

Where the goods will be transported by carrier and the seller is not obliged to hand the goods over at a particular place then the risk will pass to the buyer when the goods are handed over to the first carrier for transmission to the buyer.[126] However, risk will pass only if the goods are clearly identified to the contract by markings on the goods, shipping documents, notice to the buyer or otherwise.[127] If the goods are damaged from the time they are handed over to the first carrier the buyer will bear the loss. The seller is, however, responsible for ensuring proper packaging of the goods.[128]

Where goods are sold in transit the risk in the goods will pass to the buyer at the time the contract is concluded.[129] If the seller knows or should know that the goods have been lost or damaged and he does not disclose this information to the buyer, the loss or damage is at the risk of the seller.[130]

Where the seller is not obliged to hand the goods over at a particular place and the goods are not sold in transit, then the risk in relation to the goods will pass to the buyer when he takes over the goods or if he does not do so in due time, from the time that the goods were placed at his disposal.[131]

VII Checklist of provisions

The following checklist provides a list of the provisions that should be included in simple international commercial agreements. This agreement is intended for use in international transactions between commercial parties. Not every one of the provisions listed in the checklist is mandatory but each of them should be considered by the parties when planning, negotiating, drafting and finalising the contract.

The contract and contractual provisions reviewed below cover transactions involving the sale of goods that are finished goods, where the buyer is a commercial party as opposed to a consumer and the sale is a one-off sale. The term 'international commercial agreement' (or 'agreements') is read to mean 'international sales agreement' and if applicable 'international distribution agreement'.[132]

Where a continuing supply arrangement is contemplated by the parties they may decide to conclude a contract that establishes a framework for a number of individual sales transactions (for example a distribution agreement). In such a situation, the sales transactions concluded under the auspices of the framework agreement may each be governed by the provisions contained within the said framework agreement.[133]

Where the contract is governed by the CISG, the parties have the option if they wish to derogate from or vary the effect of the provisions of the CISG.[134]

Box 3.6 Checklist of provisions

Preface to the contract
- ✓ Cover sheet
- ✓ Table of contents (in longer contracts; optional)
- ✓ Index of defined terms

Front of the contract (section VIII)
- ✓ Title
- ✓ Introductory clause (type of agreement, date of agreement, parties to agreement)
- ✓ Recitals

Body of the contract (section IX)
- ✓ Definitions clause
- ✓ Goods (description, price, quantity)
- ✓ Payment terms (method, time and structure of payment, currency, with or without taxes, consequences of delayed payment and non-payment)
- ✓ Costs and charges (duties and taxes, insurance, handling and transport)
- ✓ Delivery (date and location), trade term, documents, transport, insurance, import and export arrangements
- ✓ Packaging and due delivery (liability for delay in delivery or non-delivery)
- ✓ Invoicing
- ✓ Restrictions on re-export (optional)
- ✓ Warranties and liabilities
- ✓ Indemnity (optional)
- ✓ Licensing and protection of intellectual property rights
- ✓ Performance
- ✓ Termination (grounds and consequences) (optional)
- ✓ Contingencies and force majeure
- ✓ Confidentiality

Boilerplate clauses (section X)
- ✓ Assignment clause
- ✓ Merger clause
- ✓ Modification clause
- ✓ Severance clause
- ✓ Notice clause
- ✓ Representation clause
- ✓ Dispute resolution (informal discussions, renegotiation, adaption, ADR, choice of jurisdiction, choice of law)
- ✓ Language clause

Back of the contract (section XI)
- ✓ Concluding clause
- ✓ Signature blocks
- ✓ Attachment (exhibits and schedules)

VIII Front of the contract[135]

The front of the contract will incorporate the following:

1. Title
2. Introductory clause noting the type and date of the agreement as well as the details of the contracting parties
3. Recitals.

Consider the following sample extract.

> *Sale agreement*
> This sale agreement is dated 12 November 2009 and is between MANCHESTER STORAGE LTD, an English company ('MANCHESTER'), and BOLTON HAULAGE INC., a New York corporation ('BOLTON HAULAGE').

The extract above incorporates:

1. a title:[136]

> *Sale agreement*

2. an introductory clause:[137]

> This sale agreement is dated 12 November 2009 and is between MANCHESTER STORAGE LTD, an English company ('MANCHESTER'), and BOLTON HAULAGE INC., a New York corporation ('BOLTON HAULAGE')

No recitals are included in this extract.[138]

IX Body of the contract[139]

Definitions clause

See corresponding section in Chapter 2.

Goods (description, price, quantity)

> *Option A*
> 1. The Seller agrees to sell to the Buyer goods ('Goods') set out in [Schedule —— *or* the Definitions clause].
> 2. The Buyer agrees to buy the Goods from the Seller.
> 3. The price for the Goods to be paid by the Buyer to the Seller is [*insert currency, amount in numbers and amount in letters*]. The price for the Goods is not subject to any adjustments.
>
> *Option B*
> The Seller agrees to sell to the Buyer and the Buyer agrees to buy from the Seller goods ('Goods') of the following kind for the price and quantity stated:

1. number of model
2. description
3. quantity
4. price [*currency, amount in numbers and amount in letters*]
5. item
6. total price.

Description of goods

Goods may be defined

1. within the body of the agreement itself (option B);
2. in a schedule annexed to the agreement (option A); or
3. in the Definitions clause (option A).

The agreement may refer to

1. specific goods;
2. lines of goods produced by the seller; or
3. the whole range of production of the seller.

The agreement may permit new lines or goods to be included under the agreement as well as permitting the discontinuance or modification of goods falling under the scope of the agreement. The agreement may include a clause stating that it ceases to apply to goods which the seller stops producing.

Goods supplied may be tangible (land, equipment) or intangible (intellectual property rights, such as patents, copyright and trade marks). Goods may be supplied alone or alongside a service (for example contracts for the sale of machinery may also include installation).

The provision relating to goods should contain a description of the goods. Description is usually needed for a contract to be treated as enforceable. Goods may be described by model number or defined by reference to some other specification (option B). For multiple goods a detailed list should be provided. If a description of the goods is missing or is not specific enough then enforcement of the contract may be impossible as the goods cannot be identified.

Price of goods

The provision relating to goods should contain not only a description of the goods but also the price of the goods. Price as well as description is usually needed for a contract to be treated as enforceable. Whilst price may be implied by the law applicable to the contract this is not always the case.[140] If the parties fail to specify price or a mechanism for determination of price the courts will be unlikely to enforce the contract.

In an international contract it would be wise to denote price using an abbreviation of the currency in which payment is to be made.

Quantity of goods

It is important to denote the quantity of goods. Where a contract relates to goods of more than one type then the quantity of each type of goods should be noted by giving the number of units or weight of goods to be sold. If goods are measured by weight, it is important to make sure that a note is made of whether the weight is net weight, dry weight or drained weight.

IX BODY OF THE CONTRACT

Payment terms (method of payment, time and structure; currency; consequences of non-payment)

Method of payment, time and structure

> All prices for the Goods are exclusive of any applicable value added tax or any other sales tax for which the Buyer shall be additionally liable.
>
> [The Buyer shall make payment in [*include currency*] by transfer to such bank account as the Seller may from time to time notify in writing to the Buyer *or* The Buyer shall remit payment to the Seller at the address stated above or at an address to be specified by the Seller.]
>
> *Option A*
> The Buyer shall pay the purchase price on or before ———.
>
> *Option B*
> The Buyer shall pay the purchase price no later than ——— days before the Delivery Date.

In commerce remuneration of some kind will usually be agreed upon. Remuneration can be monetary or non-monetary. The question of payment and the mode of remuneration should be agreed upon by the contracting parties and appropriate provisions should be included in the contract addressing these issues.

Methods of payment in international trade
In a one-off transaction or a situation when the buyer and seller are transacting for the first time, the seller will usually be inclined to demand the most secure form of payment before shipping the goods. For his part, the buyer will want to make sure that the goods are delivered before payment is made.

The buyer and seller will usually negotiate the method of payment before settling on a workable compromise. The main methods of payment used in international trade are reviewed below. Many of the methods for payment used nationally are not necessarily suited to international commerce. Cheques can be dishonoured if there are insufficient funds in the account concerned. This uncertainty hinders international trade as the seller will be averse to dispatching the goods before the cheque clears and will be wary of taking the risk of having to sue the buyer in a foreign court in the event that the cheque issued by the buyer is dishonoured.

Cash in advance protects the seller at the expense of the buyer. The seller will receive payment before dispatching the goods or providing the service, in which case the buyer has no guarantee that the seller will actually go on to supply the goods or services contracted. Payment on account, by contrast, protects the buyer at the expense of the seller. The buyer receives the goods or is supplied with the services before he dispatches payment to the seller. The seller will accordingly depend on the buyer.

To address the transactional risks associated with cash in advance and payment on account several methods have been devised, amongst them **documents against payment** and **letters of credit**. These methods help mitigate the transactional risks that each party bears. The seller for his part bears the risk of supplying the goods or services and not being paid (risk of non-payment) whilst the buyer who pays for the goods or services bears the risk of not receiving the goods or services paid for (risk of non-delivery).

Documents against payment[141]

Where the parties agree on the term 'documents against payment' the seller agrees to deliver a **bill of lading** to a bank situated in the country of the buyer in turn enabling the buyer to confirm that the goods have in fact been shipped. The bank will deliver the bill of lading to the buyer once the buyer has tendered payment.

Bill of lading[142] A **bill of lading** is an instrument issued by the ocean carrier (carrier) to the shipper. The bill of lading fulfils three key functions. Firstly it acts as a receipt for the goods issued by the carrier. Secondly it is evidence of the contract of carriage concluded between the carrier and the shipper, although it is not in itself the contract of carriage strictly speaking, as normally the contract of carriage will be concluded between the carrier and the shipper either when the space upon the vessel is booked or when the goods are presented and accepted for loading.[143] Finally the bill of lading is a document of title. According to Professor Robert Bradgate,

> the purpose of a document of title to goods is to enable an owner of the goods to deal with them, for instance by selling or pledging them, even though they are in the physical possession of a bailee, by dealing with the document.[144]

A document will qualify as a document of title to goods, in English law, if it is such that the transfer of the document itself is effective to transfer constructive possession of the goods.[145]

According to Professor R. M. Goode, a document will be recognised as a document of title to goods, in English common law, if the document in question fulfils three conditions:

1. It must be issued by the bailee of the goods.
2. It must relate to identifiable goods.
3. A custom must exist recognising that transfer of the document transfers constructive possession of the goods.[146]

Transfer of the bill of lading will transfer constructive possession only when the goods to which the bill of lading relates are identifiable.[147] As such when the bill of lading relates to goods that are comprised in a larger bulk of goods, transfer of the bill of lading will not transfer constructive possession.[148]

The transferability of the bill of lading will depend on the wording of the bill of lading.[149] A bill of lading may be transferable by delivery, or by indorsement and delivery. In the event that no consignee is named in the bill of lading, it may be transferred by simple delivery to the intended transferee. In such a case the carrier agrees to deliver the goods to the person who produces the bill of lading. In the alternative the bill of lading may be made out to a named consignee. The named consignee may be the shipper or some other party (for example the party who has acquired the goods from the shipper). If the bill of lading makes the goods deliverable 'to X or order', it may be transferred. In such a case the bill of lading must be transferred by indorsing the name of the transferee and delivering the bill to the transferee.

Three types of bill of lading can be distinguished: a **straight bill of lading**, an **order bill of lading** and a **bearer bill of lading**.

A **straight bill of lading**[150] is a bill of lading that names the consignee. Such a bill of lading does not contain the phrase 'or order' or contains phrases such as 'non-transferable' or 'non-negotiable'. When a straight bill of lading is issued the carrier can deliver the goods to the named consignee only. Where goods are shipped under a straight bill of lading, the named consignee is not able to deal with the goods whilst they are in transit. For this reason such a bill of lading is known as a non-negotiable bill of lading in so far as it is non-transferable.

The negotiability, or transferability, of a bill of lading permits the transfer of rights in the instrument, in turn permitting the holder of the instrument to sue in his own name.[151] A non-negotiable instrument forbids such a transfer of rights, whilst a negotiable instrument permits it. Apart from the transfer of rights, the transfer of a bill of lading in a negotiable form represents a constructive delivery of the goods themselves. According to Professor Michael Bridge,

> The significance of a bill of lading in negotiable form is that its transfer from seller to buyer effects a constructive delivery of the goods. Subject to the carrier's lien for unpaid freight, the buyer may demand the goods at discharge without the carrier's attornment. Whether the buyer is named at the outset as the consignee ... or has the bill of lading indorsed and delivered to him, he will need to present it to the carrier to demand the goods, for the carrier is both bound and entitled to surrender the goods only to the holder of the bill.[152]

In contrast with a straight bill of lading, an **order bill of lading** is a negotiable bill of lading. An order bill of lading is universally regarded as representing goods whilst they are in transit.[153] Indorsement and delivery of this bill of lading operates as the symbolic delivery of the cargo.[154] Property in the goods will pass by means of the indorsement and delivery of this bill of lading whenever the parties intend for property to pass, just as property would pass by an actual delivery of the goods.[155]

A bill of lading will require the carrier to deliver the goods either to the person who holds the properly indorsed bill of lading (order bill of lading to the order of a named party) or to the holder of the bill of lading (order bill of lading made out to bearer).

There is a third type of bill of lading: a **bearer bill of lading**. A bearer bill of lading is a negotiable bearer document that can be transferred from one party to another by mere delivery of the document. Due to the risk that such a document may fall into the wrong hands, bearer bills of lading are not commonly used in foreign trade.

Letters of credit[156]

As a method of payment documents against payment resolves to mitigate the transactional risks that both buyer and seller bear. However, the seller may not agree to use this mode of payment due to the risk that he assumes in the event that the buyer fails to pay him the sums due under the contract. In the event of the buyer defaulting, the seller will be obliged to go to the expense and time of suing the buyer for the monies owing to him. In a bid to enhance the seller's protection more secure modes of payment have been devised by the banks, namely the **letter of credit** and in particular the **irrevocable letter of credit**. A letter of credit is an instrument issued by a bank or on occasion another institution in response to a request by an account party (in international trade the buyer). This instrument obliges the issuer to pay the beneficiary of the letter of credit (in international trade the seller) a sum of money if the beneficiary complies with conditions stipulated by the account party, including an obligation to present documents.

Irrevocable letter of credit A letter of credit may be irrevocable or revocable. Whilst a **revocable letter of credit** can be changed or cancelled by the issuing bank at any time without prior notice to the beneficiary (in other words the seller), an irrevocable letter of credit is far more secure as it may be changed or cancelled only after all the contracting parties agree to the modification or cancellation.

The bank issuing the letter of credit has certain obligations including the obligation to pay on the letter of credit once the conditions listed within it are fulfilled by the seller. This is the case even if there is a problem between seller and buyer. Moreover the bank that issues the letter of credit must ensure that all the documents sent through by the seller are in order, though it will not need to verify the quality of the contract goods.

Letters of credit are costly. Typically the fee charged by the bank for a letter of credit will represent a percentage of the sum covered by the letter and this fee will increase as the transaction increases in complexity.

Banking practices on international letters of credit have been standardised by a set of rules issued by the ICC entitled the Uniform Customs and Practice for Documentary Credits (UCP). The first version of the UCP was published in 1933 and the current version, UCP 600, took effect on 1 July 2007.[157] The UCP will only apply in situations where the text of the credit expressly indicates that it is subject to these rules.[158]

Structure of payment
Where money is the consideration for the supply of goods or services, the contracting parties may agree to use the following methods of payment, either alone or together: the initial sum and ongoing payments.

Initial sum Where an initial sum is due then this provision will need to indicate whether the sum is due as a one-off lump sum payment (in which case, the due date and figure involved will need to be noted) or in instalments (in which case, a due date for each instalment will need to be fixed along with an indication of the sums involved).

Ongoing payments Certain contracts may also include a provision for ongoing payments. Such payments may be fixed or they may fluctuate. For example, where the cost of goods depends on market conditions then such payments may be left open or they may fluctuate upwards or downwards by a set sum.

In certain situations, the ongoing payments will be fixed as a percentage of the sales generated. In a licensing agreement, for example, the contracting parties may agree that the licensee will pay the licensor ongoing royalties on top of the lump sum due under the agreement. Payment on collection or letters of credit may also be demanded by the seller as security in this context.

Currency

In the payment provisions, the contracting parties should take care to indicate the currency to be used and the instrument of payment. The currency selected by the contracting parties should be stable and the instrument secure.

IX BODY OF THE CONTRACT

Consequences of delayed payment and non-payment

The consequences of delayed payment and non-payment and any interest payable (rate, period and activation) must also be addressed by the contracting parties when formulating, negotiating, drafting and finalising the clauses in the contract.

Retention of title

> The title to the Goods shall not pass to the Buyer until the Seller has received payment in full of the Price.

Retention of title clauses permit the seller to retain legal ownership in the goods concerned until full payment has been received from the buyer. The contracting parties should bear in mind the fact that under certain bodies of national law, provisions for the retention of title of goods intended for resale are not always effective.[159]

Rights of the seller in relation to delayed payment and non-payment

> If the Buyer fails to pay the price for all or some of the Goods within —— days after the date of the invoice therefor, the Seller shall be entitled (without prejudice to any other right or remedy it may have) to
> - cancel any further delivery to the Buyer;
> - delay any further delivery to the Buyer;
> - sell or otherwise dispose of any Goods which are the subject of any order by the Buyer, whether or not appropriated thereto, and use the proceeds of sale to offset the overdue payment; and
> - charge the Buyer interest on the sums due from the date the payment became due until the date actual payment is made (irrespective of whether the date of payment is before or after any judgment or award in respect of the same). Such interest shall be charged at the rate of —— per cent per annum above —— Bank base rate in force from time to time.

Where the buyer fails to pay the seller for the contract goods the seller would be wise to retain the right to

1. cancel or delay further deliveries planned;
2. sell or dispose of any goods which are the subject of any order placed by the buyer; and
3. charge interest on the sums due.

Costs and charges

> The Buyer is responsible for the following costs and charges [*costs and charges may be listed in a schedule or within the body of the contract*].

> The Seller is responsible for the following costs and charges [*costs and charges may be listed in a schedule or within the body of the contract*].

This clause will list any additional costs and charges that each of the parties is responsible for, inter alia duties, shipping fees and taxes such as value added tax. Where the list is lengthy it is wise to list these additional costs and charges separately in a schedule.

Delivery (date and location), trade term, transport, insurance, import and export arrangements and documents

Delivery (date and location)

> The Seller shall deliver the Goods on [*here the date of delivery or period over which delivery will be carried out should be noted*] ('Delivery Date') at [*location (optional)*].

Delivery date
The contracting parties may agree on a precise date ('2 December 2012') or a period for delivery of the contract goods ('over the week commencing 2 December 2012' or 'during the month of December 2012' or '30 days from the date of receipt of the irrevocable letter of credit by the Seller'). Where the agreement is governed by the CISG, it is advisable to consider Article 33 of the CISG, which states that the seller must deliver the goods, if a date is fixed or can be determined by the contract, on that date and, if a period of time is fixed or can be determined under the contract, at any time during the period agreed upon, unless the circumstances indicate that the buyer is to select a date for delivery.[160] In the event that the contract is governed by the CISG, the contracting parties are permitted to either exclude or modify the provisions of the CISG, including Article 33.[161]

Delivery location
The contracting parties should consider the delivery location. In this context, they should review the trade term agreed upon to see whether it addresses this matter.

Trade term, transport, insurance, import and export arrangements and documents

The contracting parties should consider their respective responsibilities under the trade term that they have selected, before finalising the provision in the contract that addresses their respective responsibilities for, amongst other matters, transport, insurance and import and export arrangements.

> *Option A*
>
> *Trade term*
> The Seller shall sell the Goods to the Buyer on the following basis: [*the chosen trade term should be noted here and reference should also be made here to the origin of the trade term used, for example under English law, under Incoterms® and so on; if Incoterms® are used here, care should be taken to denote the version used*].
>
> *Single shipment*
> The Seller shall deliver the Goods in a single shipment.

IX BODY OF THE CONTRACT

Transport and insurance
Unless otherwise agreed, the Buyer shall be liable, in addition to the price, for arranging and paying all costs of transport and insurance.

Documents
Unless otherwise agreed, the Seller shall furnish the Buyer with the following documents: [*A list of the documents that the seller is required to furnish to the buyer should be given here*].

Where the Seller agrees at the request of the Buyer to arrange for transport and insurance as agent of the Buyer, the Buyer shall reimburse the Seller the full costs thereof and all the applicable provisions of this agreement shall apply with respect to the payment of such costs as they apply to payment of the price for the contract Goods.

Option B

Trade term
The Seller shall deliver the Goods on the following basis [*the chosen trade term should be denoted here and reference should also be made here to the origin of the trade term used, for example under English law, under Incoterms® and so on; if Incoterms® are used here, care should be taken to denote the version used*].

Single shipment
The Seller shall deliver the Goods in a single shipment.

Transport, insurance
The Seller shall choose the mode of transport to the point of delivery. The Seller shall best endeavour to start transportation of the Goods in order to ensure that the Goods arrive by the Delivery Date.

The [Buyer *or* Seller] shall arrange and pay for all insurance on the Goods whilst in transit, provided that the insurance arranged will include for the protection of the [Seller *or* Buyer] coverage for the following [*here the extent of coverage should be noted*]. Confirmation of this insurance [*here the form of confirmation should be specified; for example a copy of the insurance policy, or some other statement provided by the insurer*] shall be supplied to the [Seller *or* Buyer] before the Goods are shipped.

Each Party shall obtain any other insurance for the Goods that they require.

Import and export arrangements
The Seller shall organise and provide to [*the country in question should be noted here*] customs all export documents and fees required for clearance, including the following: [*a list of the same should be included here*].

The Buyer shall organise and provide to [*the country in question should be noted here*] customs all import documents and fees required for clearance, including the following: [*a list of the same should be included here*].

The Buyer shall inform the Seller that all import requirements have been complied with. The Seller shall not be required to ship the Goods until such a time as the Buyer has supplied the Seller with evidence that the import requirements and fees have been or will be met in a timely fashion. If shipment is delayed due to a failure by the Buyer to supply such evidence in a timely fashion the Seller shall not be deemed to have breached the contract.

Title to the Goods

Title to the Goods shall pass to the Buyer at such a time as the Goods are delivered to [*specify place*] on the proviso that the Buyer has transmitted payment to the Seller by that time.

Documents

Unless otherwise agreed, the Seller shall furnish the Buyer with the following documents: [*a list of the documents that the seller is required to furnish to the buyer should be given here*].

Trade terms

More often than not in international commercial agreements, the contracting parties will use customary trading terms. The selection of such terms should be performed with care, with each contracting party paying particular attention to the point in time when title and risk pass from seller to buyer under the term selected, and the responsibilities of each contracting party under the term selected.

Insurance

Though trade terms such as Incoterms® generally address the issue of insurance it is still advisable to check that the trade term selected provides the requisite insurance cover. In the context of insurance, the following details should be specified within the body of the contract:

1. the insurance cover required
2. the details of the beneficiary of the policy
3. the date on which insurance should be taken out
4. the documents that should be supplied as satisfactory evidence of insurance.

Passage of title and risk

The provision addressing the passage of title is important as the contracting party with title will generally assume responsibility for the goods. Each contracting party should ensure that it obtains insurance for the goods for the time that it has possession, holds title or is responsible for the goods in question.

When the contracting parties select an Incoterm® within their contract, the Incoterm® will stipulate the time and place when risk and title pass from seller to buyer. If the contracting parties do not use an Incoterm® then it would be wise for them to verify that the trade term they have selected makes provision for the time and place when risk and title pass from seller to buyer. In the event that no such provision is included within the selected trade term, then it would be sensible for the contracting parties to agree on a provision setting out the following:

1. which contracting party will be responsible for carriage from the seller's premises
2. which contracting party will be responsible for insuring the goods
3. the name or type of carrier that will handle shipment of the freight (occasionally a certain carrier will be preferred in a situation where the carrier offers competitive pricing or can provide a better service)
4. the requirements for storage of the goods before and during transit
5. when and where the goods will be delivered to the buyer
6. whether notification must be given by the seller to the buyer advising the buyer that the goods are ready for delivery or collection, or tracking the location of the goods
7. issues arising where more than one carrier is involved or special care is needed due to the nature of the goods transported

IX BODY OF THE CONTRACT

8. the point in time when risk and title pass from seller to buyer.

Documents[162]

In international commercial agreements, it is commonplace for the seller to furnish the buyer with certain documents including title documents, insurance documents, permissions and so on. In this context the parties contracting should consider which documents are to be furnished under the trade term that they have agreed upon. If necessary the parties may revise or supplement this list of documents. Moreover if the parties agree to payment by letter of credit they should also take care to ensure that they are clear as to the documents that are required under the letter of credit.

Packaging and due delivery (liability for delay in delivery or non-delivery)

Packaging

The Seller shall retain discretion in relation to the packaging of the Goods so long as the following conditions are met:
1. The packaging withstands transportation of the Goods.
2. The packaging prevents damage to the Goods occurring during their transportation.
3. The packaging conforms with the laws governing [*inter alia labelling, warnings, instructions and origin marking*] as they pertain to such goods.

The Seller shall use its best endeavours to complete all packaging in time for the Delivery Date.

Liability for delay in delivery or non-delivery

In the event of a delay in delivery of the Goods:
The Seller shall notify the Buyer immediately of the delay, the reason for the delay and the projected time for completion of the delivery of the Goods. The Buyer will then have the option of
1. agreeing a new Delivery Date with the Seller which the Parties will confirm in writing as a modification to this agreement; or
2 notifying the Seller that the agreement is terminated.

Packaging

Such a provision should at the very least require the seller to package the goods in a manner that will ensure that they withstand the transportation. Where special packaging is needed in order to ensure compliance with the laws in the target market and the market expectations in the said market, the buyer should advise the seller of this fact and should ensure that this provision indicates the manner in which the goods should be packaged and labelled. Where it is agreed that the buyer should be responsible for ensuring proper packaging for sale in his country, the seller should insist on the inclusion of protective provisions for intellectual property and third party liability.[163]

Liability for delay in delivery or non-delivery

According to the CISG a delay in delivery for which the seller is responsible (in so far as it is not justified under the force majeure clause) will entitle the buyer to various remedies.[164] The provisions of the CISG may be derogated from or varied by the contracting parties[165].

The ICC Model International Sale Contract provides for a solution that is different to the one proposed under the CISG. Under this model contract, the buyer will be entitled to liquidated damages for a set period (the standard suggested by the model contract is ten weeks) and thereafter the buyer may terminate the contract.[166]

Invoicing

> The Seller shall prepare and send to the Buyer provisional and final shipment invoices relating to the Goods describing the Goods, the quantity of the Goods and their price.

In the context of international commercial agreements invoices perform two functions. Firstly they attest to the fact that shipment has taken place. Secondly they provide the requisite documentary evidence for customs clearance. The format of such invoices may be stipulated by the laws or regulations in the country of the buyer or seller. In order to ensure compliance with such laws or regulations it is important to ensure that reference is made within the terms of the contract to the specific requirements of each contracting party.

Restrictions on re-export (optional)

> The Buyer covenants that the Goods shall be shipped to and delivered in [*the country or countries should be listed here*].
> The Buyer covenants that the Goods shall not be shipped to or be delivered to any other country.
> The Buyer covenants that it shall not re-export the Goods after delivery in [*the country or countries must be specified here*].

A provision of the kind outlined above is advisable in those scenarios where the contracted goods are subject to either import restrictions or export restrictions under the laws of a particular country. This could for example be the case where an embargo is in place,[167] preventing the export of goods to specific countries.

Warranties and liabilities

> Subject as herein provided the Seller expressly warrants to the Buyer ('Warranty') that
> 1. all the Goods supplied will at the time of delivery and at the time of the Buyer's subsequent sale be of merchantable quality and will comply with any specification agreed upon by the Parties; and
> 2. the Trade Marks given in Schedule —— are registered in the name of the Seller and the Seller has disclosed to the Buyer all Trade Marks used by the Seller in connection with the Goods at the date of this agreement.
>
> Except as expressly provided for in this agreement, the Seller does not warrant the

> Goods in any manner at all. Implied warranties are disclaimed.
>
> In the event of any breach of the Warranty, the liability of the Seller shall be limited to
> 1. replacement of the Goods; or
> 2. at the discretion of the Seller, repayment of the Price where the Price has already been paid.
>
> Notwithstanding anything to the contrary in this agreement, the Seller shall not be liable to the Buyer for any consequential loss or damage arising out of or in relation to any act or omission by the Seller, resulting from any representation or implied warranty, or under the express terms of this agreement, except in relation to death or personal injury caused by the negligence of the Seller.

Warranties

The seller may be prepared to grant the buyer certain warranties in relation to the goods. Whilst it is sensible for the buyer to secure warranties in relation to the goods, the seller may try to limit or remove his liability completely. In the event that the parties contracting have agreed upon warranties, it is sensible for them to ensure that these warranties are clearly set out in the contract.

The manufacturer of goods will typically grant a warranty to the end buyer. In this case, the warranty of the manufacturer may overlap with the obligations of the seller to the end buyer under the contract of sale. In the event that the goods sold are defective, the end buyer may have a claim against both the seller and the manufacturer of the goods. In such a situation it is advisable for the parties to agree that they will cooperate in order to manage the warranty; for example, they may agree that the buyer confirm to the manufacturer the date of the on-sale to the end buyer, which is typically also the date of commencement of the warranty of the manufacturer.[168] Moreover the parties may agree that the buyer perform certain duties, for example repairing or replacing goods that are defective, on the manufacturer's behalf.[169]

Implied warranties[170]

It is also worthwhile bearing in mind that warranties may be read into the contract by operation of the law. Such warranties are known as implied warranties. The seller may look to exclude all implied warranties. Obviously the buyer may object to this attempt by the seller to compromise the protection extended to the buyer by the implied warranties.

In the event that the agreement is governed by the CISG,[171] the seller will be obliged by virtue of the provisions of the CISG[172] to not only deliver goods of the quantity, quality and description required by the contract but also to ensure that they are fit for the purposes for which goods of the same description are ordinarily used, are fit for a stated purpose (made known to the seller by the buyer), possess the qualities of the goods which the seller has held out to the buyer as a sample, and are packaged in the manner usual for such goods.

Liability for non-conforming goods

Where the goods fail to meet the warranties (express or implied), they are said to be **non-conforming**. In the event that the agreement is governed by the CISG and the goods are non-conforming the buyer has certain remedies available to him.[173] Under the ICC's Model International Sale Contract,[174] the solution suggested is one that is radically different to that suggested under the CISG. Under this model contract, the seller always retains the right to rectify the non-conformity even when the said non-conformity amounts to a fundamental breach; the buyer will be entitled to terminate the contract only if the seller cannot remedy the defects within a reasonable time.[175]

Indemnity (optional)

The seller may, but is not bound to, agree to indemnify the buyer in certain limited circumstances. The contract is likely to address the liabilities of the contracting parties if a certain event should happen: in a contract for the provision of services, the contracting parties may address liability in the event of injury; and in a contract for the supply of goods, the contracting parties may decide to make provision for liability in the event of fire, disaster and so on.

Licence and protection of intellectual property rights

1. The Seller authorises the Buyer to use the Trade Marks in the Territory on or in relation to the Goods, solely for the purposes of exercising its rights and performing its obligations under this agreement.
2. Except as provided for in clause 1 above, the Buyer shall not have rights in respect of any trade names or Trade Marks used by the Seller in relation to the Goods or of the goodwill associated therewith. The Buyer confirms that, except where expressly provided for in this agreement, it shall not obtain any rights in respect thereof and that all such rights and goodwill are and shall remain vested in the Seller.
3. The Buyer shall take all steps as the Seller may reasonably require of the Buyer in order to help the Seller maintain the validity and enforceability of the Intellectual Property of the Seller during the term of this agreement, on the proviso that the Seller shall indemnify the Buyer against all costs, claims, damages, responses or other liabilities arising from or in connection with such steps.
4. The Buyer shall, in response to a request from the Seller, execute such registered user agreements or licences in respect of the use of the Trade Marks in the Territory as the Seller may reasonably require, so long as the provisions thereof shall not be more onerous or restrictive than the provisions of this agreement.
5. Without prejudice to the right of the Buyer or any third party to challenge the validity of any Intellectual Property of the Seller, the Buyer shall not do or authorise any third party to do any act which would or might invalidate or be inconsistent with any Intellectual Property of the Seller.
6. The Buyer shall notify the Seller in a comprehensive and timely fashion of any actual, threatened or suspected infringement in the Territory of any Intellectual Property of the Seller which comes to the notice of the Buyer. The Buyer shall at the request and expense of the Seller do all such things as may be reasonably required to assist the Seller in taking or resisting any proceedings in relation to any such infringement or claim.
7. The Buyer shall notify the Seller in a comprehensive and timely fashion of any claim by a third party, of which the Buyer has knowledge.

In order to promote sales of the contract goods in the assigned territory, under the agreement the buyer will be awarded a licence to use the intellectual property belonging to the seller for the duration of the agreement. Such a grant will be subject to certain conditions laid out in the agreement which protect the intellectual property of the seller along with the seller's reputation and goodwill.

Firstly, the seller will ensure that the agreement contains provisions that effectively curtail the buyer's rights in relation to the seller's intellectual property. Such provisions will limit the buyer's use of the seller's intellectual property generally and the buyer's use of the seller's intellectual property in relation to the contract goods in the assigned territory. Such provisions may for example oblige the buyer to use the seller's intellectual property only for the purposes contemplated by the agreement and in a manner approved by the seller. Moreover the buyer may be prohibited by the agreement from tampering with or modifying the contract goods or their packaging or in any way using the intellectual property of the seller in a fashion that might prejudice their distinctiveness or validity or in some way that may impact on the goodwill of the seller.

Secondly, the seller may insist that the buyer take all necessary steps to help the seller maintain the validity and enforceability of the intellectual property. With this in mind, the seller may insist that the buyer provide notification of any actual or potential infringement of the seller's intellectual property in the assigned territory. Thirdly, to ensure that no rights are obtained by the buyer in relation to the seller's intellectual property a provision will probably be included in the agreement stating that all rights and goodwill that arise in relation of the intellectual property will remain at all times the property of the seller.

Performance

The Seller and Buyer agree that time is of the essence.

From a legal and business point of view, time is invariably of the essence and as such any provision in the contract denoting time of performance (the delivery date, the payment date and so on) is considered of paramount importance. As a result any failure to comply with such a provision is treated as a fundamental breach of the contract.

Termination (grounds and consequences) (optional)

This provision is optional in contracts for sale of goods that are one-off agreements. It is more appropriate where the contract concluded is intended to cover a continuing arrangement between the parties. In such a context, the contracting parties should consider firstly the grounds for termination and secondly the consequences of such a termination.

Grounds for termination

1. Either Party may terminate this agreement with immediate effect by notice given in writing in the following situations:
   a. The other Party commits any breach of any of the provisions of this agreement resulting in such detriment to the Party terminating so as to substantially deprive him of that which the Party terminating is entitled to expect under this agreement and, in the case of a breach capable of remedy, fails to remedy such a breach within ―― after receipt of written notice setting out the particulars of the breach and requiring the breach to be rectified.
   b. A receiver is appointed over any of the property or assets of the other Party.
   c. That other Party enters into a voluntary arrangement with its creditors or becomes the subject of an administration order.
   d. That other Party goes into liquidation.
   e. Anything analogous to any of the aforementioned under the law of any jurisdiction occurs in relation to that other Party.
   f. That other Party ceases or threatens to cease to carry on business.
   g. There is at any time a material change in the management, ownership or control of the other Party.
   h. The other Party is substantially prevented from performing its obligations under the agreement.
   i. The other Party assigns or tries to assign the agreement without prior authorisation.
2. A breach shall be considered capable of remedy if the Party in breach is able to comply with the provision concerned in all respects other than as to the time of performance, on the proviso that time of performance is not of the essence.
3. Any waiver by either Party of a breach of any provision of this agreement shall not constitute a waiver of any consequent breach of the same or any other provision thereof.
4. Any termination of this agreement shall be without prejudice to any rights or remedies of either Party in respect of the breach concerned (if any) or any other breach.

In practice, it is more likely that the contracting parties will reach an agreement allowing them both to benefit equally from the right to terminate. As such each contracting party will typically have the option of terminating by providing the other party with written notice of a set length.

The contracting parties will usually agree that either will have a right to terminate in one of the following situations:

1. Where the other party has committed a material breach. Such a right will typically be exercisable once the innocent party has given the defaulting party (the breaching party) an opportunity to remedy the breach. In such a situation the innocent party will usually send written notice to the breaching party setting out the full particulars of the breach and asking the breaching party to remedy the said breach.
2. If the other party goes into liquidation, administration or receivership, or enters into a voluntary arrangement, or stops carrying on business (or threatens

to do so). In this provision it is sensible for the contracting parties to consider stipulating that the right to terminate can be used if the other party ceases to carry on its business for a specified period of consecutive days (other than for annual holidays), in order to accommodate for those countries in which businesses close down completely over the annual holidays (France for example).

3. If the other party is substantially prevented from performing obligations under the agreement.
4. If the other party assigns or tries to assign the agreement without firstly obtaining authorisation.

Consequences of termination

Upon termination of this agreement for whatever reason:
1. The Seller may buy back from the Buyer all or part of any stocks of the Goods held by the Buyer at their Invoice Value or the value at which they stand in the books of the Buyer (whichever is the lower) and the Seller shall organise and pay for transportation and insurance.
2. The Buyer, at its own expense and within —— days of termination, shall dispatch to the Seller or otherwise dispose of in accordance with the Seller's instructions and in the presence of the Seller's duly authorised representative all samples of the Goods and any materials relating to the Goods in the possession or control of the Buyer.
3. The Buyer shall pay immediately
   a. all outstanding unpaid invoices rendered by the Seller in respect of the Goods and/or
   b. all invoices to be issued by the Seller in relation to Goods ordered pre-termination once these invoices are issued by the Seller.
4. The Buyer shall stop promoting, marketing or advertising the Goods.
5. The Buyer shall stop using the Trade Marks.
6. The Buyer shall have no claim against the Seller.
7. Subject to what is otherwise provided for in this agreement and to any rights or duties which have accrued prior to termination, neither Party shall have any further obligations to the other under this agreement.
8. The Buyer shall supply the Seller with a list of the Buyer's customers for the Goods.
9. The Buyer shall assign to the Seller at no charge all permissions, consents and licences pertaining to the Goods and shall execute all documents and do all things that are required to ensure that the Seller has the benefit of these permissions, consents and licences after the termination in question to the entire exclusion of the Buyer.

Upon termination of the agreement, for whatever reason, the contracting parties will reserve themselves certain rights. Each will usually ask for the inclusion of a provision that states that subject to anything otherwise provided for in the agreement and to any rights or obligations that accrue prior to termination, neither of the contracting parties will have any further obligations to the other under the agreement. The seller, in order to prevent a situation (post termination) of the buyer competing in some way with him or one of his distributors or agents, will be keen to protect his position by reserving himself certain rights upon termination and imposing certain duties on the buyer upon termination. With this in mind, the seller will typically reserve himself the following rights:

1. The right to ask the buyer to dispose of (in line with the directions of the seller) or return to the seller, promptly or within a set number of days, all samples and documents (whatever their nature) found in the possession or control of the buyer and pertaining to the contract goods, to the seller or to the activities of the buyer in relation to the said goods (at the expense of either the seller, the buyer or both).
2. The right to ask the buyer to sell back to the seller all or part of any stocks of the contract goods held by the buyer at a price set out in the agreement or at the price at which such goods stand in the books of the buyer, whichever happens to be the lower.
3. The right to demand payment by the buyer of outstanding unpaid invoices levied by the seller.
4. The right to demand payment of invoices for orders placed before termination but for which an invoice has yet to be raised.

The seller will also usually insist that the following duties arise automatically on termination on the buyer's part:

1. A duty to destroy in the presence of the seller (or his authorised representative) and at the buyer's expense all contract goods which are non-merchantable, obsolete, illegal, damaged, deteriorated, defective or otherwise unsuitable for resale or, where the good has a shelf life, with more than half of its shelf life expired. Such a provision is intended to prevent the buyer from selling old or defective stock of goods at distress prices, putting the reputation of these goods and the seller at risk.
2. A duty to stop promoting, marketing or advertising the contract goods.
3. In relation to leftover goods of a merchantable quality:
   a. A duty to negotiate the sale back to the seller of these goods or their transfer to a new distributor or agent (in return for a lump sum payment from the seller).
   b. A duty to stop using the trade mark belonging to the seller in any way whatsoever in the event that the goods are left with the buyer. Obviously this will not be ideal from the point of view of the seller due to the risk of competition with the seller, his distributor or agent. Such a provision may be applicable where the seller does not or is not in a position to negotiate the sale back of the goods or their disposal. Obviously in such a situation, the seller would not want the buyer to sell the goods left in the charge of the buyer using the seller's trade mark or trade marks.
4. A duty to supply the seller with a list of customers for the goods. Such a list will be of critical importance to the seller and any new buyer in the assigned territory. A provision of this nature is likely to meet with resistance from the buyer, as the buyer will regard such customers as his own and in turn as part of his goodwill. This is likely to be the case where the buyer wishes to continue on selling goods that are similar to the contract goods.
5. A duty to assign to the seller at no charge all permissions, consents and licences relating to the contract goods

and execute all documents and do anything that is required in order to ensure that the seller is in a position to take advantage of these permissions, consents and licences post termination, to the entire exclusion of the buyer. Obviously such an assignment to the seller or the appointee of the seller is essential to the business of the seller generally. In the absence of such an assignment, the buyer may have the option of holding the seller to ransom. Where the permissions and so on are personal to the buyer these will need to be assigned. Where these are non assignable the situation may prove far more problematic for the seller.

Contingencies and force majeure

Option A

1. Neither Party shall be deemed to be in breach of this agreement, to the extent that performance of their obligations (except payment of sums due hereunder) is delayed or prevented by circumstances that are beyond the reasonable control of that Party ('Force Majeure') and the Party in question could not reasonably be expected to have taken the impediment into account at the time this agreement was concluded, provided that each Party gives the other Party written notice promptly and uses its good faith efforts to cure the breach.
2. In the event of Force Majeure, the time for performance will be extended for a period equal to the duration of the event of Force Majeure.
3. If the event of Force Majeure prevails for a continuous period in excess of —— months, the Parties shall be entitled to enter into good faith discussions with a view to alleviating its effects or to agreeing upon some other alternative arrangement or arrangements as may be fair and reasonable.
4. This clause shall not relieve either Party of the obligation to use all reasonable endeavours to mitigate the effect of such circumstances in relation to its obligations under this agreement.

Option B

This agreement is deemed cancelled and neither Party will be liable to the other for losses resulting from non-performance if performance of the Parties' obligations (except payment of sums due hereunder) is delayed or prevented by circumstances that are beyond the reasonable control of one or both of the Parties ('Force Majeure') provided that each Party gives the other Party written notice promptly and each Party uses good faith efforts to cure the breach.

The contract will attempt to address the many contingencies that may arise during the course of dealings between the contracting parties and the way in which such contingencies will affect the execution of the contract. Two issues will need to be considered in such circumstances. Firstly, will the contract terminate on the happening of certain events or will it continue? Secondly, if the contract continues will new provisions kick in or will the terms of the contract need to be renegotiated?

Most of the time the contracting parties will include in the contract a provision suspending and in turn excusing performance in such circumstances until the event passes. Such a provision will permit the contracting party to resume performance of its obligations under the contract once the event passes. The contracting parties will probably also include a provision in the contract to address those situations where an event continues for a period which is longer than the one that the contracting parties set out in the contract. In such a provision, the contracting parties will probably state that they are permitted to renegotiate the terms of the contract between them in order to accommodate for this change in circumstances.

The courts will usually uphold such provisions on the basis that the contracting parties freely agreed them. If no such provision is included within the contract or the provision included is incomplete, the courts will typically apply the law governing the contract in order to resolve the difficulty.

If an event that is beyond the reasonable control of a contracting party arises, which either delays or prevents performance of obligations under the agreement, then the party whose performance is disrupted will not be deemed to be in breach of the agreement.

Under option A, the time for performance of these obligations by the contracting party will be extended for a period equal to the event; where the event lasts for a period that is longer than the agreed period, the contracting parties will have an opportunity to re-examine their options. In the alternative, under option B, the contracting parties may decide that the agreement is cancelled if performance is prevented by circumstances that are beyond the reasonable control of either one of the parties.

Confidentiality

1. Neither Party shall use information which is confidential and proprietary to the other except in performance of this agreement.
2. Neither Party shall disclose such information to third parties except in the normal course of business in its performance of this agreement under an appropriate non-disclosure agreement with the third party.
3. This obligation will remain in force after the expiry or termination of this agreement and shall subsist for as long as the information remains confidential.

In order to protect proprietary information of the contracting parties this provision obliges the parties to keep information that comes into their possession about the other party confidential for as long as the information itself remains confidential.

X Boilerplate clauses

See the corresponding section in Chapter 2.

XI Back of the contract

Schedule

The schedules accompanying a sales agreement are likely to address amongst other matters the goods and the trade marks licensed. See also the corresponding section in Chapter 2.

Summary

This chapter reviewed the law governing international sales of goods and the role of trade terms and the manner in which these trade terms operate. It also reviewed the provisions that the contracting parties should consider including in the international sales agreement. Firstly, we examined key provisions that need to be included in an international sales agreement. Secondly, in relation to each such provision, we considered its purpose and possible wording.

Useful links

General

http://www.cisg.law.pace.edu/cisg/text/treaty.html (text of CISG)
http://www.hcch.net/index_en.php?act=home.splash (Hague Conference on Private International Law)
http://www.iccwbo.org (International Chamber of Commerce)
http://www.legislation.gov.uk/ukpga/1967/45 (Uniform Laws on International Sales Act 1967 – English law)
http://www.legislation.gov.uk/ukpga/1979/54 (Sale of Goods Act 1979 – English law)
http://www.unidroit.org/english/conventions/c-ulf.htm (Convention relating to a Uniform Law on the Formation of Contracts for the International Sale of Goods, The Hague, 1 July 1964)
http://www.unidroit.org/english/conventions/c-ulis.htm (Convention relating to a Uniform Law on the International Sale of Goods, The Hague, 1 July 1964)
http://www.uncitral.org/uncitral/en/index.html (UNCITRAL)

Listing of conventions:

http://www.hcch.net/index_en.php?act=conventions.listing (on website of Hague Conference on Private International Law)
http://www.uncitral.org/uncitral/en/uncitral_texts.html (list of UNCITRAL texts and their status)
http://www.uncitral.org/uncitral/en/uncitral_texts/sale_goods.html (list of UNCITRAL texts specifically relating to international sale of goods and related transactions)

Further reading

August, Ray, Mayer, Don and Bixby, Michael (2009), *International Business Law: Text, Cases and Readings*, 5th ed., Pearson Education.
Bortolotti, Fabio (2008), *Drafting and Negotiating International Commercial Agreements: A Practical Guide*, International Chamber of Commerce.
Bradgate, Robert (2000), *Commercial Law*, 3rd ed., Butterworths.

Christou, Richard (2003), *International Agency, Distribution and Licensing Agreements*, 4th ed., Sweet & Maxwell.

Fox, William F. Jr (1992), *International Commercial Agreements: A Primer on Drafting, Negotiating and Resolving Disputes*, Kluwer Law and Taxation.

Jones, Alison and Sufrin, Brenda (2008), *EC Competition Law: Text, Cases, and Materials*, 3rd ed., Oxford University Press.

Macintyre, Ewan (2010), *Business Law*, 5th ed., Pearson Education Limited.

Murray, Carole, Holloway, David and Timson-Hunt, Daren (2007), *Schmitthoff's Export Trade: The Law and Practice of International Trade*, 11th ed., Sweet & Maxwell.

Murray, Daniel (1991), 'Risk of Loss of Goods in Transit: A Comparison of the 1990 Incoterms® with Terms from Other Voices', *The University of Miami Inter-American Law Review* 23:1, 93.

Ramberg, Jan (2011), 'Incoterms® 2010', *Penn State International Law Review* 29, 415.

Shippey, Karla C. (1999), *A Short Course in International Contracts: Drafting the International Sales Contract for Attorneys and Non-attorneys*, World Trade Press.

Tillotson, John (1995), *Contract Law in Perspective*, 3rd ed., Cavendish.

Notes

1. Conflict of laws and parties' choice of law are reviewed in Chapter 2.
2. This topic is reviewed in Chapter 2.
3. Regulation (EC) No 593/2008 of the European Parliament and the Council of 17 June 2008 on the Law Applicable to Contractual Obligations (Rome I) governs all contracts concluded after 17 December 2009 (whilst its predecessor, the Rome Convention, applies to those contracts concluded before and on 17 December 2009). Rome I and the Rome Convention before it apply to contractual obligations in situations where there is a choice between the laws of different countries. Rome I will be addressed further in Chapters 6 and 7.
4. The CISG has been ratified by more than seventy-five states. A regularly updated list of the states that have ratified the CISG is available at http://www.uncitral.org/uncitral/en/uncitral_texts/sale_goods/1980CISG_status.html (last accessed 17 January 2013).
5. This topic is reviewed in Chapter 7.
6. These model contracts will be discussed in each of the relevant chapters.
7. Murray, Carole, Holloway, David and Timson-Hunt, Daren (2007), *Schmitthoff's Export Trade: The Law and Practice of International Trade*, 11th ed., Sweet & Maxwell, Chapters 2–7.
8. The CISG 'applies to contracts of sale of goods between parties whose places of business are in different States when the States are Contracting States or when the rules of private international law lead to the application of the law of a Contracting State' (Article 1(1) CISG). It addresses different elements of contract law that are applicable to international sale transactions. Firstly it addresses the process by which a contract is formed, namely what constitutes

an offer, what constitutes an acceptance and when the offer and acceptance are effective (Part 2 CISG). Secondly it defines the obligations of the seller and buyer as well as the remedies available to them in the event of a breach (Part 3 CISG). Thirdly it defines the passage of risk (Part 3 CISG).

9. A selection of these conventions can be found on websites of the Hague Conference on Private International Law (http://www.hcch.net/index_en.php?act=conventions.listing (last accessed 17 January 2013)); and UNCITRAL (http:www.uncitral.org/uncitral/en/uncitral_texts/sale_goods.html (last accessed 17 January 2013)).
10. Firstly the Convention Relating to a Uniform Law on the International Sale of Goods (The Hague, 1 July, 1964), available at http://www.unidroit.org/english/conventions/c-ulis.htm (last accessed 17 January 2013), and secondly the Convention Relating to a Uniform Law on the Formation of Contracts for the International Sale of Goods (The Hague, 1 July 1964), available at http://www.unidroit.org/english/conventions/c-ulf.htm (last accessed 17 January 2013). They can be found in Schedule I and Schedule II respectively of the Uniform Laws on International Sales Act 1967.
11. The full title of this Act is 'An Act to give effect to two Conventions with respect to the international sale of goods; and for purposes connected therewith'. It is available at http://www.legislation.gov.uk/ukpga/1967/45 (last accessed 17 January 2013). See Murray et al. (2007: 845–2).
12. Bradgate, Robert (2000), *Commercial Law*, 3rd ed., Butterworths, 766.
13. When a contract is concluded through an agent it is the place of business of the principal as opposed to that of the agent that is relevant. See *Ocean Chemical Transport Inc. v. Exnor Craggs Ltd* [2000] 1 All ER (Comm) 519 (Court of Appeal).
14. Bradgate 2000: 766.
15. Available at http://www.legislation.gov.uk/ukpga/1979/54 (last accessed 17 January 2013). The 1979 Act is reviewed later in this chapter.
16. Bradgate 2000, Chapter 31.
17. Available at http://www.legislation.gov.uk/ukpga/1977/50 (last accessed 17 January 2013).
18. Pursuant to §26 Unfair Contract Terms Act 1977. The 1977 Act is reviewed later in this chapter.
19. The full title of this Act is 'An Act to consolidate the law relating to the sale of goods'.
20. §64(2) Sale of Goods Act 1979.
21. §1(1) Sale of Goods Act 1979 as amended.
22. Part 2 of the Sale of Goods Act 1979 as amended, consisting of §§2–15 inclusive.
23. Part 3 of the Sale of Goods Act 1979 as amended, consisting of §§16–26 inclusive.
24. Part 4 of the Sale of Goods Act 1979 as amended, consisting of §§27–37 inclusive.
25. Part 5 of the Sale of Goods Act 1979 as amended, consisting of §§38–48 inclusive.

26. Part 5 of the Sale of Goods Act 1979 as amended, consisting of §§48A–48F inclusive.
27. Part 6 of the Sale of Goods Act 1979 as amended, consisting of §§49–54 inclusive.
28. §61 Sale of Goods Act 1979 as amended.
29. §61 Sale of Goods Act 1979 as amended.
30. §12 Sale of Goods Act 1979 as amended.
31. §13 Sale of Goods Act 1979 as amended.
32. §14 Sale of Goods Act 1979 as amended.
33. §12 Sale of Goods Act 1979 as amended.
34. §12(1) Sale of Goods Act 1979 as amended.
35. §12(2) Sale of Goods Act 1979 as amended.
36. §13 Sale of Goods Act 1979 as amended.
37. §13(1) Sale of Goods Act 1979 as amended.
38. §13(2) Sale of Goods Act 1979 as amended.
39. §14 Sale of Goods Act 1979 as amended.
40. §14(2) Sale of Goods Act 1979 as amended.
41. §14(2C) Sale of Goods Act 1979 as amended.
42. §14(5) Sale of Goods Act 1979 as amended.
43. §14(2A) Sale of Goods Act 1979 as amended.
44. §14(2B) Sale of Goods Act 1979 as amended.
45. §14(3) Sale of Goods Act 1979 as amended.
46. Ibid.
47. §55(1) Sale of Goods Act 1979 as amended.
48. Ibid.
49. §55(2) Sale of Goods Act 1979 as amended.
50. The full title of this Act is 'An Act to impose further limits on the extent to which under the law of England and Wales and Northern Ireland civil liability for breach of contract, of for negligence or other breach of duty, can be avoided by means of contract terms and otherwise, and under the law of Scotland civil liability can be avoided by means of contract terms'.
51. §31(1) Unfair Contract Terms Act 1977.
52. The Unfair Contract Terms Act 1977 consists of three parts. Part I (§§1–14 inclusive) applies in England, Wales and Northern Ireland but not Scotland (§32(2) Unfair Contract Terms Act 1977); Part II (§§15–25 inclusive) applies in Scotland alone (§32(3) Unfair Contract Terms Act 1977) and Part III (§§26–32) applies to the whole of the United Kingdom (§32(4) Unfair Contract Terms Act 1977).
53. §31(2) Unfair Contract Terms Act 1977.
54. Pursuant to §12 Unfair Contract Terms Act 1977, a contracting party will be dealing as a consumer in relation to the other party if the prior party neither makes the contract in the course of business nor holds himself out as doing so and the latter party does make the contract in the course of a business. As the focus of this book is on B-to-B transactions these provisions have not been reviewed.
55. Except where the contrary is stated in §6(4) Unfair Contract Terms Act 1977.

56. §1(3) Unfair Contract Terms Act 1977.
57. §2(1) Unfair Contract Terms Act 1977.
58. §2(3) Unfair Contract Terms Act 1977.
59. §3(2) Unfair Contract Terms Act 1977.
60. §3(1) Unfair Contract Terms Act 1977.
61. §6(1) Unfair Contract Terms Act 1977.
62. §13 Sale of Goods Act 1979 addresses the sale of goods by description and §14 addresses the quality of the goods and their fitness for purpose.
63. §6(3) Unfair Contract Terms Act 1977.
64. §6(3) Unfair Contract Terms Act 1977.
65. §7 Unfair Contract Terms Act 1977.
66. §13(1)a and §13(1)b Unfair Contract Terms Act 1977 (respectively).
67. §26(1) coupled with §§26(3) and 26(4) Unfair Contract Terms Act 1977.
68. §26(2) Unfair Contract Terms Act 1977.
69. The Channel Islands and the Isle of Man are treated as different states from the UK in this context.
70. §26(1) coupled with §§26(3) and 26(4) Unfair Contract Terms Act 1977.
71. §27(1) Unfair Contract Terms Act 1977.
72. §§2–7 Unfair Contract Terms Act 1977 address: exclusion or restriction of liability for death or personal injury resulting from negligence (§2); exclusion or restriction of liability for breach of contract (§3); unreasonable indemnity clauses where a person is dealing as a consumer (§4); guarantees for consumer goods (§5); exclusion or restriction of liability for breaches of §§12–15 inclusive Sale of Goods Act 1979 (§6); exclusion or restriction of liability for breach of an obligation arising by implication of law (§7).
73. For history of ex-works, FOB (free on board) and CIF (cost, insurance and freight) contracts see Sassoon, D. M. (1967), 'The Origin of F.O.B. and C.I.F. Terms and the Factors Influencing Their Choice', *Journal of Business Law* 32. For detailed review of FOB and CIF contracts, see Murray et al. (2007), Chapter 2.
74. See below a review of certain key trade terms in English law, namely 'ex-works', 'FOB' and 'CIF'.
75. For a general review of Incoterms® see Murray, Daniel (1991), 'Risk of Loss of Goods in Transit: A Comparison of the 1990 Incoterms with Terms from Other Voices', *The University of Miami Inter-American Law Review* 23:1, 93; Ramberg, Jan (2011), 'Incoterms® 2010', *Penn State International Law Review* 29, 415. For a review of Incoterms® 2010, see Ramberg (2011).
76. http://www.iccwbo.org (homepage of the International Chamber of Commerce).
77. Ramberg 2011: 415–16, 419, 422 (the ICC has assessed the value of the commercial usages).
78. Ramberg 2011: 420.
79. Ramberg 2011: 418.
80. EXW: ex-works; FCA: free carrier; CPT: carriage paid; CIP: carriage and insurance paid; DAT: delivered at terminal; DAP: delivered at place; DDP: delivered duty paid.

81. FAS: free alongside ship; FOB: free on board; CFR: cost and freight; CIF: cost, insurance and freight.
82. For a review of these two trade terms see Ramberg (2011: 421).
83. Ramberg 2011: 421.
84. Ramberg 2011: 422. This issue is covered further in the review of trade terms under English law in Section VI below.
85. Bradgate 2000: 766–91; Murray et al. 2007, Chapter 2.
86. Bradgate 2000: 766.
87. Murray et al. 2007: 12.
88. *Davies v. McLean* (1873) 21 WR 264.
89. Unless otherwise agreed, the purchase price will be due on delivery (Murray et al. 2007: 12).
90. Murray et al. 2000: 18.
91. *Wimble, Sons & Co. Ltd v. Rosenberg & Sons* [1913] 3 KB 743.
92. Though plaintiffs are known as claimants in England, here the term 'plaintiff' is used rather than 'claimant'.
93. *Wimble, Sons & Co. Ltd v. Rosenberg & Sons* [1913] 3 KB 743, 749 (Vaughan Williams LJ); *Wimble, Sons & Co. Ltd v. Rosenberg & Sons* [1913] 3 KB 743, 752 (Buckley LJ).
94. This Act is available at http:/www.legislation.gov.uk/ukpga/1893/71/pdfs/ukpga_18930071_en.pdf (last accessed 18 January 2013).
95. *Wimble, Sons & Co. Ltd v. Rosenberg & Sons* [1913] 3 KB 743, 751 (Vaughan Williams LJ).
96. *Pyrene Co. Ltd v. Scindia Steam Navigation Co. Ltd* [1954] 2 QB 402, 424 [1954] 2 All ER 158.
97. *Pyrene Co. Ltd v. Scindia Steam Navigation Co. Ltd* [1954] 2 QB 402, 424.
98. Discussed in Bradgate (2000: 770).
99. Described in *Wimble, Sons & Co. Ltd v. Rosenberg & Sons* [1913] 3 KB 743.
100. Bradgate 2000: 770.
101. Murray et al. 2000: 18.
102. Bradgate 2000: 778.
103. *T. D. Bailey, Son & Co. v. Ross T. Smyth & Co. Ltd* (1940) 56 TLR 825, 828 (Lord Wright).
104. Professor Karl Llewellyn, cited in Tillotson, John (1995), *Contract Law in Perspective*, 3rd ed., Cavendish, 32.
105. *Johnson v. Taylor Bros & Co. Ltd* AC 144, 155-156 (Lord Atkinson).
106. Bradgate 2000: 779 (tasks noted in brackets supplement those listed by Lord Atkinson in *Johnson v. Taylor Bros & Co. Ltd* [1920] AC 144, 155–6).
107. *Johnson v. Taylor Bros & Co. Ltd* AC 144, 158 (Lord Atkinson).
108. Ibid.
109. Ibid.
110. *Johnson v. Taylor Bros & Co. Ltd* [1920] AC 144, 158–9 (Lord Atkinson).
111. *Johnson v. Taylor Bros & Co. Ltd* [1920] AC 144, 156 (Lord Atkinson).
112. Murray et al. 2000: 34.
113. Murray et al. 2000: 35.
114. Ibid.

NOTES

115. *Manbré Saccharine Co. Ltd* v. *Corn Products Co. Ltd* (1919) 1 KB 198, 202 (McCardie J).
116. *Manbré Saccharine Co. Ltd* v. *Corn Products Co. Ltd* (1919) 1 KB 198 (McCardie J citing Scrutton LJ, *Charterparties and Bills of Lading*, 8th ed., 167).
117. Ibid.
118. *Berger & Co. Inc.* v. *Gill & Duffus SA* [1984] AC 382.
119. Bradgate 2000: 779.
120. Ibid.
121. *Johnson* v. *Taylor Bros & Co. Ltd* [1920] AC 144, 156 (Lord Atkinson).
122. *Ross T. Smyth & Co. Ltd* v. *Bailey, Son & Co. Ltd* [1940] 3 All ER 60 (Lord Wright).
123. *Manbré Saccharine Co. Ltd* v. *Corn Products Co. Ltd* (1919) 1 KB 198 (McCardie J citing Scrutton LJ, *Charterparties and Bills of Lading*, 8th ed., 167).
124. Bradgate 2000: 789.
125. In the US, §2-303 UCC.
126. Article 67(1) CISG.
127. Article 67(2) CISG. If the contract relates to goods that are not then identified, the goods are considered not to be placed at the disposal of the buyer until they are clearly identified to the contract (Article 69(3) CISG).
128. Article 35 CISG.
129. Article 68 CISG.
130. Article 68 CISG.
131. Article 69 CISG.
132. In Chapter 4, reference is made to certain provisions contained in this chapter.
133. Bortolotti, Fabio (2008), *Drafting and Negotiating International Commercial Agreements: A Practical Guide*, International Chamber of Commerce, 246.
134. Pursuant to Article 6 CISG. The CISG is reviewed in Chapter 7.
135. More in Chapter 2.
136. More in Chapter 2.
137. More in Chapter 2.
138. More in Chapter 2.
139. More in Chapter 2.
140. More in Chapter 7 (determination of price under the CISG, the UNIDROIT Principles and the PECL).
141. A review of carriage of good by sea can be found in Bradgate (2000), Chapter 32; Murray et al. (2007), Chapter 15; and August et al. (2009), *International Business Law: Text, Cases, and Readings*, 5th ed., Pearson Education, Chapter 11.
142. The multilateral treaty governing bills of lading is the International Convention for the Unification of Certain Rules of Law Relating to Bills of Lading (also known as the 1921 Hague Rules and the Brussels Convention of 1924). The Hague Rules were revised in 1968 by the Brussels Protocol and

the amended 1968 version is known as the Hague-Visby Rules. The 1921 Hague Rules are available at http://www.austlii.edu.au/au/other/dfat/treaties/1956/2.html (last accessed 18 January 2013). The Brussels Protocol is available at http://www.austlii.edu.au/au/other/dfat/treaties/1993/23.html (last accessed 18 January 2013). The Hague-Visby Rules are available at http://www.jus.uio.no/lm/sea.carriage.hague.visby.rules.1968/doc.html (last accessed 18 January 2013). A review of the role of bills of lading can be found in Bradgate 2000: Chapter 32; Murray et al. 2007: Chapter 15; and August et al. (2009), Chapter 11. A general review of bills of lading can be found in Michael Bridge (1997), *The Sale of Goods*, Oxford University Press, Chapter 6.
143. Bradgate 2000: 736.
144. Bradgate 2000: 733.
145. Ibid.
146. Bradgate 2000: 733–4, citing Goode, R. M. (1989), *Proprietary Rights and Insolvency in Sales Transactions*, 2nd ed., Sweet & Maxwell, 61.
147. Bradgate 2000: 734.
148. Ibid.
149. Bradgate 2000: 735.
150. Straight bills of lading are reviewed in Bradgate (2000: 735).
151. August et al. 2009: 626.
152. Bridge 1997: 234.
153. *Sanders Bros* v. *Maclean & Co.* (1883) 11 QBD 327, 341 (Bowen LJ).
154. Ibid.
155. Ibid.
156. A review of letters of credit can be found in Bradgate (2000), Chapter 34; Murray et al. (2007), Chapter 11; August et al. (2009), Chapter 12.
157. Letters of credit opened before 1st July 2007 will continue to be governed by the previous issue of the UCP (UCP 500), which was issued in 1993.
158. Article 1 UCP 600. This is typically done by the banks in the UK when contracting with a UK party, an overseas party or other banks.
159. Bortolotti 2008: 250. The Model International Sale Contract of the ICC, published for the first time in 1997, is reviewed in Bortolotti (2008), Chapter 7. This model contract comprises Specific Conditions and General Conditions. Whilst the Specific Conditions set out the terms that are unique to the particular contract of sale concluded by the parties contracting, the General Conditions set out the standard terms that are common to all contracts that incorporate the ICC General Conditions of Sale (Bortolotti 2008: 245–6). The Specific Conditions of this model contract are reproduced in Bortolotti (2008: 254–6) and the General Conditions are reproduced in Bortolotti (2008: 257–9).
160. Article 33 CISG reads: 'The seller must deliver the goods: (a) if a date is fixed by or determinable from the contract, on that date; (b) if a period of time is fixed by or determinable from the contract, at any time within that period unless circumstances indicate that the buyer is to choose a date; or (c) in any other case, within a reasonable time after the conclusion of the contract.'

NOTES

161. Article 6 CISG reads: 'The parties may exclude the application of this Convention or, subject to Article 12, derogate from or vary the effect of any of its provisions.'
162. Bortolotti 2008: 248.
163. More in Chapter 6.
164. Force majeure is discussed later on in this chapter. The remedies of the buyer for delayed delivery and non-delivery under the CISG are reviewed in Chapter 7.
165. Article 6 CISG.
166. Bortolotti 2008: 249–50. Liability for delay is addressed in Article 10 of the Specific Conditions as supplemented by Articles 10 and 11.3 of the General Conditions in the ICC's model international sale contract (reproduced in Bortolotti (2008: 255, 258, 259)).
167. See Chapter 1 for more on trade barriers.
168. Bortolotti 2008: 250.
169. Bortolotti 2008: 250. The ICC's Model International Sale Contract makes provision for this in Article 12 (reproduced in Bortolotti (2008: 259)).
170. A review of implied terms is provided at the start of this chapter in the section reviewing the Sale of Goods Act 1979 as amended and in Chapter 7.
171. For a review of the CISG, see Chapter 7.
172. Article 35 CISG.
174. The remedies available to a buyer under the CISG for non-conforming goods are discussed in Chapter 7.
174. Reproduced in Bortolotti (2008: 254–9).
175. Bortolotti 2008: 252–3.

4
International Distribution Agreements[1]

Contents

Overview 112
Glossary 113
I Vertical integration 113
II The set-up in a distribution relationship 115
III Strategies when working with a distributor 116
IV The relationship between principal and distributor 118
V Choosing between a traditional buyer and a distributor 119
VI Choosing between an agent and a distributor 120
VII The law governing international distribution agreements 124
VIII Choice of law under European Union law 127
IX European competition law and the treatment of distribution and agency agreements 128
X Motivations and concerns of the distributor 130
XI Motivations and concerns of the principal 131
XII Distribution agreement and sales agreement 134
XIII Checklist of provisions 134
XIV Front of the contract 135
XV Body of the contract 136
XVI Boilerplate clauses 154
XVII Back of the contract 154
Summary 155
Useful links 155
Further reading 155
Notes 156

Overview

This chapter firsts consider vertical integration, before looking at the set-up in a distribution relationship, the law governing international distribution agreements and the provisions contained in standard distribution agreements.

By the end of the chapter the reader will have a better understanding of

- the set-up used in distribution agreements;
- the international law governing distribution agreements;
- which provisions the contracting parties should consider including in international distribution agreements;
- the purpose of each provision; and
- the proposed wording of these provisions.

🔍 Glossary

Agent In certain circumstances, a person (legal or natural) will appoint another to act on its or his or her behalf in relation to certain tasks. The former is the **principal** and the latter is the **agent**. The agent may act on behalf of the **principal** in order to bring about legal relations between the principal and another person (the third party) or persons (third parties).

Block exemptions Instruments effectively exempting those agreements that are at first sight in breach of Article 101(1) of the Treaty on the Functioning of the European Union on account of their beneficial nature.

Commission agent An agent instructed by the principal to either acquire or sell property on behalf of the principal.

Del credere agent Where the agent provides a del credere guarantee, he or she will be assuring due performance by all or specific customers of contracts concluded as a result of the work of the agent in question.[2]

Grey market See **parallel imports**

Horizontal agreements Agreements between parties operating at the same level of the economy, which are often actual or potential competitors.

Notices Instruments providing non-binding guidance on the policy of the European Commission by mainly addressing agreements that would not breach Article 101(1) of the Treaty on the Functioning of the European Union.

Parallel imports (or **grey market**) The importation of a legally produced good into the principal's home market without the permission of the principal.[3]

Principal In certain circumstances, a person (legal or natural) will appoint another to act on its or his or her behalf in relation to certain tasks. The former is the **principal** and the latter is the **agent**.

Privity (or **privity of contract**) A doctrine providing that rights and obligations arising out of a contract can be relied on by the contracting parties. A contract concluded between A and B cannot be relied upon by C, even if C benefits from performance of the contract.[4]

Vertical agreements Agreements between parties operating at different levels, such as between distributor and manufacturer, between licensor and licensee and between franchisor and franchisee.

1 Vertical integration[5]

Vertical integration involves 'operations that are 100 per cent owned and physically interconnected and that supply 100 per cent of the firm's needs'.[6] It will effectively entail one entity exercising control over certain integrated levels in the supply chain, such as research and development, production, pricing policy, packaging, marketing and distribution. In theory, the entity could go as far as controlling all levels in the supply chain from the factory through to the retail outlets.[7]

Vertical integration offers certain benefits to the entity.[8] Besides the fact that it can be used to attain greater control over operations, to enhance margins, to forecast costs, to require and impose changes and to improve marketing and technological intelligence, vertical integration offers the following key advantages.

Firstly it allows for economies of integration as well as cost savings. Economies of integration are attained by removing the duplicate sources of overheads, by bypassing certain steps in production and distribution and by enhancing coordination of activities. Cost savings are achieved by removing the need for price shopping, for the communication of design details and for the negotiation, drafting and enforcement of contracts. Secondly it is used to acquire and improve knowledge relating to demand, so that the goods and/or services concerned may be tailored to the needs of customers with ease and speed. Thirdly it may be used in order to guarantee the supply of raw materials and to secure access to markets for the goods. Fourthly a vertically integrated system is generally unaffected by competition law. The arrangements between the different levels in the integrated supply chain as such will not be subjected to the scrutiny of the competition authorities.

However, from the point of view of the entity, there are certain disadvantages associated with vertical integration.[9] Firstly the entity in question will have no third party with which to share risk or outlay. Secondly, since the different levels in the supply chain are integrated a situation will arise where there is less of an incentive on the part of the players at the different levels of the supply chain to take risks and win business. Whilst corporate employee incentive schemes help tackle this problem, such schemes cannot replace the motivation for example of a distributor.

Lack of expertise at a particular level in the supply chain combined with the need to absorb the overheads associated with the control of the different levels in the integrated chain may mean that the disadvantages associated with vertical integration outweigh the benefits. Accordingly, an entity would be wise to curtail the scope of vertical integration (over too many levels) since the further down the supply chain the integration goes the less likely the entity is to possess the needed expertise and the less cost effective the supply chain is likely to be.[10] A more cost-effective method may be to let a third party with expertise run a particular level in the chain, in which case the entity forfeits part of its margin for a sharing of risk and capital outlay.

Over time, the format and extent of vertical integration have changed.[11] When looking at vertical integration, reference nowadays needs to be made to breadth, stages and degree as well as the form that it takes. Vertical integration down the supply chain is often limited and each level in the chain is more likely to specialise. As such a producer is likely to focus on production leaving all other tasks to specialist wholesalers or distributors.

Box 4.1 The different levels in the supply chain and their respective roles[12]

Showrooms
Showrooms will offer a shop window for the goods produced by the principal. Typically, such operations will help with marketing and will channel prospective orders to the principal, leaving the principal to handle negotiation and contracting.

Marketing consultants
Marketing consultants are responsible for advising on sales strategy, for collecting market data and for supervising the sales operations of local agents or distributors. Like showroom operatives they do not negotiate contracts or contract themselves on behalf of the principal.

Production franchises[13]
The proprietor of a product (franchisor) franchises production and distribution to a franchisee and the franchisee in turn becomes responsible for producing the goods to strict quality standards. The franchisor will generally permit the franchisee to use his trade mark, brand and set-up so that the franchisee

can better market and sell the products that he produces. Bearing in mind the extensive outlay that the franchisee will need to incur in setting up production, distribution and marketing operations, he is only likely to accept such a risk if he feels that the brand is strong enough. Arrangements of this kind are typically used for household names such as soft drinks and beers.

Distribution franchises[14]

Franchises of this kind are commonly used at the retail level in relation to consumer goods and services. Examples include fast food chains, photocopying or printing services. The franchisor is principally concerned with maximising his returns, by means of royalties or other fee structures offered in exchange for use of the trade mark, brand and set-up. The franchisor will expend time and money training, monitoring and assisting all the franchisees on an ongoing basis, and as such he will be concerned about obtaining a corresponding level of return from the fees and royalties paid by the franchisees. This can only work if the franchisor possesses a strong brand, which will be further strengthened by advertising and marketing.

Licensing[15]

The intellectual property (IP) owner who does not necessarily possess a strong brand but owns technology will likely consider opting for a licensing agreement. He will have little direct control over the licensee's operation save for set-up requirements to monitor quality control and income streams. In return for off-loading risks and cost, the IP owner will forfeit most of the margin.

Commercial agents[16]

Using an agent is the closest that a principal will come to vertical integration without creating a branch or a wholly owned subsidiary. The principal will shift some of the risk to the agent, providing the agent with an incentive to generate profits, whilst still retaining most of the margin and much of the control over the agent. Legally speaking such a set-up does not typically involve major tax concerns nor is the principal regarded as carrying on a business in the territory, unless the agent has authority to conclude contracts for the principal or, if he has no authority to conclude contracts, he holds stock needed to fulfil orders placed with the principal. Competition law issues are unlikely to arise in relation to such an arrangement. The agent may enjoy certain protections under national or regional law.[17]

II The set-up in a distribution relationship

Distributors and principals are independent and distinct entities. Both the distributor and principal operate independently of each other, each acting on his own account and in his own name. The principal sells to the distributor and the distributor acts as a buyer and reseller, selling on the goods bought off the principal to his own customers. The distributor essentially acts as an intermediary between the principal and his own customers, and has been described as a 'wholesaler, jobber or other merchant middleman authorized by a manufacturer or supplier to sell chiefly to retailers and commercial users'.[18]

Even though the transaction involving the principal and the distributor is effectively a straightforward sale, the distributor has a continuing relationship with the principal whose goods he distributes. Unlike an ordinary dealer, the distributor buys and resells the goods of the principal on an ongoing basis. The distributor may be engaged for either a specified period or an unspecified period and is typically engaged under conditions that are set out in the agreement concluded between the distributor and the principal.

Use of distributors is an alternative to vertical integration and licensing. The principal forfeits control and a large share of the margin by using a distributor but in exchange the distributor assumes a large share (if not all) of the risk, responsibility and cost.

Distributorship arrangements[19]

Distribution of goods and/or services is commonly performed through one or more sales channels, each consisting of interdependent entities responsible for making available either the goods, services or both for consumption or use.[20] The principal may select either a single channel or a hybrid system of distribution. If he opts for a hybrid system, he must take care in ensuring that the risk of a clash between and within the channels is pre-empted and removed.[21]

Direct and indirect sales channels

The principal may use an assortment of direct and/or indirect sales channels. Direct sales channels will comprise a direct sales force, telesales, direct mail, internet and corporation-owned outlets, whilst indirect sales channels will comprise independent representatives and distributors.

Creation of a branch/subsidiary in a given market to complement distribution arrangement

The appointment of a distributor may be complemented by the establishment of a branch or a subsidiary in a given market by the principal.[22] A subsidiary may be charged for example with monitoring the efforts of the distributor and with the provision of an after-sales service.[23]

Strategic alliance to complement distribution arrangement

Besides the creation of a branch and/or subsidiary in a given market, as a complement to a distribution arrangement in the said market, the principal may consider the possibility of entering into a strategic alliance with an entity in the target market.[24] Such an alliance may be contractual in nature or may be achieved through the creation of an equity structure. The resulting equity structure may take the form of a partnership, a jointly owned corporation, a European company (SE)[25] or a European economic interest grouping (EEIG).[26]

Such a decision may be motivated by the experience and expertise of the partner in the strategic alliance or by the desire of the principal to share risks and costs. For example, the strategic alliance may permit improvement of the principal's competitive advantage through joint investment in research and development. It may be based on the expertise and experience of the partner in the alliance.

III Strategies when working with a distributor

Once the principal has sourced a suitable distributor it would be sensible for the distributor and the principal to agree on realistic joint goals. When these goals have been agreed upon, the principal should consider introducing mechanisms to persuade the distributor to move towards reaching them. This may be achieved by motivating the distributor using a variety of incentives, whilst at the same time making sure that an adequate support infrastructure is put in place and performance measures are instituted and enshrined in the terms of the contract.

A variety of methods can be used to motivate distributors. Volume discounts may for example be employed in order to provide further financial incentives to distributors buying large quantities of goods. Fees may also be offered to distributors that perform specific activities such as the supply of support services to customers.

The support infrastructure provides distributors with the tools and programmes that they need in order to succeed. Promotional support, training, sales and technical support are all part of this support infrastructure. In this context, the principal may provide assistance with the design of marketing strategies and the formulation of promotional materials. Moreover, he may offer to train the personnel of the distributor and to provide them with ongoing technical support. All these mechanisms allow the distributor to resell the goods more effectively and to promote them in a manner that is befitting to the principal.

Obligations may be imposed on distributors to ensure that a certain level of sales is generated and maintained. A principal may stipulate in the contract that the distributor place a certain minimum value of orders with the principal over a specified period of time. The principal may also place certain minimum obligations on the distributor with regard to promotion and marketing. On occasion the principal may oblige the distributor to visit prospective customers at set intervals.

Box 4.2 Right to terminate an agreement for non-performance illustrated

L. Schuler AG v. Wickman Machine Tool Sales Ltd [1974][27]

Under an agreement concluded in May 1963 between L. Schuler AG (S), the appellants, and Wickman Machines Tool Sales Ltd (W), the respondents, S agreed to give W acting as its agent the sole selling rights for panel presses in a territory encompassing the UK (these presses are machine tools used in the production of motor vehicles).

Clause 7b of the agreement between the parties stated that W should use its best endeavours to promote the products of S and it was a condition of the agreement that W send its representatives once a week to visit six firms listed in a schedule to the agreement (the six largest manufacturers of motors in the UK) for the purpose of soliciting orders for the presses.

Clause 11 of the agreement stated inter alia that the agreement might be terminated if one of the parties gave written notice to the other if the other had committed a material breach of its obligations under the agreement and had failed to remedy the same within sixty days of being asked to do so in writing. W breached the obligation contained in Clause 7 and in July 1964 S claimed a right to terminate arguing that the respondents had committed a material breach of their obligations. The dispute was referred to arbitration and in an award issued by the arbitrator (in October 1969) the arbitrator held that S was not entitled to terminate the agreement. On appeal, this finding was reversed by Mocatta J. This finding was restored by the Court of Appeal. The matter was then appealed to the House of Lords.

W argued that S was permitted to terminate the agreement only for the reasons and in the manner prescribed by Clause 11. S argued that Clause 7 permitted it to terminate, as this clause, which stated that it was a condition of the agreement, meant that any of breach of it permitted S to terminate the agreement forthwith and as the clause had been breached on several occasions and these breaches had not been waived, S was allowed to terminate the agreement.

Dismissing the appeal, the House of Lords held that the word 'condition' (used in Clause 7) had obtained more than one meaning in contracts[28] and that in the present agreement the word 'condition' (employed in relation to the obligation to carry out weekly visits) had a meaning that was equivocal. In light of the remainder of the agreement the word 'condition' (in Clause 7) meant a contractual term breach of which if unremedied gave S the right to bring the agreement to an end in line with Clause 11.[29] Use of the word 'condition' in Clause 7, the House of Lords stated, did not mean that a single breach, however minor, permitted the innocent party to terminate the whole of the agreement in the absence of any waiver.

IV The relationship between principal and distributor

In the agreement reviewed below, the distributor operates as a buyer-reseller as well as an importer. As buyer, the distributor purchases the goods from the principal. The relationship between the principal and the distributor will be that of seller and buyer with a separate sale contract being formed each time the distributor places an order with the principal for the purchase of goods.[30] As reseller, on acquisition of the goods from the principal, the distributor assumes responsibility for the sale of the goods to his customers. Such goods are sold on by the distributor in his own name and on his own account. As such, he is responsible for exercising his own personal business acumen and for assuming the risks associated with the sale of the goods. The distributor will accordingly assume responsibility for the promotion and distribution of the goods acquired from the principal and imported into the target market.

The return that the distributor makes constitutes the difference between the purchase price and the sale price. Any loss sustained will also be the responsibility of the distributor and not the principal. Such a loss may arise where market conditions necessitate a mark-down on the price of the goods. In the event that the distributor makes a profit on the sale of the goods, the profit will be his own.

As importer, the distributor will need to attend to importation of the goods purchased from the principal. The exact division of responsibilities between the principal and the distributor (in relation to the transportation, importation and insurance of the goods) as well as the question of the transfer of risk in relation to the goods acquired from principal will be matters that the parties themselves will determine. Such matters are typically governed within the contract by the trade term that the principal and distributor determine.[31]

What distinguishes a distributorship arrangement from a traditional sales agreement[32]

The distributorship arrangement has certain characteristics that distinguish it from the traditional sales arrangement. Firstly, the nature and scope of the relationship existing between distributor and principal is characterised by the dependency of the distributor on the principal, resulting in the creation of a special relationship between the distributor and the principal. Under this set-up the distributor undertakes to sell the goods of the principal in his own name and on his account, whilst at the same time the distributor is incorporated into the operations of the principal thus becoming part of the sales organisation of the principal.[33]

Secondly, the relationship between the distributor and principal is distinct from a one-off sales transaction or even a series of one-off sales transactions.[34] In a distributorship arrangement, the relationship between the principal and the distributor is more substantively regulated (by means of the terms of the distribution agreement) than the relationship between a seller and a buyer. For example, the principal may provide ongoing support and training to the distributor, the principal may insist that the distributor market the goods in a certain manner and, in a number of situations, the distributor may even be awarded exclusivity of supply and distribution in an assigned territory.

Box 4.3 Franchisee and distributor distinguished[35]

Corporation A (based in the state of Michigan) entered into a relationship with Corporation B (based in the state of Florida) for distribution of paper produced by Corporation B, after sales representatives for Corporation B approached Corporation A to act as a distributor for its products in Michigan. No written agreement was concluded between Corporation A and Corporation B. Instead they concluded an oral agreement between them.

In line with this oral agreement, orders were first telephoned or teletyped through by Corporation A to Corporation B and followed up with a written order posted by Corporation A to Corporation B. Generally Corporation B replied with a written acknowledgement indicating the shipping date and method of shipment. Corporation A was responsible not only for purchasing goods from Corporation B for later resale, but also for soliciting orders on behalf of Corporation B. As such Corporation A employed a sales team that covered several US states.

After several years, Corporation B informed Corporation A that it wished to terminate Corporation A as its distributor. Corporation A alleged that it was acting as a franchisee for Corporation B (a status that offered it certain legal protections)[36] and that Corporation B firstly had breached a duty that it owed to Corporation A to keep the franchise in place in order to permit Corporation A as franchisee to recoup its investment of time and money and secondly had terminated the franchise without good cause or justification.

The courts have recognised the investment of time and money that a franchisee is required to make and have often stated that such an arrangement cannot be terminated arbitrarily. In this case the court ruled that the agreement in question did not have the hallmarks of a franchise, namely a licence from the owner of a trade mark or trade name (licensor or franchisor) to another entity (licensee or franchisee) allowing the latter to sell its product or service using a trade mark or trade name owned by the licensor. Since Corporation A always did business in its own name, described itself as a distributor or broker, solicited orders for Corporation B and took title to the goods for resale, the court ruled that the relationship more closely resembled that of a distributorship arrangement with the distributor acting as a middleman between Corporation B and the customers of Corporation A.

V Choosing between a traditional buyer and a distributor[37]

The relationship between the principal and the distributor is different in many respects from the relationship that exists between the traditional seller and buyer. The following review looks at some of the characteristics that differentiate the two.

The nature of the relationship

The distributor–principal relationship is much more than a one-off sales transaction or even a series of one-off sales transactions, since it is based around a set of agreed terms contained within the distribution agreement, which govern the relations between the distributor and principal and set out the rights and obligations of each party in relation to the other. Pursuant to this agreement, the principal is not just supplying goods to the distributor for resale; he is committing himself to the distributor. As such he may be committed to allowing the distributor to use a trade mark belonging to him and to providing the distributor with promotional materials, training facilities and ongoing technical support.

The goods

The contract between the distributor and the principal will likely define certain key parameters that govern the ongoing relationship between the parties. Firstly, such a contract will define the goods to be sold by the principal to the distributor and to be resold by the distributor. Secondly, the contract may set out the intellectual property (belonging to the principal) that the principal will permit the distributor to use in the promotion and resale of the goods.

Duration (or term) of agreement

The contract concluded by the distributor and the principal will either set out the duration of the engagement between the parties or, if no term is defined, usually make provision for the manner in which the contract may be terminated by the parties.

Territory assigned

The contract between the distributor and the principal may also address such matters as the territory assigned to the distributor for the sale of the goods. In a number of cases, the distributor may be given a privileged position in the territory in question in the form of exclusivity of supply and exclusivity of distribution.

Provisions governing competition between the parties

The terms of the agreement that the parties conclude between them may limit or forbid the principal from selling in the territory assigned or from appointing other distributors in the territory assigned. What is more, such an agreement may limit or forbid the distributor from competing (directly or indirectly) with the principal outside the assigned territory.

VI Choosing between an agent and a distributor[38]

The relationship between the principal and distributor is not one of principal and agent[39] for a number of reasons. The following features generally distinguish an agent from a distributor.

Independence of the parties

The distributor is independent of the principal. The goods bought from the principal by the distributor are sold on by the distributor, on his own account and in his own name. As such the distributor assumes the risks associated with the resale of the goods bought from the principal and receives all the benefits ensuing from the resale of these goods.

The distributor will have no authority to create **privity** between the principal and the party to whom he resells the goods.[40] In this respect the distributor is akin to a **commission agent**.[41] A commission agent is instructed by the principal to either acquire or sell property on behalf of the principal, but unlike a traditional agent the commission agent has no authority to create privity of contract between the third party (with whom he deals) and the principal. In this respect the commission agent deals as a principal vis-à-vis the third party with whom he deals. The commission agent is a halfway house between a true agent and a distributor.[42] Unlike a commission agent, however, the distributor does not enjoy the rights that the commission agent would enjoy as agent, nor is he bound by the obligations that would bind the commission agent as a result of his status as an agent.

Like the agent, the distributor promotes the brand name and range of goods produced by the principal. But unlike the agent, the distributor resells the goods in his own right as a principal and not as an agent for the principal. In contrast with the distributor, the agent does not assume the business risks associated with dealing with the goods and is subject to the control of the principal. The nature and scope of the authority delegated by the principal to the agent will shape the activities that the agent is permitted to undertake.

As the principal has no privity of contract with the third parties to whom the distributor resells the goods, he will incur no contractual product liability to the third parties with whom the distributor contracts.[43] Moreover the principal may be able to either limit or eliminate the contractual liability to the distributor.[44] He may, however, be liable in tort to the ultimate customers.

Box 4.4 Test to distinguish an agent from a distributor

The answers to the following questions will generally indicate whether a person is an agent or distributor:[45]

1. Does the person assume all the economic risks associated with the distribution of the goods? If the answer is yes, then the person will usually be a distributor.
2. How independent is the person? The more independence the person possesses the more likely he is to be a distributor.

Notwithstanding anything to the contrary in the contract concluded between the parties, the lack of independence may lead a court to rule that the relationship between the parties is an agency relationship rather than a distributorship relationship, as the following case demonstrates.

Box 4.5 The effect of assumption of control over the operations of another corporation[46]

The operations of a grain dealer (W) were financed by another entity (C). W owed monies to another. The latter sued W and C arguing that C was jointly liable for W's indebtedness since C had acted as a principal for W. C argued that notwithstanding the fact that it financed the operations of W there was no agency relationship between C and W.

The court ruled that C by its control and influence over W became a principal with liability for transactions concluded by its agent W,[47] stating that 'agency is a fiduciary relationship that results from the manifestation of consent by one person to another that the other shall act on his behalf and subject to his control, and consent to the other so to act'.[48] The creation of an agency relationship requires agreement though it is not necessary for there to be a contract between the parties. Agreement may result in the creation of an agency relationship even though the parties themselves did not choose to call it an agency arrangement and did not intend the legal consequences of such a relationship to emerge.

The existence of an agency relationship may be demonstrated by circumstantial evidence. When such a relationship is proven by circumstantial evidence the principal must be shown to have consented to the agency as one cannot be an agent for another except by the consent of the latter.[49]

On the given facts, the court held that all the three elements of agency were present.[50] Firstly, by directing W to give effect to its recommendations C manifested its consent that W would be its agent. Secondly, W acted on behalf of C in procuring grain for C as part of its normal operations, which were financed entirely by C. Thirdly an agency relationship was created by C's interference with the internal affairs of W which amounted to de facto control of W.

C tried to argue that the relationship between itself and W was that of buyer and supplier, not that of principal and agent. Referring to Restatement (Second) of Agency Section 14K (1958), which states that 'one who contracts to acquire property for a third party and convey it to another is the agent of the other only if it is agreed that he is to act primarily for the benefit of the other and not for himself', the court held that the elements indicating that one is a supplier as opposed to an agent are[51]

1. that he receives a set price for the property irrespective of the price that he pays;
2. that he acts in his own name and acquires title to the property that he in turn transfers; and
3. that he owns an independent business which buys and sells similar property.

The court stated that before it could be said that it is not an agent, it must be demonstrated that the supplier had an independent business. Here W's operations were financed entirely by C and W sold the bulk of its grain to C. For this reason, the court ruled that the relationship between the parties was not merely that of buyer and supplier.[5]

Control over the title to the goods and the goods themselves

Unlike the agent the distributor will not be acting on behalf of the principal. For this reason, where a principal is concerned about retaining control over the goods it would probably be more sensible for him to opt for an agency rather than a distributorship arrangement. An agent acquires neither title nor possession of the goods, both of which are retained by the principal when using the services of an agent.[53]

In contrast with an agent, a distributor takes both title and possession of the goods and will be able to modify and repackage them. This could in turn adversely impact upon the goodwill of the principal, his market share and his ability to compete. For this reason, it is sensible for the principal to impose restrictions in this context on the distributor in the terms of the distribution agreement.[54]

Control over the customer base

In contrast with a distributorship arrangement, when using the services of an agent a principal retains control over his customer base. Once an agent solicits orders for the principal these orders are passed through to the principal who then decides whether to accept or reject them. When an agent is used, the principal will generally be liaising directly with the customers sourced by the agent; as such, customers that the agent sources become customers of the principal and not of the agent.[55] Notwithstanding this fact, in certain situations the agent will be delegated the authority not only to solicit orders but also to conclude contracts with these customers.

When a distributor is involved the situation is quite different as it is the distributor and not the principal who will be dealing with customers buying the goods bought from the principal. The distributor will have a direct relationship with the customer base. These customers are unlikely to have any direct dealings with the principal. The customers that the distributor sources are usually his own customers and not customers of the principal. In many circumstances the principal may not even be aware of the identity of the customers of the distributor. For this reason, an agent will have less sway over the principal than the distributor in the event of termination.

Control over pricing

A distributor who buys goods from the principal will be responsible for reselling these goods; as such he will typically have complete discretion over the pricing of the goods. Notwithstanding this fact, whilst the distributor buys the goods from the principal and is free to set resale prices, occasionally the principal will supply a recommended retail price list. An agent, on the other hand, will typically be entrusted by the principal with soliciting orders for the principal, in line with directions issued to him by the principal, he will have no discretion in relation to the resale prices of the goods concerned.

In a situation where a principal wishes to exercise control over pricing, it would be sensible for him to use an agent rather than a distributor or at the very least to supply the distributor with a recommended retail price list.

Monitoring performance

A distributor buys and resells the goods to his customers, whereas an agent is responsible for soliciting orders for the principal which he then typically transmits to the principal. It is easy for a principal to monitor the performance of an agent as he simply needs to consider the number of orders that the agent has transmitted to him. In contrast, when a distributor is used it is generally harder for a principal to directly monitor the performance of the distributor.

In order to monitor the performance of a distributor, the principal should consider including provisions in the agreement permitting him to review the sales performance and the financial status of the distributor. Moreover, he should consider instituting a mechanism that permits him to monitor the volume of purchases made by the distributor from him.

Financial control

The principal will be able to look to the distributor for payment for the goods he has sold to the distributor. In contrast, where an agent is used, the agent will ordinarily be charged with sourcing orders for the principal himself, in which case the principal will be concerned about the creditworthiness of the customers that the agent sources for him.

The situation is different when the agent is acting as a **del credere agent**. Where the agent provides a del credere guarantee, he will be assuring due performance by all or specific customers of contracts concluded as a result of his work.[56]

Typically, the principal will extend credit terms to the distributor, which the distributor will in turn extend to his customers on resale. Effectively, the distributor will be using the principal as a source of interest-free credit. Whilst the principal can try to build this risk into the prices charged, this still does not stop him from taking a credit risk on all the distributor's customers. In contrast, when the principal uses an agent the credit risk can be moderated as credit may or may not be given to the end customer.

Profit[57]

The distributor is not accountable to the principal for the profits that he makes on the sale of the goods. The profit that the distributor generates belongs to the distributor. The profit made by the distributor usually represents the difference between the price at which the goods were bought from the principal and the price at which the goods were resold.

Contractual relationship[58]

In contrast with an agency arrangement, when dealing with a distributor, the principal will have no contractual relationship with the customers of the distributor since the distributor buys the goods which he then resells to his customers. In this context, separate sets of contracts will exist between the principal and the distributor and between the distributor and his customers.

Termination

From the point of view of the principal, it is far easier to terminate a distributorship arrangement than an agency arrangement.[59] As will be seen in Chapter 5, commercial agents may be entitled to certain legal protections on termination of the agency agreement.

Competition law concerns

In contrast with agency agreements, distribution agreements may fall under the restrictions found in national and EU competition law.

VII The law governing international distribution agreements

English law

International distribution agreements are not governed by a distinct body of law in English law. Nor are they governed by a dedicated body of law internationally. Under English law, such agreements are usually governed by the general law governing contracts as well as the terms of the contract concluded between the principal and the distributor. As such the rules established by the parties in their contract are pivotal to the relationship between the parties and should be drafted with care. Legally speaking such an appointment does not come under the Council of the European Communities' Directive 86/653/EEC of 18 December 1986 on the Coordination of the Laws of Member States relating to Self-employed Commercial Agents,[60] though a distributor may be assured certain legal protections under national law.

Obviously once discussions commence with a potential distributor, the principal should seek the advice of a local lawyer in the distributor's country to verify the implications of national law on the relationship. This is advisable even in those situations where the law chosen to govern the contract is different as it may not be possible for the contracting parties to exclude certain provisions of national law.

Draft Common Frame of Reference (DCFR)[61]

The DCFR was presented to the European Commission by the Study Group on the European Civil Code and the Research Group on Existing EC Private Law in December 2008 and published in 2009. Intended to be used as a stand-alone tool with a role of its own,[62] the hope is that the DCFR will act as a source of inspiration for the resolution of private law questions.[63]

Composition and scope of DCFR

The DCFR consists of ten books, most of which are subdivided into chapters, sections, subsections and articles. Book IV, which addresses a number of different commercial contracts, is subdivided into eight parts, each dedicated to a different category of contract. Part E, which is divided into five chapters, deals with the formulation and regulation of commercial agency, franchise and distributorship agreements.

Regulation of commercial agency, franchise and distribution agreements by the DCFR

The general provisions contained in Chapter IV.E.–1 of the DCFR and the rules contained in Chapter IV.E.–2 govern all the agreements covered by Part IV.E, namely commercial agency, franchise and distribution agreements. Each of these agreements is also addressed separately by a set of dedicated and supplementary rules, each of which is contained in one of the three remaining chapters in Part IV.E: Chapter IV.E.–3 covers commercial agency agreements, Chapter IV.E.–4 covers franchise agreements, and Chapter IV.E.–5 covers distribution agreements.

General provisions and general rules governing commercial agency, franchise and distribution agreements[64]

The provisions contained in Part IV.E are intended to cover contracts for the creation and regulation of a commercial agency, franchise or distributorship agreement.[65] In addition these provisions are intended to cover other types of contract under which a party is engaged to bring the products of another party on to the market.[66] In this context the term 'product' is regarded as including not only goods but services as well.[67]

The contracting parties owe each other certain duties. Such duties will arise both before and after the conclusion of the contract. At the pre-contractual phase, each party is obliged to provide the other with sufficient information to allow it to decide on a reasonably informed basis whether or not to conclude a contract with the other party.[68] Such information must be provided within a reasonable period of time before the contract is concluded.[69] Each of the contracting parties owes a duty to the other party to cooperate,[70] to provide in due time all the information in its possession which the other party needs in order to achieve the objectives of the contract,[71] to keep information received from the other party confidential (during the course of the contractual relationship and after the contractual relationship comes to end)[72] and to not use such confidential information for any other purpose other than that of achieving the objectives of the contract.[73]

Contracts for a definite term

Each contracting party is free not to renew a contract for a definite term.[74] In the event that either one of the contracting parties wishes to renew the contract it may do so by giving the other party notice in due time of its desire to renew,[75] in which case the contract will be renewed for an indefinite period, unless the other party gives that party notice of non-renewal, not later than a reasonable time before the expiry of the contract period.[76]

Contracts for an indefinite term

Each contracting party to a contract for an indefinite term will have the right to terminate the contractual relationship by giving notice to the other.[77] In the event that the notice provides for termination after a period of reasonable length no damages are payable.[78] In the event that the notice provides for immediate termination or termination after a period which is not of reasonable length then damages will be payable.[79]

Right to a lien over property held[80]

The party bringing the products on to the market will have a right to retain movables belonging to the other party in its possession as a result of the contract until such a time as the other party performs its obligations to pay (remuneration, compensation, damages and/or indemnity).

Statement of terms[81]

Either party to the contract may ask the other for a signed statement setting out the terms of the contract in textual form on a durable medium. The parties are not permitted to exclude this duty or to derogate from or vary its effects.

Distribution agreements and the DCFR

Distribution agreements are governed by the general provisions (in Chapter IV.E.–1) and rules (in Chapter IV.E–2) reviewed above, alongside the specific provisions set out in Chapter IV.E–5. Chapter IV.E–5 is intended to cover contracts under which one party (the supplier) agrees to supply another party (the distributor) with products on an ongoing basis and under which the distributor agrees to buy these products or take and pay for them and supply them to others in the name of the distributor and on the distributor's own behalf.[82] The obligations of the supplier and the distributor are set out in Sections 2 and 3 of Chapter 5 (Part E of Book IV) (respectively).

Obligations of the supplier

The obligations of the supplier are set out in Section IV.E.–5:2. Beyond the general obligations reviewed above, the supplier is obliged to supply the products ordered by the distributor in so far as this is practicable and so long as the order is reasonable.[83] In addition, the supplier is obliged to provide the distributor with information relating inter alia to the features of the products being supplied, the prices and the terms for the supply of these products and the recommended prices and terms for the resale of these products.[84] The supplier is also expected to advise the distributor within a reasonable period of time when he foresees that his supply capacity will be significantly less than the distributor has reason to expect.[85]

Obligations of the distributor

The obligations of the distributor are set out in Section IV.E.–5:3. Beyond the general obligations reviewed above, the distributor must make reasonable efforts to promote the products of the supplier[86] and to follow reasonable instructions issued by the supplier that are intended to secure the proper distribution of the products or to maintain their reputation or distinctiveness.[87] In addition, the distributor is obliged to inform the supplier of actual or threatened claims brought by third parties in relation to the intellectual property rights of the supplier and any infringements by third parties of the supplier's intellectual property rights.[88] The distributor is also expected to advise the supplier within a reasonable period of time when he foresees that his requirements will be significantly lower than the supplier has reason to expect.[89]

VIII Choice of law under European Union law

In the European Union, the contract between the principal and the distributor will be governed by Regulation (EC) No 593/2008 of the European Parliament and the Council of 17 June 2008 on the Law Applicable to Contractual Obligations (Rome I).[90] Rome I governs all contracts concluded after 17 December 2009. Contracts concluded on or before 17 December 2009 are governed by the Convention on the Law Applicable to Contractual Obligations opened for signature in Rome on 19 June 1980 (the Rome Convention),[91] the predecessor to Rome I.

Rome I and the Rome Convention both apply to contractual obligations in situations where there is a choice between the laws of different countries.[92] Rome I is distinct from the Principles of European Contract Law (PECL), a body of contract law that is voluntary in nature and as such adopted at the discretion of the contracting parties contracting. Rome I and the Rome Convention both contain rules that define the law applicable to a contract and those rules are mandatory in application.

Freedom to choose the governing law

Whilst the contracting parties are free to choose the law applicable to the contract between them,[93] if they do not do so, Rome I will intercede to make the selection for them in accordance with the rules set out in Article 4.

Article 3.1 of Rome I permits the parties contracting to choose the law governing their contract. The parties may choose the law applicable to the whole of their contract or alternatively to just part of it.[94] Furthermore, Article 3.2 permits the parties contracting to modify by agreement the law governing the contract. Any such selection must be made expressly or clearly demonstrated by the terms of the contract or the circumstances of the case.[95]

Wherever possible, it is advisable for the contracting parties to expressly identify the law that they have chosen to govern the contract concluded between them. This will ensure certainty and clarity in their relationship and will ward against any potential litigation that could later ensue on this very question.

In the absence of a choice by the parties

Article 4.1 of Rome I sets out specific choice of law rules for particular categories of cases. Where Article 4.1 does not supply a conclusive choice of law then the general rule articulated in Article 4.2 applies. Further general displacement rules – included in Articles 4.3 and 4.4 – are intended to introduce flexibility in those situations where the application of one of the specific choice of law rules does not produce the appropriate result.

Pursuant to Article 4.1 a distribution contract will be governed by the law of the country where the distributor has his habitual residence.[96] 'Habitual residence' is defined by Article 19 of Rome I as follows:

- For companies and other bodies (corporate or unincorporated) habitual

residence will be the place of central administration.
- For a natural person acting in the course of a business activity, habitual residence will be his principal place of business.
- For a contract concluded in the course of the operations of a branch, agency or any other establishment, or if, under the contract, performance is the responsibility of such a branch, agency or establishment, the place where the branch, agency or any other establishment is located shall be treated as the place of habitual residence.

For the purposes of determining the habitual residence, the relevant point in time is the time of the conclusion of the contract.

IX European competition law and the treatment of distribution and agency agreements[97]

Article 101 of the Treaty on the Functioning of the European Union (TFEU) states:

> The following shall be prohibited as incompatible with the internal market: all agreements between undertakings, decisions by associations of undertakings and concerted practices which may affect trade between Member States and which have as their object or effect the prevention, restriction or distortion of competition within the internal market.[98]

Article 101 contains a prohibition that precludes inter alia restrictive agreements between two or more undertakings that are independent market operators,[99] whether these agreements are **horizontal** (between parties operating at the same level of the economy, which are often actual or potential competitors) or **vertical** (between parties operating at different levels, such as agreements between distributor and manufacturer or between licensor and licensee) in nature.[100]

Article 101 TFEU does not extend to agreements concluded between undertakings that form part of a single economic entity.[101] Nor, moreover, does it extend to genuine agency agreements.[102] Agency agreements will not fall under Article 101(1) TFEU if the agent bears no or only insignificant risks in relation to contracts concluded and/or negotiated by him on the principal's behalf.[103] Certain other agreements may fall outside the scope of Article 101(1), inter alia agreements of minor importance which are not capable of appreciably affecting trade between member states or of appreciably restricting competition by object or effect.

Examples of the types of restrictive agreement that infringe Article 101(1) are noted in the article itself. This list, which is intended to be illustrative rather than exhaustive, includes agreements that

1. directly or indirectly fix purchase or selling prices or other trading conditions;
2. limit or control production, markets, technical development or investment;
3. share markets or sources of supply;
4. apply dissimilar conditions to equivalent transactions with other trading parties, thereby placing them at a competitive disadvantage; or
5. make the conclusion of contracts subject to acceptance by the other parties of supplementary obligations, which, by their nature or according to commercial usage, have no connection with the subject of such contracts.

Agreements infringing Article 101(1) are automatically void pursuant to Article 101(2). Effectively an agreement caught by Article 101(1) which does not satisfy the conditions set out in Article 101(3) TFEU is automatically null, without the need for a prior decision to this effect.[104] Notwithstanding Article 101(2), the Court of Justice of the European Union has held that nullity will affect only the provisions in an agreement that are prohibited;[105] as such the agreement as a whole will be void only if the prohibited provisions within the agreement cannot be severed from the agreement.

Substantive requirements contained in Article 101 TFEU

Article 101 TFEU will apply if the following factors are met:[106]

1. There is an agreement between undertakings, a decision by an association of undertakings or a concerted practice between undertakings.
2. This agreement may affect trade between member states.
3. This agreement has as its object or effect the prevention, restriction or distortion of competition within the internal market.

Article 101(3) TFEU[107]

Article 101(1) TFEU may be declared inapplicable, pursuant to Article 101(3), in the case of an agreement which contributes to improving the production or distribution of goods or to promoting technical or economic progress, whilst allowing consumers a fair share of the resulting benefit. As such agreements caught by Article 101(1) which meet the conditions set out in Article 101(3) shall not be prohibited and no prior decision to this effect is required.[108]

Pursuant to Article 101(3), Article 101(1) may be declared inapplicable to agreements that otherwise fall foul of it when such agreements fulfil certain conditions set out in Article 101(3). These conditions consist of two sets of criteria. One set comprises two positive criteria, whilst the other comprises two negative criteria. These criteria are cumulative so that affected agreements must fulfil all four criteria.

The positive criteria contained in Article 101(3) TFEU

Article 101(1) TFEU may be declared inapplicable to agreements that firstly, contribute in some way to improving the production of goods or their distribution or to promoting technical or economic progress; and secondly, permit consumers a fair share of the resulting benefit.

The negative criteria contained in Article 101(3) TFEU

Article 101(1) TFEU may be declared inapplicable when agreements that meet the two positive criteria outlined above also fulfil the following negative criteria contained in Article 101(3) TFEU: firstly, such agreements must not contain provisions that impose on the undertakings concerned restrictions which are not indispensable to the attainment of the objectives noted above; secondly, such agreements must not include provisions that afford the undertakings concerned the possibility of eliminating competition in relation to a substantial part of the goods involved.

Vertical agreements under European competition law

Block exemptions and notices

Over the years, the European Commission (the Commission) has issued a number of notices and block exemptions in order to facilitate the operation of Article 101(3) TFEU. Whilst **notices** provide non-binding guidance on the policy of the Commission by mainly addressing agreements that would not breach Article 101(1) TFEU, **block exemptions** effectively exempt agreements that are at first sight in breach of Article 101(1) on account of their beneficial nature.

Block exemption applicable to vertical agreements

Agreements that breach Article 101(1) TFEU are automatically void[109] unless they fall within the scope of a block exemption or in default within the scope of Article 101(3).[110]

The block exemption governing vertical agreements is Commission Regulation No. 330/2010 on the Application of Article 101(3) of the TFEU to Categories of Vertical Agreements and Concerted Practices (the 2010 Regulation).[111] This regulation, which replaced the former block exemption (Commission Regulation (EC) No. 2790/1999 of 22 December 1999 on the Application of Article 81(3) of the Treaty to Categories of Vertical Agreements and Concerted Practices),[112] came into effect on 1 June 2010 and is due to expire on 31 May 2022.[113]

European competition law and agency agreements – Commission Notice Guidelines on Vertical Restraints[114]

According to the Commission Notice Guidelines on Vertical Restraints, an agent is a person (natural or legal) vested by the principal with the power to negotiate or conclude contracts on behalf of the principal for the purchase or sale of goods or services.[115]

The application of Article 101(1) TFEU to agency arrangements will be governed by the assumption of financial risk by the agent on behalf of the principal.[116] The financial risk is classified into three categories:

- 'contract-specific risks', directly related to the contracts concluded or negotiated by the agent on behalf of the principal
- 'market-specific investment risks', inherent in the type of activity undertaken by the agent on behalf of the principal
- 'associated independent risks', risks associated with other activities undertaken by the agent on the same product market to the extent that the principal requires him to undertake such activities at his own risk.[117]

The agreement will be an agency agreement for the purpose of Article 101(1) TFEU if the agent bears either no risks or minimal risks in relation firstly to the contracts negotiated and occasionally concluded on behalf of the principal, secondly to the market-specific investments for that field of activity and finally to the other activities required by the principal to be undertaken on the same product market. Risks that are deemed to be part of the general risks associated with the activities of an agent will have no bearing on the assessment of whether or not Article 101(1) will apply to the agency agreement. The fact that the agent's income will depend on his own success is an example of the kind of general risks that are inherent to an agency arrangement.

X Motivations and concerns of the distributor

In contrast with an agent, a distributor enjoys far more autonomy and generally a higher rate of remuneration. The distributor will benefit from the margin added on to the price charged to him by the principal. Where the principal is producing a leading brand, the distributor will benefit from reputation by association especially when the latter is an exclusive distributor for the allocated territory.

A distributor will ideally aspire to be the exclusive distributor of the principal for an assigned territory, as beyond the fact that there is no risk of competition in the territory in question, the distributor may be able to guarantee himself exclusivity of supply and exclusivity of representation as sole representative for the principal in the said territory. Furthermore, from the view point of the distributor, in order to enhance his function he may attempt to negotiate training and support from the principal in relation to marketing and sales activities performed by the distributor's personnel. Obviously such a set-up will also be beneficial to a principal, as the more goods the distributor resells, the more goods the principal will be selling to the distributor.

Beyond the prospect of exclusivity the distributor may aspire to obtain a return-back clause enabling him to return excess stocks of goods that he is not able to sell on. A principal will obviously be reluctant to accept such a provision.

XI Motivations and concerns of the principal

The independence of the distributor suggests a certain loss of control on the part of the principal. The question then is: why would a rational principal decide to contract with a distributor rather than choosing to enter the target market himself? There are a variety of reasons for this.[118]

Firstly, aside from being able to reduce his overheads by contracting with a distributor, the principal will be able to reduce his exposure to risk, since it is the distributor who assumes a large part of the risk. The distributor may be required inter alia to assume responsibility for the following:

1. keeping a minimum level of stock
2. buying new equipment
3. arranging for warehousing of goods and possibly components for those goods (when for example it is the distributor who is responsible for after-sales servicing)
4. hiring and training sales and technical staff to provide in-store pre-sales and post-sales assistance to customers.

From time to time, the distributor will also be asked to assume responsibility for marketing (by planning and designing promotional campaigns and literature), warranty claims and maintenance. The risk assumed by a distributor is far higher than that assumed by an agent, as unlike the agent the distributor is independent of the principal. As such it is the distributor and not the principal who is responsible for bad debts resulting from contracts concluded by the distributor.

The ability of the distributor to stock the goods is important from the standpoint of the principal. In a situation where the goods are easily stocked it may be prudent for the principal to use a distributor. Where, however, the goods cannot be easily stocked it may be more prudent for the principal to handle these sales directly.[119] It may also be prudent for the principal to handle matters directly when the decision to buy the goods is made by top management. The same is equally true when the decision-making process starts with the design of the goods and goes through a series of stages before the final goods are produced.[120]

The outlay incurred by the distributor as well as the risk that he bears will usually prompt him to insist not only on territorial exclusivity in order to prevent free-riding, but also on some form of protection against the risk of competition from contract goods that are legally produced outside his assigned territory and imported into the assigned territory.[121]

The second reason that a principal may choose to contract with a distributor is that he can rely on the distributor for his network of clients in the assigned territory and his knowledge of the national market, cultural environment and local law as well as his marketing capacity. The larger the potential client base of the distributor, the more likely it is that he will perform more effectively than the principal himself in the given market.[122] However, if the product involved is specialised it may appeal to a smaller group of potential customers, in which case it may be more effective for the principal to assume direct responsibility for sales, rather than contracting with a distributor.[123]

Certain countries regulate the manner in which foreign entities operate. Accordingly there may be situations where national law stipulates that a foreign entity use a local distributor.[124]

The third reason why a principal may choose to contract with a distributor is that the distributor's manufacturing and after-sales capacity may be essential from the point of view of the principal. The principal may rely on the distributor for final assembly of the goods: the distributor may be expected either to assemble the goods when they are shipped in pieces or to source the components required for assembly. Moreover, there may be situations when the principal relies on the distributor's ability to provide after-sale services to customers in the assigned territory, by for example repairing defects in the goods sold.

A related concern for the principal will be whether or not the distributor is capable of providing a rapid and effective after-sales service to customers. Principals will typically evaluate this parameter in terms of costs. One of the questions that the principal may ask is: how much would it cost the customer if no immediate after-sales service was available in the event that the good defaults or breaks down? When the cost is high for the customer the principal runs the risk of losing the goodwill of the customer involved and in turn market share or profitability. In such a situation, he may decide that rather than delegating the function to another (such as a distributor) it would be more sensible for him to handle the provision of after-sales service himself.[125]

When contracting with a distributor, the principal will need to bear in mind certain concerns. Firstly, he will want to limit or even eliminate the risk of the distributor and others competing with him. Where territorial exclusivity is granted to the distributor the principal may try to insist on the inclusion of a clause limiting the distributor's ability to sell the goods contracted outside the allocated territory in competition with the principal or others operating on behalf of the principal (agents, distributors and so on). Moreover, the principal will also want to address the risk of indirect competition by ensuring no other party is able to produce and sell the goods contracted in competition with the principal or those acting on his behalf (**parallel imports** or **grey market**). To guard against this risk, the principal will try to include within the distribution agreement a confidentiality clause that limits the risk of leakage of information by the distributor (his workforce and authorised agents).

A second concern that the principal will look to address when contracting with a distributor is the need to protect his revenue stream by minimising his exposure to risk in circumstances where the distributor's sales performance is poor. The principal has an incentive therefore to challenge the territorial exclusivity of the distributor, especially when the principal and distributor are working together for the first time. In a situation where the distributor has no territorial exclusivity, the principal will typically retain the right to sell the goods himself as well as through his agents and other distributors. Even when territorial exclusivity is granted to the distributor, the principal may still look to reserve himself the right to sell the goods in the assigned territory alongside the distributor.

A third concern that the principal will need to bear in mind when contracting with the distributor is the need to protect his cash flow and liquidity. The principal is likely to include a number of dedicated provisions to that end. Aside from insisting on punctual payment by the distributor, he may insist that the distributor pays for the contract goods before they are supplied. In the alternative the principal may insist that the distributor pay on delivery of the documents.[126] In this context the principal may insist on the inclusion of a reservation of title clause which reserves title in the contract goods to the principal until full payment is made by the distributor (more below).

Moreover, the principal will ensure that a provision is included in the contract that provides him with the right to recover the principal sum owing plus interest. Obviously the principal will also look to retain the option of terminating the distribution agreement as a last resort. In terms of the financial set-up the principal may try to negotiate a provision that allows for payment of a commission on sales of the contract goods generated in the assigned territory by the distributor or the payment of an initial fixed sum. In the alternative, the principal may insist on the purchase of a standing stock of contract goods by the distributor.

Fundamentally, the protection of quality assurance and brand image will be key concerns from the point of view of the principal. To this end the principal is likely to want to include a number of dedicated provisions in the agreement concluded:

- Firstly, the principal will probably include a provision requiring the distributor to maintain such stocks of the contract goods as may be required in order to meet his customers' requirements.
- Secondly, the principal may demand that the distributor use only such advertising, promotional and selling materials as the principal has first approved in writing.
- Thirdly, the principal may insist on the inclusion of a provision allowing him to be involved in marketing decisions, to audit the price lists of the distributor (if he cannot set the prices to be charged by the distributor – more about this later), to demand monthly reports from the distributor relating to sales of the contract goods, to consult with the personnel of the distributor, to visit the distributor's premises and to inspect documentation used by the distributor in connection with sales of the contract goods (including sales aids, catalogues and sales literature).
- Fourthly, the principal may insist on training the distributor's workforce in a bid to help the distributor with the marketing and sales of the contract goods in the assigned territory.
- Fifthly, the principal may restrict the manner in which his trade marks are used, by forbidding the distributor to modify either the contract goods or their packaging, to tamper with or

remove the trade marks, or to use any other trade mark or trade name on the contract goods that is likely to generate confusion or deception in the mind of the buying public. The principal may also insist in this context that the distributor assist in maintaining the validity and enforceability of the principal's intellectual property by bringing to his attention possible infringements in the assigned territory for example.

Ultimately in the case of material or persistent breaches of quality on the part of the distributor, the principal will look to reserve himself the right to terminate the agreement and if relevant the right to sue the distributor for losses that he may have sustained as a result of the acts or omissions of the distributor.[127]

XII Distribution agreement and sales agreement

Since the distribution agreement implies by definition that there is also a sales agreement between the contracting parties, the contracting parties will also need to agree on the conditions of sale (price, payment, quantity, delivery, transport, warranties, indemnities and so on).[128] In this context, the contracting parties have a number of options available to them. They may

1. make reference to the conditions of sale of one of the contracting parties;
2. agree on a set of general conditions of sale between them that they will then incorporate into their distribution agreement; or
3. refer to the General Conditions contained in the ICC model distribution contract.[129]

XIII Checklist of provisions

The following section will examine the general provisions that the parties should consider incorporating into the agreement concluded between them.[130] Where relevant, these provisions are considered in light of EU law. The checklist below provides a list of the provisions that should be included in simple international distribution agreements. This agreement is intended for use in international transactions between commercial parties. Not every one of the provisions listed in the checklist is mandatory but each of them should be considered by the parties when planning, negotiating and finalising the contract.

Box 4.6 Checklist of provisions

Preface to the contract
- ✓ Cover sheet
- ✓ Table of contents (in longer contracts; optional)
- ✓ Index of defined terms

Front of the contract (section XIV)
- ✓ Title
- ✓ Introductory clause (type of agreement, date of agreement, parties to agreement)
- ✓ Recitals

Body of contract (section XV)
- ✓ Definitions clause
- ✓ Goods (description, price and quantity)
- ✓ Territory (non-exclusivity or exclusivity)
- ✓ Relationship of the parties
- ✓ Term of the agreement (with or without an initial period; fixed or indefinite period)
- ✓ Payment terms (method, time and structure of payment, currency, with or without taxes, consequences of delayed payment and non-payment)
- ✓ Divisibility of orders

- ✓ Costs and charges
- ✓ Delivery (date and location), trade term, documents, transport, insurance and import and export arrangements
- ✓ Packaging and due delivery (liability for delay in delivery or non-delivery)
- ✓ Invoicing
- ✓ Performance
- ✓ Restrictions on re-export (optional)
- ✓ Warranties and liabilities
- ✓ Indemnity
- ✓ Permissions, consents and licences
- ✓ Licence and protection of intellectual property rights
- ✓ Obligations of the distributor
- ✓ Obligations of the principal
- ✓ Improvement and modification to goods
- ✓ Promotion of goods
- ✓ Verification
- ✓ Policies
- ✓ Termination (grounds and consequences)
- ✓ Contingencies and force majeure
- ✓ Confidentiality

Boilerplate clauses (section XVI)
- ✓ Assignment clause
- ✓ Merger clause
- ✓ Modifications clause
- ✓ Severance clause
- ✓ Notice clause
- ✓ Representation clause
- ✓ Dispute resolution (informal discussions, renegotiation, adaption, ADR, choice of jurisdiction and choice of law)
- ✓ Language clause

Back of contract (section XVII)
- ✓ Concluding clause
- ✓ Signature blocks
- ✓ Attachment (exhibits and schedules)

XIV Front of the contract[131]

The front of the contract will incorporate the following:

1. Title
2. Introductory clause noting the type and date of the agreement as well as the details of the contracting parties
3. Recitals.

Consider the following sample extract.

Distribution agreement
This distribution agreement is made [on this —— day of —— in the year —— *or* upon the date of the signature hereof] and is between:
1. —— of —— ('Principal')
2. —— of —— ('Distributor').
The Principal and the Distributor will be referred to in this agreement separately as a 'Party' or collectively as the 'Parties'.

Option A
The Principal has agreed to appoint the Distributor as its non-exclusive distributor for resale in the Territory of the Goods on the terms set out in this agreement.

Option B
The Principal has agreed to appoint the Distributor as its exclusive distributor for the resale of the Goods in the Territory on the terms set out in this agreement. The Distributor agrees to accept this appointment.

The extract above incorporates:

1. a title:[132]

> *Distribution agreement*

2. an introductory clause:[133]

> This distribution agreement is made [on this —— day of —— in the year —— *or* upon the date of the signature hereof] and is between:
> 1. —— of —— ('Principal')
>
> 2. —— of —— ('Distributor')
> The Principal and the Distributor will be referred to in this agreement separately as a 'Party' or collectively as the 'Parties'.

3. a recital:[134]

> *Option A – Non-exclusive appointment*
> The Principal has agreed to appoint the Distributor as its non-exclusive distributor for resale in the Territory of the Goods on the terms set out in this agreement.
>
> *Option B – Exclusive appointment*
> The Principal has agreed to appoint the Distributor as its exclusive distributor for the resale of the Goods in the Territory on the terms set out in this agreement.

Option A is available for use in situations when the distributor is appointed as a non-exclusive distributor for resale of the contract goods in the assigned territory. Option B is available for use in situations when the distributor is appointed as an exclusive distributor for resale of the contract goods in the assigned territory. Territorial exclusivity and non-exclusivity are reviewed below.

XV Body of the contract

Definitions clause

See corresponding section in Chapter 2.

Goods (description, price, quantity)

See corresponding section in Chapter 3. The terms 'Buyer' and 'Seller' should be replaced with 'Distributor' and 'Principal' respectively.[135]

Territory

The geographic unit (the assigned territory) for which the distributor will be responsible may be defined either within the body of the agreement or in a schedule annexed to it. Such a unit may consist of

- a country (Germany for example);
- several countries (the current and future member states of the European Union for example);
- a region within a country (the North West of England for example);
- several regions within a country; or
- the world.

The agreement may also provide for a later modification of the assigned territory. For example it may state that after a period of five years the distributor may claim an extension of the assigned territory.

Territorial exclusivity[136]

The distributor may be granted territorial exclusivity. A distributor who is in a better negotiating position than the principal may be better able to leverage such exclusivity.

Where the distributor is granted exclusivity this typically implies that the principal will not be permitted to appoint another distributor or agent in the assigned territory. Whilst this could ordinarily be implied by commercial usage, it is sensible to make sure that it is clearly set out within the terms of the agreement.

It is sensible for the contracting parties to agree in advance whether the principal will also have the right to distribute the contract goods within the assigned territory in the event that the distributor is awarded territorial exclusivity.[137] If the principal does not have this right it is sensible for the contracting parties to insert a provision to that effect within the agreement.[138] What is more, in such a situation the principal may also be obliged to refer queries from customers in the assigned territory to the distributor.

It is worthwhile bearing in mind that agreements with such provisions are likely to be regulated by European competition law.[139]

Non-exclusivity[140]
1. The Principal appoints the Distributor as its non-exclusive distributor for the resale of the Goods in the Territory on the terms set out in this agreement. The Distributor accepts this appointment.
2. The Distributor shall have the right during the continuance of this agreement to describe itself as the Authorised Distributor of the Principal for the Goods in the Territory.
3. The Distributor shall not have the right to hold itself out as the Principal's agent or as being entitled to bind the Principal in any way.

Exclusivity[141]
1. The Principal hereby appoints the Distributor as its exclusive distributor for the resale of the Goods in the Territory on the terms set out in this agreement. The Distributor accepts this appointment.
2. The Principal shall not appoint any other person in the Territory as a distributor or agent for the sale of the Goods in the Territory.
3. The Principal shall not supply to any other person in the Territory any of the Goods whether for use or resale.
4. The Principal shall not sell the Goods in the Territory itself.
5. The Principal shall not be involved either directly or indirectly in the sale of Goods in the Territory.
6. The Distributor shall have the right during the continuance of this agreement to describe itself as the Authorised Distributor of the Principal for the Goods in the Territory.
7. The Distributor shall not hold itself out as the Principal's agent or as being entitled to bind the Principal in any way.

Relationship of the parties

1. The Parties agree that the Principal is separate and independent of the Distributor.
2. The Parties agree that the Distributor is not an agent or representative of the Principal for any purpose.

3. The Parties agree that the Distributor has not got authority to bind the Principal in any way whatsoever.
4. The Parties agree that the Distributor shall not contract in the name of the Principal or on behalf of the Principal.
5. Nothing in this agreement shall create or be treated as creating between the Parties a joint venture, a partnership, an employment relationship, a fiduciary relationship, the relationship of principal and agent or any other similar relationship.
6. Each Party shall be free to recruit or employ any staff or independent contractors.
7. Neither Party shall have the power to limit or dismiss any staff or independent contractors recruited or employed by the other Party.
8. Each Party shall ensure that all staff and independent contractors recruited or employed sign an agreement not to use the Intellectual Property for any other purpose.
9. Neither Party shall be liable for the debts or obligations of the other Party.
10. Save as expressly provided for in this agreement, neither Party shall conclude or have authority to conclude an agreement or make any representation or warranty on behalf of or pledge the credit of or otherwise obligate the other Party to this agreement.

The agreement will include this standard provision clarifying the nature of the relationship existing between the distributor and the principal. The provision makes it clear that the distributor acts as a buyer and reseller and not as an agent, partner, employee and so on of the principal. It also makes it clear that the distributor and principal are separate and independent entities, which is beneficial to both parties. Such a provision prevents a situation where it may be argued that the agreement gives rise to amongst other things a partnership, joint venture, agency relationship or employment relationship between the contracting parties. Effectively, it will operate in such a way as to ringfence and curtail the power and authority of the parties to legally commit the other.

Term of the agreement (with or without an initial period; fixed or indefinite period)

Option A – Without an initial period
1. This agreement shall come into force [on this —— day of —— in the year —— or upon the date of the signature of this agreement].
2. (Subject to earlier termination permitted by the terms of this agreement) this agreement shall continue in force unless or until terminated by either Party giving the other not less than —— written notice.

Option B – With an initial period
1. This agreement shall come into force [on this —— day of —— in the year —— or upon the date of the signature of this agreement].
2. (Subject to earlier termination permitted by the terms of this agreement) this agreement shall continue in force for an initial period of —— years and thereafter, unless and until terminated by either Party giving to the other not less than —— months' written notice.
3. (*optional*) Neither Party shall give notice before the end of the initial period.

Such a provision will stipulate the date on which the agreement will commence and if appropriate the term of the agreement. The term will determine the overall duration of the contract. A contract will typically run its course unless there is some reason for its premature termination. The term may be for a set period with or without the possibility for extension. In the alternative the contract may run until a specific future event occurs.

Fixed or indefinite period

An agreement may be concluded for a fixed period or for an indefinite period with either party having the right to terminate the agreement by providing the other party with written notice of a fixed period. If the agreement contains no provision for its termination, a party may give the other notice of a reasonable length.[142] Such a provision may either stipulate the date on which the agreement commences or refer to date of the signature of the agreement as the date on which it shall come into force.

In a fixed-term agreement, the distributor may be tempted towards the end of the term to put in less effort than if he had opted for an agreement for an indefinite term. For this reason, the parties may agree on an indefinite-term agreement.

Initial period or no initial period

Option A provides for an agreement without an initial period. Option B provides for an agreement with an initial period. The distributor will probably insist on an initial period due to the sizeable investment required of him and the risk that he takes when building up the market for the contract goods.[143]

The distributor is likely to insist on exclusivity in the assigned territory for the same reasons. He will be concerned about other parties taking advantage of the investment that he has made in building up a market for the contract goods (free-riding).[144] He will also be concerned about his distribution rights being terminated at will by the principal.

The agreement may include an initial period along with a provision stating that the agreement cannot be terminated during that period (clause 3, option B above). The contracting parties may agree that the agreement can be terminated in specific situations (for example if one of the parties is declared insolvent) or if specific obligations are not met by either party.

Payment terms (method, time and structure of payment, currency, with or without taxes, consequences of delayed payment and non-payment)

See corresponding section in Chapter 3. The terms 'Buyer' and 'Seller' should be replaced with 'Distributor' and 'Principal' respectively.

Divisibility of orders

1. Each order for Goods shall constitute a separate agreement.
2. Any default by the Principal in relation to any one order shall not permit the Distributor to treat this agreement as terminated.

The principal will endeavour to protect his position by ensuring that a provision is included in the agreement stating that each order will be treated as a distinct agreement and that the distributor is prevented from terminating the agreement as a whole in the event of a problem with a specific order.

Costs and charges

See corresponding section in Chapter 3. The terms 'Buyer' and 'Seller' should be replaced with 'Distributor' and 'Principal' respectively.

Delivery (date and location), trade term, documents, transport, insurance and import and export arrangements

See corresponding section in Chapter 3. The terms 'Buyer' and 'Seller' should be replaced with 'Distributor' and 'Principal' respectively.

Packaging and due delivery (liability for delay in delivery or non-delivery)

See corresponding section in Chapter 3. The terms 'Buyer' and 'Seller' should be replaced with 'Distributor' and 'Principal' respectively.

Invoicing

See corresponding section in Chapter 3. The terms 'Buyer' and 'Seller' should be replaced with 'Distributor' and 'Principal' respectively.

Performance

See corresponding section in Chapter 3. The terms 'Buyer' and 'Seller' should be replaced with 'Distributor' and 'Principal' respectively.

Restrictions on re-export (optional)

See corresponding section in Chapter 3. The terms 'Buyer' and 'Seller' should be replaced with 'Distributor' and 'Principal' respectively.

Warranties and liabilities

1. Subject as herein provided, the Principal expressly warrants to the Distributor that
   a. all Goods will at the time of delivery and at the time of the subsequent sale by the Distributor be of merchantable quality and will comply with any specification agreed upon by the Parties;
   b. the Trade Marks listed in Schedule ——— are registered in the name of the Principal and the Principal has disclosed to the Distributor all trade marks used by the Principal in connection with the Goods at the date of this agreement; and
   c. it is not aware of any rights or claims by any other party in the Territory which could or would render the sale of the Goods, or the use of the Trade Marks on or in relation to the Goods, unlawful.
2. Except as expressly provided for in this agreement, the Principal does not warrant the Goods in any manner at all. Implied warranties are disclaimed.
3. In the event of any breach of the warranty in subsection 1, the Principal's liability shall be limited to replacement of the Goods in question; or, at the discretion of the Principal, repayment

XV BODY OF THE CONTRACT

> of the Price (where the Price has already been paid).
> 4. Notwithstanding anything to the contrary in this agreement, the Principal shall not be liable to the Distributor, except in relation to death or personal injury caused by the negligence of the Principal, by reason of any representation or implied warranty, or under the express terms of this agreement, for any consequential loss or damage arising out of or in connection with any act or omission on the part of the Principal.

The principal may agree to offer extended or limited warranties or no warranties at all in relation to the quality of the contract goods. On the one hand, such warranties, if offered, are intended to protect the distributor by providing certain assurances in relation to the quality of the contract goods and the ownership of the intellectual property. On the other hand, such a provision if properly drafted is able to contain and ringfence the liability of the principal. As such the distributor should take care to check the scope of the warranties negotiated and included in the agreement. In certain circumstances where the contract goods are ordered for a specific purpose that the distributor has discussed with the principal, a warranty should be included in the agreement confirming this.

In addition to the warranties expressly provided by the principal, certain warranties may be inserted into an agreement by the law governing the said agreement. In other words, these warranties are said to be implied into the agreement. Such warranties are known as implied warranties.[145] The principal may look to exclude all implied warranties. Obviously the distributor may object to this attempt by the principal to compromise the protection extended to him by the implied warranties.

In the event that the agreement is governed by the CISG,[146] the principal will be obliged by virtue of the provisions of the CISG[147] not only to deliver goods of the quantity, quality and description required by the contract but also to ensure that the goods are fit for the purposes for which goods of the same description are ordinarily used, are fit for a stated purpose (made known to the principal by the distributor), possess the qualities of goods which the principal has held out to the distributor as a sample and are packaged in the manner usual for such goods.

Indemnity

See corresponding section in Chapter 3. The terms 'Buyer' and 'Seller' should be replaced with 'Distributor' and 'Principal' respectively.

Permissions, consents and licences

> 1. The Distributor shall be responsible for securing, at his own expense, all requisite authorisations in order to allow the Distributor to market, distribute, sell and service the Goods in the Territory and to ensure the functioning of this agreement.
> 2. The Distributor shall be responsible for paying for all applicable customs charges, duties and taxes pertaining to the import of the Goods into the Territory and the resale of the Goods in the Territory.
> 3. If such authorisations are not secured and fully operational within a period of —— from the date of commencement

> of this agreement, the Principal shall have the right to terminate the agreement immediately by giving written notice to the Distributor. The Distributor shall not be entitled to any compensation on the termination of this agreement by reason of this provision.
>
> 4. In respect of each order for Goods, the Principal shall be responsible for obtaining, at his own expense, all necessary export licences, certificates of origin or other governmental approval required in order to export the Goods from [*country of export*].

The contracting parties may agree that the distributor assume responsibility for obtaining all the permissions, consents and licences needed locally in order to allow him to market, distribute, sell and service the contract goods.[148] The distributor may also be required, firstly, to register the agreement with the local authorities so that he can import the contract goods and then remit monies abroad; and, secondly, to obtain the authority to market and service the contract goods, especially where such goods are subject to regulation under local law. Regulation is likely in the case of foods and electrical and electronic goods, as well as chemicals and pharmaceuticals.[149] Such regulation will affect the composition of the goods as well as their packaging, labelling and the instructions accompanying the goods. This is the situation in the European Union, where the law regulates the goods and their packaging, labelling and instructions.

In the event that permissions, consents and licences are not forthcoming within a stipulated period of time, the principal will probably look to retain the right to terminate the agreement immediately (on the provision of notice in writing to the distributor). The distributor is unlikely to be able to market and accordingly sell the contract goods until the licences and so forth are issued. Accordingly in an agreement with a fixed period, the question will arise as to whether the term starts to run from the date on which licences are obtained and marketing can commence (favourable to the distributor) or from the date of the agreement itself, so that the time required to acquire the said licences eats into the fixed period (favourable to the principal as it gives the distributor an incentive to get the licence as rapidly as possible).[150]

In either case, the principal's hands will be tied if the distributor has the exclusive right to market in an assigned territory since the only route the principal will have is termination. In the absence of this right to terminate, the principal's sole option will be to rely on the distributor's failure to meet his obligation to exercise due diligence, which the principal would need to prove.[151] The principal is likely to insist that the distributor be denied compensation on termination of the agreement in this context. It is worth noting that in certain countries, compulsory compensation may be due to the distributor in such a situation. Where local law does not provide for compulsory compensation, a claim in contract may still arise if there is a plausible case for breach of contract. The position should be checked in advance of contracting with a local legal advisor.

Licence and protection of intellectual property rights[152]

1. The Principal authorises the Distributor to use the Intellectual Property, including but not limited to the Trade Marks, in the Territory on or in relation to the Goods, for the purposes only of exercising its rights and performing its duties under this agreement.
2. Except as provided in clause 1 above, the Distributor shall have no rights in relation to any Intellectual Property used by the Principal in relation to the Goods or in any goodwill associated therewith.
3. Except as expressly provided for in this agreement, the Distributor acknowledges that he shall not acquire any rights in relation to any Intellectual Property used by the Principal in relation to the Goods or in any goodwill associated therewith and that any such rights and goodwill are and shall remain vested in the Principal.
4. The Distributor shall not register any Intellectual Property without the prior written authorisation of the Principal.
5. The Distributor shall provide the Principal, prior to use of any Trade Mark, a sample of the documentation displaying the Trade Mark, including but not limited to publicity, catalogues, price lists, informational booklets, technical manuals and packaging. The Distributor shall make use of any such documentation only once the Principal has specifically approved in writing the proofs of such documentation.
6. The Distributor shall take all steps as the Principal may reasonably require to assist the Principal in maintaining the validity and enforceability of the Intellectual Property of the Principal during the term of this agreement, on the proviso that the Principal shall indemnify the Distributor against all costs, claims, damages or other liabilities arising from or in connection with such steps.
7. The Distributor shall, at the request of the Principal, execute such registered user agreements or licenses in respect of the use of the Trade Marks in the Territory as the Principal may reasonably require, on condition that the provisions shall not be more onerous or restrictive than the provisions of this agreement.
8. Without prejudice to the right of the Distributor or any third party to challenge the validity of any Intellectual Property of the Principal, the Distributor shall not do or authorise any third party to do any act that would or might invalidate or be inconsistent with any Intellectual Property of the Principal.
9. The Distributor shall promptly and fully notify the Principal of any actual, threatened or suspected infringement in the Territory of any Intellectual Property of the Principal which comes to the notice of the Distributor.
10. The Distributor shall promptly and fully notify the Principal of any claim by any third party that comes to his notice that the import of the Goods into the Territory or their sale in the Territory violates any rights of any other person.
11. The Distributor shall at the request of the Principal and at the expense of the Principal execute all acts reasonably required in order to help the Principal in taking or resisting any proceedings in relation to any such infringement or claim.

In order to promote sales of the contract goods in the assigned territory, the agreement between distributor and principal will grant the distributor the right to use the intellectual property belonging to the principal in the assigned territory in relation to the contract goods during the term of the agreement. Such a grant will be made subject to certain strict conditions included in the agreement which are intended to protect the intellectual property of the principal, as well as his reputation and goodwill. In this context, the principal will ensure that the agreement contains provisions that curtail the distributor's rights in relation to the principal's intellectual property. Such provisions will restrict the distributor's use of the principal's intellectual property generally as well as the use of the same on or in relation to the contract goods in the assigned territory.

The agreement will typically oblige the distributor to use the intellectual property only for the purposes contemplated by the agreement. In particular, during the term of the agreement, the distributor will be obliged under the agreement to ensure that the intellectual property is used in a manner approved by the principal. Moreover, under the agreement the distributor will be prohibited from[153]

1. tampering with or modifying the contract goods themselves or their packaging; and/or
2. using the intellectual property of the principal in a way that might prejudice its distinctiveness or validity or in some other way that could or does impact on the goodwill of the principal.

The distributor will usually be required to take all steps to help the principal maintain the validity and enforceability of the intellectual property under the agreement. Accordingly, the distributor will be obliged to advise the principal of any actual or potential infringement in the assigned territory. To ensure that no rights are obtained by the distributor in relation to the intellectual property owned by the principal, the principal will insist that the distributor agree that all rights and goodwill that arise in relation of the intellectual property will remain at all times the property of the principal.

In some countries, it may not possible for the distributor to import goods bearing a trade mark without the distributor being registered as owner or user of the said trade mark. In such situations, it is essential that a registered user agreement be concluded between the principal and the distributor. Such an agreement will need to be registered in compliance with local law. Under it, the distributor will have the right to use the trade mark without gaining ownership rights in the said trade mark. Without such an agreement, the distributor may in time acquire rights in the trade mark.

In order to ensure protection of proprietorship rights in trade marks, the distributor will be forbidden from using the trade marks on other items that are not the contract goods and the principal will stipulate that he has exclusive rights in the trade marks. Moreover, the distributor will be obliged to take steps to protect such rights.

Obligations of the distributor[154]

1. The Distributor shall during the course of the agreement
   a. serve the Principal diligently and faithfully as his distributor in the Territory;
   b. use his best endeavours to increase the goodwill of the Principal in the Territory;
   c. use his best endeavours to increase the sales of Goods in the Territory;
   d. keep adequate supplies of the Goods to fulfil the requirements of his customers;
   e. promote, sell and service the Goods sold to customers in the Territory by the Distributor;
   f. recruit staff to sell, distribute and promote the sale of the Goods in the Territory;
   g. recruit staff to service the Goods sold to customers in the Territory by the Distributor;
   h. ensure that staff execute promptly and diligently the obligations of the Distributor under this agreement;
   i. buy all his supplies of the Goods in packaging from the Principal;
   j. store the Goods under such conditions as to prevent their deterioration and on the instructions of the Principal, store particular Goods under such conditions as may be appropriate considering the particular characteristics and needs of the Goods;
   k. use his best endeavours to ensure that Goods clear as rapidly as possible through customs in the Territory;
   l. pending such clearance, use his best endeavours to ensure that the Goods are stored in the manner mentioned above;
   m. upon the provision of reasonable notice by the Principal, permit the Principal or his authorised representative/s to examine the Goods whilst the Goods are in storage controlled by the Distributor;
   n. ensure compliance with all laws and regulations that exist or may come into effect in the Territory;
   o. meet the targets defined in Schedule —— accompanying this agreement;
   p. ensure that each reference to and use of any of the Trade Marks by the Distributor will be in a manner that is approved, from time to time, by the Principal;
   q. ensure that each reference to the Trade Marks and use of any of the Trade Marks by the Distributor will be accompanied by an acknowledgement in a form approved by the Principal that the same is a trade mark (or registered Trade Mark) of the Principal;
   r. at the request of the Principal and within —— days from the date of the Principal's request, supply the Principal with an inspection report relating to shipments of Goods received by the Distributor and the quality and performance of the Goods supplied (*optional:* the inspection report should accord with the template provided to the Distributor by the Principal);
   s. indemnify the Principal against all liabilities, losses or damages sustained as a consequence of a breach or omission by the Distributor under this agreement;
   t. in relation to each order of Goods to be supplied, ensure the accuracy of

the order and provide the Principal with all the information needed in order to enable him to process the order; and

u. provide the Principal with a written estimate not later than —— days before the first day of each Quarter of the quantities of Goods required to be delivered by the Principal in each such Quarter and shall promptly inform the Principal of any change in circumstances which affects the requirements of the Distributor. This estimate is not binding on the Principal or Distributor.

2. The Distributor shall not during the course of this agreement
   a. do anything that is capable of adversely affecting the sale of Goods in the Territory;
   b. do anything that is capable of adversely affecting the goodwill of the Principal;
   c. reproduce, alter or construct the Goods or any part thereof for use, sale or any other purpose;
   d. assist any third party in reproducing, altering or constructing the Goods or any part or parts thereof for use, sale or any other purpose;
   e. make any changes to the Goods or their packaging;
   f. alter, remove or tamper with the Trade Marks, numbers or other means of identification used on or in relation to the Goods;
   g. use any of the Trade Marks in a manner which may prejudice their distinctiveness or validity or the goodwill of the Principal therein;
   h. use in relation to the Goods any trade mark other than the Trade Mark(s) without first obtaining the written authorisation of the Principal; and
   i. use in the Territory any trade mark or trade name so resembling a trade mark or trade name of the Principal that is likely to cause confusion or deception.

3. Nothing in this agreement shall entitle the Distributor to any priority of supply in relation to the Goods as against the Principal's other distributors or customers.

4. Nothing in this agreement shall be read as giving the Distributor any right or remedy against the Principal if any of the Goods are sold in the Territory by any person outside the Territory other than the Principal.

Optional clauses

5. (*non-compete clause*) The Distributor shall not during the course of this agreement (and for a period of —— after the end of this agreement), without the prior written authorisation of the Principal
   a. seek customers, establish any branch or maintain any distribution depot for the Goods outside the Territory;
   b. manufacture or sell in or import into the Territory any goods which compete with the Goods; or
   c. be concerned or interested, directly or indirectly, in the manufacture, sale, import or distribution in the Territory of any goods which compete with the Goods.

   This provision shall not apply to those goods (if any) that are listed in Schedule —— accompanying this agreement.

6. (*retail units*)
   a. The Distributor shall open at least —— retail units in the Territory within —— after the date this agreement comes into effect.

> b. The opening of further retail units will remain within the discretion of the Distributor.
> 7. (*full line forcing*)[155]
>   a. During the course of this agreement, the Distributor shall ensure at all times at least —— stock of the Goods.
>   b. During the course of this agreement and at the request of the Principal, the Distributor shall, within —— days from the date of the Principal's request, provide the Principal with written reports noting stock levels and movements. (*optional:* Such a report shall accord with the template furnished to the Distributor by the Principal).

The agreement will spell out the distributor's obligations in order to protect the interests of the principal in general and specifically in the context of the agreement. Below is a list of obligations that are typically incorporated in a distribution agreement. This list is by no means exhaustive.

1. To enhance the goodwill of the principal, the distributor will have an obligation to act with due diligence using his best efforts.[156] Such a provision is especially important bearing in mind the fact that the principal has licensed the distributor the right to sell the contract goods using his trade mark or brand name.
2. To protect the level of sales in the assigned territory, the distributor will be obliged to do nothing capable of adversely affecting the volume of contract goods sold in the assigned territory. Such a requirement is especially important in the event that the agreement is terminated, as during the period of notice the distributor may be less inclined to act in the interests of the principal. Such a provision is also important in non-exclusive agreements.
3. To ensure that sales levels are met and maintained, the principal will commonly insist that the distributor retain adequate stocks of the contract goods so that customer needs can be met promptly. The principal may require that the distributor carry at all times at least several months' worth of stock in order to fulfil customer orders as and when these are received. The principal will usually note the number of months' worth of stock that the distributor will be required to carry. This practice is known as full line forcing.[157] In this context, the principal may also insist on reporting requirements and impose minimum staffing requirements on the distributor.
4. To protect the reputation and goodwill of the principal and prevent legal action against him, the distributor will be obliged to make sure that contract goods manufactured, distributed and sold in the assigned territory conform to local law in terms of labelling, packaging, permitted ingredients, warnings and instructions. Such a provision is important when the principal is relying on the distributor to ensure compliance with local law.[158] Obviously compliance is important from the point of view of the distributor as well. Failure to comply will expose the distributor to legal action and will in turn impact on his reputation and goodwill.
5. To protect the contract goods against for example deterioration or damage, the principal should insist that the

distributor store the contract goods in a manner suited to the goods concerned.

6. To ensure import formalities are dealt with in a timely fashion by the distributor, the principal should insist that the distributor clear the contract goods through customs in the assigned territory as rapidly as possible.[159] Moreover the principal should insist on the inclusion of a provision that stipulates that the distributor should be responsible for making sure that the contract goods are stored in a suitable fashion pending such clearance. Storage is essential when the contract goods are either perishable or fragile. Problems with the condition of such goods will adversely affect the reputation and goodwill of the principal as well as the distributor.

7. To ensure a steady flow of cash, the principal may require the distributor to either sell a set quantity of contract goods (by reference for example to a minimum number of units) or buy off the principal a set quantity of contract goods (by reference for example to a minimum number of units), either throughout the whole term of the agreement or during a set period of time at the start of the term.[160]

8. To protect his position the principal should insist on the inclusion of a non-compete clause. Such a provision may state that during the term of the agreement the distributor will not be permitted to compete directly or indirectly with the principal in the assigned territory. In the provision used above the distributor is prohibited from producing, selling or importing goods that compete with the contract goods or otherwise being interested in an operation that produces, sells or imports goods that compete with these goods in the territory in question. In the event that the distributor wishes to retain the right to sell competing goods, it may be sensible for him to negotiate and include in the agreement a list of such competing goods that he may sell as well as to reserve the right to extend the list at a later date by agreement with the principal.[161] Such a provision should be drafted in such a way as to be limited to the sales of competing goods, as opposed to the sale of all goods, as most jurisdictions will not enforce contracts that stop an independent contractor selling goods that are not in direct competition with the contract goods.

9. The principal will want to preserve his right to sell the contract goods outside the assigned territory either himself or through another. With this in mind, it would be sensible for the principal to ensure that a provision is included in the agreement[162]
    a. forbidding the distributor from selling the contract goods outside the allocated territory either directly or indirectly;
    b. curtailing the distributor's ability to source customers outside the assigned territory;
    c. prohibiting the distributor from being involved directly or indirectly with any operation for the promotion or sale of the contract goods outside the assigned territory; and
    d. obliging the distributor to relay any enquiries from customers outside the assigned territory to the principal.

10. To protect the livelihood of the principal the distributor will be forbidden to copy, produce or modify the contract goods or any parts thereof and to help another party do the same. Such a prohibition is required since a distributor

will usually possess substantial technical information pertaining to the contract goods, making it far easier for him to reproduce the contract goods and parts of these goods.[163]
11. The distributor will not be permitted to interfere with notices or marks which the principal affixes to the contract goods, which would effectively undermine the principal's rights in relation to these goods.[164]
12. The distributor will be obliged to indemnify the principal in relation to acts or omissions for which it is responsible. Such a provision, which reinforces to a certain degree the position of the law, is sensible as it operates to remind the distributor of the obligations owing to the principal whilst at the same time ensuring indemnification in circumstances which are not otherwise provided for by the governing law.[165]
13. In order to protect the cash flow of the principal, it is sensible for the principal to insist on the inclusion of a provision stating that the distributor is obliged to buy all his requirements for the contract goods from the principal.[166] Such a provision will prevent a situation from arising where the distributor is tempted to acquire cheaper goods elsewhere.

Obligations of the principal

1. The Principal shall deliver to the Distributor, within ——, all Goods for which the Distributor places orders, unless the delivery is delayed due to a fault on the part of the Distributor or if delivery becomes impossible as provided for in this agreement. (*Alternatively*: The Principal shall use his best endeavours to supply the Goods to the Distributor in accordance with the orders of the Distributor.)
2. The Principal shall deliver the Goods ordered by shipment to the locations assigned by the Distributor within the Territory.
3. (*in exclusive distribution agreements*) The Principal shall not sell any Goods to any other party in the Territory other than the Distributor.
4. The Principal shall immediately relay to the Distributor all leads, prospects, enquiries and analogous information that the Principal acquires regarding prospective customers for the Goods in the Territory.[167]
5. The Principal shall provide the Distributor with his suggested list of retail prices for the Goods. Such prices are not binding on the Distributor.

The contracting parties must take care when negotiating the provision in the agreement relating to the retail prices for the contract goods, due to the potential breach of competition law associated with such a provision.[168] An agreement reached between a principal and distributor which includes a provision fixing minimum resale prices to be charged by the distributor will be held to have as its object the restriction of competition.[169] In contrast, a principal may furnish a distributor with price guidance so long as there is no concerted practice between the parties.[170]

Improvement and modification to the goods

1. The Principal shall not be under any obligation to continue the manufacture of all or any of the Goods.
2. The Principal may enhance or alter the Goods in any way he chooses without notifying the Distributor.
3. Where the Distributor is notified of any such enhancement or alteration to the Goods, he may change or cancel any orders for the Goods placed before receipt of such notice, save to the degree that such orders may be met by supply of Goods which do not incorporate the enhancement or alteration notified.
4. The Distributor shall effect such changes or cancellation of orders by notifying the Principal within —— of receipt of the relevant notice by the Distributor.
5. The rights of cancellation under this provision shall be the only remedy that the Distributor has at his disposal.

The principal will typically want to reserve the right to make modifications and improvements to the contract goods during the term of the agreement. As such he will look to reserve the right to do this without giving prior notice to the distributor.[171] In the event that the principal attempts to negotiate such a provision, the distributor may attempt to counter by reserving himself the rights to be notified in advance of any modification or improvement and to cancel or change any orders he placed with the principal before the date on which the modification or improvement was made, except that is to the extent that such an order or orders may be met by the supply of contract goods that do not include the modification or improvement in question.

In the event that the distributor uses this right, the principal should consider conditioning it by stating that the distributor's only recourse would be to cancel or change the order. This would prevent the distributor from seeking any other form of redress from the principal such as compensation. Moreover the principal has the option of refining this right by stating that it may be exercised by the distributor only when

1. the order placed cannot be met by the supply of contract goods that do not incorporate the modification or improvement; and
2. the distributor notifies the principal within a set period of time from the date on which he was informed of the modification or improvement.

Promotion of goods[172]

1. The Distributor shall ensure that in all his dealings with his customers (actual and prospective) and in the context of the promotion and marketing of the Goods it is made clear that he is acting as a distributor of the Goods and not as an agent for the Principal.

Option A: promotion is the responsibility of the Principal

2. The Principal shall supply the Distributor at no cost to the Distributor with all promotional literature.
3. The Principal shall be solely responsible for the cost of promoting the Goods in the Territory.

Option B: promotion is the responsibility of the Distributor

2. Unless otherwise agreed, the Distributor shall be solely responsible for the cost of promoting the Goods in the Territory.
3. During the first year of this agreement
   a. the Principal shall make available to the Distributor at such time as may be agreed and for a period not exceeding —— the services of a suitably qualified employee of the Principal to assist the Distributor in the marketing of the Goods; and
   b. the Distributor may send to the Principal's premises at such time as may be agreed upon with the Principal and for a period not exceeding ——, up to —— suitably qualified employees of the Distributor for training by the Principal in matters relating to the Goods and their marketing.
4. The services provided by the Principal will be free of charge, but the Distributor shall
   a. reimburse the Principal all travelling, accommodation and other expenditure reasonably incurred by the employees of the Principal; and
   b. remain liable for all salaries and other employment expenses of and all travelling, accommodation and incidental expenses incurred by employees of the Distributor who are sent to the Principal's premises.

Option B1

5. The Distributor may subject to the provisions in this agreement
   a. promote and market the Goods in the Territory in such manner as it deems fit; and
   b. resell the Goods to its customers at such prices as it may set.

Option B2

5. The Distributor shall inform the Principal and agree with the Principal not later than the end of —— in each year, any promotional programme for the Goods for the next year.
6. The Distributor may revise the programme agreed with the Principal, from time to time, as required by the market conditions present in that year.
7. The Distributor shall expend on the programme no less than an amount equivalent to —— per cent of the actual proceeds of sale of the Goods obtained over the year. The Distributor may discount this sum by the expenditure dispensed by him in fulfilment of his obligations under any other clause in this agreement and any compensation that he has credited to his customers in relation to the return of Goods.

Promotional activities in the assigned territory may be the responsibility of the principal, the distributor or both. Where they are the responsibility of the principal then Option A is appropriate. Where they are the responsibility of the distributor then Option B is appropriate.

Responsibility of the principal (Option A)

If the principal is responsible for such programmes then he will supply the distributor with promotional materials bearing the cost of all the advertising that the distributor undertakes in the assigned territory.

Responsibility of distributor (Option B)

In the event that the distributor is responsible for such programmes the principal may reserve the right to be notified and approve all such programmes before implementation. In order to enhance the level of sales in the assigned territory the principal may also try to negotiate a provision within the agreement requiring the distributor to spend a minimum sum over a set period (annually for example) on promotional programmes. An annual expenditure of 5 per cent of the actual proceeds of sale of the contract goods (received in the year preceding the one in question) is not atypical.[173]

The principal for his part will have an incentive to increase this percentage as the sums come out of the distributor's margin and act as a motivational tool encouraging the distributor to increase his sales in the assigned territory.[174] This sum will usually be discounted by sums expended by the distributor under the other provisions of the agreement as well as monies paid out by the distributor to his customers (for example in relation to returned goods).

Verification[175]

1. The Distributor shall maintain and preserve accounts and retain all documents in support of these accounts (including but not limited to copies of invoices and documentation showing all orders for the supply of Goods by the Principal to the Distributor and by the Distributor to its customers).
2. The Distributor shall permit inspection, auditing and/or copying of the accounts and supporting documentation by the Principal or the authorised representative(s) of the Principal at all reasonable times whether this agreement is terminated or not, in order inter alia to verify the information furnished by the Distributor to the Principal and to confirm compliance by the Distributor with his obligations under this agreement.
3. The Distributor shall provide the Principal, by the —— day following the end of each calendar month, with a written report confirming sales of the Goods in the Territory during the month in question, together with marketing information and any other operational information as the Principal may require.
4. The Principal shall supply to the Distributor standard forms forming the basis for these reports.

In order to monitor the quantities of contract goods sold by the distributor, to implement a product recall in the assigned territory where needed and to ensure inter alia that the distributor has not been competing with the principal, the principal is likely to insist on a provision which permits either the principal or the representatives of the principal to audit the records kept by the distributor[176] and requires the distributor to submit regular reports including sales figures, marketing efforts and other operational information. Typically the distributor will be provided with a template report by the principal listing the parameters that the principal is interested in finding out more about.

To safeguard the goodwill and reputation of the principal and the contract goods produced by him, he may reserve himself the right to audit price lists and sales materials used by the distributor. He

XV BODY OF THE CONTRACT

may even go so far as to reserve the right to interview members of the distributor's workforce and visit the premises used by the distributor.

Policies

> 1. The Distributor shall adhere to the general policies of the Principal.
> 2. The Principal shall have the right to supply instructions, from time to time, to the Distributor to ensure such adherence.

The principal will generally ensure the inclusion of a provision that requires the distributor to adhere to the strategies and policies of the principal. In such a situation, the principal will also reserve the right to issue directions to the distributor in order to ensure conformity with these strategies and policies.[177] Such a catchall provision will cover all those situations that do not fall under any of the other provisions in the agreement.

Termination (grounds and consequences)

Grounds for termination[178]

In an agreement with a minimum sales target (typical in exclusive distribution agreements), the principal will usually look to reserve the right to terminate if the distributor fails to meet the target agreed upon. The minimum sales target may be defined in the body of the agreement or in a schedule.[179] An alternative remedy available to the principal (though not necessarily worthwhile) is the right to revoke the exclusivity provision in such a situation.[180] This would in turn permit either the principal or another party on the principal's behalf (distributor, agent and so on) to supply the contract goods in the assigned territory alongside the distributor who would now be operating on a non-exclusive basis.

Usually the principal will not have the incentive to supply the contract goods in the assigned territory. If he had been motivated to do so then he would have done so instead of opting for a distribution agreement in the first place. What is more, the principal is unlikely to be able to source an alternative distributor in the assigned territory. Such a distributor, if one can be found, which is uncertain if the principal agreed to an exclusivity arrangement initially, will be unlikely to want to distribute when the existing distributor is still free to sell the contract goods in the assigned territory albeit on a non-exclusive basis.

Consequences of termination[181]

> 1. Upon termination of this agreement for whatever reason
>   a. the Principal may (but is not obliged to) buy back all or part of any stocks of the Goods held by the Distributor at their Invoice Value or at the value at which they stand in the books of the Distributor, whichever is the lower;
>   b. the [Principal or Distributor] shall be responsible for organising and for paying the cost of transport and insurance of these stocks;
>   c. at the discretion of the Principal, the Distributor shall at his own expense, within —— days of termination, send to the Principal or

otherwise dispose of (in accordance with the directions of the Principal and in the presence of the Principal's duly authorised representative) all samples of the Goods and any materials relating to the Goods found in the possession or in the control of the Distributor;

d. the Distributor shall pay immediately all outstanding unpaid invoices issued by the Principal in respect of the Goods;

e. the Distributor shall pay immediately all invoices pertaining to Goods ordered pre-termination once these invoices are provided by the Principal;

f. the Distributor shall stop promoting, marketing or advertising the Goods;

g. the Distributor shall stop using the Trade Marks in any way whatsoever;

h. the Distributor shall free of charge dispose of, in accordance with the instructions of the Principal, or return to the Principal, all documentation utilising such Trade Marks found in the control or in the possession of the Distributor; and

i. the Distributor shall have no claim against the Principal.

2. Subject to what is otherwise provided for in this agreement and to any rights or duties which have accrued before the termination, neither Party shall have any further obligations to the other under this agreement.

Optional provisions

1. The Distributor shall upon termination of this agreement provide the Principal with the details of all his customers for the Goods.

2. The Distributor shall upon termination of this agreement assign to the Principal all authorisations at no charge pertaining to the Goods and shall execute all documents and perform any actions required in order to ensure that the Principal has the sole benefit of these authorisations.

Contingencies and force majeure

See the corresponding section in Chapter 3.

Confidentiality

See the corresponding section in Chapter 3.

Schedules

The schedules accompanying a distribution agreement are likely to address amongst other matters goods, territory, trade marks and intellectual property,

XVI Boilerplate clauses

See the corresponding section in Chapter 2.

XVII Back of the contract

See the corresponding section in Chapter 2.

purchase targets and competing goods. An example of a schedule addressing purchase targets is given below.

During the course of this agreement during each consecutive period of twelve months, the Distributor agrees to meet the following minimum targets for purchases from the Principal:

| Period | Target |

Summary

This chapter reviewed the concept of vertical integration, different levels in the supply chain and each player's role in the supply chain. It looked at the distinction between agent and distributor and the difference between buyer and distributor. It explored the international law governing distribution agreements and principals' and distributors' concerns when opting for a distribution agreement. The second part covered

- which provisions the contracting parties should consider including in international distribution agreements;
- the purpose of each provision; and
- these provisions' proposed wording.

Useful links

http://ec.europa.eu/internal_market/company/se/index_en.htm (background information about European companies or *societates Europaeae* (SE))

http://ec.europa.eu/justice/policies/civil/docs/dcfr_outline_edition_en.pdf (outline edition of Draft Common Frame of Reference (DCFR))

http://eur-lex.europa.eu/LexUriServ/LexUriServ.do?uri=OJ:C:2010:083:0047:0200:en:PDF (consolidated version of Treaty on the Functioning of the European Union (TFEU))

http://europa.eu/legislation_summaries/internal_market/businesses/company_law/l26015_en.htm (information about EEIGs)

Further reading

Bortolotti, Fabio (2008), *Drafting and Negotiating International Commercial Agreements: A Practical Guide*, International Chamber of Commerce.

Bradgate, Robert (2000), *Commercial Law*, 3rd ed., Butterworths.

Christou, Richard (2003), *International Agency, Distribution and Licensing Agreements*, 4th ed., Sweet & Maxwell.

Fox, William F. Jr (1992), *International Commercial Agreements: A Primer on Drafting, Negotiating and Resolving Disputes*, Kluwer Law and Taxation.

Graupner, Rudolf (1969), 'Sole Distributorship Agreements: A Comparative View', *International and Comparative Law Quarterly* 18:4, 879.

Hlavacek, James D. and McCuistion, Tommy J. (1983), 'Industrial Distributors: When, Who, and How?', *Harvard Business Review*, March, 96.

Jones, Alison and Sufrin, Brenda (2011), *EU Competition Law: Text, Cases, and Materials*, 4th ed., Oxford University Press.

Moosa, Imad (2002), *Foreign Direct Investment: Theory, Evidence and Practice*, Palgrave.

Murray, Carole, Holloway, David and Timson-Hunt, Daren (2007), *Schmitthoff's Export Trade: The Law and Practice of International Trade*, 11th ed., Sweet & Maxwell.

Shippey, Karla C. (1999), *A Short Course in International Contracts: Drafting the International Sales Contract for Attorneys and Non-attorneys*, World Trade Press.

Staubach, Fritz (1977), *The German Law of Agency and Distributorship Agreements*, Oyez.

Yelpaala, Kojo (1994), 'Strategy and Planning in Global Product Distribution: Beyond the Distribution Contract', *Law and Policy in International Business* 25:3, 839.

Notes

1. This topic is reviewed further in Shippey, Karla (1999), *A Short Course in International Contracts: Drafting the International Sales Contract for Attorneys and Non-attorneys*, World Trade Press, Chapter 19; Murray, Carole, Holloway David and Timson-Hunt, Daren (2007), *Schmitthoff's Export Trade: The Law and Practice of International Trade*, 11th ed., Sweet & Maxwell, Chapter 30; Christou, Richard (2003), *International Agency, Distribution and Licensing Agreements*, 4th ed., Sweet & Maxwell, Chapters 4, 5; Staubach, Fritz (1977), *The German Law of Agency and Distributorship Agreements*, Oyez, 229–30. This topic is also reviewed in the following articles: Meek, Marcellus R. (1966), 'Overseas Distributorship Agreements', *Business Lawyer* 21, 661; Meek, Marcellus R. and Feltham, Ivan R. (1967), 'Foreign Sales, Distribution, Licensing and Joint Venture Agreements', *DePaul Law Review* 17, 46; Graupner, Rudolf (1969), 'Sole Distributorship Agreements: A Comparative View', *International and Comparative Law Quarterly* 18:4, 879; Jones, Robert T. (1972), 'Practical Aspects of Commercial Agency and Distribution Agreements in the European Community', *International Lawyer* 6, 107; Salter, Leonard M. (1971), 'Expanding Horizons: New Legal Worlds to Conquer', *Commercial Law Journal* 76, 90; Puelinckx, A. H. and Tielemans, H. A. (1981), 'The Termination of Agency and Distributor Agreements: A Comparative Survey', *Northwest Journal of International Law and Business* 3, 452; Saltoun, André and Spudis, Barbara (1983), 'International Distribution and Sales Agency Agreements: Practical Guidelines for US Exporters', *Business Lawyer* 39, 883; Berwind, Michael (1983), 'Strategies for Entering Foreign Markets', *Hastings International and Comparative Law Review* 7, 293; Handel, Stephen (1992), 'Entering International Markets: An Experimental Guide', *Currents* 1:2, 23; Yelpaala, Kojo (1994), 'Strategy and Planning in Global Product Distribution: Beyond the Distribution Contract', *Law and Policy in International Business* 25:3, 839.
2. More in Chapter 5.
3. This definition is derived from the definition found in the WTO glossary, available at http://www.wto.org/english/thewto_e/glossary_e/parallel_imports_e.htm (last accessed 21 January 2013).
4. Lillenthal, Jesse (1887), 'Privity of Contract', *Harvard Law Review*, 1:5, 226.
5. For a detailed review, see Harrigan, Kathryn Rudie (2003), *Vertical Integration, Outsourcing, and Corporate Strategy*, Beard, Chapter 9; Hill, Charles W. L. and Jones, Gareth R. (2010), *Strategic Management Theory: An Integrated Approach*, 9th ed., South-western Cengage Learning; Christou (2003), Chapter 23.
6. Harrigan 2003: 1. Vertical integration has since changed from this image, and as such when looking at vertical integration, reference needs to be made to the breadth, stages, degree and form that it takes.
7. Christou 2003, Chapter 23.
8. Harrigan 2003: 3–5; Christou 2003, Chapter 23.
9. Christou 2003, Chapter 23.
10. Ibid.

11. Ibid.; Harrigan 2003: 1–3.
12. The classification is provided by Christou (2003), Chapter 23. For a detailed review, see ibid.
13. More on franchising agreements in Chapter 6.
14. More on franchising agreements in Chapter 6.
15. More in Chapter 6.
16. More in Chapter 5.
17. In the EU, pursuant to Council Directive 86/653/EEC of 18 December 1986 on the Coordination of the Laws of Member States Relating to Self-employed Commercial Agents (more in Chapter 5).
18. United States – *Aaron E. Levine & Co.* v. *Calkraft Paper Co.*, 429 F. Supp. 1039 (ED Mich. 1976), at 1050, citing *Rubinger* v. *International Tel. & Tel. Corp.*, 310 F. 2d 552 (2d Cir. 1962), cert. Denied, 375 US 820 (1962).
19. Berwind 1983; Handel 1992; Yelpaala 1994; Christou 2003, Chapter 23.
20. Christou 2003, Chapter 23.
21. Yelpaala 1994: 877.
22. Yelpaala 1994: 877–915 (in this part of the article, there is a review of the structures available to the principal, as well as the concerns and legal ramifications associated with these structures; there is also a review of case studies).
23. Yelpaala 1994: 927.
24. Yelpaala 1994: 915–26 (in this part of the article, there is a review of the structures for strategic alliances).
25. A European company or *Societas Europaea* (SE) is governed by a mixed regime consisting of European Union law, national law and the provisions of that particular SE's constitution. Background information about SEs can be found at (last accessed 21 January 2013). The following books and articles review SEs: Andenas, Mads and Woolridge, Frank (2009), *European Comparative Company Law*, Cambridge University Press; Becker, Arnd and Oelmüller, Mark (2009), 'Die SE für den Mittelstand – Theorie und Praxis der SE-Gründung, *Praxishefte zum Europäischen Privatrecht* 5; Bouloukos, Marios (2004), 'Le Régime juridique de la société européene (SE): vers une société européenne "à la carte"? The Legal Status of the European Company (SE): Towards a European Company "à la carte"', *Revue de Droit des Affairs Internationales/International Business Law Journal* 2004:4, 489; Bouloukos, Marios (2007), 'The European Company (SE) as a Vehicle for Corporate Mobility within the EU: A Breakthrough in European Corporate Law?' *European Business Law Review* 18, 535; Craig, Adam, Van den Hurk, Hans, Mueller, Stefan, Rainer, Anno, Roels, Jan, Thoemmes, Otmar and Tomsett, Eric (2004), 'The European Company is Born', *International Tax Review*, November; Deau, Veronique and Montfort, Roland (2006), 'Establishing a European Company ("SE"): A New Eldorado for European Group Companies and for Practitioners? A French Perspective', *International Company and Commercial Law Review* 17:9, 271; Di Luigi, M. Christina (2008), 'An Invasive Top-down Harmonization or a Respectful Framework Model of National Laws? A Critique of the Societas Europaea Model', *International Company and Commercial Law Review* 19:2, 58; Drobek, Daniel

(2007), *Die Societas Europaea (SE): eine alternative Rechtsform für grenzüberschreitend tätige Unternehmen?*, GRIN; Donald, David C. (1991), 'Company Law in the European Community: Toward Supranational Incorporation', *Dickinson Journal of International Law* 9, 1 (1991); Ebert, Sabine (2003), 'The European Company on the Level Playing Field of the Community', *European Business Law Review* 14:2, 183; Ebert, Sabine (2004), 'The Law Applicable to Groups of Companies Involving European Companies (Societas Europaea)', *Company Lawyer* 25:4, 108; Edbury, Mike (2004), 'The European Company Statute: A Practical Working Model for the Future of European Company Law Making?', *European Business Law Review* 15:6, 1283.
26. Information about EEIGs can be found at http://europa.eu/legislation_summaries/internal_market/businesses/company_law/l26015_en.htm (last accessed 21 January 2013).
27. *L. Schuler AG* v. *Wickman Machine Tool Sales Ltd* [1974] AC 235, 247–9 (facts and arguments summarised by Lord Reid).
28. Lord Reid stated that in relation to agreements, the word 'condition' may mean a prerequisite (something that must occur or be done before the agreement may take effect) or some state of affairs that must continue to exist if the agreement is to remain in force (*L. Schuler AG* v. *Wickman Machine Tool Sales Ltd* [1974] AC 235, 251).
29. Lord Reid stated that the word 'remedy' (used in Clause 11) was read to mean 'cure' so that matters are put right for the future, adding that he was inclined to the view that breaches of the obligation in Clause 7 should be held to be capable of remedy within the meaning of Clause 7 (*L. Schuler AG* v. *Wickman Machine Tool Sales Ltd* [1974] AC 235, 249–250).
30. Bradgate, Robert (2000), *Commercial Law*, 3rd ed., Butterworths, 135.
31. The matter of trade terms is addressed in Chapter 3.
32. More in Chapter 3.
33. Staubach, Fritz (1977), *The German Law of Agency and Distributorship Agreements*, Oyez, 229–30.
34. More in Chapter 3.
35. United States – *Aaron E. Levine & Co.* v. *Calkraft Paper Co.*, 429 F. Supp. 1039 (ED Mich. 1976).
36. More on this below.
37. Graupner, Rudolf (1969), 'Sole Distributorship Agreements: A Comparative View', *International and Comparative Law Quarterly* 18:4, 879–95; Yelpaala 1994.
38. Bradgate 2000, Chapter 3 (notably section 3.2.4); Christou 2003, Chapter 23; Staubach 1977: 229–30; Yelpaala 1994.
39. The relationship between principal and agent is covered in Chapter 5.
40. Bradgate 2000: 135.
41. Bradgate 2000: 133. See Chapter 5 for more on commission agents.
42. Bradgate 2000: 133.
43. Pursuant to the terms implied by §§ 13–15 Sales of Goods Act 1979 (English law).
44. Bradgate 2000: 135.
45. Yelpaala 1994.

NOTES

46. United States – *A. Gay Jenson Farms Co.* v. *Cargill Inc.* 309 NW 2d 285 (Minn. 1981).
47. *A. Gay Jenson Farms Co.* v. *Cargill Inc.* 309 NW 2d 285, 290.
48. Ibid.
49. Ibid. Here reference is made to the decision in *Larkin* v. *McCabe*, 211 Minn. 11, 299 NW 649 (1941).
50. *A. Gay Jenson Farms Co.* v. *Cargill Inc.* 309 NW 2d 285, 291.
51. *A. Gay Jenson Farms Co.* v. *Cargill Inc.* 309 NW 2d 285, 291–2. Here reference is made to Restatement (Second) of Agency §14K Comment a (1958).
52. *A. Gay Jenson Farms Co.* v. *Cargill Inc.* 309 NW 2d 285, 292.
53. More in Chapter 5.
54. More below.
55. As will be seen in Chapter 5, commercial agents are afforded certain protections under European Union law as a result of Council Directive 86/653/EEC of 18 December 1986 on the Coordination of the Laws of Member States relating to Self-employed Commercial Agents.
56. More in Chapter 5.
57. Murray et al. 2007: 808.
58. Ibid.
59. Bradgate 2000: 135.
60. See Chapter 5 for more on international agency agreements.
61. The DCFR is reviewed in Chapter 7.
62. Paragraph Intr. 7 DCFR (Introduction, paragraph 7).
63. Paragraph Intr. 8 DCFR.
64. Contained in Chapters 1 and 2 of Part E of Book IV (respectively).
65. Paragraph IV.E.–1:101(1) DCFR (Book IV, Part E, Chapter 1, Section 1, subsection 1, paragraph 1).
66. Ibid.
67. Paragraph IV.E.–1:101(2) DCFR.
68. Subsection IV.E.–2:101 DCFR.
69. Ibid.
70. Subsection IV.E.–2:201 DCFR.
71. Subsection IV.E.–2:202 DCFR.
72. Paragraph IV.E.–2:203(1) DCFR.
73. Paragraph IV.E.–2:203(2) DCFR.
74. Subsection IV.E.–2:301 DCFR.
75. Ibid.
76. Ibid.
77. Paragraph IV.E.–2:302(1) DCFR.
78. Paragraph IV.E.–2:302(2) DCFR.
79. Ibid. Calculation of the length of a reasonable period is addressed in subsection IV.E.–2:302. Calculation of damages for termination with inadequate notice is addressed in subsection IV.E.–2:303.
80. Subsection IV.E.–2:401 DCFR.
81. Subsection IV.E.–2:402 DCFR.

82. Subsection IV.E.–5:101 DCFR. This subsection also defines an exclusive distribution agreement and a selective distribution agreement.
83. Subsection IV.E.–5:201 DCFR.
84. Subsection IV.E.–5:202 DCFR.
85. Subsection IV.E.–5:203 DCFR.
86. Subsection IV.E.–5:301 DCFR.
87. Subsection IV.E.–5:304 DCFR.
88. Subsection IV.E.–5:302 DCFR.
89. Subsection IV.E.–5:303 DCFR.
90. Available at http://eur-lex.europa.eu/LexUriServ/LexUriServ.do?uri=OJ:L:2008:177:0006:0006:en:PDF (last accessed 21 January 2013).
91. Available at http://eur-lex.europa.eu/LexUriServ/LexUriServ. do? ur i= CELEX:41980A0934:EN:HTML (last accessed 21 January 2013).
92. Where states have several territorial units each of which has its own rules of law in relation to contractual obligations then each territorial unit will be treated as a country for the purposes of identifying the law applicable under Rome I (Article 22.1 Rome I).
93. Article 3 Rome I.
94. Article 3(1) Rome I.
95. Ibid.
96. Article 4(1)e Rome I.
97. Further reading on European competition law generally and specifically on Article 101 of the Treaty on the Functioning of the European Union (TFEU) and vertical agreements can be found in Jones, Alison and Sufrin, Brenda (2011), *EU Competition Law: Text, Cases, and Materials*, 4th ed., Oxford University Press.
98. The full text of Article 101 TFEU can be viewed at http://eur-lex.europa.eu/LexUriServ/LexUriServ.do?uri=OJ:C:2010:083:0047:0200:en:PDF (last accessed 11 February 2013).
99. For a detailed review of Article 101 see Jones and Sufrin (2011), Chapter 3.
100. Vertical agreements are addressed by two key instruments: firstly the Commission Notice Guidelines on Vertical Restraints SEC(2010)411 Final (the 2010 Guidelines), and secondly the Commission Regulation No. 330/2010 on the Application of Article 101(3) of the TFEU to Categories of Vertical Agreements and Concerted Practices (the 2010 Regulation). Vertical agreements are defined as 'agreements or concerted practices entered into between two or more undertakings each of which operates . . . at a different level of the production or distribution chain'. (Article 1, 2010 Regulation). See Jones, Alison and Sufrin, Brenda (2001), *EC Competition Law: Text, Cases and Materials*, Oxford University Press, 85; Cases 56/64 and 58/64 *Consten & Grundig* v. *Commission* [1966] ECR 299, [1966] CMLR 418.
101. The question of what constitutes a single economic entity is discussed in Jones and Sufrin (2011: 134–9).
102. Case C-73/95 *Viho Europe BV* v. *Commission* [1996] ECR I-5457, [1997] 4 CMLR 419.
103. More on this below.

104. Article 1(1), Council Regulation (EC) No 1/2003 of 16 December 2002 on the Implementation of the Rules on Competition Laid Down in Articles 81 and 82 of the Treaty (Regulation 1/2003). Article 101(3) TFEU is reviewed below.
105. Case 56/65 *Société Technique Minière* v. *Maschinenbau Ulm GmbH* [1966] ECR 235 (English). For further review, see Jones and Sufrin (2011), Chapter 15.
106. For a detailed review of the requirements see Jones and Sufrin (2011: 121).
107. For a review of the relationship between Articles 101(1) and 101(3) TFEU, see Jones and Sufrin (2011), Chapter 4.
108. Article 1(2) Regulation 1/2003.
109. Pursuant to Article 101(2) TFEU.
110. See inter alia judgments in Cases 56/64 & 58/64 *Consten & Grundig* v. *Commission* [1966] ECR 299, [1966] CMLR 418; Case 56/65 *Société Technique Minière* v. *Maschinenbau Ulm* [1966] ECR 235 (English); Case T-77/92 *Parker Pen Ltd* v. *Commission* [1994] ECR II-549.
111. Available at http://eur-lex.europa.eu/LexUriServ/LexUriServ.do?uri=OJ:L:2010:102:0001:0007:EN:PDF (last accessed 22 January 2013).
112. Available at http://eur-lex.europa.eu/LexUriServ/LexUriServ.do?uri=OJ:l:1999:336:0021:0025:en:PDF (last accessed 22 January 2013).
113. Article 10, 2010 Regulation.
114. Commission Notice Guidelines on Vertical Restraints SEC (2010) 411 Final (2010 Guidelines) is available at http://eur-lex.europa.eu/LexUriServ/LexUriServ.do?uri=SEC:2010:0411:FIN:EN:PDF (last accessed 22 January 2013).
115. Paragraph 12, 2010 Guidelines.
116. See judgments in Case T-325/01 *Daimler Chrysler AG* v. *Commission* [2005] ECR II-3319; Case C-217/05 *Confederación Española de Empresarios de Estaciones de Servicio* v. *CEPSA* [2006] ECR I-11987; Case C-279/06 *CEPSA Estaciones de Servicio SA* v. *LV Tobar e Hijos SL* [2008] ECR I-668.
117. According to the 2010 Guidelines.
118. A fuller review can be found in Yelpaala (1994: 870*ff.*).
119. Yelpaala 1994: 875, citing Hlavacek, James D. and McCuistion, Tommy J. (1983), 'Industrial Distributors: When, Who, and How?', *Harvard Business Review*, March, 96, 97.
120. Yelpaala 1994: 875, citing Hlavacek and McCuistion (1983: 97).
121. Yelpaala 1994: 870–1.
122. Yelpaala 1994: 875.
123. Ibid., citing Hlavacek and McCuistion (1983: 96).
124. For further discussion of this point, see Yelpaala (1994), footnotes 101 and 102.
125. Yelpaala 1994: 875, citing Hlavacek and McCuistion (1983: 97).
126. See the sections dedicated to documentary collections and letters of credit in Chapter 3.
127. *Sport International Bussum BV* v. *Hi Tec Sports Ltd* (No. 1) [1988] RPC 329.
128. See Chapter 3.
129. The General Conditions are reproduced in Bortolotti, Fabio (2008), *Drafting and Negotiating International Commercial Agreements: A Practical Guide*, International Chamber of Commerce, 353–8.

130. This topic is reviewed further in Shippey (1999), Chapter 19; Murray et al. (2007), Chapter 30; Christou (2003), Chapters 4 and 5; Staubach (1977: 229–30). See also Meek (1966); Meek and Feltham (1967); Graupner (1969); Jones (1972); Salter (1971); Puelinckx and Tielemans (1981); Saltoun and Spudis (1983); Berwind (1983); Handel (1992); Yelpaala (1994).
131. For background see Chapters 2 and 3.
132. More in Chapter 2.
133. More in Chapter 2.
134. More in Chapter 2.
135. See also 'Improvements and modifications to the goods' below.
136. For a further review, see discussion at the start of this chapter and Murray et al. (2007: 806).
137. Christou 2003: 175.
138. Ibid.
139. For a further review, see discussion at the start of this Chapter.
140. For a further review, see discussion at the start of this Chapter.
141. For a further review, see discussion at the start of this Chapter.
142. In English law, *Decro-Wall International SA* v. *Practitioners in Marketing Ltd* [1971] 2 All E.R. 216; (1970) 115 S.J. 171; [1971] 1 WLR 361; *Martin-Baker Aircraft Co. Ltd* v. *Canadian Flight Equipment Ltd* [1955] 2 QB. 556, at 571.
143. Christou 2004: 195.
144. Ibid.
145. A review of implied warranties is provided in Chapter 3.
146. For a review of the CISG, see Chapter 7. Case law generally distinguishes between distribution agreements and sales agreements with regard to the application of the CISG. Whilst sales agreements are treated as falling within the scope of the CISG, distribution agreements are not (Appellate Court in Germany 11 July 1996, Appellate Court in Düsseldorf (lawn mower engines case) http://cisgw3.law.pace.edu/cases/96071191.html).
147. Article 35 CISG, which address conformity of goods, states: '1. The seller must deliver goods which are of the quantity, quality and description required by the contract and which are contained or packaged in the manner required by the contract. 2. Except where the parties have agreed otherwise, the goods do not conform with the contract unless they: a. are fit for the purposes for which goods of the same description would ordinarily be used; b. are fit for any particular purpose expressly or impliedly made known to the seller at the time of the conclusion of the contract, except where the circumstances show that the buyer did not rely, or that it was unreasonable for him to rely, on the seller's skill and judgement; c. possess the qualities of goods which the seller has held out to the buyer as a sample or model; d. are contained or packaged in the manner usual for such goods or, where there is no such manner, in a manner adequate to preserve and protect the goods.'
148. Christou 2003: 196.
149. Ibid.
150. Christou 2003: 197.
151. Ibid.

152. Christou 2003: 186.
153. Ibid.
154. A detailed review of the obligations of the distributor is provided in Christou (2003: 175–86).
155. Christou 2003: 193.
156. Christou 2003: 176.
157. Christou 2003: 193.
158. Christou 2003: 176.
159. Christou 2003: 177.
160. Ibid.
161. Christou 2003: 178.
162. Christou 2003: 187.
163. Christou 2003: 178–9.
164. Christou 2003: 186.
165. Ibid.
166. Christou 2003: 188.
167. Christou 2003: 187.
168. See relevant section at the start of this chapter. Retail price maintenance is discussed in detail in Jones and Sufrin (2011: 656). In Case 161/84 *Pronuptia de Paris GmbH* v. *Pronuptia de Paris Irmgard Schillgallis* [1986] ECR 353, paragraph 25, the Court of Justice of the European Union held that provisions that undermine the freedom of a franchisee to set his own prices would be trade restrictive. In case 26/76 *Metro SB-Großmärkte GmbH & Co. KG* v. *Commission of the European Communities* [1977] ECR 1875, paragraph 21, the Court of Justice of the European Union stated that price competition was so important that it cannot be eliminated.
169. Jones and Sufrin 2011: 657.
170. Ibid., citing Case 161/84 *Pronuptia de Paris GmbH* v. *Pronuptia de Paris Irmgard Schillgallis* [1986] ECR 353, paragraph 25.
171. Christou 2003: 189.
172. Christou 2003: 190–2.
173. Christou 2003: 191.
174. Ibid.
175. Christou 2003: 190.
176. Further discussion can be found at the start of this Chapter, in the section that reviews the factors that need to be taken into account when choosing between an agent and distributor.
177. Christou 2003: 192.
178. See also corresponding section in Chapter 3.
179. Christou 2003: 200.
180. Ibid.
181. See corresponding section in Chapter 3 for a review of the provisions in this section. The terms 'Buyer' and 'Seller' should be replaced with 'Distributor' and 'Principal' respectively. A review of the effects of termination can be found in Christou (2003: 201-3).

5
International Agency Agreements[1]

Contents

Overview 164
Glossary 165
I Agency arrangements – when and why? 166
II Fundamentals of agency law 166
III Common types of agency relationship 167
IV The sources of law governing the agency relationship 168
V Governing law under European Union law 169
VI Formation of the agency agreement 170
VII Creation of an agency relationship 171
VIII Consequences of agency 173
IX Termination of the agency agreement 175
X Liability of the principal to the third party 175
XI Disclosed and undisclosed agency 179
XII Civil law contrasted with common law 180
XIII General concerns of the parties 180
XIV Agency agreements under EU law 184
XV Agency law and international instruments 187
XVI Checklist of provisions 191
XVII Front of the contract 192
XVIII Body of the contract 193
XIX Boilerplate clauses and back of the contract 215
Summary 216
Useful links 217
Further reading 217
Notes 218

Overview

This chapter looks at the various issues that concern international agency agreements.

Firstly, it looks at the fundamental characteristics of the agency relationship. In this context, a review is given of the use and structure of this set-up, the distinction between independent and dependent agents, the sources of law governing this set-up, formation of the agency agreement, the methods used to create the agency relationship, termination of the agency agreement, the liability of the principal to the third party and the concerns of the different parties involved in the agency set-up.

Secondly, this chapter examines the treatment of commercial agency arrangements under European Union law. In this context, a review is given of the protections invoked under the directive governing commercial agents (Council Directive 86/653/EEC of 18 December 1986 on the Coordination of the Laws of the Member States relating to Self-employed Commercial Agents). Thirdly, this chapter looks at the key provisions that the contracting parties should consider including within an international agency agreement, their purpose and proposed wording.

By the end of this chapter the reader will have a better understanding of

- the law governing agency relationships;
- the provisions that the contracting parties should consider including within their agency agreement; and
- the purpose and proposed wording of each provision.

Glossary

Agent In certain circumstances, a person (juristic or natural) will appoint another (the **agent**) to act on its or his or her behalf in relation to certain tasks. The former is the **principal** and the latter is the **agent**. The **agent** may act on behalf of the **principal** in order to bring about legal relations between the **principal** and another person (the third party) or persons (third parties).

Artificial person See **juristic person**.

Broker In English law, a party entrusted with negotiation of contracts on behalf of the principal. The broker will not be given possession of the goods.

Commercial agent A self-employed **agent** with a continuing authority to negotiate or to negotiate and conclude contracts for the sale or purchase of goods on behalf of the principal and in the name of the principal.

Commission agent An **agent** who buys or sells goods on behalf of the principal but has no authority to create privity of contract between the principal and the third party.[2]

Del credere agent An **agent** who negotiates contracts for the principal and in turn guarantees to the principal that the third party (or parties) will pay all sums due to the principal under the contract.

Disclosed agency An agency is disclosed when the third party is aware that the **agent** is an agent, whether the principal has been named (named principal) or not (unnamed principal).

Estoppel A bar raised by the law that stops a person from alleging or from denying a certain fact or a certain set of facts, on account of the person's previous statement or conduct or as a result of a final adjudication of the matter by a court of law.[3]

Factor (or **mercantile agent**) An **agent** whose business it is to sell goods, consign goods for the purpose of sale, buy goods or raise money on the security of goods, on behalf of the principal.

Juristic person (or **artificial person**) An entity that is regarded as having legal personality. Under English law, a corporation is regarded as a juristic person.

Mercantile agent See **factor**.

Natural person A human being.

Notarisation In certain jurisdictions, the signing of the contract needs to be notarised. Which effective means that a notary public is required to certify to the vailidity of a signature on the contract.

Principal In certain circumstances, a person (juristic or natural) will appoint another to act on its or his or her behalf in relation to certain tasks. The former is the **principal** and the latter is the **agent**.

Third party The **agent** may act on behalf of the **principal** in order to bring about legal relations between the **principal** and another person (the **third party**) or persons (**third parties**).

Undisclosed agency An agency is undisclosed when the third party believes the **agent** is acting on his own behalf rather than representing another.

I Agency arrangements – when and why?[4]

Many businesses use intermediaries to handle transactions on their behalf with others. An **agent** is one such intermediary.

Agency in English law is a legal relationship involving three parties: the principal, the agent and the third party.[5] In English law, the agent acts on behalf of another person (the **principal**) in order to affect legal relations between the principal and another person (the **third party**) or other persons (**third parties**). Dealings between the principal and the agent may be for a single transaction or on an ongoing or permanent basis.

Agents are selected for their expertise and understanding of a market, service or commodity[6] and are used in order to save costs and in an effort to overcome the fact that the principal is not able to be physically present to source a client and indeed to conclude a contract. This may happen because the principal is a **juristic person** and as such is reliant on natural persons to do its bidding or where the principal is a **natural person** and is unable to be physically present in a number of places at the same time. As Diplock LJ stated, 'a corporation cannot do any act, and that includes making a representation, except through its agent'.[7] Entities that are regarded as having legal personality are juristic persons (or **artificial persons**). Under English law, a corporation is regarded as a juristic person. A human being is a natural person.

Agents may be used for an array of purposes. They may be responsible for marketing goods and services. In the alternative, they may be responsible for sourcing clients for the principal with the principal assuming responsibility for negotiating and then concluding the contract with the given client. On occasion, an agent will be responsible not only for sourcing the client but also for negotiating and concluding contracts with the said client on behalf of the principal. Sometimes agents will be used to source and buy goods or services for the principal.

> Very few persons are able to transact all their business, supply all their wants and accomplish all their purposes, without sometimes employing another person to represent them, and act for them, and in their stead. Such person becomes their agent, and the person employing an agent is his principal.[8]

Care must be exercised when using the terms 'agent' or 'agency' since both terms have legal ramifications (powers, rights and duties). Not all parties referred to in commercial parlance as agents are in fact agents in the legal sense. Conversely parties who are not referred to as agents may in fact be deemed agents in law.

II Fundamentals of agency law[9]

A three-sided relationship

Three different and distinct parties are involved in an agency arrangement: the agent, the principal and the third party. Such parties may be natural persons or juristic persons. Agency permits one party (the principal) to contract with another (the third party) from a distance using the services of the agent, who acts on behalf of and for the benefit of the principal. The agent can be viewed as an 'instrument of the principal'; the principal authorises the agent to carry out certain acts in its stead with the principal assuming the relations produced, acquiring the resulting rights and incurring the resulting obligations (these are effectively treated as an extension of the principal's acts).

The agent assumes no responsibilities under the contract

It is important to stress that the role of the agent is that of facilitator: whilst he is instrumental in concluding the contract (as he is, for example, responsible for securing the order of the third party, for introducing the parties to each other, or for negotiating and concluding the contract between the principal and the third party), he usually has no responsibilities under the contract and is not a party to the ensuing contract.

One-off or more permanent arrangement

The agent may be acting on a one-off basis or on a more permanent basis. He may be an employee of the principal or contracted to the principal for a certain purpose.

Three distinct relationships[10]

Agency will involve three distinct relationships:

1. the principal–agent relationship
2. the agent–third party relationship
3. the principal–third party relationship.

The first relationship (principal–agent) is the contract of agency and settles the rights and responsibilities of the agent and principal. The third relationship (principal–third party) is an ordinary sale contract, though it may be affected by the fact that the seller entered into the sale agreement through the efforts of an agent. The second relationship (agent–third party) will only occur in exceptional situations.[11]

Box 5.1 Examples of agency relationships

Agency relationships exist where the following are involved: sales agents, officers and directors of companies, and professional agency agreements involving lawyers, accountants and auditors.

An estate agent appointed to take charge of the rental of property by the owner of the property will be acting as an agent for the owner (the principal). Whilst the tenants renting the said property (the third parties) will deal with the agent rather than the principal, any contract concluded with the tenants will give rise to rights and obligations from the point of view of the principal.

A director of a corporation charged with employing members of staff will be an agent for the corporation for which he works. In dealings with members of staff, the director will be representing the corporation as principal. Any contracts of employment concluded by the director on behalf of the corporation will bind the corporation.

III Common types of agency relationship[12]

Factors and brokers

In English law, the term **factor** (or **mercantile agent**) is used to describe an agent whose business involves the sale of goods, the consignment of goods for the purpose of sale, the acquisition of goods or the raising of capital (on the security of goods), on behalf of the principal.[13] To this end the factor is given possession of the goods. In contrast, the term **broker** is used in English law to refer to a party entrusted with negotiation of contracts on behalf of the principal. The broker will not be given possession of the goods.

Legally speaking the distinction

between a broker and a factor is important in English law as the law grants factors certain statutory powers.[14] Where a factor possesses goods or the documents of title to goods with the consent of the principal, he may sell, pledge or otherwise dispose of them in the ordinary course of business as if he had the principal's express authorisation to do so, so long as the recipient of the goods acts in good faith and is not aware at the time of the transaction that the factor has no authority to carry out the transaction.[15]

Del credere agents[16]

A **del credere agent** will negotiate contracts for the principal and will in turn guarantee to the principal that the third party will pay all sums due to the principal under the contract. Such a guarantee will be important when the third party is not known to the principal. The del credere agent will receive a higher commission in exchange for extending such a guarantee to the principal.

Commission agents[17]

A **commission agent** buys or sells goods on behalf of the principal but has no authority to create privity of contract between the principal and the third party with whom he deals. Vis-à-vis the third party, the agent effectively contracts in his own right. For this reason, the commission agent is contractually liable to the third party. Nevertheless, a commission agent owes the principal the same duties that are ordinarily owed by an agent to his principal. A commission agent thus falls between an agent in the true sense of the word and an independent contractor who buys and resells the goods in his own right. Such a set-up is typical in civil law systems and is recognisable to a certain degree in common law systems.[18]

Commercial agents[19]

A **commercial agent** is a self-employed agent with a continuing authority to negotiate or negotiate and conclude contracts for the sale or purchase of goods on behalf of the principal and in the name of the principal.

IV The sources of law governing the agency relationship

> **Box 5.2 The sources of law governing the agency relationship**
> Agency relationships are governed by
> 1. the contract between the parties (here the agent and the principal);
> 2. national law, and
> 3. international law (including EU law)

The agency relationship will be governed in different and distinct ways. Firstly, the relationship between agent and principal is governed by the terms of the agreement concluded between them (the agency agreement). In order to avoid legal difficulties further down the line, it is advisable to draw up a written contract. This contract will not only be evidence of the terms agreed between the parties, but will also clearly delineate the authority vested by the principal in the agent.

Beyond the contract concluded by the parties, the relationship between principal and agent is governed by the law of the country where the agent is based. It may also be governed in certain circumstances by regional law and indeed international law. The law governing the relationship may be specific (the law governing agency) or more general in application, so that the law governing contracts may also impact on the agency relationship. The relationship between a principal and a commercial agent both operating in England will be governed not only by the terms of the contract concluded between them but also by European Union law, which affects the relationship between the principal and commercial agent in a situation where the agent is based in a member state of the European Union (such as the United Kingdom).

Occasionally the relationship between the principal and agent will be affected by the law in the jurisdictions in which the principal and the third party are respectively located. Such laws may impose certain obligations on the agent as well as granting the agent certain rights, by protecting his stream of revenue and providing him with job security.

V Governing law under European Union law

In the European Union, the contract between the principal and the agent will be governed by Regulation (EC) No 593/2008 of the European Parliament and the Council of 17 June 2008 on the Law Applicable to Contractual Obligations (Rome I).[20]

Freedom to choose the governing law

Whilst the contracting parties are free to choose the law applicable to the contract between them,[21] if they do not do so, Rome I will intercede to make the selection for them in accordance with the rules set out in Article 4.

Article 3.1 of Rome I permits the parties contracting to choose the law governing their contract. The parties may choose the law applicable to the whole of their contract or alternatively to just part of it.[22] Furthermore, Article 3.2 permits the parties contracting to modify by agreement the law governing the contract. Any such selection must be made expressly or clearly demonstrated by the terms of the contract or the circumstances of the case.[23]

Wherever possible, it is advisable for the contracting parties to expressly identify the law that they have chosen to govern the contract concluded between them. This will ensure certainty and clarity in their relationship and will ward against any potential litigation that could later ensue on this very question.

In the absence of a choice by the parties

Article 4.1 of Rome I sets out specific choice of law rules for particular categories of cases. Where Article 4.1 does not supply a conclusive choice of law then the general rule articulated in Article 4.2 applies. Further general displacement rules – included in Articles 4.3 and 4.4 – are intended to introduce flexibility in those situations where the application of one of the specific choice of law rules does not produce the appropriate result.

Pursuant to Article 4.1 a contract for the sale of goods is governed by the law of the country where the seller has his habitual residence[24] whereas a contract for the provision of services is governed by the law of the country where the service provider has his habitual residence.[25] Pursuant to Article 19 of Rome I, which defines the phrase 'habitual residence', where a contract is concluded in the course of the operations of a branch, agency or any other establishment, or if, under the contract, performance is the responsibility of such a branch, agency or establishment, the place where the branch, agency or any other establishment is located shall be treated as the place of habitual residence. For the purposes of determining the habitual residence, the relevant point in time shall be the time of the conclusion of the contract.

VI Formation of the agency agreement[26]

An agency relationship is a 'consensual relationship in which one (the agent) holds in trust for and subject to the control of another (the principal) a power to affect certain legal relations of that other'.[27] In this statement, the phrase 'in trust for' is taken to mean 'for the benefit of',[28] whilst the term 'control' encompasses 'the idea of consent by the principal'.[29]

The agent has the power to act on behalf of the principal and may in turn impact on the legal position of the principal.[30] The relationship that exists between the principal and the third party (the external relationship) will in turn depend on the scope of the power of the agent, whilst the relationship that exists between the principal and the agent (the internal relationship) will depend upon consent.[31] In law, the agent is treated as having the power to act on behalf of the principal when the principal has consented to the agent having such power. In such a situation, the agent is said to possess the 'authority' to act on behalf of the principal.[32]

In law, the agent may also be treated as having the power to act on behalf of the principal, even when the principal has not expressly consented to the agent having such power.[33] There are four scenarios where the law recognises the agent as having the power to bind the principal:

1. in a situation where the principal has granted advance consent to the actions of the agent (in which case the agent has 'actual authority');
2. in a situation where acts carried out in the name of the principal but without his authority are consented to by the principal after the fact (through the process of ratification);
3. in a situation where the agent acts without the consent of the principal, but the law regards the principal as having consented (agency of necessity); and
4. in a situation where the agent acts without the consent of the principal but the principal is not permitted to deny the authority of the agent (the agent is said to possess 'apparent authority').[34]

The trend is to define the power of the agent to bind the principal, even when the principal has not consented to the actions of the agent, in terms of the different categories of authority (more below).

Scope of authority

The agent acts for and represents the principal and the principal will delegate a portion of its power to the agent to enable him to do so. The question of whether the agent acts properly will depend on the scope of authority extended by the principal to its agent. Such authority will be either contractual or implied.[35]

The relationship between principal and agent determines not only their respective rights and obligations, but also the rights and obligations of the third party. Where an agent contracts with a third party, the question will arise as to whether the third party's interest is affected by an agent acting within the authority granted to him by his principal. In the event that the agent acts outside such authority, then the agent may be personally liable to the third party.

VII Creation of an agency relationship[36]

An agency relationship may be created in a number of ways, directly through the express appointment of an agent and, to a certain degree, by means of ratification, or indirectly by implication, out of necessity or as a result of the doctrine of estoppel.

Box 5.3 The ways in which an agency relationship is created

Direct	Indirect
Express appointment (before the fact)	Agency by implication
Ratification (after the fact)	Agency out of necessity
	Agency by means of estoppel

Express appointment[37]

The most common type of principal–agent relationship will arise where the principal specifically appoints the agent for a certain purpose or more generally. In the case of a corporation, for example, directors will be appointed to represent the corporation on a daily basis, whilst from time to time certain unique powers will be delegated by the board of the directors to a specific director.

In certain jurisdictions, the contract with the agent will need to be written and yet still, on occasion, such contracts will also need to be notarised. In other jurisdictions, the appointment of an agent may be made verbally. Where the agent is given the power to execute deeds in the name of the principal, then he may need to be appointed by means of a deed (known as a power of attorney).

Ratification[38]

An agency created by ratification will occur where a person who has no authority purports to contract with a third party on behalf of a purported principal. Ratification will permit an act done by a person not assuming to act for himself but for the other, though without any precedent authority, to be regarded as the act of the principal, provided the principal subsequently ratifies the act in question.[39] Ratification will be by means of subsequent and retrospective acceptance by the purported principal of the said contract executed by the purported agent with the third party.

Agency by implication[40]

An action of the agent is implicitly authorised when even though the action is not sanctioned by the express agreement between the agent and the principal, the principal is regarded as having given implied consent to the action in question.[41] Agency by implication may come about in a number of ways.[42] In the most extreme situation, the appointment of the agent may be wholly implicit. More commonly, the authority of an agent who is expressly appointed may be extended by implication, so that an agent who is provided with express authority to execute a certain task has additional authority to do such acts that are reasonably incidental to enabling him to execute his authorised task.[43]

Agency out of necessity[44]

When an emergency requires one party to take action on behalf of another in order to protect the interests of the latter, it is possible that agency may arise out of necessity. Agency out of necessity may occur where there is no agency agreement in place (thereby creating an agency relationship where none previously existed) or in a situation where, though there is an agency agreement in place, the surrounding circumstances call for the agent to exceed his authority.

Agency by means of estoppel[45]

Agency by means of estoppel occurs where the principal has led a third party to believe that a certain person has the authority to represent the interests of the principal. The authority possessed by that person, the apparent agent, is apparent authority. Even though no agency relationships actually exist between the principal and the apparent agent, by operation of the law the principal is not permitted to deny the existence of the principal–agent relationship. In other words, the principal is estopped from denying the existence of the agency relationship. In turn, the principal is bound by the acts of the apparent agent vis-à-vis the third party, which acted on the belief that an agency relationship existed.

In order for agency by estoppel to arise certain conditions must be fulfilled. Firstly, the principal must have made a representation in relation to the authority of the agent which the third party relied upon. Secondly, the acts of those who take it upon themselves to act for the corporation must be within the limits of their apparent authority. Thirdly, the party seeking to rely on estoppel must do so in good faith.

Box 5.4 Corporations and their agents (scenario one)

When a contract is concluded by the secretary of a corporation ostensibly for the benefit of the corporation for which he is secretary and the corporation then refuses to respect this contract, the question that the third party is confronted with is: what rights, if any, does he have against the corporation?

A corporation secretary hired cars ostensibly for the corporation for which he was secretary, from a car hire firm. However, he ended up using these cars himself and not for the business of the corporation. The hire charges were not paid and the hire firm sued the corporation for these charges. The corporation denied liability for the charges. On appeal it was held that the corporation secretary had ostensible authority to conclude hire contracts and that the corporation was obliged to respect those hire contracts. Accordingly the corporation was obliged to pay for the hire. The reasoning of the court was that a corporation secretary has implied (ostensible) authority to enter into contracts in the name of the corporation in the context of the daily running of the corporation[46] and may be regarded as held out as having authority to do such things on behalf of the corporation. As such he is entitled to sign contracts connected with the administrative side of the affairs of a corporation, such as the employment of staff and the ordering of cars for the corporation.[47]

Box 5.5 Corporations and their agents (scenario two)

In *Freeman & Lockyer v. Buckhurst Park Properties Ltd*,[48] a director of a corporation had contracted with a firm of architects (the plaintiff in this case). Once the firm had completed its work it looked to the corporation for payment of its fees. The corporation challenged this claim, arguing that the director himself was responsible for the fees. The director in question regularly contracted on behalf of the corporation as if he were its managing director even though the directors of the corporation had never appointed him as such and had not delegated to him any of their powers. Nevertheless, the other directors of the corporation were aware of the conduct of the director in question and acquiesced in it. Furthermore, they did not challenge the authority of the director in question and did nothing to correct the false impression given by this director to others.[49]

On appeal, it was ruled that the corporation was liable for the fees of the plaintiff, as the act of engaging the plaintiff fell within the ordinary scope of authority of a managing director and the plaintiff was not required to check whether the director had been appointed, as from the perspective of the plaintiff it was enough that under the articles of association there was a power to appoint the director as such. The agent whose authority was relied on had been acting to the knowledge of the corporation as a managing director and the act of contracting with the plaintiff had been one that fell within the ambit of the powers of a managing director in the transaction of the affairs of the corporation.[50]

Willmer LJ referred to the words of Lopes LJ,[51] who stated that a corporation is bound by the acts of those who take it upon themselves to act for the corporation with the knowledge of the directors. So long as such persons are acting within the limits of their apparent authority and that the strangers deal on a bona fide basis with such persons then they have the right to assume that such persons have been duly appointed. Willmer LJ stated that a party seeking to set up an estoppel must show that it relied on the alleged representation (whether this representation was given in words or through conduct),[52] adding that where an act is one ordinarily within the powers of a certain officer then the corporation cannot dispute the authority of the officer to do the act, whether the directors had or had not actually invested the officer in question with authority to do the act.

In conclusion, Willmer LJ indicated that the plaintiff relied on the fact that the director was acting throughout as a managing director, to the knowledge of the board of directors of the corporation, and was therefore being held out by the board as a managing director. The act of the director in engaging the plaintiff was clearly within the scope of authority of a managing director and for this reason the plaintiff did not need to verify whether the director had been appointed properly. From the point of view of the plaintiff, it was sufficient that under the articles of the corporation there was in fact the power to appoint the director as a managing director.

VIII Consequences of agency[53]

A number of consequences will ensue from the creation of an agency relationship. Besides the fact that the principal will acquire certain rights and obligations in relation to third parties, contractual or otherwise, the existence of the agency relationship will result in substantive obligations and rights between the parties themselves (the agent and the principal).

Rights and obligations from the point of view of the principal

The first consequence of the creation of an agency relationship is that in law the agent will be recognised as being able to affect the legal position of the principal, creating by his actions rights and obligations enforceable both by the principal and against the principal. As an exception to the doctrine of privity,[54] the agent is able to conclude contracts on behalf of the principal that are in turn treated in law as contracts of the principal himself. Accordingly such contracts may be enforced by and against the principal.

In addition, the acts of the agent have the potential of affecting the principal in a variety of other ways. The agent is, for example, capable of making statements that will bind the principal contractually and otherwise. Moreover, if the agent bribes a foreign official, such acts may render the principal criminally liable.[55]

In the event that non-conforming goods are sold, the ultimate customer will typically have a right to sue the principal directly and the agent will usually bear no liability to the ultimate customer. Where goods are sold by an agent, they will remain the property of the principal until they are sold. As such contracts with customers are enforceable directly by the principal, which can then claim the sums owing directly from the customer.

Sums received by the agent from the customer are held by him in his fiduciary capacity, in which case such sums are also treated as the property of the principal. This is important if the agent happens to become insolvent, as in such a situation the principal will be in a legal position to recoup the goods held by the agent. It can also claim the proceeds of sales collected by the agent by means of a proprietary claim, as opposed to having to pursue a claim as a creditor (of the agent).

The relationship between the agent and the principal[56]

The second consequence of the creation of an agency relationship is that the law will impose obligations on the principal and the agent vis-à-vis the third party and extend rights to the principal as well as the agent in relation to each other. The agent will acquire a fiduciary position vis-à-vis the principal and as such will owe the principal certain duties. The agent for his part will be extended certain rights in law by virtue of the agency relationship.[57] At common law, an agent has the right to be indemnified against expenses incurred in the course of representing the principal. The agent in common law may also have the right to be paid for his work.

Consensual and non-consensual

The third consequence of the creation of an agency relationship is the assumption of consent between the parties. It is worth noting here that in law the parties may be deemed to have consented to an agency relationship without their express agreement to this effect or without them even realising it.[58]

Box 5.6 A master's liability for the criminal acts of his servant

A butcher employed an assistant who was charged with preparing parcels for clients and ticketing them. Whilst the butcher was absent, the assistant affixed tickets to the parcels which displayed overcharges. Both butcher and assistant were charged. Whilst the assistant was convicted, informations against the butcher were dismissed.

The prosecutor appealed on the grounds that the butcher was vicariously liable for the acts of his servant, the servant having breached an express statutory provision containing an absolute prohibition requiring no knowledge. Parliament, the prosecution submitted, placed on the seller of meat an absolute duty not to allow even an act that was preparatory to the sale of the meat at an overcharge.

The question on appeal that the court posed was whether a master could be liable for the acts of his servant in such a set of circumstances.[59] A master who is not *particeps criminis* (an accomplice in crime) can be criminally liable for acts committed by his servant only in a situation where the wording of the statute creating the offence does so in terms which impose an absolute prohibition, in which case the question of knowledge or intent will not arise as the state of mind of the perpetrator will be deemed irrelevant.[60] This will not mean that a master will necessarily be criminally liable if his servant commits an act which is forbidden by law, as liability will depend on whether the wording of the statute imposes liability in such a situation.[61]

Parker J stated that liability in such a case will depend on the application of a principle articulated in an earlier case[62] by Atkin J to the facts of the present case.[63] According to Atkin J, whilst prima facie a principal is not to be deemed liable in criminal law for acts of his servant, legislation forbidding an act or imposing a duty may use words that render the act forbidden or the duty imposed absolute, in which case the principal is liable if the act is performed by his servants. Regard must be had to the following in order to determine the impact of the legislation: the aim of the legislation, the wording employed in the provision or provisions, the attributes of the duty, the person upon whom the duty is imposed, the person by whom the duty would ordinarily be performed and the person upon whom the penalty is imposed.

Upon reading the legislation in light of the principle enunciated by Atkin J, Parker J ruled in the present case that so far as the provisions in this case are concerned both knowledge and intent are necessary components to constitute an offence and are in turn needed for both an attempt and a preparatory act to the commission of the substantive offence.[64]

IX Termination of the agency agreement[65]

The agency agreement may be terminated by operation of the law or by the parties themselves. The agency arrangement may come to an end if

1. the term agreed on by the parties has come to an end;[66]
2. an event has occurred upon which termination of the agency has been made contingent;[67] or
3. the agent has completed the task which he was assigned under the agency agreement.

X Liability of the principal to the third party[68]

Box 5.7 Situations where principal will be liable to a third party for the acts of an agent

The principal will be liable to a third party for the acts of the agent in a number of situations:
1. if the agent has actual authority (which may be expressed or implied)
2. if the agent has apparent (ostensible) authority to act for and to bind the principal
3. if there has been a ratification of the unauthorised acts of the agent
4. if agency emerges out of necessity.

The agent will need to have authority to contract in order to bind his principal, thus providing the third party with the means to take legal action under the contract not only against the agent but also against the agent's principal. An agent will bind a

he has actual authority. The most direct manner in which an agent is entrusted with authority occurs where the principal confers authority on an agent.

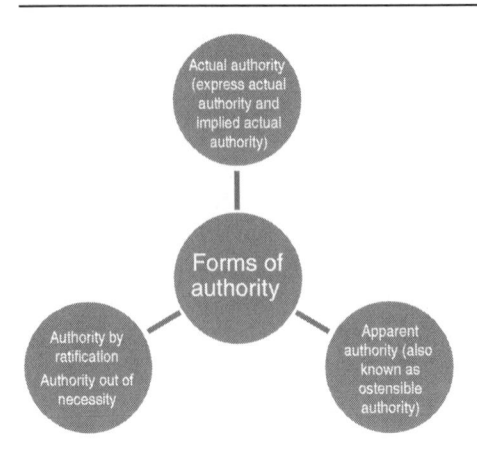

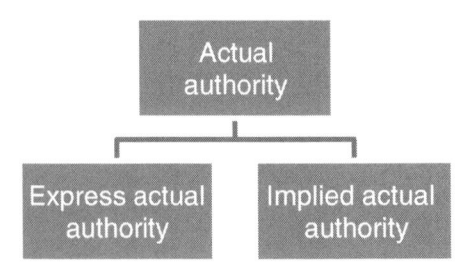

In English law, traditionally there have been no formal requirements for the appointment of an agent, though an agent appointed to execute a deed will need to be appointed by means of a power of attorney. This traditional stance must now be considered in light of Article 13 of the Council of the European Communities' Directive 86/653,[70] which imposes some formalities where a commercial agent is engaged. According to this article, the agent and the principal are entitled to receive from the other on request a signed written document setting out the terms of the agency contract. Exclusion of this right is not permitted.

Actual authority is of two kinds: express actual authority or implied actual authority.

Express actual authority[71]

The grant of authority to the agent may be expressly made by deed, in writing or verbally (though the latter will typically entail evidential problems). As such authority is explicitly granted by the principal to the agent.

The principal and agent will often agree that there is an agency arrangement between them and may agree on the terms of the arrangement, including the agent's tasks and powers (other terms will include the term of the agreement, remuneration of the agent, the responsibilities of the principal and so forth). The scope of the agency agreement will be governed by these terms as well as by the rules of contractual construction.[72]

Implied actual authority[73]

Where the agreement between principal and agent does not expressly cover all

principal to contracts that the agent has entered into, when the agent has actual authority, the agent has apparent authority or the principal ratifies the unauthorised actions of the agent. Where authority is either expressly given or implied by law it is essential to determine its extent, scope and duration.

Whilst express actual authority will arise as a result of an agreement between the agent and the principal, for the remaining forms of authority, the agency relationship will arise even if there is no such agreement or where there is such an agreement but the agent has exceeded the scope of the authority vested in him by the agreement, in other words where he has exceeded the actual authority given to him.

Actual authority[69]

An agent is able to bind his principal to contracts entered into by the agent if aspects of the agent's role, authority may be implied, in which case the agent is said to possess implied actual authority. Implied actual authority will permit the scope of express authority to be extended, so that the third party can assume that an agent in a certain position has all the powers ordinarily extended to such an agent. Without actual knowledge to the contrary, the third party can assume the agent has the usual authority associated with such a position.

The scope of implied actual authority is determined by examining the factual context, in other words by examining the relationship between the parties, the conduct of the parties, the circumstances surrounding the appointment of the agent, the manner in which the agent has conducted and continues to conduct business on the principal's behalf as well as the events surrounding the transaction concerned.[74] Moreover reference may be made to the custom generally adopted in the particular trade.[75]

The agent may perform acts that are incidental to those acts that are expressly authorised. The implied authority that the agent possess will permit him to carry out acts which are either necessary for, or ordinarily incidental in the normal course of things to the performance of, acts which have been authorised by the principal.[76] Such acts must be reasonable and should not conflict with the scope of the agent's express actual authority.

Box 5.8 The actual authority of the corporation director and its impact

The actual authority of a corporation director may be express or implied. It will be express if the director has been given specific authority by the corporation to carry out certain tasks. For example this could occur when the board of directors passes a resolution that permits two directors to sign cheques.[77] The actual authority will be implied if a director has been appointed to some office which carries with it authority to conclude contracts of a certain kind, or when the board of directors appoints one of their own to be managing director, in which case the board is implicitly authorising the managing director to carry out all tasks that fall within the usual scope of the office of managing director.[78]

Actual authority, whether it takes the express form or the implied form, will be binding between the corporation and the agent and between the corporation and third parties, whether these third parties are within the corporation (employees of the corporation for example) or outside the corporation (contractors for example).

Apparent authority (ostensible authority)

Box 5.9 Characteristics of ostensible or apparent authority

Ostensible or apparent authority is
1. the authority of an agent as it appears to others[79] (the authority which the agent appears to possess but which has not actually been granted to him by the principal);
2. intended to protect the third party; and
3. based on
   a. words of the principal;
   b. acts of the principal; or
   c. the knowledge that the principal has allowed the agent to engage in certain activities over a lengthy period.

In those situations where the third party does not know exactly what, if any, authority the agent possesses, it will need to rely on the authority of the agent as it appears to be.[80] Whereas actual authority, express and implied, is based on the agreement between the principal and the agent, to which the third party is not privy, apparent authority will be based on representations that the principal has made to the third party that do not involve the agent.[81]

In many commercial transactions when concluding a contract the third party will be relying on apparent rather than actual authority.[82] In order to determine the scope of the apparent authority vested in the agent reference needs to be made to dealings between the third party and the principal. Apparent authority will be based on whether a third party enters into a contract in reliance on an appearance created by the principal that the agent has authority.

Box 5.10 Liability of entity for representations made to third parties illustrated

Where an entity makes a representation to a third party that a particular person has authority to act as the entity's agent without actually appointing that person as its agent, the entity making the representation will then be bound by the actions of the apparent agent. It will be liable for the acts of an apparent agent where it knew that the apparent agent was claiming to be its agent and it did nothing to correct this flawed impression.[83]

Ratification

Where an entity contracts an agent in circumstances where he has neither actual nor apparent authority, the putative principal may ratify the actions of the purported agent, thus taking on the contractual rights and obligations incurred by him. In such a case, the principal is bound by the act of ratification, whether the act is detrimental or advantageous to it.[84] Ratification has a retrospective effect;[85] as such the act done for another by a person who does not assume to act for himself but for some other person, though without any authority for the act, can become the act of the principal, if the principal ratifies the act after the fact.[86]

Consequences of ratification

As a result of ratification, the three parties will be put into a position as if the agent had express authority. This will have several consequences. Firstly, the principal and third party may enforce the agreement against each other; secondly, the agent will no longer be treated as having exceeded his authority; thirdly, the agent will no longer be liable in person to the third party.[87]

Requirements of ratification

To constitute a valid ratification, three conditions must be fulfilled.[88] Firstly, 'the agent whose act is sought to be ratified must have purported to act for the principal';[89] secondly, 'at the time the act was done the agent must have had a competent principal';[90] thirdly, 'at the time of the ratification the principal must be legally capable of doing the act itself'.[91]

XI Disclosed and undisclosed agency[92]

> **Box 5.11 Categories of agency relationships**
> - Undisclosed agency
> - Disclosed agency (named or unnamed principal)

Where an agent is appointed by the principal, in his interactions with the third party he may comport himself in one of two ways, as a disclosed or undisclosed agent. This distinction is important since it determines firstly the ability of the principal to ratify acts of the agent and secondly the liability of the agent to the third party.

A **disclosed agency**[93] covers those situations in which the third party is aware that the agent is an agent, whether the principal has been named or not. A disclosed agency could arise in one of two situations. Firstly, the agent may inform the third party that a principal exists but keep its identity a secret from the third party. This may occur at the election of the agent, the principal or both parties. In such a case, the agent is effectively acting for an **unnamed principal**. Secondly, the agent may advise the third party of the existence and identity of the principal. In such as case, the agent is effectively acting for a **named principal**.

An **undisclosed agency**[94] covers those situations in which the third party believes the agent is acting on his own behalf rather than representing another. The agent may either fail to advise the third party that a principal exists or expressly choose not to do so. The principal is effectively undisclosed and the agent is said to be acting for an undisclosed principal. In such a case, the agent will effectively be contracting with the third party in his own name.

Disclosed agency

If the agent discloses his representative capacity to the third party with whom he is contracting, he will be treated in law merely as a conduit for the principal, on the proviso that he is acting within the scope of his actual or apparent authority. In such a situation, the agent will usually disappear completely from the picture once the contract is finalised between the principal and the third party, unless he agrees to be personally liable to the third party.[95]

Undisclosed agency

An undisclosed agency will arise in situations where the third party believes the agent is acting on his own behalf rather than representing another. In such a situation, the principal is effectively undisclosed and the agent is said to be acting for an undisclosed principal. In such a case, the agent will effectively be contracting with the third party in his own name.[96]

> **Box 5.12 Undisclosed agency illustrated**
> An undisclosed agency may arise in a number of circumstances:
> - When the agent fails to mention to the third party that a principal exists.
>
> This could happen when neither the principal nor the agent thinks of disclosing the principal's involvement to the third party.

- When the agent expressly chooses not to mention to the third party that a principal exists. This could happen when the principal intends to keep his involvement a secret. In the alternative, the agent himself may choose to keep the existence of the principal a secret in order to block an attempt by the third party to bypass him in a bid to gain direct access to the principal.

Undisclosed agency arrangements are permissible in law.[97] Legally speaking, when an agent acts for an undisclosed principal, to all intents and purposes he is the principal from the point of view of the outside world. The outside world is permitted to treat him as the principal.

XII Civil law contrasted with common law[98]

The concept of agency can be traced back to Hellenic law and was later developed by Roman law.[99] The manner in which agency emerged as a concept in the common law system is different to how it emerged in the civil law system. As such the common law approach to agency is defined by a separate and distinct set of societal interests than that found in civil law countries.[100] For this reason, the concept of agency manifests itself differently in the two systems.

Beyond the general distinction between agency law in the civil and common law countries, the law governing agency differs from jurisdiction to jurisdiction. Whilst *agency*, *représentation*, *rappresentanza* and *vertegenwoordiging* all seem to represent the same concept in fact they have very distinct definitions in their respective legal systems.[101] In common law systems, the concept of agency has a far broader definition. It covers those situations in which a person (the principal) allows another (the agent) to act on his behalf in order to bring about legal relations with a third party.[102] It is immaterial whether the agent advises the third party that he is representing another and whether the agent provides the third party with the identity of the principal. In civil law systems, a distinction is traditionally made between direct agency and indirect agency, which depends on whether the agent in his dealings with the third party acts in the name of the principal or in his own name.[103] In the prior instance, the agent will bind the principal directly. In the latter instance, the agent is party to the contract with the third party even in a situation where the third party knew that he was dealing with an agent.

XIII General concerns of the parties

Box 5.13 General concerns of the parties

Concerns of the principal
- Disclosed or undisclosed agency
- Advertising and marketing
- Dealing with foreign officials
- Ringfencing agent's authority
- Liability for agent's non-contractual activities
- Regulation of relationship in law.

Concerns of the agent
- Scope of mandate
- Agent's liability
- Regulation of relationship in law.

Concerns of the third party
- Agent's authority to bind principal for contracts
- Actual authority? If not, apparent authority? If not, ratification or estoppel?

Concerns of the principal

Retention of an agent leads to liability and responsibilities on the part of the principal.

Disclosed and undisclosed agency

One concern from the point of view of the principal will arise where there is in place an undisclosed agency, for reasons discussed above.

Advertising and marketing

Advertising in the target market is a concern for both the principal and the agent. If either plans to advertise in a given market, they should seek the advice of a local lawyer before planning their advertising campaign. In most countries, at least formally, false advertising is prohibited. In many countries, advertising is regulated especially when targeted at children.

Dealing with foreign public officials

Liability for the bribery of foreign public officials is governed by national law, which may give effect to international legal instruments. One of the main legal instruments governing the bribery of foreign public officials is the 1997 OECD Convention on Combating Bribery of Foreign Public Officials in International Business Transactions (the 1997 Convention). As at January 2103, thirty-four OECD member countries and six non-member countries had adopted the 1997 Convention.[104]

Bribery Act 2010[105]
Applicable throughout the United Kingdom, the Bribery Act 2010 (the 2010 Act) received Royal Assent on 8 April 2010. Pursuant to the Act a person (natural or juristic) will be guilty of an offence if the person is deemed to have bribed a foreign public official.[106]

Liability of the person (natural or juristic) for bribery of a foreign public official under the 2010 Act Pursuant to the 2010 Act, a person will be guilty of an offence of bribing a foreign public official if the certain requirements are met:

1. The person who commits the act of bribing a foreign public official must intend to influence the said official in the official's capacity as a foreign public official.
2. The person must intend to obtain or retain business or an advantage in the conduct of business.
3. The person must, directly or through a third party, offer, promise or give financial or other advantage to the said official or to another, in response to a request from the official or with the assent or acquiescence of the said official.
4. The said official must not be permitted or required by written law applicable to him to be influenced in his capacity as foreign public official by the offer, promise or gift.[107]

Liability of a commercial organisation under the 2010 Act The 2010 Act creates a criminal offence for commercial organisations in circumstances when a person associated with the commercial organisation bribes another person in order to attain or retain business or some commercial advantage for the commercial organisation.[108]

The term 'commercial organisation' is widely defined in the 2010 Act. It encompasses bodies incorporated in and outside the United Kingdom.[109] A corporation incorporated under English law which operates outside England will fall under the 2010 Act, as will a corporation incorporated outside England that carries on a business or some elements of its business in England.

> **Box 5.14 Risk management to address bribery of foreign officials**
>
> Where an agent offers, promises or gives any financial or other advantage to a foreign public official in order for example to secure or to ensure retention of existing licences or government contracts (for example the grant of mining rights, planning permissions, contracts for the supply of electronic equipment and so on), both the agent and the principal may face criminal prosecution.
>
> *Tips and techniques 110*
> Due to the potential criminality of such acts, a commercial organisation should take care when dealing with foreign public officials or persons connected to it or working for it. The Ministry of Justice has issued guidance on the procedures which commercial organisations can introduce in order to prevent persons associated with them from bribing.[111] This guidance is intended to assist commercial organisations of all sizes and sectors understand the kinds of procedures that they may implement in order to prevent bribery pursuant to Section 7(1) of the 2010 Act.[112]
>
> Commercial organisations are encouraged in the guidance to carry out periodic assessments of potential external and internal risks of bribery on behalf of persons associated with those organisations.[113] Such risk assessment should cover the operations in the UK and elsewhere and, in relation to each such operation, should isolate the types of risk to which the organisation is exposed.[114] The risk assessment procedures should be proportionate to the size and structure of the organisation and to the nature of its activities[115] and should enable it to accurately identify and prioritise the risks that it faces.[116]
>
> Once risks are identified, organisations are encouraged to introduce adequate procedures designed to prevent bribery by persons associated with the commercial organisation.[117] Such procedures, which include bribery prevention procedures, may either stand alone or form part of wider guidance for the organisation.[118]
>
> Where such an organisation is using the services of an agent or representative it should carry out due diligence procedures in relation to the person or persons who perform or will perform services for or on behalf of the commercial organisation.[119] The same is true when the associated person(s) are incorporated, in which case information should be requested in relation to the relevant individuals involved in the performance of services by the company.[120] Due diligence procedures may be performed internally or externally (by outside consultants) and should look to identify and to mitigate the bribery risk.[121] In low-risk situations, commercial organisations may decide that there is no need to conduct much in the way of due diligence, whereas in higher-risk situations, due diligence may need to be twofold: firstly taking the form of direct enquiries, indirect investigations or general research pertaining to the proposed associated persons; and secondly taking the form of ongoing monitoring of recruited or engaged associated persons.[122]

Ringfencing agent's authority

When negotiating and finalising the terms of its relationship with an appointed agent, it is essential that the principal take care to clearly define the agent's ability to contract and thus bind the principal. Accordingly the principal should make sure that the mandate of its agent is clearly defined and precisely written.

Liability for agent's non-contractual activities[123]

It is essential that a principal carry out due diligence before hiring an agent by requesting inter alia references and following such references through, to manage the potential risks associated with the non-contractual activities of the agent.

Regulation of relationship in law[124]

The principal should be aware of any minimum guarantees implied into the agency agreement by virtue of national law that may increase the potential liability of the principal. Whilst the law in the United States for example imposes few restrictions on the agency relationship,[125] other countries commonly regulate the substance of the relationship between principal and agent in a bid to protect the rights of the (local) agent. Such minimum guarantees will increase the potential liability of the principal and should be considered by the principal before negotiation of terms. It is sensible for a principal to instruct a local lawyer to provide advice on its liabilities in this context.

In common law countries, an agent will generally enjoy certain basic protections.[126] Such protections may be supplemented by the contract concluded between the agent and the principal. The following rights are amongst those enjoyed by an agent under English law:

1. The right to claim remuneration for services rendered. Typically the agreement with the agent will spell out the mode of payment (in the form of a wage, a commission or both). Where no such provision is included in the contract then the court will imply a provision into the contract requiring reasonable remuneration of the agent.
2. The right to demand indemnification of expenditure legitimately incurred in the performance of services on behalf of the principal.
3. The right to exercise a lien over property owned by the principal in relation to sums owed by the principal to the agent where the property has lawfully come into the possession of the agent.

It is important for a principal using an agent based in the European Union to seek the advice of a lawyer in the member state where the agent is operating before negotiation of the agency agreement.

Concerns of the agent

Scope of mandate

The agent will need to know that he has the necessary mandate otherwise he will need to seek further authority before carrying out tasks which may otherwise be unauthorised.

Agent's liability

The liability of the agent is addressed in the section above reviewing the liability of the principal.

Regulation of relationship in law

The agent typically owes certain duties in law which may be supplemented by the terms of the agreement reached between the parties. The duties that an agent owes in English law include

1. the duty to perform an undertaking in compliance with instructions given by the principal;-
2. the duty to act with due care and skill;
3. the duty to carry out instructions personally;

4. the duty to account to the principal for sums received and property recovered in the execution of the agent's duties;
5. the duty to avoid situations involving conflicts of interests – an agent must not act if there is, or there is a significant risk that there will be, a conflict between the interests of the principal and those of the agent;
6. the duty not to make a secret profit – if a profit is made using information obtained from the principal or in the context of the agency relationship then the agent is obliged to account to the principal for it;
7. the duty not to misuse confidential information pertaining to the principal; and
8. the duty not to take a bribe.[127]

Concerns of the third party

The agent will need to have authority to contract in order to bind its principal, thus providing the third party with a course of action against the principal. To this end, a third party will need to determine whether the agent has actual authority and in the absence of actual authority, apparent authority. In default of actual or apparent authority, the third party will need to rely on ratification or estoppel.[128]

XIV Agency agreements under EU law[129]

Beyond the potential impact of European competition law on such arrangements[130] the relationship between the agent and the principal is governed by Council Directive 86/653/EEC of 18 December 1986 on the Coordination of the Laws of the Member States Relating to Self-employed Commercial Agents (the Directive).[131] The Directive, enacted to harmonise the laws of the different member states as they apply to independent (self-employed) commercial agents, is largely inspired by the law of those member states that afford agents the highest levels of protection (notably France and Germany).[132]

The Directive came into force on 1 January 1990 in all member states except the United Kingdom, Ireland and Italy. These three were given a longer period of implementation. Italy had to give full effect to the Directive by 1 January 1993, whilst the UK and Ireland had until 1 January 1994 to introduce implementing legislation covering all agency agreements old and new.

The Directive aims to protect the interests of the agent, by protecting the agent's stream of revenue as well as imposing notice provisions on the principal. It is worthwhile noting that notwithstanding the implementation of this harmonising directive, the national laws of the various member states still differ substantially. The Directive achieved only partial harmonisation. Certain important issues were left out, allowing member states the freedom to address such matters using national law.

Applicability of the Directive

The Directive applies to commercial agents, defined as self-employed intermediaries who have continuing authority to negotiate the sale or purchase of goods on behalf of a principal or to negotiate and conclude such agreements on behalf of and in the name of the principal.[133] For a party to qualify as a commercial agent, he must fulfil certain prerequisites:

1. He must be acting on behalf of another.
2. He must have authority to negotiate agreements on behalf of that other party

or the authority to negotiate and conclude agreements on behalf of that other party.
3. He must have continuing authority to do so.[134]

Acting on behalf of another[135]

The agent must be acting on behalf of the principal in order to fall under the scope of the Directive.[136] Whereas an agent negotiates on behalf of the principal, a party that negotiates and sells or buys in his own interest is excluded from the scope of the Directive.[137] Since the commercial agent acts on behalf of the principal, this distinguishes him from a person acting in his own name such as a distributor or indeed an agent acting for an undisclosed principal.[138]

A distributor who negotiates and resells the goods that he has acquired from the principal is transacting in his own interest rather doing so on behalf of another party. For this reason, distribution agreements are not covered by the Directive.[139]. A commercial agent who undertakes transactions in his own name without revealing the existence of the principal is therefore also excluded from the scope of the Directive.[140]

Authority to negotiate on behalf of another[141]

In order for a party to quality as a commercial agent, he must have authority to engage in the act of negotiation.[142] The term 'negotiate' has been given its dictionary meaning.[143] An agent will be regarded as negotiating when he deals with, manages or conducts a matter, exercising in the process some skill or consideration.[144] An agent does not need to be involved in the process of bargaining, in the sense of invitation to treat, offer, counteroffer and finally acceptance.[145]

This criterion seems to exclude those persons who lack the requisite authority to negotiate for the putative principal. Accordingly, persons who act as conduits charged with transmitting orders to the putative principal for fulfilment may fall outside the scope of the Directive.[146] For the same reason, persons who have no authority to discuss the contractual terms with the third party may also be excluded from the scope of the Directive.[147] For example, a petrol station attendant who dispenses petrol and sells merchandise and who possess no authority to negotiate the terms of sale will not qualify as a commercial agent and will accordingly fall outside the scope of the Directive.[148]

This criterion also appears to exclude those persons who lack the requisite authority or power to bind the putative principal to a contract.[149]

The separate and distinct act of concluding the contract, by entering into the contract on behalf of the principal and thus creating a legal relationship between the principal and the third party, is optional.

Continuing authority[150]

The agent must have continuing authority to negotiate the sale or the purchase of goods or to negotiate and conclude such transactions to be covered by the Directive.[151] In other words, he must have authority to act on behalf of the principal in more than one transaction during the period of the agency agreement.[152] This criterion would appear to exclude someone appointed on a one-off basis to negotiate a contract on behalf of his principal. Accordingly, brokers or lawyers who only act on a one-off basis are excluded from the scope of the Directive.[153]

Exclusions

In addition to the three prerequisites mentioned above, the applicability of the Directive is limited in two further ways. Firstly, the contract must involve the sale or purchase of goods for the Directive to apply. Secondly, the Directive will not apply to certain categories of persons.

Sale or purchase of goods[154]

The contract negotiated or negotiated and concluded by the agent on behalf of the principal must involve the sale or purchase of goods for the Directive to apply.

Mixed contracts

No guidance is given as to the applicability of the Directive to mixed contracts involving the supply of both goods and services.[155] Notwithstanding this fact, however, in certain member states, national legislation has been introduced that extends the scope of the Directive to agency agreements for the supply of services. It is therefore wise for the principal to consult with a local lawyer before instructing a prospective agent.

Land and interests in land

As the contract negotiated or negotiated and concluded by the agent on behalf of the principal must involve the sale or purchase of goods for the Directive to apply, this criterion excludes those transactions involving land or interests in land.[156]

Excluded categories of persons[157]

Certain categories of persons who may otherwise be classed as commercial agents are excluded from the scope of the Directive.[158] Pursuant to the Directive, the term 'commercial agent' does not include the following persons: firstly, persons empowered to enter into commitments binding on a corporation in their capacity as officers; secondly, a partner who is lawfully authorised to enter into commitments on behalf of his fellow partners; thirdly, a receiver, a liquidator and a trustee in bankruptcy.[159] The Directive also does not apply to the following people, even though they are termed commercial agents: firstly, the commercial agent whose activities are unpaid; secondly, the commercial agent operating on the commodity exchanges or in the commodity market; thirdly, the body known as the Crown Agents for the Overseas Governments and Administrations, created under the Crown Agents Act 1979 in the UK.[160] Pursuant to the Directive, each of the member states retains the power to provide that the Directive shall not apply to those persons whose activities as commercial agents are regarded as secondary by the law of the member state in question.[161]

Formalities

The Directive allows member states to determine questions of formality. Each member state has the autonomy to decide whether their national law will require the agreement to be written, verbal or notarised.[162]

Either contracting party is permitted to ask the other to provide him with a document noting the terms of the agreement, including those terms subsequently agreed upon.[163] The right of either party to request this signed document cannot be waived by the parties.[164] Accordingly, in those situations where the commercial agency agreement is not required to be entered into in writing either contracting party can still ask the other for a signed written document setting out the terms of the agreement.¹⁶⁵ What is more, either contracting party may ask the other for a signed written document setting out subsequent modifications agreed upon by the parties.¹⁶⁶

Appointment

The Directive leaves open the question of whether an appointment can be exclusive or not. Moreover it permits appointments of agents by reference to either a territory or a group of customers.

Reciprocal and compulsory obligation of good faith¹⁶⁷

A mandatory obligation of good faith is imposed by the Directive on both the principal and the agent. Given the position of this obligation in the body of the Directive it appears to have been intended to be considered in advance of all other obligations in the Directive.¹⁶⁸

This obligation is defined by the Directive in two steps. Firstly, the Directive obliges the contracting parties to act dutifully and in good faith.¹⁶⁹ Secondly, it defines specifically how each party must act in this context.¹⁷⁰ The agent in particular must make proper efforts to negotiate and where appropriate to conclude the transactions that he is instructed to take care of, to communicate to the principal all necessary information available to him and to comply with reasonable instructions issued to him by the principal.¹⁷¹

The principal for his part must provide his agent with the documentation needed relating to the goods concerned and must furnish his agent with the information necessary for the performance of the agency contract. In particular, the principal must notify the agent within a reasonable period once he anticipates that the volume of commercial transactions will be significantly lower than that which the agent could normally have expected.¹⁷² What is more, the principal must inform the agent within a reasonable period of his acceptance, refusal or any non-execution of a commercial transaction which the agent has procured on behalf of the principal.¹⁷³

In spite of the apparent detail provided, the Directive remains silent on the precise meaning of the idea of good faith.¹⁷⁴

XV Agency law and international instruments

Efforts have been made to introduce some uniformity into international law in the context of agency law. The 1978 Hague Convention on the Law Applicable to Agency (the 1978 Hague Convention) and the 1983 Geneva Convention on Agency in International Sale of Goods (the 1983 Geneva Convention) are examples of such instruments.

The 1978 Hague Convention entered into force on 1 May 1992 but only in a limited number of states.¹⁷⁵ The 1983 Geneva Convention, adopted on 17 February 1983, has not entered into force as the requisite number of ratifications is missing. Ten ratifications are needed in order for the said convention to enter into force,¹⁷⁶ but only five countries have ratified it so far.¹⁷⁷

To date efforts to produce binding instruments have produced rather limited results and have met with little practical success.¹⁷⁸ Accordingly there is a lack of internationally agreed uniform rules governing agency arrangements (unlike for example international sales transactions, which are governed to a large degree by the CISG).¹⁷⁹ In such situations, the parties contracting are required to rely on national laws governing agency, which may not take account of needs that are specific to international trade, as bodies of national law are enacted in the main for domestic arrangements and substantially differ from one country to the next.

Whilst the Directive (discussed above and below in relation to the relevant contractual provisions) introduces some harmonisation between the national laws of the different member states in the EU, it does not cover all issues that are relevant in the context of agency agreements and leaves member states the discretion to select alternative solutions in relation to a variety of issues. For these reasons, calls have been made and are being made for the formulation of new non-legislative means of unifying or harmonising the law governing international agency arrangements[180] and the elaboration of existing non-legislative instruments such as the UNIDROIT Principles of International Commercial Contracts and the Principles of European Contract Law (PECL).

Some of these calls have been for the formulation of international commercial custom, such as model provisions and contracts formulated by interested business circles utilising current trade practices as they relate to specific categories of transactions.[181] One such instrument is the model commercial agency contract produced by the ICC. The ICC has produced this model contract in a long form and a short form.[182] It is intended for use in international agency agreements concluded with self-employed agents acting in relation to the sale of goods.[183] The working group that drafted the model contract endeavoured to achieve a balance between the needs of the contracting parties.[184] The ICC believes that there is a

> space for an alternative solution, consisting in the use of uniform contractual rules, not based on any specific national law, but incorporating the prevailing practice in international trade, as well as the principles generally recognised by domestic laws on agency.[185]

The ICC's model contract offers the contracting parties two options in terms of governing law.[186] The parties can select to have their contract governed either by national law or by the provisions of the model contract itself as supplemented by the general principles of law recognised in international trade as applicable to agency agreements (lex mercatoria) as well as the UNIDROIT Principles of International Commercial Contracts (the UNIDROIT Principles), which are applicable to agency agreements. The hierarchy suggested in the model contract is as follows: the contractual clauses of the model contract itself, general principles of law, trade usages and the UNIDROIT Principles.[187] The first option mentioned above (selection of national law to govern the agency agreement) is intended for when the parties contracting prefer to submit their contract to the jurisdiction of national courts rather than arbitration.

Other calls have been made for the elaboration of an international restatement of general principles of contract law.[188] The UNIDROIT Principles and the PECL are examples of such restatements.[189]

Sphere of application of the international law instruments

Whilst the PECL and the Draft Common Frame of Reference (DCFR, see below) are intended for use in the European Union,[190] the different editions of UNIDROIT, the 1978 Hague Convention and the 1983 Geneva Convention are all intended for international use.[191] The PECL, the 1983 Geneva Convention and UNIDROIT 2010 (and before it UNIDROIT 2004)[192] focus on the relationship between the principal or the agent on the one hand and the third party on the other (the external relation)[193] rather than addressing the substantive nature of the relationship between the principal and the agent (the internal relation) in the manner that both the Directive (discussed above) and the DCFR do. The PECL and UNIDROIT 2010 leave the matter of the substantive nature of the relationship between the principal, on the one hand, and the agent, on the other hand, to national law.[194]

Draft Common Frame of Reference (DCFR)[195]

The DCFR was presented to the European Commission by the Study Group on the European Civil Code and the Research Group on Existing EC Private Law in December 2008 and published in 2009. Intended to be used as a stand-alone tool with a role of its own,[196] the hope is that the DCFR will act as a source of inspiration for the resolution of private law questions[197]. The DCFR incorporates the PECL in a partly revised form, developing what the drafters of the DCFR term a clearer and more consistent use of terminology and updating certain of the PECL's articles.[198]

Composition and scope of the DCFR

The DCFR consists of ten books, most of which are subdivided into chapters, sections, subsections and articles. Book IV, which addresses a number of different commercial contracts, is subdivided into eight parts, each dedicated to a different category of contract. Part E, which is divided into five chapters, deals with the formulation and regulation of commercial agency, franchise and distributorship agreements.

Regulation of commercial agency, franchise and distribution agreements by the DCFR

The general provisions contained in Chapter IV.E.–1 of the DCFR and the rules contained in Chapter IV.E.–2 govern all the agreements covered by Part IV.E, namely commercial agency, franchise and distribution agreements. Each of these agreements is also addressed separately by a set of dedicated and supplementary rules, each of which is contained in one of the three remaining chapters in Part IV.E: Chapter IV.E.–3 covers commercial agency agreements, Chapter IV.E.–4 covers franchise agreements, and Chapter IV.E.–5 covers distribution agreements.

General provisions and general rules governing commercial agency, franchise and distribution agreements[199]

The provisions contained in Part IV.E are intended to cover contracts for the creation and regulation of a commercial agency, franchise or distributorship agreement.[200] In addition these provisions are intended to cover other types of contract under which a party is engaged to bring the products of another party on to the market.[201] In this context the term 'product' is regarded as including not only goods but services as well.[202]

The contracting parties owe each other certain duties. Such duties will arise both before and after the conclusion of the contract. At the pre-contractual phase, each party is obliged to provide the other with sufficient information to allow it to decide on a reasonably informed basis whether or not to conclude a contract with the other party.[203] Such information must be provided within a reasonable period of time before the contract is concluded.[204] Each of the contracting parties owes a duty to the other party to cooperate,[205] to provide in due time all the information in its possession which the other party needs in order to achieve the objectives of the contract,[206] to keep information received from the other party confidential (during the course of the contractual relationship and after the contractual relationship comes to end)[207] and not to use such confidential information for any purpose other than that of achieving the objectives of the contract.[208]

Contracts for a definite term

Each contracting party is free not to renew a contract for a definite term.[209] In the event that either one of the contracting parties wishes to renew the contract it may do so by giving the other party notice in due time of its desire to renew,[210] in which case the contract will be renewed for an indefinite period, unless the other party gives that party notice of non-renewal, not later than a reasonable time before the expiry of the contract period.[211]

Contracts for an indefinite term

Each contracting party to a contract for an indefinite term will have the right to terminate the contractual relationship by giving notice to the other.[212] In the event that the notice provides for termination after a period of reasonable length no damages are payable.[213] In the event that the notice provides for immediate termination or termination after a period which is not of reasonable length then damages will be payable.[214]

Right to a lien over property held[215]

The party bringing the products on to the market will have a right to retain movables belonging to the other party in its possession as a result of the contract until such a time as the other party performs its obligations to pay (remuneration, compensation, damages and/or indemnity).

Statement of terms[216]

Either party to the contract may ask the other for a signed statement setting out the terms of the contract in textual form on a durable medium. The parties are not permitted to exclude this duty or to derogate from or vary its effects.

Commercial agency agreements and the DCFR

Commercial agency agreements are governed by the general provisions (Chapter IV.E.–1) and rules (in Chapter IV.E.–2) reviewed above, alongside the specific provisions set out in Chapter IV.E.–3. Section 1 of Chapter IV.E.–3 defines the scope of the chapter and Sections 2 and 3 contain the obligations of the commercial agent and principal respectively. The provisions contained in Chapter IV.E.–3 are similar to the provisions found in the Directive (discussed above), in terms not only of their scope but also of the substantive obligations of the commercial agent and the principal.

Definition of a commercial agent under the DCFR

The rules contained in Chapter IV.E.–3 will apply to contracts under which one party (the commercial agent) agrees to act on a continuing basis for remuneration as a self-employed intermediary, to negotiate contracts on behalf of another party (the principal) or to conclude contracts on behalf of this party.[217] To qualify as a commercial agent under these rules, the party must fulfil certain conditions: firstly, he must be acting on a continuing basis; secondly, he must be remunerated for his activities; thirdly, he must be self-employed; fourthly, he must be an intermediary; and finally, he must have the authority to negotiate or to conclude contracts on behalf of the other party.

Obligations of parties under the DCFR

Pursuant to these rules, the agent and the principal will owe each other duties.

Agent's obligations

The agent owes the principal several specific obligations on top of the general obligations noted above. Firstly, he must use reasonable efforts in order to negotiate contracts on the principal's behalf and to conclude those contracts which he is instructed to conclude.[218] Secondly, he is obliged to follow the instructions given to him by the principal so long as these instructions are reasonable and do not substantially affect his independence.[219]. Thirdly, the agent owes a general duty to the principal to keep him informed.[220] A non-exhaustive list of matters is provided in this regard,[221] including an obligation to inform the principal of contracts negotiated or concluded; of market conditions and of the solvency of clients. Fourthly, the agent is obliged to keep proper accounts detailing the contracts negotiated or concluded on the principal's behalf.[222] Finally, on receipt of a request from the principal, the agent is obligated to permit reasonable access to the accounts mentioned above to an independent accountant appointed by the principal.[223]

Principal's obligations

The principal owes the agent several specific obligations on top of those noted above. Firstly, the principal must pay commission to the agent. This obligation will arise during the term of the agency agreement[224] as well as after the agency agreement has come to an end.[225] Secondly, the principal owes the agent a duty to pay him the commission due no later than the last day of the month following the quarter in which the agent became entitled to it.[226] This duty cannot be excluded or derogated from and its effects cannot be varied.[227] Thirdly, the principal owes a general duty to keep the agent informed.[228] A non-exhaustive list of matters is provided in this regard, including an obligation to inform the agent of the features of the goods or services as well as their prices and conditions of sale or purchase.[229]. Moreover the principal is obliged to advise the agent of his decision to accept or reject a contract negotiated by the agent on the principal's behalf,[230] or of non-performance under such a contract;[231] of foreseeable decreases in the volume of contracts that the principal will be able to conclude;[232] and of the commission due and the mechanism used in order to calculate this commission.[233]

XVI Checklist of provisions[234]

The section below reviews the provisions that the parties contracting should consider including in their international agency agreement. Where relevant, these provisions are considered in light of EU law. The following checklist provides a list of the provisions that should be included in simple international agency agreements. This agreement is intended for use in international transactions between commercial parties. Not every one of the provisions listed in the checklist is mandatory, but each of them should be considered by the contracting parties when planning, negotiating and finalising the contract. The ICC has produced a model commercial agency contract[235] intended for use in relation to international agency agreements concluded between a principal and self-employed commercial agent acting for the sale of goods[236].

> **Box 5.15 Checklist of provisions**
>
> *Preface to the contract*
> ✓ Cover sheet
> ✓ Table of contents (in longer contracts; optional)
> ✓ Index of defined terms
>
> *Front of the contract (section XVII)*
> ✓ Title
> ✓ Introductory clause (type of agreement, date of agreement, parties to agreement)
> ✓ Recitals
>
> *Body of the contract (section XVIII)*
> ✓ Definitions clause
> ✓ Appointment of agent
> ✓ Territorial exclusivity
> ✓ Term of the agreement
> ✓ General obligations of parties
> ✓ Obligations of agent
> ✓ Obligations of principal
> ✓ Promotion
> ✓ Annual sales targets or guaranteed minimum target (optional)
> ✓ Licence and protection of intellectual property
> ✓ Termination (grounds and consequences)
> ✓ Force majeure
> ✓ Confidentiality
>
> *Boilerplate clauses (section XIX)*
> ✓ Assignment clause
> ✓ Merger clause
> ✓ Modifications clause
> ✓ Severance clause
> ✓ Notice clause
> ✓ Representation clause
> ✓ Dispute resolution (informal discussions, renegotiation, adaption, ADR, choice of jurisdiction and choice of law)
> ✓ Language clause
>
> *Back of the contract (section XIX)*
> ✓ Concluding clause
> ✓ Signature blocks
> ✓ Attachment (exhibits and schedules)

XVII Front of the contract[237]

The front of the contract will incorporate the following:

1. Title
2. Introductory clause noting the type and date of the agreement as well as the details of the contracting parties
3. Recitals.

Consider the following sample extract:

Agency agreement	
This agency agreement is made [on this —— day of —— in the year —— *or* upon the date of the signature hereof] and is between:	1. —— of —— ('Principal') 2. —— of —— ('Agent'). The Principal and the Agent will be referred to in this agreement separately as a 'Party' or collectively as the 'Parties'.

The extract above incorporates:

1. a title:[238]

Agency agreement

2. an introductory clause:[239]

This agency agreement is made [on this —— day of —— in the year —— *or* upon the date of the signature hereof] and is between:
1. —— of —— ('Principal')
2. —— of —— ('Agent')

The Principal and Agent will be referred to in this agreement separately as a 'Party' or collectively as the 'Parties'.

Recitals[240]

Recitals are optional. No recitals are included in this extract. The recitals when included will vary in length.

Examples of the types of recital that can be used in agency agreements are listed below. Under option A the agent is appointed to market the sale of the contract goods in the assigned territory whilst under option B the agent is also appointed to negotiate and contract in relation to these goods in the said territory.

Option A
The Principal appoints the Agent as its [exclusive *or* non-exclusive] agent to market the sale of the Goods in the Territory on the terms set out in this agreement.

Option B
The Principal appoints the Agent as its [exclusive *or* non-exclusive] agent to market the sale of the Goods in the Territory, as well as negotiate and contract in respect of the sale of the Goods in the Territory on the terms set out in this agreement.

XVIII Body of the contract

Definitions clause

See corresponding section in Chapter 2.

Appointment of agent (exclusive or non-exclusive)[241]

1. The Principal appoints the Agent to be its [exclusive *or* non-exclusive] agent in the territory defined in Schedule — ('Territory') for the goods defined in Schedule —— ('Goods').
2. The Principal may decide to sell other goods in the Territory. In which case, the Principal shall provide the Agent with prior written notice of its intention to include these goods, so that the Parties may discuss the possibility of including these goods within the Goods defined in Schedule ——.
3. The Principal may decide to remove goods from Schedule ——. In which case, the Principal shall provide the Agent with prior written notice of its intention to remove these goods from Schedule ——.

Option A
4. The Agent shall be responsible for marketing the sale of Goods to customers

> residing, or carrying on business, in the Territory.
> 5. The Agent shall be responsible for procuring requests for quotations or orders from such customers and conveying these to the Principal.
> 6. The Principal shall have the sole right to negotiate and conclude contracts for the sale of Goods in the Territory.
>
> *Option B*
> 4. The Agent shall be responsible for marketing the sale of Goods in the Territory with customers in the Territory.
> 5. The Agent shall also be responsible for negotiating and contracting in respect of the sale of Goods in the Territory with customers in the Territory.

This provision defines the scope of an agent's authority. Under option A, the agent is permitted to procure orders for the contract goods in the designated territory. Such orders must then be transmitted to the principal, which is in turn responsible for negotiating and then concluding the agreement with the customer sourced by the agent. Under option B, the agent is entitled not only to market the contract goods in the assigned territory but also to negotiate and conclude agreements on behalf of the principal.

An agent may hold stock of the goods in order to fulfil the orders placed with him. The stock will remain the property of the principal.[242]

Territorial exclusivity[243] (applicable where the agent is an exclusive agent)

> 1. The Principal shall give the Agent the exclusive right to act as agent for transactions involving the Goods in the Territory.
> 2. The Principal shall not during the continuance of this agreement grant another party within the Territory the right to engage in transactions involving the Goods.
>
> *Option A*
> 3. The Principal may deal directly with customers in the Territory without the intervention of the Agent.
> 4. In respect of such sales the Agent shall be entitled to commission in accordance with Schedule —— unless otherwise stipulated.
>
> *Option B*
> 3. The Principal may deal directly with customers and/or the transactions listed in Schedule —— without the intervention of the Agent.
> 4. In respect of such sales the Agent shall be entitled to commission in accordance with Schedule —— unless otherwise stipulated.

The grant of agency will either be on an exclusive or a non-exclusive basis in the territory assigned. Where exclusivity is granted the principal will typically want to reserve the general right to transact in the assigned territory or in the alternative the right to deal with certain clients or transactions. In which case, it would be sensible for the parties to include option A or B (above) in the agreement. In such a situation, to ensure certainty of transaction, the agent will probably endeavour to ensure that the category (or categories) of customers and/or transactions reserved for the principal is (or are) clearly defined within the agreement (option B above).

Term of the agreement[244]

An agreement for a definite term
This agreement shall run [for a period of —— years from —— or from the date of the signature of this agreement]. This agreement is automatically renewed for successive periods of ——, unless terminated by one Party giving prior written notice to the other Party of no less than ——.

Definite term agreement with minimum notice periods (optional)
This agreement shall run [for a period of —— years from —— or from the date of the signature of this agreement]. This agreement is automatically renewed for successive periods of ——, unless terminated by one Party giving the other Party prior written notice of no less than the relevant period noted below:
1. during the first year of the agreement, one month's notice
2. during the second year of the agreement, two months' notice
3. during the third and any subsequent years of this agreement, three months' notice.

An agreement for an indefinite term

Option A – Without an initial period
1. This agreement shall come into force [on this —— day of —— in the year —— or upon the date of the signature of this agreement].
2. (Subject to earlier termination permitted by the terms of this agreement) this agreement shall remain in force unless terminated by one Party giving the other Party prior written notice of no less than —— [*minimum notice periods may be stipulated by the contracting parties as per sample clause below (optional)*].

Option B – With an initial period
1. This agreement shall come into force [on this —— day of —— in the year —— or upon the date of the signature of this agreement].
2. (Subject to earlier termination permitted by the terms of this agreement) This agreement shall continue in force for an initial period of —— years from —— and thereafter, unless or until terminated by one Party giving the other Party prior written notice of no less than —— (*optional: minimum notice periods may be stipulated by the contracting parties as per sample clause below*).

No termination during initial period (optional)
Neither Party shall give notice before the end of the initial period.

Minimum notice periods (optional)
Unless or until terminated by one Party giving the other Party prior written notice of no less than the relevant period noted below:
1. during the first year of the agreement, one month's notice
2. during the second year of the agreement, two months' notice
3. during the third and any subsequent years of this agreement, three months' notice.

Most agency agreements will run for a set period of time (initial period) and thereafter will be determinable by a reasonable period of notice. Such an initial period is required in order to motivate the agent to invest time and effort in promoting the contract goods.[245] The agent will only be motivated to promote the contract goods if he knows with certainty that the initial period will permit him to accrue sufficient commission to reward him for his efforts.

Under the Directive

Articles 14 and 15 of the Directive envisage two types of agency agreement operating within the European Union, a fixed-term agency agreement (an agreement with a defined term) and an indefinite agency agreement (an agreement with no defined term). Whilst a fixed-term contract will not require any formal method of termination, an indefinite term contract can only be terminated through due notice.[246] Such notice may be given by either party to the other party.

The contracting parties may opt to convert a fixed-term agency agreement into an indefinite one by continuing to perform their obligations under the agreement when the term envisaged under the agreement comes to an end.[247] In such a case the duration of the fixed-term will be referred to for the purpose of calculating the notice for termination.[248] The notice period required to terminate an indefinite agency agreement will vary according to the duration of the contract. The period of notice is incremental in this context: one month for the first year of contract, two months for the second year commenced, three months for the third year commenced and subsequent years.[249] These periods represent minimum notice periods and are subject to the right of member states to increase them up to a maximum of six months.[250]

The contracting parties may use longer notice periods in their agreement, so long as both parties use the same notice periods.[251] The Directive does not allow the contracting parties to agree on shorter periods of notice than those stipulated in the Directive.[252]

Unless otherwise agreed, the period of notice must expire at the end of a calendar month.[253]

General obligations of parties

1. In performance of their duties under this agreement, each Party shall act in accordance with the duties of good faith and fair dealing.
2. The Agent agrees to use best endeavours to *either* market and promote the sale of Goods to customers residing or operating in the Territory *or* carry on business in the Territory and convey requests for quotes or orders from customers residing or operating in the Territory to the Principal.
3. During the period of this agreement, the Agent shall act as an agent for the Principal under the terms of this agreement [with all due and proper diligence *or* acting dutifully and in good faith], taking care of the interests of the Principal and inter alia complying with all reasonable directions provided to it by the Principal, [using its best endeavours *or* making proper efforts] to negotiate and, where appropriate, to conclude those transactions, on behalf of the Principal, that it is instructed to take care of by the Principal.
4. During the period of this agreement, the Agent shall convey to the Principal

> all information available to it needed by the Principal.
> 5. During the period of this agreement, the Agent shall do all that it is able to do in order to increase sales of the Goods in the Territory and improve the goodwill of the Principal in the Territory.

Reference in this provision to the obligation to act with all due and proper diligence or dutifully and in good faith will usually be nothing more than a statement of intent. In circumstances where the agent has committed no specific breach but is not performing to a satisfactory level the principal will have the option of using this provision against the agent.[254] Reference in this provision to the goodwill of the principal is important as it makes it clear that the agent is working for the principal. It is therefore the principal who enjoys the prime relationship with the customers and as such the customers and goodwill generated by the agent belong to the principal and not the agent.[255]

Under the Directive[256]

The parties are not permitted to derogate from their obligations arising under the Directive. Notwithstanding this fact, they retain the freedom to supplement the obligations imposed by the Directive.

Obligations of agent

Beyond his obligations in law (reviewed at the start of this chapter), under the contract the agent will have additional duties.[257]

The agent will typically be responsible for

1. transmitting complaints;
2. providing and maintaining proper facilities;
3. providing regular market updates;
4. ensuring compliance with local law;
5. ensuring confidentiality;
6. ensuring he complies with restrictions on authority;
7. collecting and depositing payments on behalf of the principal;
8. not competing with the principal;
9. complying with restrictions on his ability to negotiate terms; and
10. providing certain assurances (del credere guarantee) where he is a del credere agent.[258]

Obligations of agent under the Directive[259]

The agent has a non-derogative obligation to look after the interests of the principal and to act dutifully in good faith.[260] In particular he must ensure proper efforts are made when negotiating with prospective customers in the assigned territory and when concluding agreements with such customers on behalf of the principal.[261] Furthermore, he must ensure proper efforts are made to communicate transactions to the principal, to transmit all information needed by the principal to the principal and to comply with reasonable instructions given by the principal.[262]

The Directive permits the use of non-compete clauses (otherwise known as restraint of trade clauses) restricting the business activities of an agent following the termination of the agency agreement so long as such provisions are concluded in writing and relate to a territory or a group of customers. The Directive limits the scope of such provisions to a certain degree by stipulating that such provisions can only last for a period of two years from the termination of the agency contract. The enforceability and scope of such provisions will also depend on national law.[263]

The provisions detailed below defining the obligations of the agent are compatible with the Directive.

Transmitting complaints

1. The Agent shall promptly inform the Principal of complaints relating to the Goods that are communicated to the Agent by customers.

2. The Parties shall address such complaints rapidly and with due consideration.

Proper facilities[264]

The Agent shall keep and furnish at its own expense and to the reasonable satisfaction of the Principal such premises as may be required for the satisfactory execution of its obligations under this agreement, including but not limited to offices.

Such a provision is typically found in long-term agency agreements, as it permits the principal to make sure that the agent is maintaining his initial level of commitment to the agency relationship.[265]

Regular market updates[266]

1. The Agent shall promptly inform the Principal and pass to the Principal all information of which the Agent becomes aware and of which it is aware, useful to the business of the Principal, relating to but not limited to
   a. marketing and sales prospects;
   b. the quality and reliability of the Goods;
   c. the activities of the competitors of the Principal;
   d. laws and regulations applicable in the Territory with which the Goods must comply;
   e. laws and regulations relating to the operations and activities of the Principal; and
   f. any unauthorised use of the trade marks, patents or other intellectual or industrial property rights belonging to the Principal.

2. (*optional*) The Agent shall provide the Principal with a written report every —— addressing all such issues for the period in question using the template report supplied by the Principal.

The value of ongoing information cannot be overstated. This information will allow the principal to redesign and improve the contract goods as well as modify marketing and sales strategies.

Compliance with local law[267]

1. The Agent shall comply [in all material respects] with all relevant laws, rules and regulations in force in the Territory affecting the activities of the Agent in the Territory and relating to, but not limited to, the import, resale and/or use of Goods in the Territory.

2. (*optional*) The Agent shall indemnify the Principal in full against any and all costs, claims, expenses, demands and proceedings incurred by and made against the Principal resulting from a breach by the Agent of such laws, rules and regulations that are in force.

Such a provision is common in agency agreements and permits the principal to ringfence its liability for the activities of the agent. In addition, in the event of any such claim, this provision can be relied on by the principal to demonstrate its good faith.[268]

Confidentiality[269]

1. The Agent shall keep strictly confidential all information irrespective of the source of such information relating to the Goods and Principal, its subsidiaries and associated corporations.
2. The Agent shall only use such information in connection with its own activities under this agreement.
3. The Agent shall disclose such information to its staff and independent contractors (including but not limited to officers, directors, employees and advisors) who require access to this information to complete the activities agreed upon under this agreement. The Agent shall ensure that any staff and independent contractors with access to such information agree, prior to being provided with any or all of the information, to be bound by the terms of this agreement.
4. Except as otherwise stated, the Agent shall not disclose such information to any third person(s). In this agreement the term third person shall be read as including any corporation, company, group, partnership, agency or individual, including but not limited to corporations or companies in the same group as the one to which the Agent belongs, as well as employees of the Agent not employed at the branch, office or local establishment in the Territory.
5. To prevent unauthorised disclosure of such information, the Agent shall safeguard such information with the same degree of care as the Agent uses in order to safeguard its own information of a similar nature but in no case less than reasonable care.
6. The Agent shall not utilise such information in any way to compete with the Principal at any time or provide such information to a third person to enable it to compete with the Principal.
7. This provision shall survive the expiry or termination of this agreement.

This provision is suited to situations where the agent is not in possession of detailed, technical know-how. Where the agent is in possession of such detailed, technical know-how, a more comprehensive provision will be required or a specific agreement addressing confidentiality.[270] This provision will cover situations where the agent is part of a multinational and the principal wants to ringfence the information provided by warranting against such information being provided to other entities making up the multinational.[271]

Restrictions on authority and notification of status[272]

1. Unless expressly stipulated in this agreement or expressly authorised by the Principal, the Agent shall not in relation to the Goods or the Principal generally
   a. incur any obligations on behalf of the Principal;
   b. pledge the credit of the Principal;
   c. make any representations on behalf of the Principal;
   d. supply any warranty on behalf of the Principal; or
   e. have authority to take part in any dispute, issue or defend any dispute, settle or try to settle any dispute.
2. The Agent shall promptly inform the Principal of all or any such matters.
3. The Agent shall follow the instructions of the Principal given in relation to such matters. The Principal shall indemnify the Agent against any costs, expenses or liabilities incurred by the Agent as a result of so acting except where the same are incurred as a result of a failure or negligence on the part of the Agent.
4. The Agent shall ensure that a statement that it is acting as —— for the Principal is
   a. printed on all documents, including but not limited to letterheads, brochures and invoices;
   b. displayed on a plaque at the Agent's registered office;
   c. displayed on a plaque at all other places of business of the Agent; and
   d. included in all publicity materials in which reference is made to the Goods or Principal.
5. The Agent shall not describe itself either expressly or impliedly as acting in any capacity whatsoever other than in accordance with such a statement.

Option A
6. The Agent shall negotiate under this agreement as agent for sales of the Goods between the Principal and customers in the Territory.
7. The Agent shall transmit to the Principal all requests for quotes and details of prospective orders. The Principal shall solely be responsible for concluding the contract with these customers. Acceptance of purchase orders will be at the discretion of the Principal.
8. Unless otherwise agreed with the Principal, the Agent shall only negotiate using the Principal's current terms and conditions including but not limited to the Principal's Standard Conditions of Sale (in Schedule ——).
9. Unless otherwise agreed with the Principal, the Agent shall have no authority to make binding sale offers or accept purchase orders on behalf of the Principal.

Option B
6. The Agent shall conduct itself under this agreement as agent for sales of the

Goods, between the Principal and customers in the Territory. 7. The Agent shall sell the Goods on behalf of the Principal.	8. The Principal will deliver the Goods to the respective customers and will invoice the Goods to the respective customers.

This provision sets out and in turn limits the actual authority of the agent, accordingly limiting his ability to bind the principal. Notwithstanding such a provision, in most common law jurisdictions, the principal may not be able to escape liability by relying on such a provision in circumstances where the third party is able to rely on the doctrine of ostensible authority. In any event, the principal will still retain a right to sue the agent to recover monies paid out in respect of such claims, though this will very much depend on the agent's ability to pay any sums ordered by an arbiter.[273]

To mitigate the risk of ostensible authority being made available to third parties a notification of status provision is commonly used in such agreements (included in the provision above).

Collecting and depositing payments on behalf of the principal[274]

1. Where the Principal has authorised the Agent to receive payments for and on behalf of the Principal, the Agent shall remit such payments if at all possible by cheque (in [*currency*]), [within a reasonable time *or* immediately] to the Principal's registered office or as otherwise indicated by the Principal from time to time. 2. The Agent shall make such remittances in full. 3. The Agent shall not make deductions from such payment or payments, other than deductions relating to taxes that the Agent must deduct under the law of the Territory and in relation to commission payable to the Agent pursuant to Schedule ——.	4. Payment will include inter alia cash, cheques, draft and negotiable instruments. *Optional provisions* 5. Where payment or payments are held by the Agent pending remittance to the Principal, the Agent shall hold such payment or payments on trust for the Principal. 6. Where the Agent deposits the payment or payments made into a bank account, the Agent shall deposit the same into a separate bank account set up as a trust account in the name of the Agent as trustee for the Principal.

In those circumstances where the agent is entrusted with collection of monies for the principal, this provision operates in a manner that protects the interests of the principal.[275] Such a provision is especially important if the agent becomes insolvent, as such monies do not form part of the assets of the (insolvent) agent. Accordingly, the principal will be permitted to recoup them.

Not competing with the principal[276]

1. Without prior written agreement from the Principal, the Agent shall not during the course of this agreement nor for a period of —— after termination of this agreement either directly or indirectly
   a. market or promote the Goods outside the Territory;
   b. procure orders for the Goods from outside the Territory; and
   c. market or promote goods that in any way compete or interfere with the sale of the Goods in the Territory.
2. Clause 1 shall apply when the Agent's negotiations with customers in the Territory result in contracts for the sale of Goods to customers residing or operating outside the Territory.

Such a provision is recommended as it limits the ability of the agent to compete with the principal. The scope and enforceability of such a provision will largely depend on the law applicable to the contract. Accordingly the position should be verified with a lawyer specialising in the applicable law.

Complying with restrictions on his ability to negotiate terms

1. The Principal shall transmit to the Agent all requests for quotes relating to the sale of Goods in the Territory, save in those situations when the Principal at its sole discretion decides that it would be inappropriate for the Agent to act in relation to a particular transaction. In those situations, the Principal shall
   a. inform the Agent of the actions taken by the Principal; and
   b. pay the Agent any commission due on such sales (if at all) in accordance with the provisions found in Schedule ——.
2. The Agent shall immediately inform the Principal of all potential business.
3. The Agent shall at all times promote the Goods [and secure requests for quotes and orders for the Goods *or* negotiate and contract on behalf of the Principal the sale of Goods] in the Territory using the prices and terms determined by the Principal and provided by the Principal to the Agent (from time to time).[277]
4. All sales of the Goods negotiated by the Agent shall be for use by persons within the Territory.

As mentioned above, the principal may want to reserve the right to handle certain transactions or clients (for example a deal involving a large client), in circumstances where the agent is acting as an exclusive agent. In such situations, the agent will probably require that the scenarios be defined, by class of client or type of transaction, to ensure certainty of transaction.

Providing certain assurances in relation to the customers (with del credere guarantee as an optional subprovision)[278]

> 1. The Agent shall use all reasonable efforts to verify the creditworthiness of customers whose orders it conveys to the Principal.
> 2. The Agent shall not transmit the orders of customers whose creditworthiness the Agent knows or ought to know is questionable without first notifying the Principal.
> 3. The Agent shall provide reasonable help to the Principal in order to recover monies owed to the Principal by customers for the Goods in the Territory.
> 4. (*optional*) With the express agreement of the Agent and the Principal, the Agent shall act as del credere agent in accordance with the conditions stipulated in Schedule ——.

The optional provision sets out the responsibilities that the agent owes the principal in relation to customers that he refers to the principal. Pursuant to that provision and the accompanying schedule,[279] which are known together as a del credere guarantee, the agent guarantees due performance by all – or specific – customers of contracts concluded as result of the efforts of the agent. Such an agreement may be separate from the agency agreement.[280] In any event an agreement of this type should be concluded in writing and be in a form agreed on by the contracting parties, otherwise in certain jurisdictions the agent may be able to successfully challenge this guarantee.

Obligations of principal

Beyond his obligations in law (reviewed at the start of this chapter), under the contract the agent will have additional duties.[281]

The principal will typically owe the agent certain supplementary obligations including the obligation to

1. supply samples and marketing literature;
2. refer to the agent quotes received from customers in the assigned territory;
3. cover certain expenses incurred by the agent;
4. organise or help in the organisation of marketing efforts within the said territory;
5. fund (fully or partially) such marketing efforts;
6. deal with orders referred to it by the agent; and
7. account to the agent for commission.

Obligations of principal under the Directive[282]

The Directive imposes certain non-derogative obligations on the principal. As such the Principal is obliged to act dutifully and in good faith,[283] especially when providing the agent with documentation pertaining to the contract goods, sourcing information required by the agent for the execution of his duties, advising the agent of an anticipated reduction in the volume of commercial transactions when compared with the volume which the agent is habitually accustomed to and advising the agent of the acceptance, rejection or non-execution of certain commercial transactions which the agent procured for the principal.[284]

Supplying documentation, information and samples[285]

1. The Principal shall provide the Agent, at no charge to the Agent, with all necessary written information relating to the Goods, including but not limited to price lists, samples, template contracts, shipping documentation and documentation required by the Agent under national law, as well as all other information needed by the Agent in order to carry out its obligations under this agreement.

Option A

2. The Principal shall supply the Agent with samples in accordance with a special agreement between the Principal and Agent to be concluded separately in each case.

Option B

2. The Principal shall supply the Agent with samples on the following terms:
   a. The Principal shall supply samples free of charge for a period of —— commencing on ——.
   b. The Principal shall ship such samples to the Territory on the following basis: [*the parties are free to select the appropriate trade term*].[286]
3. The Agent shall hold such samples at its own risk.
4. Such samples shall remain the property of the Principal.

The documentation and information that the principal should supply the agent with should be listed in the agreement between the parties. To ensure flexibility this list should be non-exhaustive. To achieve this, the list should be preceded by a phrase such as 'including but not limited to'.

The situation with promotional literature and samples is very much at the discretion of the parties (unless an EU agency agreement is involved – see below). Typically, such documentation will include sales literature, price lists, product information, manuals, template contracts, shipping documentation and documentation needed by the agent under national law (enabling the agent to register the agency agreement with the appropriate national authority for example).

The cost of a sample will typically dictate whether it is provided free of charge.[287] In any event, when samples are supplied, the principal will have an interest in retaining some control over the manner in which they are used by the agent in order to protect the reputation and goodwill of the principal and the reputation of the goods.

Under the Directive

Under the Directive, the principal has a non-derogative obligation to supply the agent with the documentation needed pertaining to the contract goods.[288] The wording of the Directive leaves open the question of which documents need to be supplied.[289]

Direct quotation in the territory assigned[290]

| 1. The Principal shall not enter into negotiations with any person in the Territory without first obtaining the written authority of the Agent. | 2. The Principal shall not execute sales to any person in the Territory without first obtaining the written authority of the Agent. |

Such a provision is suited to exclusive agency agreements[291] as it ringfences the principal's authority vis-à-vis the agent.

Expenditure of agent[292]

| The Principal shall refund the Agent all expenditure specifically and reasonably | incurred by the Agent in response to a request by the Principal. |

Typically the agent will be responsible for expenses incurred unless the principal has asked him to complete certain tasks which he would not ordinarily execute without compensation.[293]

Accepting orders

| 1. At the end of each month, the Principal shall notify the Agent in writing, without undue delay, of its acceptance, refusal and/or non-execution of any business transmitted to it by the Agent during the month in question.
2. The Principal shall notify the Agent of any relevant communication with customers in the Territory. | 3. The Principal shall not be obliged to accept business conveyed to it by the Agent.
4. The Principal may decide the terms on which it will accept such business.
5. The Principal shall not unreasonably reject orders transmitted to it by the Agent. |

This provision will be used when the agent has no authority to conclude agreements on behalf of the principal.[294] In such situations, the agent will transmit orders procured from customers in the assigned territory to the principal, leaving the principal to decide which of them to accept.

Under the Directive
Under the Directive, the principal retains the discretion to decide whether it wishes to accept or reject an order transmitted to it by the agent. In such a situation, however, the principal will need to inform the agent within a reasonable period of time of its decision.[295] The Directive permits the principal to change its mind. As such a principal may accept an order and then refuse to execute it, so long as

1. the principal informs the agent within a reasonable period of time of any orders

that it has accepted and which it has failed to execute; and
2. the principal pays the agent any commission due on orders not executed when the failure to execute is the fault of the principal.[296]

Payment of commission[297]

1. The Principal shall pay commission to the Agent in line with Schedule —— on all sales of Goods made during the continuance of this agreement to customers in the Territory.
2. The Principal shall pay commission to the Agent if the Agent when dealing with customers in the Territory generates orders, which the Principal accepts, resulting in contracts for the sale of Goods to customers outside the Territory. Such commission shall be set at a specific rate to be determined on a case-by-case basis.
3. The Principal shall pay the Agent commission if another agent procures orders from customers established outside the Territory which result in contracts for the sale of Goods with customers in the Territory. Such commission shall be set at a specific rate to be determined on a case-by-case basis.
4. Unless otherwise agreed upon in writing between the Parties, the commission shall cover all expenses incurred by the Agent in the execution of its duties under this agreement.

Optional provisions

5. The Principal shall pay the Agent commission in relation to orders conveyed to the Principal by the Agent or received by the Principal from customers in the Territory before this agreement expires or is terminated which result in contracts, within no more than —— months after the expiry or termination of this agreement.
6. The Principal shall not be obliged to pay the Agent commission in relation to contracts concluded on the basis of orders received after expiry or termination of this agreement unless the transaction is mainly attributable to the work of the Agent during the continuance of this agreement and the following conditions are fulfilled:
   a. The contract is entered into within a reasonable period of time after the expiry or termination of the agreement.
   b. The Agent provided the Principal with written notice of the pending negotiations giving rise to the commission pursuant to this clause, before expiry or termination of this agreement.
7. The Principal shall supply the Agent with a written annual sales forecast on ——.
8. The Principal shall notify the Agent in writing if the Principal anticipates that the volume of commercial transactions will be significantly lower than that which the Agent can normally expect by reference to Schedule ——.

The principal usually has an obligation to pay the agent. Such an obligation may take the form of commission payable in relation to transactions concluded during the term of the agency agreement and in certain situations after the agreement comes to end.

Under the Directive
The Directive imposes strict obligations on the principal in this regard (more below). The type of obligations that the Directive imposes on a principal can be used by an agent outside the EU to supplement the contractual obligations imposed on the principal in order to better protect his position. The principal for its part will want to limit the obligations imposed in order to reduce liability.

Right to remuneration and associated rights[298] The Directive deals with one method of remuneration, namely commission. Commission is defined by the Directive as 'any part of the remuneration which varies with the number or value of business transactions'.[299]

The Directive permits the contracting parties to choose the method of remuneration that is most suited to their needs. Where there is no agreement between the contracting parties in this regard the Directive states that the agent shall be entitled to the remuneration that commercial agents appointed for the goods forming the subject matter of the agency contract are customarily entitled to in the place where the agent carries on his activities.[300] In the event that there is no customary practice to draw on, the Directive adds that the commercial agent is entitled to what it terms reasonable remuneration ascertainable by taking into account all aspects of the transaction.[301] Importantly, whilst the Directive spells out detailed rules addressing the accrual and calculation of and the moment of payment of commission it does not displace the application of compulsory provisions of national law governing the levels of remuneration.[302]

The Directive extends two rights to the agent which cannot be derogated from to the detriment of the agent.[303] Firstly, the principal is obligated to provide the agent with a statement of commission due, which should be furnished no later than the last day of the month following the quarter in which the commission has become due.[304] Such a statement will set out the main components used to calculate the commission payable to the agent.[305] Secondly, the agent is granted the right to request from the principal all the information and in particular extracts from books available to the principal which the agent needs in order to verify the amount of commission due to him.[306]

The accrual of the right to be remunerated[307] The right of the agent to be remunerated arises at the point in time when the commercial transaction is concluded between the principal and the third party. In this context a distinction is drawn by the Directive between those transactions concluded during the term of the agency agreement[308] and those concluded after the termination of the agency agreement but within a reasonable time after termination.[309]

Loss of right to remuneration The right to commission will be lost when the contract between the third party and the principal is not executed due to a reason for which the principal is not to blame.[310] This is so even in circumstances when the agent is in no way responsible for the failure of the principal to execute. This provision cannot be derogated from to the detriment of the agent.[311] In such circumstances, the agent will be obliged to refund any commission already received from the principal.[312]

Transactions concluded during the term of the agency agreement In relation to transactions concluded during the term of the agency agreement, the Directive distinguishes between direct transactions and indirect transactions.[313]

The agent, pursuant to the Directive, will be entitled to commission on commercial transactions concluded during the term of the agreement where the transaction in question is concluded either as a result of the work of the agent[314] or with a third party previously acquired by the agent for the principal as a customer for transactions of the same kind (repeat business).[315] In such a case the customer need not pass directly through the agent for the agent to have a right to remuneration for the transaction. Such transactions are considered direct transactions.

The agent, pursuant to the Directive, is also entitled to claim commission for indirect transactions: transactions concluded during the term of the agreement when the agent did not actually participate in the sale. This right arises if the following provisos are met:

1. The agent was either entrusted with the assigned territory or group of customers or had exclusive rights to the said territory or group of customers.[316]
2. The transaction has been entered into with a customer in that said territory or group of customers.[317]

After the agency agreement comes to an end[318]   The agent will be entitled to commission on commercial transactions concluded after the agreement has come to an end in the following three situations: firstly, the transaction is mainly attributable to the efforts of the agent during the term of the agreement and the transaction was entered into within a reasonable period of time after the agreement came to an end;[319] secondly, the order from the third party reaches the principal or agent before the agreement is terminated[320] and results from the work of the agent;[321] thirdly, the order from the third party reaches the principal or agent before the agreement is terminated[322]

and the transaction involves a customer belonging to the territory or group of customers entrusted to the agent.[323]

To ensure that the principal does not pay commission twice for the same transaction, the Directive states that a new commercial agent is not entitled to a commission when it is payable under Article 8 of the Directive to a previous commercial agent, unless it is equitable because of the circumstances for such a commission to be shared between the commercial agents.[324]

Time commission becomes due   To ensure that the principal does not hold back payment of commission unduly, the Directive determines the time at which the commission will become due. According to Article 10(1), commission becomes due as soon as one of the following situations arises:

- The principal has executed the transaction.
- The principal should have executed the transaction pursuant to the contract concluded between the principal and the third party.
- The third party has executed the transaction pursuant to the contract concluded between the third party and the principal.

At the latest commission becomes due when the third party has executed its part of the transaction or would have done so had the principal executed its part of the bargain.[325] The commission must be paid no later than the last day of the month following the quarter in which the commission became due.[326]

The rules set out above and contained within Articles 10(2) and 10(3) of the Directive are not capable of being derogated from to the detriment of the agent.[327]

Sales forecast and economic conditions alarm

The principal is expected to notify the agent, within a reasonable period of time, if it anticipates that the volume of commercial transactions will be 'significantly lower' than that which the agent can 'normally' expect.[328] In order to better clarify this obligation, it would be sensible for the agreement to include not only a note of the volume of the commercial transactions which the agent would normally expect, but also an obligation on the principal to provide a written sales forecast to the agent.

Promotion

Option A
1. The Principal may at its sole discretion promote and market the Goods in the Territory.
2. The Agent shall not be permitted to promote and market the Goods in the Territory or on the internet without the prior written approval of the Principal. Such approval shall not be unreasonably withheld by the Principal.
3. The Parties may from time to time agree on the promotional activities to be carried out in the Territory, in which case
   a. the format of promotional activities and the content of promotional literature shall be approved by the Principal;
   b. the cost of promotional activities shall be [the responsibility of the [Principal *or* Agent] *or* apportioned in accordance with Schedule —— between the Parties].

Option B
1. The Agent shall be responsible for promoting and marketing the Goods in the Territory.
2. The cost of promotional activities shall be [the responsibility of the [Principal *or* Agent] *or* apportioned in accordance with Schedule —— between the Parties].

Option A provides the principal with responsibility for promotional activities whilst permitting the principal to involve the agent at its discretion. Option B provides the agent with responsibility for promotional activities.

Annual sales targets and guaranteed minimum target (optional)[329]

Optional provision A – Annual sales target
Once a year, the Parties may agree on sales targets for the forthcoming year ('Annual Sales Target'). The Parties shall use their best endeavours to meet the Annual Sales Target. If a Party fails to meet the Annual Sales Target this will not constitute a breach of the contract by the Party unless that Party is clearly at fault. The Parties may agree on a Guaranteed Minimum Target.

Optional provision B – Guaranteed minimum target
During each year, the Agent shall transmit to the Principal orders for no less than [*the*

said target may be determined by reference to sums of money, volume of Goods or a percentage of the Annual Sales Target reviewed above] ('Guaranteed Minimum Target'). If for reasons for which the Principal cannot be held responsible, at the end of the year the Guaranteed Minimum Target has not been met by the Agent, the Principal may by prior written notice given to the Agent of no less than ——
1. terminate this agreement; or
2. revoke the exclusivity of the Agent.

The ICC model rules provide for two options,[330] namely an annual sales target and an annual guaranteed minimum target. The annual sales target is agreed upon from year to year by the contracting parties and generally its non-attainment will not constitute a breach of contract. Where a guaranteed minimum target is incorporated into the contract by the parties, it is implied that in the event of non-attainment a possible contractual termination or revocation of exclusivity (if applicable) will result.

Licence and protection of intellectual property[331]

1. The Principal allows the Agent to use the Intellectual Property in the Territory, including but not limited to the Trade Marks, on the Goods or in relation to the Goods, for the purposes only of exercising its rights and performing its duties under this agreement.
2. Except as provided in Clause 1 above, the Agent shall enjoy no rights in relation to any Intellectual Property, including but not limited to the Trade Marks, used by the Principal in relation to the Goods or in any goodwill associated therewith and the Agent confirms that save where expressly provided for in this agreement
   a. the Agent shall not acquire any rights in respect thereof; and
   b. any such rights and goodwill are and shall remain vested at all times in the Principal.
3. The Agent shall not register any Intellectual Property, including but not limited to the Trade Marks, without the prior written authorisation of the Principal.
4. The Agent shall provide the Principal, prior to use of any Trade Mark, with a sample of the proposed documentation containing the Trade Mark. The Agent shall only utilise such documentation once the proofs of such documentation have first been approved in writing by the Principal.
5. The Agent shall take all steps as the Principal may reasonably require to help the Principal maintain the validity and enforceability of the Intellectual Property of the Principal during the term of this agreement, on condition that the Principal shall indemnify the Agent against all costs, claims or other liabilities arising from or in connection with such steps.
6. Without prejudice to the right of the Agent or any third party to challenge the validity of any Intellectual Property of the Principal, the Agent shall not do or allow another party to do any act which would or might invalidate or be inconsistent with any Intellectual Property of the Principal.

7. The Agent shall promptly and fully notify the Principal of any actual, threatened or suspected infringement in the Territory of any Intellectual Property of the Principal which comes to the notice of the Agent.
8. The Agent shall promptly and fully notify the Principal of any claim by a third party that comes to its notice that the import into the Territory of the Goods or the sale of the Goods in the Territory breaches any rights of any other person.
9. In response to a request from the Principal and at the expense of the Principal, the Agent shall take all reasonable steps needed in order to help the Principal take proceedings in relation to any such infringement.
10. Upon termination of this agreement, the Agent shall
    a. immediately cease using the Intellectual Property including but not limited to the Trade Marks as well as any other trade marks or trade or brand names belonging to the Principal.
    b. at no charge to the Principal and in line with the instructions of the Principal, dispose of or return to the Principal all documentation making use of the Intellectual Property including but not limited to the Trade Marks as well as any other trade marks or trade or brand names belonging to the Principal found in the possession or control of the Agent.

Termination (grounds and consequences)[332]

1. Either Party may terminate this agreement with immediate effect by notice given in writing in the following situations:
   a. The other Party commits any breach of any of the provisions of this agreement resulting in such detriment to the Party terminating so as to substantially deprive him of that which the Party terminating is entitled to expect under this agreement and, in the case of a breach capable of remedy, fails to remedy such a breach within —— after receipt of written notice setting out the particulars of the breach and requiring the breach to be rectified.
   b. A receiver is appointed over any of the property or assets of the other Party.
   c. That other Party enters into a voluntary arrangement with its creditors or becomes the subject of an administration order.
   d. That other Party goes into liquidation.
   e. Anything analogous to any of the aforementioned under the law of any jurisdiction occurs in relation to that other Party.
   f. That other Party ceases or threatens to cease to carry on business.
   g. There is at any time a material change in the management, ownership or control of the other Party.
   h. That other Party is substantially prevented from performing its obligations under the agreement.
   i. That other Party assigns or tries to assign the agreement without prior authorisation.
2. A breach shall be considered capable of remedy if the Party in breach is able to

comply with the provision concerned in all respects other than as to the time of performance, on the proviso that time of performance is not of the essence.
3. Any waiver by either Party of a breach of any provision of this agreement shall not constitute a waiver of any consequent breach of the same or any other provision thereof.
4. Any termination of this agreement shall be without prejudice to any rights or remedies of either Party in respect of the breach concerned (if any) or any other breach.

Grounds of termination

See corresponding section in Chapter 3.

Consequences of termination[333]

Option A
1. The Agent shall not be allowed any compensation, indemnity, damages or other form of payment in relation to [termination *or* expiry] of this agreement [except to the extent provided for under the governing law of this agreement].
2. This provision does not prejudice the Agent's right to claim damages for a breach of contract under this agreement.

Option B1
1. The Agent shall be entitled to an indemnity if and to the degree that the Agent has brought the Principal new customers or the Agent has significantly increased the volume of business with existing customers and the Principal continues to obtain substantial benefits from the business with such customers and payment of an indemnity is equitable in view of all the circumstances and specifically bearing in mind the commission that the Agent has lost on the business transacted with such customers.
2. Indemnity shall not exceed a figure equivalent to an indemnity for one year calculated from the Agent's average annual remuneration over the previous ―――― years. If the contract goes back less than ―――― indemnity shall be calculated on the basis of the average for the period in question.
3. The Agent shall not be entitled to the indemnity if the Agent fails to notify the Principal in writing of an intention to pursue this entitlement within ―――― following termination of the agreement.
4. The Agent shall not be entitled to the indemnity in the following situations:
   a. where the Principal has terminated the agreement due to a fault attributable to the Agent justifying immediate termination of the agreement under national law;
   b. where the Agent has terminated the agreement, unless such a termination is justified by circumstances attributable to the Principal or on the grounds of age, infirmity or illness of the Agent in consequence of which the Agent cannot reasonably be expected to continue their business; or
   c. where, with the agreement of the Principal, the Agent assigns his rights and obligations under the agreement to another.

Option B2
1. The Agent shall be entitled to compensation for the damage sustained by the Agent as a result of the termination of this agreement.
2. Such damage shall be deemed to have occurred if termination occurs in circumstances that
   a. deprive the Agent of the commission which proper performance of the agreement would have procured the Agent whilst providing the Principal with substantial benefits linked to the activities of the Agent; and/or
   b. prevent the Agent from recouping the expenditure that the Agent has incurred in the performance of the agreement on the Principal's advice.
3. The Agent shall not be entitled to the compensation if the Agent fails to notify the Principal in writing of an intention to pursue this entitlement within —— following termination of the agreement.
4. The Agent shall not be entitled to the compensation in the following situations:
   a. where the Principal has terminated the agreement due to a fault attributable to the Agent justifying immediate termination of the agreement under national law;
   b. where the Agent has terminated the agreement, unless such a termination is justified by circumstances attributable to the Principal or on the grounds of age, infirmity or illness of the Agent in consequence of which the Agent cannot reasonably be expected to continue their business; or
   c. where, with the agreement of the Principal, the Agent assigns his rights and obligations under the agreement to another.

Option C1
1. The Agent shall not be entitled to compensation, indemnity, damages or other form of payment in relation to [termination *or* expiry] of this agreement unless the Agent is a commercial agent under Council Directive 86/653/EEC on the Coordination of the Laws of Member States Relating to Self-employed Commercial Agents ('Directive').
2. In which case, in the event of a termination in respect of which the Agent is entitled to compensation or indemnity pursuant to Article 17 of the Directive, then the Parties agree that the Agent shall be entitled to the compensation or indemnity in accordance with the Directive.

Option C2
1. The Parties confirm that the Agent is a commercial agent governed by Council Directive 86/653/EEC on the Coordination of the Laws of Member States Relating to Self-employed Commercial Agents ('Directive').
2. The Parties agree that in the event of a termination in respect of which the Agent is entitled to compensation or indemnity pursuant to Article 17 of the Directive, then the Agent shall be entitled to the compensation or indemnity in accordance with the Directive.

Option A
In certain countries, the agent will not qualify for indemnity or compensation on termination or expiry of the agreement, although the agent may qualify for damages under the terms of the agreement itself, if for example the agreement stipulates that the termination qualifies as a breach of the contract by the principal. In such countries, option A will be appropriate. This

option provides for no compensation or indemnity.

Option B
In other countries, upon the expiry or termination of the agency agreement, the agent will be entitled to an indemnity or compensation. He will qualify for an indemnity in relation to the goodwill that he has brought to the principal from which the principal derives substantial benefits. The agent may for example have procured new customers for the principal or he may have been able to generate a significant increase in the volume of business with existing customers. The compensation that the agent will qualify for will relate to the loss of commission that he would have earned had the contract lasted for a longer duration.

Option B stipulates that the Agent will receive indemnity (option B1) or compensation (option B2). Option B is based on the indemnity and compensation provisions found in the Directive.

Option C
The Directive sets out certain obligations which the contracting parties cannot contract out of in the context of termination. It should be noted that it has been ruled that the rules of indemnity will apply if the agent performs his contractual activity within the European Union, even if the contracting parties have agreed to submit the agreement to the law of a country that is not in the EU.[334]

Minimum notice period (evergreen terms)
See review of periods of notice under the Directive in the 'Term of the agreement' section above.

Reasons for termination
In addition to the methods of termination reviewed above, nothing in the Directive will affect the rights of the contracting parties under national law (in the various member states) to opt for immediate termination of the agency agreement in exceptional circumstances or in situations when there is a failure by one party to carry out all or part of its obligations.[335] Broadly speaking, material breaches of the terms of the agreement, force majeure or impossibility of performance are all circumstances that national law may recognise as permitting immediate termination.[336]

Compensation and indemnification
The Directive envisages payment of compensation or indemnification when the agreement is terminated[337] or brought to an end by the death of the agent.[338] Indemnity and compensation have been held to be available when the agreement between the contracting parties comes to an end by the effluxion of time, subject the exceptions discussed below.[339]

The principal's obligation to pay compensation or to indemnify the agent is curtailed in certain situations: firstly, where the agent fails to notify the principal of his intention to pursue such a claim, within the period of one year following the termination;[340] and secondly, when the termination of the agreement or the failure to renew the said agreement, is caused by a fault or voluntary act on the part of the agent.[341] Examples of situations where the agent will lose his right to claim compensation or indemnity include the following:

1. where the principal decides to terminate the agreement due to a fault attributable to the agent which would justify immediate termination of the agency agreement under national law;
2. where the agent terminates the agreement himself, unless the decision to termination is justified by circumstances attributable to the principal or the agent

decides to terminate due to old age, infirmity or illness, as a result of which he can no longer reasonably be expected to continue executing his duties under the agreement; and

3. where the agent assigns his rights and obligations under the agreement to another, in which case it is expected that the agent will receive remuneration from the assignee in any event.[342]

Option C above allows the contracting parties to incorporate the provisions of the Directive.

Force majeure

See corresponding section in Chapter 3.

Confidentiality

See corresponding section in Chapter 3.

XIX Boilerplate clauses and back of the contract

See corresponding sections in Chapter 2.

Schedules

Schedule: apportionment of costs associated with promotional activities

The Parties agree that the costs of promotional activities shall be apportioned between them as following: • Principal —— per cent	• Agent —— per cent. If the figures left blank in the paragraph above remain blank then each Party will bear its own costs.

Schedule: commission[343]

1. Commission shall be calculated as a percentage of the net amount of the invoices. The net amount of invoices shall be the sales price less a. any discounts; b. any additional charges (including but not limited to transport, insurance and packaging); and c. customs duties or taxes, so long as such additional charges are denoted separately in the invoice. 2. The Principal shall pay the Agent commission after the full payment by customers of the invoiced price. 3. The Principal shall pay the Agent a proportional payment in the event of a partial payment by a customer of the invoiced price.	4. The Principal shall supply the Agent with a statement every —— setting out the commission due to the Agent and the business in relation to which the commission is payable. 5. The Principal shall pay the commission to the Agent not later than ——. 6. The Agent shall be entitled to all the information that the Principal has in its possession or control required by the Agent in order to verify the commission due to it. 7. The Principal shall permit inspection of all such information by an independent auditor specifically appointed for this purpose by the Agent. The Agent shall bear the costs of such an inspection.

8. Where governmental approval is needed before the Principal can transfer monies due to the Agent, the Principal shall pay the Agent once the said approval is received by the Principal. The Principal shall take all steps required in order to acquire the said approval.
9. Unless otherwise agreed, commission shall be calculated in the currency of the sales contract in respect of which commission is due.
10. Any taxes due on the commission in the Territory are the Agent's sole responsibility.

Optional provisions
11. Commission shall not be due on requests for quotes or orders sent through to the Principal by the Agent which the Principal has not accepted.
12. The Agent shall be entitled to commission in the event that a contract concluded by the Principal as a result of the Agent's efforts is not then put into effect, unless the non-performance of the contract is due to reasons for which the Principal is not responsible.

Schedule – Del credere agent[344]

The Agent shall act as a del credere agent on the following terms:
1. The Agent shall refund the Principal sums unpaid which the Principal is entitled to receive from customers where such sums have not been paid for reasons for which the Principal bears no responsibility.
2. The Agent shall be responsible for all business that it sends through to the Principal *or* the Agent shall be responsible only for customers expressly agreed upon on a case-by-case basis.
3. The Agent shall bear unlimited liability *or* The Agent shall bear liability limited to —— per cent of the sums not recovered or limited to —— times the agreed commission.

Other schedules

Other schedules accompanying an agency agreement are likely to address the following matters:

- goods
- territory
- trade marks and intellectual property
- designated customers
- designated transactions
- principal's standard conditions of sale
- anticipated volume of commercial sales.

Summary

In this chapter we looked at various issues that concern international agency agreements: firstly, the fundamental characteristics of the agency relationship; secondly, the treatment of agency arrangements under European Union law; and thirdly, the key provisions that the parties contracting should consider including in international agency agreements. In relation to each such provision, we considered its purpose and its possible wording.

Useful links

http://www.hcch.net/index_en.php?act=conventions.text&cid=89 (Hague Convention on the Law Applicable to Agency)

http://www.idiproject.com (International Distribution Institute, providing background information on international instruments governing agency)

http://www.jus.uio.no/lm/eu.contract.principles.parts.1.to.3.2002/ (Principles of European Contract Law 2002)

http://www.oecd.org/document/21/0,3746,en_2649_34859_2017813_1_1_1_1,00.html (Organisation for Economic Co-operation and Development's Convention on Combating Bribery of Foreign Public Officials in International Business Transactions)

http://www.unidroit.org/english/conventions/1983agency/main.htm (Geneva Convention on Agency in International Sale of Goods)

http://www.unidroit.org/english/principles/contracts/main.htm (UNIDROIT Principles of International Commercial Contracts)

http://www.unidroit.org/english/principles/contracts/principles2010/translations/blackletter2010-main.htm (UNIDROIT Principles of International Commercial Contracts 2010 in various languages)

http://www.unilex.info (case law relating to UNIDROIT Principles and CISG)

http://www.unilex.info/dynasite.cfm?dssid=2376&dsmid=14315 (case law, articles and commentary relating to CISG)

http://www.unilex.info/dynasite.cfm?dssid=2377&dsmid=14311 (case law, articles and commentary relating to UNIDROIT Principles)

Further reading

Bortolotti, Fabio (2008), *Drafting and Negotiating International Commercial Agreements: A Practical Guide*, International Chamber of Commerce.

Bowstead, William (2007), *A Digest of the Law of Agency*, Lawbook Exchange.

Bradgate, Robert (2000), *Commercial Law*, 3rd ed., Butterworths.

Brown, Ian (1992), 'Authority and Necessity in the Law of Agency', *Modern Law Review* 55:3, 414.

Cheng, Chia-Jui (ed.) (1988), *Clive M. Schmitthoff's Select Essays on International Trade Law*, Martinus Nijhoff.

Christou, Richard (2003), *International Agency, Distribution and Licensing Agreements*, 4th ed., Sweet & Maxwell.

Demott, Deborah (2003), 'Statutory Ingredients in Common Law Change: Issues in the Development of Agency Doctrine', in Worthington, Sarah (ed.), *Commercial Law and Commercial Practice*, Hart.

Fox, William F. Jr (1992), *International Commercial Agreements: A Primer on Drafting, Negotiating and Resolving Disputes*, Kluwer Law and Taxation.

Guyénot, Jean (1976), *The French Law of Agency and Distributorship Agreements*, Oyez.

Lando, Ole (2001), 'Salient Features of the Principles of European Contract Law: A Comparison with the UCC', *Pace International Law Review* 13:2, 339.

Munday, Roderick (2010), *Agency: Law and Principles*, Oxford University Press.
Murray, Carole, Holloway, David and Timson-Hunt, Daren (2007), *Schmitthoff's Export Trade: The Law and Practice of International Trade*, 11th ed., Sweet & Maxwell.
Saintier, Séverine (2002), *Commercial Agency Law: A Comparative Analysis*, Ashgate Dartmouth.
Seavey, Warren (1920), 'The Rationale of Agency', *Yale Law Journal* 29, 859.
Shippey, Karla C. (1999), *A Short Course in International Contracts: Drafting the International Sales Contract for Attorneys and Non-attorneys*, World Trade Press.
Staubach, Fritz (1977), *The German Law of Agency and Distributorship Agreements*, Oyez.
Verhagen, Hendrick (2006), 'Agency and Representation', in Smits, Jan M. (ed.), *Elgar Encyclopedia of Comparative Law*, Edward Elgar.
Yelpaala, Kojo (1994), 'Strategy and Planning in Global Product Distribution: Beyond the Distribution Contract', *Law and Policy in International Business* 25:3, 839.

Notes

1. This topic is reviewed in the following books and articles: Fisher, Simon and Fisher, Damien (1998), *Export Best Practice: Commercial and Legal Aspects*, Federation Press, Chapters 2 and 3; Christou, Richard (2003), *International Agency, Distribution and Licensing Agreements*, 4th ed., Sweet & Maxwell, Chapters 2 and 3; Jones, Robert T. (1972), 'Practical Aspects of Commercial Agency and Distribution Agreements in the European Community', *International Lawyer* 6, 107; Staubach, Fritz (1977), *The German Law of Agency and Distributorship Agreements*, Oyez, 229–30; Puelinckx, A. H. and Tielemans, H. A. (1981), 'The Termination of Agency and Distributor Agreements: A Comparative Survey', *Northwest Journal of International Law and Business* 3, 452; Saltoun, André and Spudis, Barbara (1983), International Distribution and Sales Agency Agreements: Practical Guidelines for U.S. Exporters, *Business Lawyer* 39, 883.
2. Privity of contract is reviewed in Chapter 4.
3. Black's Law Dictionary, 2nd Edition, available at http://thelawdictionary.org (last accessed 11 February 2013).
4. Bradgate, Robert (2000), *Commercial Law*, 3rd ed., Butterworths, 125–32.
5. Munday, Roderick (2010), *Agency: Law and Principles*, Oxford University Press, 9.
6. Bradgate 2000: 125.
7. *Freeman & Lockyer* v. *Buckhurst Park Properties (Mangal) Ltd* [1964] 2 QB 480, 504 (Diplock LJ).
8. Parsons, Theophilus (1866), *The Law of Contracts*, 5th ed., Little, Brown, vol. 1, 38.
9. Bradgate 2000, Chapters 3–6; Saintier, Séverine (2002), *Commercial Agency Law: A Comparative Analysis*, Ashgate Dartmouth; Murray, Carole, Holloway, David and Timson-Hunt, Daren (2007), *Schmitthoff's Export Trade: The Law*

NOTES

     and Practice of International Trade, 11th ed., Sweet & Maxwell, Chapter 27; Munday 2010.
10. Bradgate, Robert and White, Fidelma (2006), *Commercial Law*, Oxford University Press, 67; Murray et al. 2007: 27-002.
11. For a further discussion, see ibid.
12. Bradgate 2000: 132–4.
13. §1(1) Factors Act 1889, available at http://www.legislation.gov.uk/ukpga/Vict/52-53/45 (last accessed 23 January 2013).
14. §2 Factors Act 1889.
15. §2(1) Factors Act 1889.
16. Bradgate 2000: 132.
17. Bradgate 2000: 133.
18. *Aluminium Industrie Vaassen BV* v. *Romalpa Aluminium Ltd* [1976] 1 WLR 676.
19. Bradgate 2000: 132.
20. Available at http://eur-lex.europa.eu/LexUriServ/LexUriServ.do?uri=OJ:L:2008:177:0006:0006:en:PDF (last accessed 21 January 2013). Rome I is reviewed in Chapter 2.
21. Article 3 Rome I.
22. Article 3(1) Rome I.
23. Ibid.
24. Article 4.1(a) Rome I.
25. Article 4.1(b) Rome I.
26. Bradgate 2000, Chapter 4.
27. Seavey, Warren (1920), 'The Rationale of Agency', *Yale Law Journal* 29, 859, 868.
28. Ibid.
29. Ibid.
30. Bradgate 2000: 139.
31. Ibid.
32. Ibid.
33. Ibid.
34. Ibid.
35. Ibid.
36. Bradgate 2000, Chapter 4.
37. Bradgate 2000: 141–2.
38. Bradgate 2000: 154–60.
39. *Keighley, Maxsted & Co.* v. *Durant* [1901] AC 240, 246–7 (Lord Macnaghten).
40. Bradgate 2000: 142–4.
41. Bradgate 2000: 142.
42. Ibid.
43. Ibid.
44. Bradgate 2000: 153.
45. Bradgate 2000: 144–53.
46. *Panorama Developments (Guilford) Ltd* v. *Fidelis Furnishing Fabrics Ltd* (1971) 2 QB 711.

47. *Panorama Developments (Guilford) Ltd* v. *Fidelis Furnishing Fabrics Ltd* (1971) 2 QB 711, 716–17 (Lord Denning MR).
48. *Freeman & Lockyer* v. *Buckhurst Park Properties (Mangal) Ltd* [1964] 2 QB 480.
49. *Freeman & Lockyer* v. *Buckhurst Park Properties (Mangal) Ltd* [1964] 2 QB 480, 491 (Willmer LJ).
50. *Freeman & Lockyer* v. *Buckhurst Park Properties (Mangal) Ltd* [1964] 2 QB 480, 495 (Willmer LJ).
51. *Biggerstaff* v. *Rowatt's Wharf Ltd* [1896] 2 Ch. 93, 104 (Lopes LJ).
52. *Freeman & Lockyer* v. *Buckhurst Park Properties (Mangal) Ltd* [1964] 2 QB 480, 494 (Willmer LJ).
53. Bradgate and White 2006, Chapter 6.
54. Privity is reviewed in Chapter 4.
55. Bribery is reviewed below in section on dealing with foreign officials.
56. Bradgate and White 2006, Chapter 7.
57. Reviewed in section entitled 'regulation of relationship in law' below.
58. Reviewed above in section on creation of agency relationships.
59. *Gardner* v. *Akeroyd* [1952] 2 QB 743.
60. *Gardner* v. *Akeroyd* [1952] 2 QB 743, 749 (Lord Goddard CJ).
61. Ibid.
62. *Mousell Brothers Ltd* v. *London and North Western Railway Co.* [1917] 2 KB 836, 845 (Atkin J).
63. *Gardner* v. *Akeroyd* [1952] 2 QB 743, 746 (Parker J).
64. *Gardner* v. *Akeroyd* [1952] 2 QB 743, 747 (Parker J).
65. For a fuller review of termination, see Munday (2010), Chapter 13.
66. The term of a contract is reviewed below in this chapter.
67. Grounds for termination are reviewed below in this chapter.
68. This topic is reviewed in Bradgate (2000), Chapters 4 and 5.
69. Bradgate 2000: 141–2; Munday 2010, Chapter 3.
70. Council Directive 86/653/EEC of 18 December 1986 on the Coordination of the Laws of the Member States Relating to Self-employed Commercial Agents, available at http://eur-lex.europa.eu/LexUriServ/LexUriServ.do?uri=OJ:L:1986:382:0017:0021:EN:PDF (accessed 23 January 2013).
71. Bradgate 2000: 141–2; Bradgate and White 2006: 69; Munday 2010: 42.
72. *Freeman & Lockyer* v. *Buckhurst Park Properties (Mangal) Ltd* [1964] 2 QB 480.
73. Bradgate 2000: 142–4; Bradgate and White 2006: 69–70; Munday 2010: 48.
74. Munday 2010: 44.
75. Munday 2010: 54.
76. Bowstead, William ([1896] 2007), *A Digest of the Law of Agency*, Lawbook Exchange, Article 35; Reynolds, F. M. B. (1994), 'Apparent Authority', *Journal of Business Law*, March, 144.
77. Example given by Lord Denning MR in *Hely-Hutchinson* v. *Brayhead Ltd and Another* [1968] 1 QB 549, 583.
78. Example given by Lord Denning MR in *Hely-Hutchinson* v. *Brayhead Ltd and Another* [1968] 1 QB 549, 583.

NOTES

79. Bradgate 2000: 144–52; Bradgate and White 2006: 71–2.
80. 'Ostensible or apparent authority of an agent as it appears to others' (ibid.).
81. Bradgate and White 2006: 71.
82. *Freeman & Lockyer* v. *Buckhurst Park Properties (Mangal) Ltd* [1964] 2 QB 480, 502 (Diplock LJ).
83. Ibid.
84. *Wilson* v. *Tumman* (1843) 6 Man. & G. 236, 242 (Tindal CJ).
85. *Boston Deep Sea Fishing and Ice Co. Ltd* v. *Farnham (Inspector of Taxes)* [1957] 2 Lloyd's Rep. 238, 244 (Harman J).
86. *Wilson* v. *Tumman* (1843) 6 Man. & G. 236, 242 (Tindal CJ).
87. Murray et al. 2007: 27-008.
88. *Firth* v. *Staines* [1897] 2 QB 70,75 (Wright J); *Boston Deep Sea Fishing and Ice Co. Ltd* v. *Farnham (Inspector of Taxes)* [1957] 2 Lloyd's Rep. 238, 244 (Harman J).
89. *Boston Deep Sea Fishing and Ice Co. Ltd* v. *Farnham (Inspector of Taxes)* [1957] 2 Lloyd's Rep. 238, 244 (Harman J).
90. Ibid.
91. Ibid.
92. A detailed review of this area can be found in Bradgate (2000), Chapter 5; Bradgate and White (2006), Chapter 6; Munday (2010), Chapter 10.
93. Bradgate and White 2006:79.
94. Ibid.
95. *Plant Engineers (Sales) Ltd* v. *Davies* (1969) 113 Sol Jo 484.
96. Bradgate and White 2006: 80.
97. Jacob J, *Oystertec Plc's Patent* [2003] RPC 29.
98. For a fuller review see Cheng, Chia-Jui (ed.) (1988), *Clive M. Schmitthoff's Select Essays on International Trade Law*, Martinus Nijhoff, Chapter 22; Bonnell, Michael Joachim (2004), 'Agency', in Hartkamp, Arthur and Hesselink, Martijn (eds), *Towards a European Civil Code*, 3rd ed., Kluwer Law International.
99. Cheng 1988.
100. Ibid.
101. Bonnell 2004.
102. Ibid.
103. Ibid.
104. The 1997 Convention is available at http://www.oecd.org/corruption/oecdantibriberyconvention.htm (last accessed 24 January 2013). Links to implementing legislation are available at http://www.oecd.org/document/30/0,3746, en_2649_34859_2027102_1_1_1_1,00.html (last accessed 24 January 2013).
105. Bribery Act 2010 (2010 Chapter 23). The Bribery Act 2010 used for this review was the one posted in April 2012 on http://www.legislation.gov.uk/ukpga/2010/23/pdfs/ukpga_20100023_en.pdf
106. §6 Bribery Act 2010.
107. Ibid.
108. §7(1) Bribery Act 2010.

109. §7(5) Bribery Act 2010.
110. Guidance issued by the Ministry of Justice relating to compliance with the Bribery Act 2010 can be found in the Ministry of Justice document entitled 'Guidance about the Procedures Which Relevant Commercial Organisations Can Put into Place to Prevent Persons Associated with Them from Bribing (Section 9 of the Bribery Act 2010)' (hereafter MoJ Guidance), available at http://www.justice.gov.uk/downloads/legislation/bribery-act-2010-guidance.pdf (last accessed 11 February 2013).
111. Ibid.
112. MoJ Guidance, 6.
113. MoJ Guidance, 25.
114. Ibid.
115. MoJ Guidance, 25–6 (Principle 3).
116. Ibid.
117. MoJ Guidance, 21 (Principle 1 calls for the introduction of proportionate procedures following an initial risk assessment).
118. Ibid.
119. MoJ Guidance, 27.
120. MoJ Guidance, 28.
121. MoJ Guidance, 27–8.
122. MoJ Guidance, 28.
123. Huffcut, Ernest W. ([1895] 1999), *Elements of the Law of Agency*, Beard.
124. Information about applicable laws in different countries is available at www.idiproject.com (last accessed 4 February 2013).
125. Qualified in those states that have adopted statutory rules on sales representatives.
126. Bradgate 2000: 182–8; Bradgate and White 2006: 91–2.
127. Bradgate 2000:188–205: Bradgate and White 2006: 88–90.
128. This topic is reviewed at the start of this chapter.
129. Fisher and Fisher 1998, Chapter 3; Saintier 2002, Chapter 3; Murray et al. 2007, Chapter 27.
130. Reviewed in Chapter 4.
131. Available at http://eur-lex.europa.eu/LexUriServ/LexUriServ.do?uri=OJ:L:1986:382:0017:0021:EN:PDF (accessed 23 January 2013).
132. Fisher and Fisher 1998: 56.
133. Article 1(2) Directive reads: 'A self-employed intermediary who has continuing authority to negotiate the sale or purchase of goods on behalf of another person, hereinafter called the principal, or to negotiate and conclude such transactions on behalf of and in the name of the principal.'
134. Article 1(2) Directive.
135. Ibid.
136. Ibid.
137. In *AMB Imballaggi Plastici Srl* v. *Pacflex Ltd* [1999] 2 All ER 249 (Court of Appeal) Gibson LJ stated: 'The plain implication of the language of the Directive . . . is that if the sale or purchase of goods is negotiated by the intermediary in its own interest rather than on behalf of the principal,

the intermediary is not a commercial agent. The paradigm example of an intermediary so negotiating is as a distributor purchasing goods from the manufacturer but re-selling the goods for a profit on the mark-up.'
138. Saintier 2002: 100.
139. Ibid.
140. Fisher and Fisher 1998: 54.
141. Article 1(2) Directive.
142. Ibid.
143. *Parks* v. *Esso Petroleum Company Ltd* [2000] E.C.C. 45; [2000] Eu. L.R. 25; (1999) 18 Tr. L.R. 232 (Morritt LJ).
144. Ibid.
145. Ibid.
146. Fisher and Fisher 1998: 54.
147. *Parks* v. *Esso Petroleum Company Ltd* [2000] E.C.C. 45; [2000] Eu. L.R. 25; (1999) 18 Tr. L.R. 232 (Morritt LJ).
148. Ibid.
149. Fisher and Fisher 1998: 54.
150. Article 1(2) Directive.
151. Ibid.
152. *Mercantile International Group plc* v. *Chuan Soon Huat Industrial Group Ltd* [2002] 1 All ER (Comm) 788.
153. Saintier 2002: 100.
154. Article 1(2) Directive.
155. Saintier 2002: 101.
156. Fisher and Fisher 1998: 54.
157. Articles 1(3) and 2(1) Directive.
158. Ibid.
159. Article 1(3) Directive.
160. Article 2(1) Directive.
161. Article 2(2) Directive.
162. Article 13(2) Directive.
163. Article 13(1) Directive.
164. Ibid.
165. Ibid.
166. Ibid.
167. Saintier 2002: 104.
168. Ibid.
169. Articles 3(1) and 4(1) Directive.
170. Articles 3(2) and 4(2) Directive.
171. Article 3(2) Directive.
172. Article 4(2) Directive.
173. Article 4(3) Directive.
174. Saintier 2002: 105.
175. The four contracting states to the 1978 Hague Convention are Argentina, France, the Netherlands and Portugal (as at January 2013).
176. Pursuant to Article 33, 1983 Geneva Convention.

177. The countries that have ratified the 1983 Geneva Convention are France, Italy, Mexico, the Netherlands and South Africa (as at January 2013).
178. Bonnell 2004.
179. More in Chapters 3 and 7.
180. 'Introduction to the 1994 Edition', in *UNIDROIT Principles of International Commercial Contracts 2010*, xxii.
181. Ibid.
182. The long form of the model contract is reproduced in Bortolotti, Fabio (2008), *Drafting and Negotiating International Commercial Agreements: A Practical Guide*, International Chamber of Commerce, 282–304 and the short form of the model contract is reproduced in Bortolotti (2008: 308–14). The short form of the model contract is intended for use in those situations where the parties contracting are looking for a simpler solution (Bortolotti 2008: 305).
183. A detailed review of scope of application is provided in Bortolotti (2008: 279–81).
184. Bortolotti 2008: 274.
185. Bortolotti 2008: 273.
186. Article 24 of the long form of the model contract (reproduced in Bortolotti (2008: 294)) and Article 6 of the Special Conditions of the short form (reproduced in Bortolotti (2008: 309)).
187. Bortolotti 2008: 275.
188. 'Introduction to the 2004 Edition', in *UNIDROIT Principles of International Commercial Contracts 2010*, xvi.
189. The UNIDROIT Principles and the PECL are reviewed in Chapter 7.
190. Article 1:101(1) PECL reads: 'These Principles are intended to be applied as general rules of contract law in the European Communities.'
191. Paragraph 1, Preamble, UNIDROIT 2010 reads: 'These Principles set forth general rules for international commercial contracts.'
192. Article 3:101(3) PECL; Article 1(3), 1983 Geneva Convention; Articles 2.2.1(1) and 2.2.1(2) UNIDROIT 2010. Article 3:101(3) PECL reads: 'This Chapter does not govern the internal relationship between the agent or intermediary and its principal.' Article 1(3), 1983 Geneva Convention reads: 'It (the Convention) is concerned only with relations between the principal or the agent on the one hand, and the third party on the other.' Article 2.2.1 UNIDROIT 2010 reads: '1. This Section governs the authority of a person ("the agent") to affect the legal relations of another person ("the principal") by or with respect to a contract with a third party, whether the agent acts in its own name or in that of the principal. 2. It governs only the relations between the principal or the agent on the one hand, and the third party on the other.'
193. Termed as such by comment 1 to Article 2.2.1 UNIDROIT 2004 (Article 2.2.1 is identical in UNIDROIT 2004 and UNIDROIT 2010).
194. Bonnell 2004.
195. The DCFR is reviewed in Chapter 7.
196. Paragraph Intr. 7 DCFR.
197. Paragraph Intr. 8 DCFR.

NOTES

198. Ibid.
199. Contained in Chapters IV.E.–1 and IV.E.–2.
200. Paragraph IV.E.–1:101(1) DCFR (Book IV, Part E, Chapter 1, Section 1, subsection 1, paragraph 1).
201. Ibid.
202. Paragraph IV.E.–1:101(2) DCFR.
203. Subsection IV.E.–2:101 DCFR.
204. Ibid.
205. Subsection IV.E.–2:201 DCFR.
206. Subsection IV.E.–2:202 DCFR.
207. Paragraph IV.E.–2:203(1) DCFR.
208. Paragraph IV.E.–2:203(2) DCFR.
209. Subsection IV.E.–2:301 DCFR.
210. Ibid.
211. Ibid.
212. Paragraph IV.E.–2:302(1) DCFR.
213. Paragraph IV.E.–2:302(2) DCFR.
214. Ibid. Calculation of the length of a reasonable period is addressed in subsection IV.E.–2:302. Calculation of damages for termination with inadequate notice is addressed in subsection IV.E.–2:303.
215. Subsection IV.E.–2:401 DCFR.
216. Subsection IV.E.–2:402 DCFR.
217. Subsection IV.E.–3:101 DCFR.
218. Subsection IV.E.–3:201 DCFR.
219. Subsection IV.E.–3:202 DCFR.
220. Subsection IV.E.–3:203 DCFR.
221. Ibid.
222. Paragraph IV.E.–3:204(1) DCFR.
223. Paragraph IV.E.–3:204(3) DCFR.
224. Subsection IV.E.–3:301 DCFR.
225. Subsection IV.E.–3:302 DCFR.
226. Subsection IV.E.–3:304 DCFR.
227. Ibid.
228. Subsection IV.E.–3:307 DCFR.
229. Ibid.
230. Subsection IV.E.–3:308 DCFR.
231. Ibid.
232. Subsection IV.E.–3:309 DCFR.
233. Subsection IV.E.–3:310 DCFR.
234. The substantive provisions of international agency agreements are reviewed in Christou (2003), Chapters 2 and 3 and Bortolotti (2008), Chapter 7.
235. The long form of this model contract and annexes is reproduced in Bortolotti (2008: 282–304). The short form is reproduced in Bortolotti (2008: 308–14). This short form consists of two parts (Special Conditions, particular to the contracting parties, and General Conditions, which are standardised terms intended for all contracts of this type).

236. Scope of application is reviewed in Bortolotti (2008: 279–81).
237. For background see Chapters 2 and 3.
238. More in Chapter 2.
239. More in Chapter 2.
240. More in Chapter 2.
241. For a further review, see Christou (2003: 60–1).
242. Christou 2003: 60.
243. Reviewed in Chapter 4
244. Reviewed in Chapter 4. A detailed review of the Directive and its impact on the provision addressing term is provided in Christou (2003: 108–9). The wording of such provisions is addressed in Christou (2003: 60, 107).
245. Christou 2003: 61.
246. Article 15(1) Directive.
247. Article 14 Directive.
248. Article 15(6) Directive.
249. Article 15(2) Directive.
250. Articles 15(2) and 15(3) Directive.
251. Article 15(4) Directive.
252. Article 15(2) Directive.
253. Article 15(5) Directive.
254. Christou 2003: 61.
255. Ibid.
256. The reciprocal and compulsory obligation of good faith is addressed earlier in this chapter.
257. The obligations of the agent under English law and under the Commercial Agents (Council Directive) Regulations 1993 are reviewed in Bradgate (2000: 188–206).
258. Del credere agents are addressed earlier in this chapter. Further discussion will follow at the end of this chapter.
259. The obligations of the agent under the Directive are reviewed in Bradgate (2000: 206) and Christou (2003: 109–12).
260. Article 3 Directive.
261. Ibid.
262. Article 3(2)c Directive.
263. Article 20(4) Directive.
264. Christou 2003: 62.
265. Ibid.
266. Christou 2003: 63.
267. Ibid.
268. Ibid.
269. Christou 2003: 63–4.
270. Ibid.
271. Ibid.
272. Christou 2003: 64–6.
273. Christou (2003: 64).
274. Christou 2003: 66–7.

275. Ibid.
276. Christou 2003: 65.
277. Reviewed by Christou (2003: 65–6).
278. Bortolotti 2008: 301. Del credere guarantees are reviewed later in this chapter.
279. Reviewed at the end of this chapter.
280. Christou (2003: 67).
281. Reviewed in Bradgate (2000: 182–6).
282. Reviewed in Bradgate (2000: 186–8) and Christou (2003: 112–14).
283. Article 4(1) Directive.
284. Article 4 Directive.
285. Samples and their treatment are reviewed in Christou (2003: 69).
286. More on trade terms in Chapter 3.
287. Christou 2003: 69.
288. Article 4(2)a Directive.
289. Christou 2003: 112.
290. This provision is reviewed by Christou (2003: 70).
291. Ibid.
292. Ibid.
293. Ibid.
294. Christou 2003: 113.
295. Article 4(3) Directive.
296. Article 11(1) Directive.
297. Payment and calculation of commission are addressed in the ICC model commercial agency contract (in both the short and long forms). Article 6 of the short form General Conditions is reproduced in Bortolotti (2008: 312–13). Article 16 and Annex 6 of the long form are reproduced in Bortolotti (2008: 289, 302–3 respectively).
298. Remuneration under the Directive is reviewed in Saintier (2002: 105–9).
299. Article 6(2) Directive.
300. Article 6(1) Directive. It is interesting that the Directive looks not only at the subject matter of the contract but also at the place of business of the agent when assessing what is customary remuneration. Such a rule could prove useful in those cases where there is a dispute over the law applicable, in effect in situations where the contracting parties are located in different countries (Saintier 2002: 105, citing from Ferrier, D. (1991), 'Commentaire de la loi du 25 juin 1991 sur l'agence commercial', *Semaine Juridique: Edition Générale* 1, 32).
301. Article 6(1) Directive.
302. Saintier (2002: 105, 105 n114).
303. Article 12(3) Directive.
304. Article 12(1) Directive.
305. Ibid.
306. Article 12(2) Directive.
307. Articles 5–9 Directive.
308. Article 7 Directive.

309. Article 8 Directive.
310. Article 11(1) Directive.
311. Article 11(3) Directive.
312. Article 11(2) Directive.
313. Article 7(1) Directive. Terms employed by Saintier (2002: 106).
314. Article 7(1)a Directive.
315. Article 7(1)b Directive.
316. The selection of the option here is at the discretion of the member state (Article 7(2) Directive). Saintier (2002: 106–7) suggests that the difference between the two options available does not seem very significant as the agent will be entitled to receive such indirect commissions. See Case C-104/95 *Georgios Kontogeorgas* v. *Kartonpak AE* [1996] ECR I-6643.
317. Article 7(2) Directive.
318. Article 8 Directive.
319. Article 8(a) Directive.
320. Article 8(b) Directive.
321. Article 7(1) Directive.
322. Article 8(b) Directive.
323. Article 7(2) Directive.
324. Article 9 Directive.
325. Article 10(2) Directive.
326. Article 10(3) Directive.
327. Article 10(4) Directive.
328. Article 4(2)b Directive.
329. Annual sales targets and guaranteed minimum targets are reviewed in the context of the ICC's model commercial agency contract in Bortolotti (2008: 285, 300). This provision is based on the terms set out in those passages.
330. Article 7 and Annex IV of the long form ICC model commercial agency contract, reproduced in Bortolotti (2008: 285, 300).
331. See corresponding section in Chapter 4. The scope of this provision is reviewed by Christou (2003: 72) and Bortolotti (2008: 286–7).
332. The scope of this provision is reviewed by Christou (2003: 73) and Bortolotti (2008: 291).
333. The consequences of termination outside the EU are reviewed in Christou (2003: 73–4). The consequences of termination inside the EU are reviewed in Christou (2003: 115–44). This provision is based on the terms set out in those passages.
334. Case C-381/98 *Ingmar GB Ltd* v. *Eaton Leonard Technologies Inc.* [2000] ECR I-9305.
335. Article 16 Directive.
336. In the spirit of Article 16 Directive.
337. Article 17(1) Directive.
338. Article 17(4) Directive.
339. Lord McEwan, *Frape* v. *Emreco International Ltd* [2002] SLT 271; David J, *Tigana Ltd* v. *Decoro Ltd* [2003] EWHC 23 QBD.

340. Article 17(5) Directive.
341. Article 18 Directive.
342. Christou 2003: 121.
343. Commission is reviewed in Christou (2003: 75–8) (outside the EU) and Christou (2003: 150–66) (inside the EU). Provisions governing commission are contained in the ICC's model commercial agency contract (long form) at Articles 15 and 16 (reproduced in Bortolotti (2008: 288–9)) as supplemented by Annex 6 (reproduced in Bortolotti (2008: 302–3)). Provisions governing commission are contained in the ICC's model commercial agency contract (short form) at Article 4 (reproduced in Bortolotti (2008: 309)) and at Article 6 of the accompanying General Conditions (reproduced in Bortolotti (2008: 312–13)).
344. Del credere guarantees are addressed in the ICC's model commercial agency contract (long form) at Article 10.2 as supplemented by Annex 5 (reproduced in Bortolotti (2008: 286, 301 respectively)).

6
International Licensing Agreements

Contents

Overview 230
Glossary 231
I Intellectual property defined 231
II Intellectual property law defined 232
III The role of intellectual property law 232
IV The role of intellectual property 232
V The concerns of the different actors 232
VI Characteristics of intellectual property rights 233
VII Main categories of intellectual property rights 233
VIII The role of international licensing agreements 237
IX The role of licensing 238
X General format of a licensing agreement 238
XI Main categories of international licensing agreements 239
XII Licensing a patent 239
XIII Licensing a trade mark 240
XIV Licensing a copyright 241
XV Technology transfer agreement 241
XVI Franchising 241
XVII The principal's benefits under a licensing agreement 246
XVIII The licensee's benefits under a licensing agreement 246
XIX General concerns of the parties 247
XX Governing law under European Union law 251
XXI Checklist of provisions 252
XXII Front of the contract 253
XXIII Body of the contract 254
XXIV Boilerplate clauses 272
XXV Back of the contract 272
Summary 273
Useful links 273
Further reading 273
Notes 274

Overview

This chapter looks at the various issues that concern international licensing agreements. Firstly, it reviews the fundamental characteristics of intellectual property law, looking at the definition of intellectual property, the importance of intellectual property rights and the characteristics of certain of these rights. Secondly, it reviews the role of international licensing agreements, exploring the different types of agreement that exist, as well as the benefits and concerns of the parties to such agreements. Thirdly, it looks at the key provisions that contracting parties should consider including within an international licensing agreement.

By the end of this chapter the reader will have a better understanding of

- the fundamental characteristics of intellectual property law;
- the role of international licensing agreements;

Glossary

Advance A sum paid to the principal by the licensee in exchange for the grant of intellectual property rights.

Franchise The grant of a right by the **franchisor** to the **franchisee** to trade using a business method developed by the **franchisor** under the trade mark, service mark, trade name or other form of branding owned by the **franchisor**, in exchange for a fee or other consideration paid by the **franchisee**.

Franchisee[1] The licensee of a franchise.

Franchisor[2] The owner of a business method developed under a trade mark, service mark, trade name or other form of branding owned by the **franchisor**.

Grant-back provision A provision requiring the licensee to transfer to the principal any improvements, new products and so on it acquires using the property licensed by the principal. Such an obligation may be unilateral or reciprocal. Whilst the prior requires one party (typically the licensee) to transfer improvements, new products and so on that it acquires, the latter obliges both parties to do so.[3]

Registered user agreement A licensing agreement pertaining to a registered trade mark.

Royalties Payments paid to the principal by the licensee at regular intervals in exchange for the grant of intellectual property rights.

User agreement A licensing agreement pertaining to a trade mark that is not registered.

1 Intellectual property defined

Intellectual property has been given various definitions over the centuries. One definition was provided in 1868 by Frederick Gerhard, who defined intellectual property in his book dedicated to the Members of the US Congress as follows:

> A person's ideas or thoughts are his intellectual property only so long as they remain unuttered and unknown to others; but the moment he communicates them to the public, by speech, designs, writing, or any other mode, they cease to be his exclusive property and belong thenceforth to the community at large; for from that moment he has lost control of them, he can no longer alter or destroy them at will ... We may therefore define the term 'intellectual property' as a man's thoughts and ideas, as long as they are not made public. The versification of the poet, the results of the philosopher's experiments, the ideas of the inventor, the patterns of the manufacturer, the fashions of the modiste, all are intellectual property until made the common property of everybody by verbal or written description, design, model, or any other mode. Once published and the poet cannot efface his poem from the memory of his readers, the philosopher hinder the utilization of his discovery, the inventor limit the benefits of his invention, the manufacturer withdraw his new pattern, or the modiste prevent the general adoption

of the fashion introduced by her; all these thoughts and ideas cease to be the property of the individual and become the property of the many.[4]

II Intellectual property law defined

Just as law acknowledges ownership of tangible possessions, so it grants ownership rights in intangible property as well. Intellectual property law groups together the legal principles that govern such intangible, or intellectual, property. Such principles address inter alia ownership of intellectual property, the rights of the owners and the circumstances when the owner can stop others from using their property.

Regardless of its form, intellectual property is a creature of national law, though international law has and does put into place certain guidelines. Such international instruments aim to guarantee uniformity in terms of definitions, protection, assignment and licensing of rights, making it easier for rights' owners to acquire other such rights in different countries.

III The role of intellectual property law

Intellectual property law plays a pivotal role by encouraging investment in research and development and the marketing of new technology for the benefit of the nation as a whole. 'The future of the nation depends in no small part on the efficiency of industry, and the efficiency of industry depends in no small part on the protection of intellectual property.'[5]

IV The role of intellectual property

Intellectual property represents not only an engine of growth but an important source of employment and trade worldwide. In 2002, the copyright industries accounted for roughly 12 per cent of the US gross domestic product ($1.25 trillion) and employed 8.41 per cent of the US workforce (11.47 million workers), comparable to the total level of employment in the entire US manufacturing sector (14.5 million in twenty-one manufacturing industries).[6]

V The concerns of the different actors

Three actors are affected by a specific intellectual property. The first actor is the owner of the intellectual property (inventor, artist and so on). The second is the producer who would like to make use of the intellectual property. The third is the consuming public. Each actor has divergent and occasionally conflicting interests. It is this conflict that is addressed in national and international law as well as during the negotiation of any licensing agreement – the agreement governing the use of intellectual property rights (IPR).[7]

The inventor will be concerned about

1. capitalising on his invention or creation; and
2. receiving the highest possible return on his invention in the form of a lump sum (paid as a one-off payment or in instalments) or a running **royalty** licence with the highest royalty rate.

The producer will be concerned about

1. easy and cheap access to the new invention (product or process) so that he is able to add the product to his existing line or incorporate it into his existing product or make use of the new process in order to improve his manufacturing process;
2. being able to take advantage of the invention for as long as possible;

3. being the exclusive producer on a given market with the right to exploit the invention;
4. delaying exploitation of the invention until a time that suits him; and/or
5. blocking exploitation of the invention completely.

The body of consumers will be concerned about

1. guaranteed access to a continuous flow of new and improved products at the lowest prices possible; and
2. ensuring a wide dissemination of the state of the art for existing and future products so that product development is stimulated and consumer choice is guaranteed.

VI Characteristics of intellectual property rights[8]

Geographical boundaries

Traditionally IPRs were creatures of national law and as such they were confined to the territory in which they were created.[9] However, as a piece of music can be played anywhere in the world, a book translated into a multitude of languages and published in a variety of countries, it is clear that in fact such rights know no borders. It is this transcendent nature that the various international instruments aim to address, by ensuring protection of IPRs across national frontiers.

A patent is territorial, for example, so that it is only valid in the territory of the state that granted it. It is this problem of territoriality of protection that international instruments were devised to address.

Distinct and independent property rights

The different types of intellectual property are proprietary in nature and are largely independent of each other.[10] The existence of a patent in relation to a new product will not for example prevent registration of a trade mark used in relation to the product in question.

Divisibility

IPRs can be divided up. A right can be licensed to various businesses in different countries. Each type of intellectual property groups together a collection of rights, so that a copyright for example will include the right to reproduce the work, issue copies of the work to the public and perform the said work in public.

Dynamism

Intellectual property law is dynamic in nature, needing to change in order to reflect developments in technology and in society. As intellectual property can be accessed by foreign businesses as well as local ones, its protection is a matter of concern for countries. This was the impetus that ultimately resulted in the conclusion of international instruments, protecting and enforcing intellectual property, and the creation of bodies to administer such instruments.

VII Main categories of intellectual property rights

Licences may be granted in relation to one or more categories of intellectual property and IPRs. The most frequent subject matter of a licensing agreement is the patent.[11]

Patent[12]

To be awarded a patent by the patent authorities in a given country, the inventor must create a product that the patent authorities consider to be patentable. To be deemed patentable the product or process must fulfil certain criteria set out in law. Since a patent is generally limited to the country issuing the patent, the principal will need to make sure that he applies for patents in other countries in order to enjoy protection in these countries.[13]

Patents under English law

The main piece of patent legislation in the United Kingdom is the Patents Act 1977.[14] A patent may be granted only in relation to an invention which fulfils the following conditions:

1. It must be new.
2. It must involve an inventive step.
3. It must be capable of industrial application.
4. The grant of a patent to the said invention must not be excluded under Section 1(2) or Section 1(3) of the Act.[15]

A patent cannot be granted in relation to an invention the commercial exploitation of which would be contrary to either public policy or public morality.[16]

Amongst other things the following are not deemed inventions under the Act:

- anything consisting of a discovery, scientific theory or mathematical method
- a technique for performing a mental act
- a business technique
- a technique for playing a game
- presentation of information.[17]

This list is non-exhaustive and may be varied in order to address developments in science and technology.[18]

An invention fulfilling these conditions would be classed as a patentable invention.

Patents under US law

The United States Congress has adopted the Patent Statutes found in Title 35 of the US Code, which contains the criteria that must be fulfilled in order for an invention to qualify for a patent. Firstly, the invention must fall into one of five statutory categories: a process, a machine, an article of manufacture, a composition or a new use of one of the first four.[19] Secondly, the invention must be useful – it must have some functional value – or, if a design patent is involved, ornamental.[20] Thirdly, the invention must possess something that is different in some way from anything previously invented. It must be novel and to be novel it must be different from all previous developments made available to the public. In other words, it must be different from what is termed in law 'prior art'. Fourthly, the invention must be unobvious to a party possessing ordinary skill in the specific technology involved in the invention.[21]

Trade marks[22]

The owner of a trade mark has property rights in the mark, which represents a product or service. As such he can protect his mark by stopping others from using it.[23] This right is pivotal where counterfeiting is involved, in other words where items are produced and sold as 'real' versions.

In US law[24] a trade mark includes any word, name, symbol or device or any combination thereof used by an entity in order to identify and distinguish its goods from goods produced or sold by others and to indicate the source of the goods. Such a mark is used to alert the buying public to the origin and source of the product or service. In English law[25] a trade mark is defined as any sign that is capable of being represented graphically which is capable of distinguishing goods or services of one entity from those of other entities and could include words, designs, letters, numerals or the shape of the goods or their packaging.[26] A trade mark is not limited to a word or logo but can encompass the shape of an object, its colour or even its smell, when these are consistently attached to a good or its packaging, distinguishing it from other goods on the marketplace.

The right to claim rights in a mark is rooted in prior use.[27] Trade mark rights do not generally arise from registration as the 'registration does not create the underlying right in a trade mark. That right, which accrues from the use of a particular name or symbol, is essentially a common law property right.'[28]

Copyright[29]

Copyright is a right permitting the author of an artistic work rights (pecuniary and moral) in their work (their copy, so to speak) for a defined period of time.

The ownership of a copyright is separate from and independent of the ownership of the physical object itself. This has several manifestations, which can be illustrated by considering a person who draws a cartoon. Firstly, the cartoonist will own the copyright to the cartoon even if she is no longer in possession of the piece of paper on which the cartoon was sketched. Secondly, the act of mailing the piece of paper with the cartoon on it to another person will not divest the artist of her copyright interest in the cartoon. Thirdly, the act of mailing the piece of paper with the cartoon on it to another person will not have the result of investing the recipient of the cartoon with a copyright interest in it.[30]

Copyright is in actual fact a grouping of rights. These rights are divisible and as such each right can be separately owned, transferred or even subdivided.[31] The principal will grant a licence to a licensee. The licensee can sublicense the right licensed to another entity for a defined period of time subject to the terms in the licensing agreement.

Copyright is the child of the printing press[32]. The creators of literary works had to wait until after the advent of printing made the mass production of books a reality for any general recognition in law of their work.[33] The earliest rights were awarded to publisher-printers by means of a special grant. In 1469 the Republic of Venice granted John of Speyer the right to print the letters of Cicero and of Pliny for five years. In 1481, the Duke of Milan issued a copyright to a printer of local history. Similar copyrights were issued to various printers across Europe at around the same time.[34]

The Statute of Anne[35] was the first fully fledged copyright act. Introduced in England in 1709, during the reign of Queen Anne, in a bid to promote learning[36] and encourage 'learned men to compose and write useful books',[37] it granted authors rights in their work without requiring them to obtain an individual grant from the sovereign, thereby allowing them to stop others from delivering their work to the public without their authority. Similar legislation followed elsewhere and in 1886, several European countries (including Britain, France, Germany, Italy and Spain) signed the Berne Convention, the first international treaty governing copyright. The Statute of Anne was not only the first act to protect literary property but has also been used as a template for legislative acts introduced to protect literary property.[38]

The development of copyright law in the US came about in the eighteenth century. The framers of the first legislative acts on the subject looked at the promotion of public welfare through the diffusion of knowledge and the encouragement of literature and genius as well as the protection of authors in their property.[39] As the preamble to an act passed in Massachusetts in 1783 states,

> whereas the improvement of knowledge, the progress of civilization, the public weal of the community, and the advancement of human happiness, greatly depend on the efforts of learned and ingenious persons in the various arts and sciences: As the principal encouragement such persons can have to make great and beneficial exertions of this nature, must exist in the legal security of the fruits of their study and industry to themselves; and as such security is one of the natural rights of all men, there being no property more peculiarly a man's own than that which is produced by the labour of his mind.[40]

It was in this spirit that the framers of the US Constitution empowered Congress 'to promote the Progress of Science and useful Arts, by securing, for limited Times to Authors and Inventors the exclusive Right to their respective Writings and Discoveries'.[41]

With developments in technology, new types of work are created that are not covered by traditional law. For this reason, law in this area is dynamic, accommodating for new forms of work. An illustration of this is the fact that copyright law has been updated in various countries to incorporate computer programs into the definition of works.[42]

Copyright under English law

The Copyrights, Designs and Patents Act 1988[43] contains the primary legislation on copyright. This Act, which came into force on 1 August 1989, has been successively amended.

Copyright is defined under the Act as a property right subsisting in a variety of works, including but not limited to original literary, dramatic, musical or artistic works and sound recordings, films or broadcasts.[44] A copyright can be transmitted by assignment as personal or moveable property.[45] Such assignment may be limited so that it applies to one or more, but not all, of the things that the copyright owner has the exclusive right to do (a list of these things is given below). In the alternative, the assignment may be limited in terms of duration, so that it may apply to part but not the whole of the period for which the copyright subsists.

The owner of a copyright in a work has the exclusive right to perform the following acts in the United Kingdom:

1. to copy the work;
2. to issue copies of it to the public;
3. to lend or rent it to the public;
4. to perform it in public;
5. to communicate it to the public; and
6. to make an adaption of it.[46]

The duration of a copyright (the period for which it subsists before it expires) is determined by the type of work involved. For example the copyright in a literary work will generally expire seventy years after the end of the calendar year in which the author of the work dies.[47]

Copyright in a work is infringed by a person who does or permits another to do any of the acts restricted by the copyright without the licence of the copyright owner.[48]

Copyright under US law

Copyright law protects against an infringement of certain exclusive rights in 'original works of authorship fixed in any tangible medium of expression, now known or later developed, from which they can be perceived, reproduced, or otherwise communicated, either directly or with the aid of a machine or device'.[49] The categories of work eligible for copyright protection (copyrightable works) include the following,[50] whether published or unpublished:[51]

1. literary works
2. musical works (and any accompanying words)
3. dramatic works (including any accompanying music)
4. pantomimes and choreographic works
5. pictorial, graphic and sculptural works
6. motion pictures and other audiovisual works
7. sound recordings
8. architectural works
9. compilations and derivatives of such work.

VIII The role of international licensing agreements[52]

In addition to direct exporting, a business entity looking to expand beyond national markets may elect to use a variety of different entry strategies, including licensing a foreign entity, entering into a partnership with an existing entity in the target market, forming a new entity in the target market either alone or in partnership with another local entity, acquiring an existing entity in the target market or merging with one.[53] Before making a decision about which of these entry strategies to use, a business entity should consider the advantages and disadvantages associated with each one.

Licensing will require little or no capital investment on the principal's part, as the principal will usually be relying on foreign production by the licensee. It is an option that is available to small as well as large businesses as it requires good ideas and good products rather than a large capital investment. However, from the point of view of the principal there is always a risk that the foreign licensee may become a competitor. For example, after the agreement comes to an end there is a danger that the licensee will use the acquired know-how and technology to produce competing goods, which it may then try to sell in its market or in a foreign market. This danger is likely outweighed by the advantages associated with the relationship between the parties, namely the possibility that the licence may be extended to other producers, the likelihood that the parties will both share in the improvements made by each and the exchange of know-how.

From the perspective of the principal, an alternative to an outright licensing agreement would be an agreement pursuant to which the principal would transfer technology as a contribution to a joint venture abroad, in exchange for a share of the joint venture. Such a joint venture would in turn use the technology transferred in order to produce goods and perhaps market the goods or its components.[54]

When considering the possibility of licensing, the principal should give due regard to the system of law in place in the target market, the need to find a suitably qualified licensee, the qualifications of the licensee, the ability of the principal to communicate with the staff of the licensee and any concerns associated with the different backgrounds of the personnel employed by the principal on the one hand and the licensee on the other. Such differences may be the result of the disparities between the educational, technical, economic and legal standards in the target market and in the principal's country.[55]

In order to source a suitable licensee, the principal looking to expand operations abroad should consider contacting the chamber of commerce in the target market or in its own home market as well as trade and industrial associations. In addition, by attending trade fairs at home and abroad the principal will be able to meet up with prospective licensees as well as gauge their suitability.[56]

In terms of qualifications it is important to consider that the relationship with the licensee is intended to be a long-term one. For this reason, the principal should carry out a complete investigation of the potential licensee, considering in particular the licensee's technical know-how, its financial position and reputation in the target market, and its manufacturing and marketing capacities.[57]

IX The role of licensing

Licensing permits the principal to capitalise on the investment made in the development of an invention, a work of art, a trade mark and so on. After years spent on development of a trade mark, know-how, a process, a product or a creative work, using licensing, the principal is finally able secure itself a return on its investment of time and money.

Under and in accordance with the terms of the licensing agreement, a licensee will be permitted to take advantage of amongst other things the principal's trade mark, patent, copyright or know-how.

X General format of a licensing agreement

Term

A licence is granted under negotiated terms either indefinitely until expiry of the licensed intellectual property (patent and so forth) or for an agreed period (definite term).

Grant[58]

Under the licensing agreement the licensee is granted the licence to make use of the IPRs owned by the principal.

Consideration (monetary and non-monetary)

In exchange for the grant made to the licensee, the licensee is typically obliged to provide the principal with monetary consideration. Non-monetary consideration may also be furnished by the licensee in exchange for the grant of the licence. Such non-monetary consideration may take the form for example of improvements and new products which the licensee has developed. Effectively, under the licensing agreement, the parties may agree that the licensee grants the principal rights in improvements and new products it has developed.

In exchange for the licence, the principal may also be granted equity in the operation of the licensee or indeed in a joint operation that the principal establishes with the licensee.

Monetary consideration

Monetary consideration may take the form of

1. an **advance**, which is an initial sum paid at once or in instalments; and/or
2. **royalties**, which are payments made at regular intervals.

Advance
Where an advance is agreed upon the principal will want to ensure that the sum is paid either up front or in instalments.

Royalties

Under the terms of the licensing agreement, the licensee may also be bound to make regular payments to the principal. Such payments may be either fixed or percentage based, reflecting the profits generated by the licensee. As an added protection for the principal, it will probably try to ensure that if royalties drop below a certain level, it will have the right to either terminate the agreement, revoke exclusivity (if exclusivity is granted to the licensee under the agreement) and/or modify the territory allocated to the licensee.

XI Main categories of international licensing agreements

Licences may be granted in relation to one or more categories of intellectual property. The most frequent subject matter of a licensing agreement is the patent.[59]

Licences may be grouped into three categories,[60] namely technical licensing, artistic licensing and commercial licensing. Each category is differentiated by the subject matter underlying the licence. In technical licensing, the principal permits the licensee to imitate its products or processes. Usually such a set-up involves the transfer of technology and the intellectual property involved will generally consist of patents, engineering drawings, industrial designs or know-how.[61] In artistic licensing, the principal allows the licensee to reproduce original work written or created by the principal. This work may for example be literary, dramatic, musical or artistic.[62] In commercial licensing, the principal permits the licensee to imitate the business of the principal. The licensee under such a licensing agreement is permitted to use the name by which the goods or the business of the principal are known. Commercial licensing is usually associated with a larger licensing package involving artistic or technical licensing.[63]

XII Licensing a patent

The patent owner (known as either the patentee or licensor) will grant to the licensee under a licence pertaining to a patent a right or a bundle of rights including the right to produce, to use and/or to sell the patented goods or processes.

Exclusive and non-exclusive rights in relation to the patent

The right or bundle of rights granted to the licensee by the patent owner may be either exclusive or non-exclusive.[64] Where the right granted to the licensee is exclusive, the patent owner will be granting the licensee alone the right to produce, use and/or sell in the territory allocated within the licensing agreement. In this case, the licensee will be the only party in the territory designated in the licensing agreement with the right to produce, use and/or sell the patented goods or processes. Where exclusivity is granted to the licensee then the right licensed or the bundle of rights licensed are exercised to the exclusion of others, including on occasion the patent owner itself, by the exclusive licensee.[65]

In contrast, under a non-exclusive licensing agreement, the patent will be licensed by the patent owner not only to the licensee. In effect there may be a number of licensees in a given territory with the right to produce, use and/or sell the patented goods or processes.

Type of patent licence

Patent licences will take a number of different forms depending on the right or rights licensed by the patent owner to the licensee.[66] Licenses pertaining to patented goods or processes may extend one or more of the rights to the licensee.

The right granted by the patent owner under a patent licence may be limited to manufacturing of the product by the licensee, who will either use or sell the product; such an agreement is called a manufacturing agreement. The right granted may be limited to using the patented good; such an agreement is called a leasing agreement. The right granted may be limited to distribution and sale; such an agreement is called a distributor agreement. Another type of licence may permit the licensee to assemble components that comprise the patented good; this type of licence is commonly used in the car, electrical and electronics industries.

Box 6.1 Licensing a patent illustrated

Case study 1
An inventor wishes to capitalise on her invention after securing her exclusive rights by obtaining a patent. She does not have the financial means or know-how needed in order to exploit her invention on a national or worldwide scale and for this reason she agrees to enter into an agreement with an entity that has both the means and know-how to help her take full advantage of her invention. Under the agreement that she concludes with the entity she grants the entity permission to produce, sell and even use her invention in exchange for a royalty and advance.

Case study 2
The research department at a leading university has secured several patents for products that it has developed. The university has entered into a licensing agreement with a pharmaceutical company that will produce and sell the patented products in Europe. The pharmaceutical company also reserves itself the right to sublicense the patent to its subsidiaries in Japan, China and the United States. Under the terms of the licensing agreement, the pharmaceutical company has insisted on an exclusivity clause enabling it alone to enjoy worldwide exclusivity for the patents licenced to it.

XIII Licensing a trade mark

Trade mark licence agreements are another form of licensing agreement. The right to use a trade mark will typically be extended to the licensee along with manufacturing agreements based on patents or know-how.[67]

Box 6.2 Licensing a trade mark illustrated

Case study 1
A small business in the north of England has developed a successful line of biscuits using a trade mark that it has developed and promoted over the decade that it has been selling its products. The business as an owner of the trade mark is hoping to capitalise on the time and money invested in getting the trade mark known; as such it decides to license the trade mark to another business that produces a similar line of biscuits in the south of England. The business as an owner of the trade mark decides to licence the right to use the trade mark to this other business in exchange for a royalty and advance.

Case study 2
A well-known chain of hairdressers established in the 1970s has developed a recognisable trade mark on the high street in the United

> Kingdom. The owner of the chain decides to capitalise on the trade mark by licensing the manufacturer of a line of shampoos and hairdryers to use the trade mark on products that it manufactures and sells in Europe.

Where the owner of a trade mark decides to licence another party to exploit the trade mark that it owns, the agreement that the parties will conclude will either be called a **registered user agreement** or **user agreement**. A registered user agreement is a licensing agreement pertaining to a registered trade mark, whilst a user agreement is a licensing agreement pertaining to a trade mark that is not registered.

The licensor of a trade mark will usually enforce certain procedures and standards that the licensee of the trade mark will need to comply with in relation to the preparation, presentation, marketing, selling and the standard of the goods carrying the trade mark. Such provisions enable the licensor of the trade mark to protect the reputation associated with the trade mark.

XIV Licensing a copyright

Under such an agreement, the owner of a copyright may grant the licensee the right to exploit the copyright in a country, region or worldwide either for a defined period or indefinitely. A copyright licence may be exclusive or non-exclusive.[68]

XV Technology transfer agreement

A technology transfer agreement permits the exchange of technology and manufacturing know-how between different entities. International technology transfer agreements permit the exchange of technology and manufacturing know-how between entities in different countries through arrangements such as licensing agreements. Aside from the transfer of know-how and technology, the licensee may benefit from training provided by the principal or on behalf of the principal in relation to the use of the know-how and technology.

In certain countries such set-ups are regulated by local governments. Such regulation is usually intended to guarantee modernisation and development within the country, especially when the owner of the technology is from a highly industrialised country and the licensee is located in a developing country. In such situations, the government is likely to restrict the terms of the licensing agreement in a manner that benefits its own country. Government regulation may for example require the owner of the technology to train workers in the use of the technology or permit sublicensing of the said technology.

XVI Franchising[69]

The difficulty in formulating a definition for the term **franchise** stems from the fact that the term is used to designate a large number of marketing systems.[70] However, as will be seen below, many of these systems possess a number of common underlying characteristics.

Franchising is by no means a new concept in law or marketing. Martin Mendelsohn has stated that franchising as a technique 'did not derive from one moment of inventiveness by an imaginative individual. It evolved from the solutions developed by businessmen in response to the problems with which they were confronted in their business operations'.[71]

It is generally believed that franchising emerged in the United States when, after the end of the Civil War, the Singer Sewing Machine Company instituted a dealer network.[72] At the start of the twentieth century in began to be used in the US beverage and motor industries 'followed by a trickle of developments until the 1930s, when Howard Johnson started his famous chain in the USA, and the 1940s and 1950s, which saw the birth of so many of the modern giants of the franchising community'.[73]

Franchising now involves all levels in the chain from manufacturing to consumer. Franchising can be found between

1. manufacturers and retailers;
2. manufacturers and wholesalers;
3. wholesalers and retailers; and
4. retailers and retailers.[74]

Franchises are regulated in certain countries by

- franchise disclosure laws (protecting investors);
- approval schemes (where governmental approval of the franchise operation is required); and
- laws covering the import of supplies (affecting food products, pharmaceutical products, electrical and electronic products and so on).

Characteristics of franchising[75]

A franchise agreement is a mechanism permitting the franchisor to distribute goods or services through a network of independent entities (franchisees). Under a franchise agreement, the franchisee is

1. allowed to offer goods or services to the public using a business model developed by the **franchisor** under the trade name, trade mark, service mark or other form of branding developed and owned by the franchisor;
2. provided with a range of services furnished by the franchisor which are intended to ensure as best as possible that the **franchisee** enjoys the same level of success as the franchisor, such services including selection of trading sites, training in the operation of the business model, the provision of know-how and other trade secrets, and
3. provided with ongoing support from the franchisor (which usually includes operational support, marketing support, research and development).[76]

From the point of view of the franchisee, the franchisor

1. supplies specialised knowledge and experience;
2. provides initial training and support and ongoing assistance and back-up;
3. furnishes 'the benefit of a name and reputation (a brand image) and goodwill which are already well established in the mind and eye of the consumer';[77] and
4. promotes the trade mark, service mark or trade name.[78]

From the point of view of the franchisor, the franchisee

1. supplies the capital investment and the manpower;
2. takes on the vast majority of the capital risk;
3. takes charge of the day-to-day running of the business;
4. provides entrepreneurial commitment; and
5. furnishes on-site management and local knowledge.[79]

Franchising is defined in US case law as 'the license from the owner of a trademark or trade name permitting another to sell his product or service under that name'.[80] It is a model that has developed over the years out of a series of business transactions and practices which share a number of key characteristics:

1. ownership by one party of a name, idea, process or piece of equipment with the accompanying goodwill
2. the grant of a licence for exploitation of the same by the owner to another party (the licensee)
3. the inclusion of directions within the licensing agreement governing the operation of the business in the conduct of which the licensee exploits his rights under the licensing agreement
4. the payment by the licensee of a royalty or other consideration for the rights extended under the licensing agreement.[81]

These same features characterise every single licensing arrangement. In addition to the four elements described above, with a franchise a fifth element is present, which is the presence of a continuing relationship between the franchisor and the franchisee consisting of the franchisee receiving the full and ongoing support of a comprehensive range of expert know-how in the running of the operation.[82]

The term 'franchising' is used to describe inter alia the dealer appointed by the car manufacturer and the petrol station owner appointed by the oil company. As an operational tool, franchising is commonly used in many industries, amongst them fast-food retailing, hotels, video rental stores and cinema chains. The difference between a franchisee and any other party establishing a business is the presence of pre-opening training and an external entity which assumes responsibility for the provision of ongoing training, support and guidance.

From the point of view of the franchisor, a franchise is distinct from a branch. A branch invariably involves dealing with a branch manager with all the problems associated with operating a branch in terms of motivation, control and responsibility. A franchise involves dealing with a business owner (the franchisee).[83] The motivation, control and responsibility of the franchisee are rarely going to be an issue from the point of view of the franchisor.

Many of the difficulties associated with creating and running a business (lack of capital, a bad business concept, a poor trading position, lack of specialised know-how, failure to pinpoint risks and so on) should not typically be present in a franchising operation. The knowledge of the franchisor should ensure that these difficulties are pre-empted and addressed[84] through the pre-opening training and ongoing support structure.[85]

Total business franchise[86]

Though many transactions are referred to as franchises, each has a different application. The main type of franchise is the 'total business' franchise.[87] In a 'total business' franchise a party develops a complete method for founding and operating a business and grants licences to others to trade using the same particular business method.[88]

The 'total business' franchise concept entails the exploitation of the goods or services identifiable by a trade mark, trade name, service mark or other brand name developed and owned by the franchisor, and the sale of the blueprint of how to successfully operate the business.[89] The blueprint developed by the franchisor aims to reduce the risks typically associated with the creation of a new business.[90] Such a blueprint will cover all aspects of the business and will include the parameters used to select sites for the positioning of the business, training of parties buying the business in the business methods used to distinguish it from other similar businesses, and training of parties in the methods of marketing.[91]

The party acquiring this franchise will obtain the blueprint developed by the franchisor coupled with the continuing support of the franchisor. In return the franchisee will pay a fee or other consideration to the franchisor.[92]

Draft Common Frame of Reference (DCFR)[93]

The DCFR was presented to the European Commission by the Study Group on the European Civil Code and the Research Group on Existing EC Private Law in December 2008 and published in 2009. Intended to be used as a stand-alone tool with a role of its own,[94] the hope is that the DCFR will act as a source of inspiration for the resolution of private law questions[95].

Regulation of franchise agreements by the DCFR

The general provisions contained in Chapter IV.E.–1 of the DCFR and the rules contained in Chapter IV.E.–2 govern all the agreements covered by Part IV.E, namely commercial agency, franchise and distribution agreements. Each of these agreements is also addressed separately by a set of dedicated and supplementary rules, each of which is contained in one of the three remaining chapters in Part IV.E: Chapter IV.E.–3 covers commercial agency agreements, Chapter IV.E.–4 covers franchise agreements, and Chapter IV.E.–5 covers distribution agreements.

General provisions and general rules[96]

The provisions contained in Part IV.E are intended to cover contracts for the creation and regulation of a commercial agency, franchise or distributorship agreement.[97] In this context the term 'product' is regarded as including not only goods but services as well.[98]

The contracting parties owe each other certain duties. Such duties will arise both before and after the conclusion of the contract. At the pre-contractual phase, each party is obliged to provide the other with sufficient information to allow it to decide on a reasonably informed basis whether or not to conclude a contract with the other party.[99] Such information must be provided within a reasonable period of time before the contract is concluded.[100] Each of the contracting parties owes a duty to the other party to cooperate,[101] to provide in due time all the information in its possession which the other party needs in order to achieve the objectives of the contract,[102] to keep information received from the other party confidential (during the course of the contractual relationship and after the contractual relationship comes to end)[103] and not to use such confidential information for any purpose other than that of achieving the objectives of the contract.[104]

In the context of franchising, the franchisor is also required at the pre-contractual phase to furnish the putative franchisee with information regarding the business and experience of the franchisor; the scope and structure of the network involved; the relevant intellectual property rights; the franchise method and operation; the proposed terms of the franchise agreement; and the fees, royalties or other periodical payments.[105]

Contracts for a definite term

Each contracting party is free not to renew a contract for a definite term.[106] In the event that either one of the contracting parties wishes to renew the contract it may do so by giving the other party notice in due time of its desire to renew,[107] in which case the contract will be renewed for an indefinite period, unless the other party gives that party notice of non-renewal, not later than a reasonable time before the expiry of the contract period.[108]

Contracts for an indefinite term

Each contracting party to a contract for an indefinite term will have the right to terminate the contractual relationship by giving notice to the other.[109] In the event that the notice provides for termination after a period of reasonable length no damages are payable.[110] In the event that the notice provides for immediate termination or termination after a period which is not of reasonable length then damages will be payable.[111]

Statement of terms[112]

Either party to the contract may ask the other for a signed statement setting out the terms of the contract in textual form on a durable medium. The parties are not permitted to exclude this duty or to derogate from or vary its effects.

Rules specific to franchise agreements

Franchise agreements are governed by the general provisions (Chapter IV.E.–1) and rules (Chapter IV.E.–2) reviewed above, alongside the specific provisions set out in Chapter IV.E.–4. Chapter IV.E.–4 is intended to cover contracts concluded between a franchisor and a franchisee under which the franchisor grants the franchisee the right to conduct business within the network of the franchisor, using the trade name or trade mark of the franchisor along with any other intellectual property belonging to the franchisor, as well as the franchisor's know-how and business method.[113]

The obligations of the franchisor and the franchisee are set out in Sections IV.E.–4:2 and IV.E.–4:3 respectively. The franchisor is obliged inter alia

- to provide the franchisee with the right to use the IPRs to the extent needed to operate the franchise business;[114]
- to provide the franchisee with assistance including training, guidance and advice without additional charge;[115]
- to keep the franchisee informed about market conditions, relevant communication between the franchisor and customers in the territory and marketing campaigns;[116] and
- to ensure the supply of products ordered by the franchisee within a reasonable time.[117]

The franchisee is obliged inter alia

- to pay the franchisor the agreed fees, royalties or other periodical payments;[118]
- to keep the franchisor informed about claims brought or threatened by third parties in relation to the franchisor's IPRs;[119]
- to keep the franchisor informed about infringements of its IPRs by third parties[120];
- to adhere to the business method of the franchisor;[121] and
- to provide the franchisor with the opportunity to inspect the franchisee's premises and accounting books.[122]

XVII The principal's benefits under a licensing agreement

A business looking to expand beyond its national market may elect to do so by licensing an established entity in the target market. Under a licensing agreement the principal will be extending the licensee the right to produce, use and sell products using the IPRs owned by the principal.

Licensing a foreign entity has certain advantages over exporting from the point of view of the principal. Using licensing, the principal can secure greater penetration into the foreign market, whilst enjoying more control over the manner in which the foreign entity produces, packages and markets the goods produced using the licensed intellectual property. The principal avoids transportation costs as well as the risks associated with transportation and delivery. As the goods are typically produced locally, transportation can be dispensed with, so that the associated costs, time and risks are no longer an issue. Furthermore, as the goods are being produced in the target market, tariff and non-tariff barriers will no longer be a concern.

Licensing a foreign entity also has certain advantages over creating a branch or establishing a subsidiary in the target market. When compared with setting up a branch or subsidiary in the target market, licensing offers the principal the opportunity to limit its legal, financial and political exposure. Licensing will usually require little to no capital investment on the principal's part as it will usually rely on the licensee's investment. Since the licensee usually assumes responsibility for foreign production, marketing and sales, it will typically be responsible for employing and training personnel, for concluding contracts locally and for obtaining local permissions and consents (the latter two elements will usually relate to the production, marketing and sale of the goods produced). As such the principal is able to reduce his legal exposure and his political risks in the target market.

Licensing is also a good way of capitalising on an investment made in development of intellectual property, inter alia trade mark, service mark, know-how, patent and copyright, whilst at the same time securing a constant stream of revenue in the form of royalties. The latter is particularly important during periods of recession.[123] Götz Pollzien and George Bronfen give the example of a firm based in the US that sees a drop in its domestic sales during a period of recession whilst its revenue from licensees outside the US increases.

Aside from the financial rewards associated with licensing, the principal benefits from development of brand recognition in a new geographic market. Moreover, it is expanding its operation into a new geographic market with the help of another entity (the licensee) which has an established network of customers and distributors, know-how of the market and local law and regulations, and a pre-existing share of the market targeted by the principal.

XVIII The licensee's benefits under a licensing agreement

The licensee will benefit from the principal's investment in the development of its intellectual property, inter alia trade mark, service mark, know-how, patent and copyright, which the licensee is now licensed to use in the target market when producing, promoting and selling. In turn, the licensee will make a saving on the costs and risks associated with development of the intellectual property including the costs and risks inherent in research and development and promotional activities (in relation to a trade mark for example).

The licensee may benefit from the

association with the licensed intellectual property. For example when an established trade mark is licensed, the licensee will benefit from the association with the said trade mark. This association will be likely in turn to improve the reputation and goodwill of the licensee, which may enable it to attract other potential principals and to expand market share. Such an association will also provide the licensee with know-how and staff training.

The licensee may be able to negotiate territorial exclusivity, in which case it will not need to worry about competition from other parties licensed by the principal in the same geographic market. A licensee may also be able to reap additional financial rewards, aside from the earnings made using the licensed intellectual property, by securing a right to sublicense the licensed intellectual property.

When negotiating a licensing agreement, the licensee will want to secure the right to use new products and improvements developed firstly by the principal and secondly by the licensee using the licensed intellectual property.

XIX General concerns of the parties

The following section considers the concerns of the principal and the licensee in the context of the licensing agreement.

Box 6.3 General concerns of the parties

Principal's concerns
- Financial incentive
- Promotional activities
- Anti-competition restrictions
- Right to grant rights to more than one licensee
- Confidentiality
- Right to improvements and new goods developed by the licensee
- Unauthorised use of licensed property
- Protection of intellectual property
- Quality control
- Sublicensing
- Regulation of the licensing agreement.

Licensee's concerns:
- Support services
- Exclusivity
- Right to improvements and new goods developed by the principal
- Minimum outlay
- Restrictions on use of licensed property
- Warranties.

The principal's concerns

Beyond the financial incentive other concerns should be considered with care by the principal.

Promotional activities

A principal will be concerned by the efficiency of the promotional and marketing activities of the licensee, as the principal's economic return will depend on the marketing success of the licensee, as will its market share, its reputation and in turn its goodwill. For this reason, the principal should consider incorporating into the licensing agreement provisions that address the promotional and marketing activities of the licensee. Within this context it would be wise for the principal to give due consideration to the inclusion of provisions within the licensing agreement requiring the licensee

1. to use its best efforts to develop a market for the products manufactured with the intellectual property licensed;
2. to comply with specific marketing quotas (more below); and
3. to pay the principal a guaranteed annual minimum payment.

This last provision not only protects the principal's cash flow but also acts as a motivational tool prompting the licensee to generate a regular annual return.

Anti-competition restrictions

A principal should take into account the risk that the licensed intellectual property may come back into the principal's home market in the form of products that will compete with its own products. This phenomenon is known as the grey market or parallel imports.

A grey market could arise after the expiry of the licence and its anti-competition restrictions, in a situation where either the licensee or another party produces the licensed goods using the intellectual property of the principal. Alternatively, it could arise even before the expiry of licence, where the licensee or a third party sells the licensed goods in the home market of the principal in competition with the latter.

There is no set view on parallel trade amongst the different jurisdictions. In certain countries, for example, the benefits of price competition are considered to be more important than the concerns of the principal.

Right to grant rights to more than one licensee

See 'Territorial exclusivity' subsection in Section XXIII, 'Body of the contract', below.

Confidentiality

See 'Confidentiality' subsection in Section XXIII, 'Body of the contract', below.

Right to improvements and new goods developed by the licensee

See 'Licensee's obligations' subsection in Section XXIII, 'Body of the contract', below.

Unauthorised use of licensed property

The principal should endeavour to ring-fence the manner in which the licensee exploits and uses the licensed intellectual property, in order firstly to address the risk of losing control over the licensed intellectual property, which could have an adverse effect on the business of the principal, and secondly to prevent the establishment of a potential competitor to the principal. In this context, the principal may insist on certain restrictions on use in the licensing agreement, in turn preventing unauthorised use of licensed intellectual property by the licensee, the licensee's personnel or another entity in the licensee's country.

Firstly, the principal may insist that the licensee neither use the licensed intellectual property in competition with the principal (non-compete clause) nor disclose the intellectual property licensed to another entity (confidentiality clause). Secondly, the principal may impose geographic limitations on the licensee's manufacturing or marketing activities by assigning a licensed territory. Thirdly, the principal may impose limitations on the licensee's field of use by restricting the applications for which the licensee may employ the intellectual property licensed, the output of the licensee and/or the customer base of the licensee.

Protection of intellectual property

Protection of intellectual property is largely a matter of national law. The principal will accordingly need to ensure protection under the national law in the target market. It has two options in this context: firstly, it may decide to delegate the protection of the intellectual property licensed to the licensee; or secondly, it may assume responsibility for protection of the licensed intellectual property. This option is beneficial from the point of view of the principal since it ensures certainty whilst allowing the principal to ensure effectiveness of protection.

Quality control

Quality control is an issue that will concern the principal. Poor quality control by the licensee will have an adverse effect on the reputation and goodwill of the principal and any intellectual property that the principal owns (a trade mark, service mark and so on). To avoid such problems, it is sensible for the principal to ensure that certain provisions are included in the agreement addressing such issues:

- firstly, a provision permitting the principal the right to inspect the facility or facilities where the contract goods are produced;
- secondly, a provision requiring the licensee to furnish samples of the contract goods produced using the licensed intellectual property of the principal;
- thirdly, a provision addressing training of the personnel working for and on behalf of the licensee; and
- fourthly, a provision allowing the principal to approve promotional campaigns and promotional literature involving the licensed intellectual property.

Sublicensing

The licensee may want to acquire the right to sublicense the licensed intellectual property. A sublicence will enable the licensee to license the licensed intellectual property belonging to the principal to another entity, thereby generating revenue for the licensee. This is a concern for the principal in terms of loss of control and loss of confidential information developed and owned by the principal.

A number of options are available to the principal in this context. Firstly, it may include a provision in the licensing agreement prohibiting sublicensing. Secondly, it may decide to permit sublicensing, subject to certain conditions that it defines. The principal may decide to do this as the sublicensing may benefit it in financial terms (it may receive a portion of the royalties received from the sublicensee for example) and in terms of research and development in view of any investment in that area that may be made by the sublicensee.

If a principal decides to permit sublicensing, it should consider including certain provisions in the licensing agreement addressing the question of sublicensing:

- firstly, a provision ensuring that the licensee obtains the prior written consent of the principal before sublicensing; and
- secondly, a provision requiring the sublicensee to enter into an agreement with the principal as a precondition for the grant of the sublicence.

Regulation of the licensing agreement

Competition law implications[124] will need to be considered alongside tax issues and legal regulation of the substantive terms of the licensing agreement. Target market regulation of the terms of the licensing agreement will be a major concern for the principal,[125] as the following case illustrates.[126]

Box 6.4 Regulation of franchise agreements illustrated

William Mariniello t/a J & B Shell Station, Inc. v. Shell Oil Company[127]

In 1960 a franchising agreement was concluded pursuant to which Mr Mariniello (M) would run a Shell Oil Company (S) petrol station as a franchisee. Until 1969 the franchise agreement, consisting of two separate agreements (a lease for the premises and an agreement granting M the right to buy S's goods and to use their trade mark), was renewed annually. In 1969 a three-year lease and a three-year dealership agreement were executed. The lease permitted S to terminate at will on its expiry whilst the dealership agreement permitted termination at any time with a notice of ten days.

In 1972 S advised M that neither of the agreements would be renewed. M challenged this decision and filed an action in court for continuance of both agreements.

The case involved an earlier decision of the New Jersey Supreme Court allowing a franchisor to terminate a franchise agreement when there is good cause justifying the termination in question; as a matter of public policy it was stated that clauses in franchise agreements that permit termination at will are unenforceable.[128] The issue that the court addressed in this present case was whether this earlier rule formulated by the New Jersey Supreme Court upon which M relied is violative of the US Constitution.[129] In the present case, the court concluded that the rule in question neither operated in a manner that compromises the aims of the Lanham Act[130] nor violated the Supremacy Clause. The aims of the Lanham Act, the court stated, are the need for public confidence that it will get the product that it asks for and wants to get; and the need of the owner of a trade mark, who has invested time, money and energy in presenting the product to the public, to be protected in his investment from misappropriation of its trade mark by pirates and cheats.[131]

The court also stated in this case[132] that the interpretation and enforcement of contracts is traditionally a matter that falls within the province of state courts and that the invalidation of contractual clauses that are held to be repugnant to state public policy is a proper exercise of the state judicial function. When a state law is challenged as violative of the Supremacy Clause of the US Constitution,[133] as the present state law was, the federal court is responsible for determining if in fact the state law is an impediment to the achievement and execution of the full purposes and objectives of Congress.[134] Where a conflict is alleged between state law and federal law, the court stated that reference needs to be made to the specific aim of the federal act to determine any potential erosion of the federal plan as a result of state law.[135] For this reason, in this case reference was made to the intent of Congress in enacting the Lanham Act.

The government in the target market may demand that licensing agreements be registered and in some cases national law may stipulate prior approval of the licensing arrangement, in a bid to ensure that the licensing agreement and its provisions have no potential adverse effect on the local economy and its growth.[136] Such schemes will have not only the effect of increasing the expenditure and time involved in getting the licensing operation up and running, but may also increase the risk of leakage of confidential information.[137] In certain countries, for example, attempts by a principal to restrict or prohibit sublicensing will not be permitted, due to the perceived importance such sublicences have for the local economy and its growth. Other provisions which may be open for scrutiny include grant-back requirements, export restrictions, price-fixing, non-competition clauses, exclusivity clauses and territorial restrictions.[138]

The licensee's concerns

Support services

See 'Support services' subsection in Section XXIII, 'Body of the contract', below.

Exclusivity

See 'Territorial exclusivity' subsection in Section XXIII, 'Body of the contract', below.

Right to improvements and new goods developed by the principal

See 'Improvements and new goods' subsection in Section XXIII, 'Body of the contract', below.

Minimum royalty payments if at all

See 'Fixing the royalty rate' subsection in Section XXIII, 'Body of the contract', below.

Minimum outlay

The licensee may want to keep its outlay to a minimum by reducing the payments due to the principal.

Restrictions on use of licensed property

The licensee may want to ensure that it retains the freedom to use the licensed intellectual property by for example securing the right to sublicense.

Warranties

See 'Warranties' subsection in Section XXIII, 'Body of the contract', below.

XX Governing law under European Union law

In the European Union, the contract between the principal and the licensee will be governed by Regulation (EC) No 593/2008 of the European Parliament and the Council of 17 June 2008 on the Law Applicable to Contractual Obligations (Rome I).[139] Rome I governs all contracts concluded after 17 December 2009. Contracts concluded on or before 17 December 2009 are governed by the Convention on the Law Applicable to Contractual Obligations opened for signature in Rome on 19 June 1980 (the Rome Convention),[140] the predecessor to Rome I.

Rome I and the Rome Convention both apply to contractual obligations in situations where there is a choice between the laws of different countries.[141] Rome I is distinct from the Principles of European Contract Law (PECL), a body of contract law that is voluntary in nature and as such adopted at the discretion of the contracting parties. Rome I and the Rome Convention both contain rules that define the law applicable to a contract and those rules are mandatory in application.

Freedom to choose the governing law

Whilst the contracting parties are free to choose the law applicable to the contract between them,[142] if they do not do so, Rome I will intercede to make the selection for them in accordance with the rules set out in Article 4.

Article 3.1 of Rome I permits the parties contracting to choose the law governing their contract. The parties may choose the law applicable to the whole of their contract or alternatively to just part of it.[143] Furthermore, Article 3.2 permits the parties contracting to modify by agreement the law governing the contract. Any such selection must be made expressly or clearly demonstrated by the terms of the contract or the circumstances of the case.[144]

Wherever possible, it is advisable for the contracting parties to expressly identify the law that they have chosen to govern the contract concluded between them. This will ensure certainty and clarity in their relations and will ward against any potential litigation that could later ensue on this very question.

In the absence of a choice by the parties

Article 4.1 of Rome I sets out specific choice of law rules for particular categories of cases. Where Article 4.1 does not supply a conclusive choice of law then the general rule articulated in Article 4.2 applies. Further general displacement rules – included in Articles 4.3 and 4.4 – are intended to introduce flexibility in those situations where the application of one of the specific choice of law rules does not produce the appropriate result.

Pursuant to Article 4.1 a franchise contract shall be governed by the law of the country where the franchisee has his habitual residence.[145] 'Habitual residence' is defined in Article 19, which also decrees:

- For companies and other bodies (corporate or unincorporated) habitual residence will be the place of central administration.
- For a natural person acting in the course of a business activity, habitual residence will be his principal place of business.
- For a contract concluded in the course of the operations of a branch, agency or any other establishment, or if, under the contract, performance is the responsibility of such a branch, agency or establishment, the place where the branch, agency or any other establishment is located shall be treated as the place of habitual residence.

For the purposes of determining the habitual residence, the relevant point in time shall be the time of the conclusion of the contract.

XXI Checklist of provisions

The following section will examine the general provisions that the parties should consider incorporating into the agreement concluded between them. The checklist below provides a list of the provisions that the contracting parties should consider when planning, negotiating and finalising their licensing agreement. This agreement is intended for use in international transactions between commercial parties. Not every one of the provisions listed in the checklist is mandatory, but each of them should be considered by the contracting parties when planning, negotiating and finalising the contract.

XXII FRONT OF THE CONTRACT

Box 6.5 Checklist of provisions

Preface to the contract
- ✓ Cover sheet
- ✓ Table of contents (in longer contracts; optional)
- ✓ Index of defined terms

Front of the contract (section XXII)
- ✓ Title
- ✓ Introductory clause (type of agreement, date of agreement, parties to agreement)
- ✓ Recitals

Body of the contract (section XXIII)
- ✓ Definitions clause
- ✓ Grant
- ✓ Term of the agreement
- ✓ Relationship of the parties
- ✓ Obligations of the licensee
- ✓ Obligations of the principal
- ✓ Termination (grounds and consequences)

Boilerplate clauses (section XXV)
- ✓ Assignment clause
- ✓ Merger clause
- ✓ Modifications clause
- ✓ Severance clause
- ✓ Notice clause
- ✓ Representation clause
- ✓ Dispute resolution (informal discussions, renegotiation, adaption, ADR, choice of jurisdiction and choice of law)
- ✓ Language clause

Back of the contract (section XXVI)
- ✓ Concluding clause
- ✓ Signature blocks
- ✓ Attachment (exhibits and schedules)

XXII Front of the contract

The front of the contract will incorporate the following:

1. Title
2. Introductory clause noting the type and date of the agreement as well as the details of the contracting parties
3. Recitals.

Consider the following sample extract.

> Technology transfer/patent/trade mark licensing agreement[146]
>
> This [*note type of licensing agreement involved*] agreement is made [on this —— day of —— in the year —— or upon the date of the signature hereof] and is between:
>
> 1. —— of —— ('Principal')
> 2. —— of —— ('Licensee')
>
> The Principal and the Licensee will be referred to in this agreement separately as a Party or collectively as the Parties.

The extract above incorporates:

1. a title:[147]

> Technology transfer/patent/trade mark licensing agreement

2. an introductory clause:[148]

This [note type of licensing agreement involved] agreement is made [on this —— day of —— in the year —— or upon the date of the signature hereof] and is between:

1. —— of —— ('Principal')
2. —— of —— ('Licensee')

The Principal and Licensee will be referred to in this agreement separately as a Party or collectively as the Parties.

Recitals[149]

Recitals are optional and will vary in length. None is included in the extract above, but the recital sampled below can be used when concluding a technical licensing agreement. Under such licensing agreements the principal grants the licensee the right to imitate the products or processes of the principal. Usually such a set-up involves the transfer of technology and the intellectual property involved will generally consist of patents, engineering drawings, industrial designs or know-how.[150]

The Principal has developed and obtained [insert details of the technology here which may include but is not limited to patents technology, know-how and related trade marks] ('Licensed Property'). Licensed Property is defined in Schedule ——.

The Principal is willing to grant a licence to the Licensee in relation to the Licensed Property.

The Licensee is presently involved in the business of —— and is looking to develop its business using the Licensed Property.

The Licensee desires to receive a licence in relation to the Licensed Property.

Optional provisions:
The Licensee desires to receive training and support from the Principal during the term of this agreement.

The Licensee desires to produce and sell [*the type of goods may be listed here or in a schedule; if the latter option is used reference should be made here to the pertinent schedule, e.g. 'the goods listed in Schedule ——'*] ('Licensed Goods') using [and carrying] the Principal's Licensed Property in the territory defined in Schedule —— ('Licensed Territory').

XXIII Body of the contract

Definitions clause

See corresponding section in Chapter 2.

Grant[151]

1. The Principal shall grant the Licensee a licence limited to the Licensed Territory.
2. The Agent shall negotiate separately with the Principal any sales or exports of the Licensed Goods outside the Licensed Territory.

Option A: non-exclusive licence
3. The agreement is non-exclusive.

Option B: exclusive licence
3. The Principal hereby grants the Licensee an exclusive licence in relation to the Licensed Property.
4. The Licensee may exclusively produce, have produced or use the Licensed Goods in the Licensed Territory to the exclusion of other parties [including the Principal].
5. The Licensee may exclusively sell the Licensed Goods in the Licensed Territory to the exclusion of other parties [including the Principal] [with the trade marks licensed by the Principal defined in Schedule —— ('Licensed Trade Marks')].
6. The Licensee may exclusively use the technology licensed by the Principal defined in Schedule —— ('Licensed Technology') in the Licensed Territory to the exclusion of other parties [including the Principal].

This provision grants the licensee a licence in the intellectual property owned by the principal. The intellectual property licensed is referred to in this agreement as the licensed property.

The grant provision is pivotal to the agreement since it fulfils a number of key functions that are central to the relationship between the parties. Firstly, in the grant provision the principal provides the licensee with the right to use the licensed property belonging to the principal in the licensed territory. In this provision mention should be made of whether the licence granted is exclusive or non-exclusive. Secondly, in this provision the principal sets out scope of the licence endowed upon the licensee. The principal may reserve itself the right to grant further licences to other parties aside from the licensee, in circumstances where a non-exclusive licence is involved. It may also reserve itself the right to use the licensed property in the licensed territory effectively in competition with the licensee.

Territorial exclusivity[152]

The grant of a licence will either be on a non-exclusive basis (option A) or on an exclusive basis (option B) in the territory assigned. Parties to agreements granting such rights should take care to define the terms that they use in their agreement, since such terms are interpreted differently in different countries.[153]

Option A: non-exclusive licence
A non-exclusive licence is a licence that does not curtail the ability of the principal to grant further licenses in the assigned territory to other parties aside from the licensee. Such an arrangement may appeal to a principal for a number of reasons. Firstly, it may appeal to a principal which is using a rolling royalty licensing agreement to generate a continuous return on its licensed property and is hoping to spread its risk amongst several different players in the assigned territory. Secondly, this arrangement may appeal to a principal looking to enter into a new geographic market in circumstances where it wants to test the capability of the different potential licensees on that market in the short term before entering into a longer-term arrangement with the most competent licensee. Thirdly, this arrangement may appeal to a principal that is looking to use the licensed property itself in the assigned territory.

Option B: exclusive licence
An exclusive licence is one that curtails the ability of the principal to grant further licenses in the assigned territory. The grant of exclusivity in the territory will be advantageous from the point of view of the licensee as it will not be subject to direct competition in the assigned territory.

The licensee for its part is likely to insist on exclusivity in the assigned territory for two reasons. Firstly, the licensee will have to make a significant investment in terms of energy, time and money, especially in a situation where the principal is a newcomer to the market. As such the licensee will need to build up demand for the licensed goods and recognition of the licensed property. The licensee may also for example need to invest in developing recognition of certain trade marks licensed by the principal to the licensee. Secondly, the licensee is initially taking a risk when building up a new market. For these reasons the licensee will be reluctant to allow another party (another licensee, a distributor, the principal itself and so on) to come along and benefit from its work in a given market (free-riding).

From the point of view of the principal, exclusivity may not necessarily be advisable. It will effectively mean that the principal will be putting all its eggs in one basket, and this may result in a reduction of potential revenue from the market in question if the licensee does not fare well. In such an eventuality, in circumstances where the licensee enjoys exclusivity, the principal will typically need to wait until the term expires or, if permitted, to attempt to terminate the agreement on the grounds of a breach by the licensee.

In such circumstances, it is sensible for the principal to try and conclude an agreement that contains the following provisions, which help to a certain degree to offset the risk, from the principal's point of view, associated with exclusivity. Firstly, the principal should try to include a provision stipulating a guaranteed annual minimum payment;[154] secondly, the principal should try to include a provision permitting him to convert the exclusive licence into a non-exclusive licence in the event that the licensee fails to meet set royalty rates.

Term of the agreement[155]

Option A1: an agreement for an indefinite term without an initial period
1. This agreement shall come into force [on this —— day of —— in the year —— *or* upon the date of the signature of this agreement].
2. [Subject to earlier termination permitted by the terms of this agreement] This agreement shall remain in force unless terminated by one Party giving the other Party prior written notice of no less than ——.

Option A2: an agreement for an indefinite term with an initial period
1. This agreement shall come into force [on this —— day of —— in the year —— *or* upon the date of the signature of this agreement].
2. [Subject to earlier termination permitted by the terms of this agreement] This agreement shall continue in force for an initial period of —— years and thereafter, unless terminated by one Party giving the other Party prior written notice of no less than ——.

> 3. (*optional: no termination during initial period*) Neither Party shall give notice before the end of the initial period.
>
> *Option B – An agreement for a definite term*
> 1. This agreement shall run [for a period of —— years from —— *or* from the date of the signature of this agreement].
> 2 This agreement is automatically renewed for successive periods of ——, unless terminated by one Party giving prior written notice to the other Party of no less than ——.

Such a provision may stipulate the date on which the agreement will commence and if appropriate the term of the agreement. Where the parties contracting agree on a definite term (option B) or an initial period (option A1), they should take care to ensure that the definite term or initial period is sufficiently long in order to permit the licensee to develop a profitable business and to recoup his sunk investment.

An agreement for an indefinite term

Where the parties agree to conclude an agreement for an indefinite term, the relevant provision will state that the agreement will continue unless and until it is terminated by one party giving the other written notice of a specified period.

The principal will need to take particular care when the agreement is indefinite as such an agreement may in certain countries be treated as giving rise to an agency arrangement. This will in turn subject the principal to agency laws in the country in question. Such laws may be stricter than the rules governing licensing arrangements.[156]

An agreement for a definite term

The provision fixing a term for the agreement will determine the overall duration of the contract. In this context the term is the period of time during which the licensee is permitted by the principal to exploit the licensed property in the assigned territory.

Where a term is definite, in other words fixed, the contract will run its course unless there is some reason for its premature termination.[157] The term may be for a set period with or without the possibility for extension.

The provision reproduced above in option B states that the agreement is automatically renewed for successive periods, unless it is terminated by one of the contracting parties giving prior written notice to the other contracting party.

Relationship of the parties

See the corresponding section in Chapter 4. The term 'distributor' should be replaced with the term 'licensee'.

Obligations of the licensee

The following obligations imposed on the licensee under the licensing agreement are intended to protect the principal's interests, inter alia its reputation, goodwill and earnings. From the point of view of the principal, it will want to ensure the incorporation of provisions into the agreement that protect its interests in an effective and comprehensive manner.[158] The licensee for its part will probably look to ringfence these obligations as best as it can. As mentioned above[159] certain provisions may be open to scrutiny in different countries. These include grant-back requirements, export restrictions imposed on the licensee, price-fixing requirements, non-compete clauses, exclusivity clauses and territorial restrictions.[160] The provisions that follow are representative of the provisions that the principal is likely to want to incorporate into the agreement and of the interests that it is likely to want to protect.

Firstly, beyond a financial commitment on the part of the licensee,[161] the principal will want make sure that the licensee cannot compete with it either during the course of the agreement and, if at all possible, after the end of the term of the agreement. To this end it will try to secure a non-compete clause that is as widely drafted as possible, bearing in mind the licensee's willingness to agree to such a provision and the position under national law, which may restrict the parameters of such a provision.

Secondly, due to the risks associated with the principal's loss of control over the property that it has licensed to the licensee (the licensed property) and the potential loss of proprietary information belonging to it, the principal will endeavour to secure

1. either a prohibition or limitation on sublicensing;
2. the inclusion of a confidentiality clause which is as wide in scope as possible; and
3. a provision restricting the use of the licensed property.

Thirdly, to ensure retention of ownership in the property that it has licensed to the licensee (the licensed property), the principal would be sensible to insist on the following provisions:

1. a provision clearly stating that the licensee shall obtain no rights in relation to the licensed property;
2. a provision stating that all rights and goodwill in the licensed property are and shall remain vested in the principal;
3. a provision obliging the licensee to update the principal if an infringement of the licensed property becomes known to it; and
4. a provision obliging the licensee to assist the principal in maintaining the validity and enforceability of the licensed property (maintenance of licensed property clause).

Fourthly, in order to ensure that a correct level of quality is maintained by the licensee, it is sensible for the principal to secure the following provisions amongst others:

1. a provision permitting the principal to carry out inspections of the facility or facilities belonging to or run by the licensee; and
2. a provision requiring the licensee to provide the principal with samples of the goods produced using the licensed property either at set intervals or in response to a request from the principal.

Fifthly, the principal will be interested in preserving its rights in relation to new goods and improvements developed by the licensee using the licensed property. To this end, it is sensible for the principal to insist on a provision permitting it to exploit new goods and improvements developed by the licensee (**grant-back provision**).[162]

Payment (paid-up licence or running royalty licence)[163]

This part of the licensing agreement sets out the licensee's financial commitments to the principal. A licensing agreement can take the form of either a paid-up licence or a licence that includes a running royalty provision.

Paid-up licence

1. The Licensee shall pay the Principal the sum of —— ('Initial Sum') in exchange for the rights and licenses granted under this agreement by the Principal to the Licensee [and for the transfer of technology and know-how *(in transfer of technology agreements)*].

Option A
2. The Licensee shall pay the Principal the Initial Sum in full on ——.

Option B
2. The Licensee shall pay the Principal the Initial Sum by means of instalments as follows:
   a. The Licensee shall pay the first instalment of —— on ——;
   b. The Licensee shall pay the second instalment of —— on ——;
   c. [...]

A paid-up licence is one in which a set amount is paid by the licensee to the principal, either as a lump sum or in instalments over a period of time and in accordance with a schedule of payments. Once the sum is fixed by the contracting parties it does not fluctuate, whether the sales made by the licensee are high, low or non-existent.[164] Notwithstanding this fact, the future sales anticipated by the contracting parties may be used to calculate the sum paid as royalty, so that the greater the anticipated sales, the higher the sum the principal will demand from the licensee. Market-testing will provide an indication of the expected sales.[165] Paid-up licences are better suited to those situations where the future earnings of the licensee are relatively predictable as the contracting parties are less likely to dispute the figure to be paid over.[166]

A paid-up licence is more certain from the point of view of the principal than a running royalty licence if the financial viability of the licensee is questionable (for example when the licensee is a start-up company) or there are risks associated with the licensed property (where for example the potential for litigation in relation to possible infringements is high).[167] Such a licence may also be more convenient for the contracting parties than a running royalty licence due to the complexities associated with accounting and processing a running royalty licence.[168] When using a running royalty licence, the principal will first need to go to the time and expense of negotiating and agreeing (alone or with the help of a lawyer) the royalty rate (used to calculate the royalty due) and the frequency with which the royalty is paid. Then it must ensure that the licensee accounts for all the sums earned under the agreement. Furthermore, it may need to insist on regular audits of the licensee's accounts by an independent third party.[169]

Short-term licences are commonly paid-up licences. Such licences are typically used when the licensee is only after a short-term commitment or if the licensed property is due to expire.

Running royalty licence

1. The Licensee shall pay the Principal in consideration of the licence for the [Licensed Patents *or* Licensed Technology *or* Licensed Trade Marks *or* technical assistance to the Licensee and so forth] a royalty equal to —— per cent on the direct sales ('Royalty').
2. The Licensee shall pay the Principal the Royalty in [*currency*] within —— days of the end of each calendar quarter of each year.
3. The Licensee shall furnish the Principal with a written report with each Royalty payment setting out
   a. the total number of units sold;
   b. the total sum invoiced by the Licensee;
   c. the sales price for sales for the period covered by the Royalty; and
   d. *(optional)* the permitted sublicenses granted by the Licensee.
4. The Principal may terminate this agreement and all the Licensee's rights under this agreement immediately and without notifying the Licensee if the Licensee fails to pay the Royalty within —— from the date it falls.
5. The Licensee shall maintain separate internal accounting records ('Accounting Records') relating to
   a. the exploitation of the [Licensed Patents *or* Licensed Technology *or* Licensed Trade marks and so forth] in the Licensed Territory; and
   b. the sales of Licensed Goods in the Licensed Territory.
6. The Licensee shall permit an independent accounting firm selected by the Principal to have reasonable access to the Accounting Records to confirm the sums provided by the Licensee. The Principal shall be responsible for the fees and expenses of the accounting firm.

Optional provisions

7. If during any year ending on an anniversary date specified in the table below, the sales made by the Licensee drop below the corresponding minimum sums detailed below ('Minimum Sums') the applicable royalty in subsection 1 above will be calculated on the basis of the Minimum Sums.
8. If during any year ending on an anniversary date specified in the table below, the aggregate payments paid by the Licensee to the Principal, pursuant to subsection 1 above, drop below the applicable royalty as calculated on the basis of the Minimum Sums then the Licensee shall pay the Principal in [*currency*] within —— days of the end of such year, the difference.

Table setting out the anniversary date of this agreement and the corresponding minimum sums

Anniversary date of this agreement	Minimum sums

A running royalty licence may be suited to the following scenarios:

1. where the contracting parties are unable to agree on anticipated future sales;
2. where the contracting parties are looking to share in the success of the venture; and
3. if the licensee has limited cash flow.[170]

Once the parties agree to use a running royalty licence, the next step is to agree on the royalty rate.

Fixing the royalty rate[171] The rate at which the royalty is set should be such as to ensure that the contracting parties share the benefits produced by the contract equally. Obviously the principal will endeavour to secure a higher rate whilst the licensee will try for a lower one. Royalty payments may be calculated using the per-unit rate or some other parameters such as quantity produced measured using for example weight or length.[172] Reference should also be in made the provision drawn up by the parties as to whether the royalty is payable after manufacture or upon sale.[173]

Box 6.6 Negotiation strategies of each contracting party in relation to royalty rates

The principal's arguments in favour of a higher royalty rate

In order to secure a higher royalty rate, the principal may try to use the following arguments:[174]

1. It was the principal's energy, time and money that generated the licensed property. In such a context, it may state 'I spent the time and money developing this trade mark'.
2. It took on the risks associated with acquiring the requisite legal protection. An inventor in such a context may argue that he carried out all the searches prior to applying for a patent and then made the application for the patent.
3. Use of the licensed property will mean that the licensee may be in a position to charge for the provision of after-sales service.

The licensee's counterarguments in favour of a lower royalty rate

In order to counter the principal's arguments in favour of a higher royalty rate, the licensee may try to use the following arguments:[175]

1. The sums of which the principal is speaking are sunk costs that the principal would have had to put in.
2. The licensee assumes the lion's share of the investment since it is the party that is taking on the responsibility for producing, promoting, distributing and selling the item.
3. The licensee assumes the higher risk since it is the party that will need to promote, distribute and sell the goods manufactured using the licensed property.
4. Both parties will receive a portion of the monies received for after-sales service.

Certain relevant factors when fixing the royalty rate

Other factors that have been deemed to be relevant when fixing the royalty rate include[176]

1. the duration of the patent;
2. the term of the licence granted;
3. the likely (or established) profitability of the product made using the licensed property;
4. the advantages that the patent has over old products or processes;
5. the proportion of the profit that is attributable to the invention rather than the non-patent components including the manufacturing process; and
6. whether or not the licence is exclusive, as an exclusive licence will generally carry a higher royalty rate than a non-exclusive one.

Guaranteed annual minimum payment The principal has an incentive to ensure that the licensee is motivated to generate as many sales as possible each year. To this end it may be sensible for the principal to insist on the inclusion of a guaranteed annual payment provision in the running royalty licence (subsections 7 and 8 in the sample licence featured above). The licensee, for its part, will try either to challenge the inclusion of such a provision or to negotiate the minimum sums involved.

In exclusive licensing agreements, to offset the benefit of exclusivity obtained by the licensee, the principal may insist that the licensee pay a base sum should its earnings drop below a set minimum.

Anti-competition restrictions[177]

1. The Licensee shall not during the course of this agreement enter into any agreement under which the Licensee obtains rights in the Licensed Territory to make, have made, use, promote or sell goods which directly compete with the Licensed Goods.

Optional provisions

2. The Licensee shall not for a period of —— after the end of this agreement enter into any agreement under which the Licensee obtains rights in the Licensed Territory to make, have made, use, promote or sell goods which directly compete with the Licensed Goods.

3. This provision shall not apply to the goods listed in Schedule ——. The goods listed in Schedule —— may be modified by an agreement of the Parties.

The principal will want to ensure that the licensee does not compete with it either during the course of the agreement or if at all possible after the term of the agreement. To this end, it will insist on the inclusion of a non-compete clause covering the period of the agreement and, if possible under national law, after the term of the agreement. The use of such provisions is regulated in various countries.[178] If such a provision is too wide (temporally and geographically speaking) it may be rendered invalid under the applicable law. Such a provision should be drafted so as to be limited to the sales of competing goods, as opposed to the sale of all goods, as most jurisdictions will not enforce a contract that stops a licensee from being involved in the production, marketing and sale of goods that are not in direct competition with the licensed goods.

In the event that the licensee wishes to retain the right to sell competing goods, it may be sensible for it to negotiate and include in the agreement the following provisions:

1. a list of competing goods which it is permitted to sell (optional provision above); and
2. a provision that such a list can be extended, if necessary, by later agreement of the contracting parties (optional provision above).

Restrictions on sublicensing[179]

The Licensee shall not grant any sublicence(s), under the licence(s) granted, to another party without the prior written permission of the Principal.

Confidentiality[180]

1. The Licensee agrees that all information made available to the Licensee by the Principal is confidential irrespective of the source of such information. Such information shall include but is not limited to technical information and information about the Licensed Goods and the Principal, its subsidiaries and associated corporations.
2. The Licensee agrees that such information is made available to it solely for the purpose of its use in accordance with the terms of this agreement.
3. The Licensee shall keep confidential all such information.
4. The Licensee shall use such information only in connection with its activities under this agreement.
5. The Licensee may provide all or some of the information to [its officers, directors, employees and advisors, agreed upon by the Parties and listed in Schedule —— *(option A)* or its officers, directors, employees and advisors who require such information to execute the activities agreed upon under this agreement *(option B)*], once [these officers, directors, employees or advisors have agreed to be bound by the terms of this agreement *(option C)* and/or these officers, directors, employees or advisors have signed a confidentiality and non-exploitation agreement on terms to be agreed between the Parties *(option D)*].
6. The Licensee shall protect such information to prevent unauthorised disclosure, with the same degree of care, no less than reasonable care, that it employs to protect its own information of a similar nature.
7. The Licensee shall not disclose such information to any third person(s) unless the same is expressly provided for in this agreement. Third person(s) in this context include(s) but is/are not limited to a corporation, company, group, partnership, agency, or individual, including but not limited to corporations or companies in the same group as the one to which the Licensee belongs, as well as any employees of the Licensee not employed at the branch, office or local establishment in the Territory.
8. The Licensee shall not use such information to compete with the Principal at any time or provide such information to a third party to compete with the Principal.
9. This provision shall survive the expiry or termination of this agreement.

Optional provisions

10. The Licensee shall not disclose such information to others or sell to or license others to use any such information without the prior written consent of the Principal.
11. Any sublicences granted by the Licensee under the terms of this agreement shall contain confidentiality requirements that are no less restrictive than the obligations that apply to the Licensee under this agreement.

In this provision, the principal requires the licensee to keep proprietary information confidential. In addition in order to enhance management of the risk of leakage, it would be sensible for the principal to also insist on one or more of the following provisions:

1. The licensee ensures that those with access to the information agree to be bound by the terms of the agreement (option C).
2. Those with access to the information enter into confidentiality and non-exploitation agreements (option D).
3. The parties agree on who should have access to the information and those people are listed in a schedule (option A).

The provisions above are drafted in such a way as to encompass those situations where the licensee is part of a multinational and the principal is looking to ringfence the information provided to the licensee. Optional provision 10 (above) will permit the disclosure of information to another with the prior written agreement of the principal. The optional provisions above are suitable for those situations where sub-licensing is a possibility.[181]

Retention of title[182]

1. Except as provided for in this agreement, the Licensee shall not obtain rights in relation to the Licensed Property.
2. The Licensee acknowledges that, except as expressly provided for in this agreement, it shall not obtain any rights in respect of the Licensed Property and all such rights and goodwill are, and shall remain, vested in the Principal.

Quality control[183]

1. The Licensee shall ensure that the Licensed Goods produced by it or for it meet the specifications set by the Principal and detailed in Schedule ——.
2. The Principal may by means of inspection and sampling ascertain the quality of the Licensed Goods which the Licensee produces or has produced [*optional:* together with the quality of the use of Trade Marks].
3. Upon the provision of written prior notice to the Licensee by the Principal,
   a. the Licensee shall permit duly authorised representatives of the Principal to inspect the facility (or facilities) used for the production of the Licensed Goods. [*optional:* The Licensee shall not be obliged to allow such visits to the degree that such visits hinder the operations of the Licensee].
   b. the Licensee shall provide the Principal with free samples of the Licensed Goods which the Licensee produces or has produced. [*optional:* The Principal agrees that the standards of verification shall be reasonable.] [*optional:* The Principal agrees that it shall not unreasonably object to the quality of the Licensed Goods.]
4. The Licensee shall comply with directions issued by the Principal on the question of quality. Such directions shall not be unreasonable in terms of practicality or financial cost.

Maintenance of licensed property[184]

During the course of this agreement:
1. The Licensee shall promptly advise the Principal of any infringement, actual or threatened, of the Principal's Licensed

Property of which the Licensee is or becomes aware.
2. The Licensee shall take all steps reasonably required of it by the Principal to assist the Principal in maintaining the validity and enforceability of the Licensed Property.
3. The Principal shall indemnify the Licensee against all reasonable costs, damages and/or liabilities resulting from or in connection with such steps.
4. The Principal shall pay all maintenance fees or taxes and shall at its own expense take all required actions needed from time to time to maintain the Licensed Property in force until the expiry date(s) thereof.

Restrictions on use of licensed property[185]

1. The Licensee shall include a notice in all materials used on or in connection with the Licensed Goods indicating that the Principal owns the Licensed Property and the Licensee is an authorised licensee of the Principal.
2. The Licensee shall prepare or have prepared at its own expense a design or plan for the Licensed Goods and all promotional materials displaying the Licensed Property.
3. The Licensee shall submit such a design or plan to the Principal for its approval within —— of the effective date of this agreement.
4. The Licensee shall not modify the Licensed Property in any way.

[*optional:* The Licensee shall ensure that Trade Marks appear in a legible indelible manner on all Licensed Goods produced in the Licensed Territory].
5. The Licensee shall not market the Licensed Property in connection with any goods that are not Licensed Goods.
6. The Licensee shall not use the Licensed Property in any way which may prejudice the distinctiveness or validity of the Licensed Property or the goodwill of the Principal therein.
7. The Licensee shall not use any trade mark which resembles the Licensed Trade Mark which is likely to cause confusion or deception.

Improvements and new goods[186]

Improvements
1. During the course of this agreement
   a. each Party agrees to notify the other Party promptly of Improvements of which it becomes aware; and
   b. each Party shall have the exclusive right to file a patent in relation to Improvements made or acquired by it.

Option A
2. The Licensee shall grant the Principal the right to use Improvements, in relation to which the Licensee shall have the right to grant such licences, on the same terms as found in this agreement.

Option B
2. In relation to Improvements made by the Licensee and with respect to all patent rights therein, during the term

of this agreement, the Licensee shall grant to the Principal, at the request of the Principal
  a. during the term of this agreement, a [non-exclusive *or* exclusive] royalty-free licence for the whole world save for the Licensed Territory; and
  b. after the expiry or term of this agreement, a non-exclusive royalty-free licence for the whole world.

New Goods

3. During the course of this agreement each Party shall notify the other Party promptly of New Goods and all technology and know-how relating thereto. Each party shall have the exclusive right to file a patent in relation to New Goods developed or acquired by it.

Option C

4. The other Party shall then have the right to use free of charge New Goods and all related technology and know-how [during the course of this agreement *or* during the course of this agreement and after this agreement expires or is terminated].

Option D

4. For —— following notice of the availability of any such New Goods, the notified Party shall have the right to agree with the other Party on a mutually acceptable price for any such New Goods and all related technology and know-how. In default of such an agreement, the New Goods may be sold or licensed to a third party.

The right to use improvements and to exploit new goods developed using the licensed property is a right that will be important for the licensee and for the principal. In this context, it is sensible for the parties contracting to distinguish between the terms 'improvements' and 'new goods' in the agreement.

The principal is likely to negotiate the right to use new goods and/or improvements developed by the licensee (Options A and B) using the licensed property at least during the course of the agreement. In such circumstances, it is likely to try to negotiate either an automatic grant-back to it of ownership in new goods and/or improvements, or at a minimum the automatic right to be granted a licence to use new goods and/or improvements during the course of the agreement and even after the agreement expires or is terminated.

The licensee, for his part, will probably attempt to reserve himself the following rights:

1. the right to sell any new goods developed by the licensee if the principal is not prepared to pay a mutually acceptable price for them (Option D); and
2. the right to extend a non-exclusive licence to the principal in relation to the improvements so that the licensee is in a position to grant a licence in relation to improvements to parties besides the principal (Option B).

Obligations of the principal

The licensee will want to ensure the incorporation of certain provisions in the licensing agreement in order to protect his interests. To this end, the following obligations are imposed on the principal.

Firstly, the licensee will want to limit his exposure to competition in the assigned territory. For this reason he will attempt to secure exclusivity or at the very least a non-compete clause which is as widely drafted as possible (such a clause and its scope will depend on the principal's willingness to agree to the same).

Secondly, the licensee will endeavour to secure training and support in the use of the technology and know-how licensed. To this end, he will insist on a provision requiring the principal to provide him and his staff with support and training.

Thirdly, the licensee will be interested in preserving his interests in any new goods and improvements that he has developed. Moreover, he will be interested in securing rights in relation to new goods and improvements developed by the principal. To this end, he will insist on provisions that govern the rights of the contracting parties to new goods and improvements.

Fourthly, the licensee will be concerned about protecting any proprietary information relating to his operations that becomes available to the principal. Accordingly he will try to insist on the inclusion of a suitably drafted confidentiality clause.

Fifthly, the licensee will be concerned about preserving his peaceful enjoyment of the licensed property. To this end, he will endeavour to negotiate the inclusion of both a warranties clause and an indemnity clause. The warranties clause will include the warranties that the principal is providing to the licensee. The indemnity clause will include the principal's promise that it will indemnify the licensee if he sustains any loss due to a claim by a third party in relation to the licensed property.

Exclusivity[187]

Non-compete

1. The Principal represents that, as of the date of this agreement, neither it nor any of its Affiliates has
   a. provided or made available the Licensed Property Technology (or any part of it) to a third party in the Licensed Territory; and/or
   b. granted any rights under the Licensed Patents [*optional:* and Licensed Property] to any third party in the Licensed Territory.
2. The Principal agrees that, during the term of this agreement, neither it nor any of its Affiliates shall
   a. provide or make available the Licensed Technology (or any part of it) [*optional:* or the Licensed Patents or Licensed Property] to a third party in the Licensed Territory;
   b. produce directly or indirectly the Licensed Goods in the Licensed Territory; or
   c. use the Licensed Technology [*optional:* and Licensed Property] in the Licensed Territory.

Support services

1. The Principal shall, during the term of this agreement, supply and make available to the Licensee, at reasonable times and places in the Licensed Territory and on reasonable notice
   a. technical assistance in relation to the use of Licensed Property; and
   b. the services of technical personnel to train and assist the Licensee in using the Licensed Property to develop, produce and test the Licensed Goods.

2. The Principal shall, during the term of this agreement, allow visits by representatives of the Licensee at reasonable times and upon the provision of reasonable notice, to the —— in order to view aspects of the [*manufacturing and testing operations and so on*] and obtain hands-on training in relation to such operations.

3. The costs incurred by the Principal in relation to the technical assistance provided by the Principal, under the terms of this agreement, will be the sole responsibility of the [Principal *or* Licensee]. [*optional:* Such costs shall be paid within —— days from the date on which the invoice was issued for these costs.]

Support services provided by the principal to the licensee will benefit both parties. From the principal's point of view such arrangements will help improve sales whilst also ensuring the quality of production and service, in turn protecting the principal's reputation and goodwill as well as the image of the intellectual property owned by the principal. From the point of view of the licensee such arrangements will not only improve sales but also add value to his workforce.

Improvements and new goods[188]

Improvements

1. During the course of this agreement
    a. each Party agrees to notify the other Party promptly of Improvements of which it becomes aware; and
    b. each Party shall have the exclusive right to file a patent in relation to Improvements made or acquired by it.

Option A

2. The Principal shall grant the Licensee the right to use Improvements, in relation to which the Principal shall have the right to grant such licences, on the same terms as found in this agreement.

Option B

2. In relation to Improvements made by the Principal (and its Affiliates) and with respect to all patent rights therein, during the term of this agreement, the Principal shall grant to the Licensee, at the request of the Licensee
    a. a [non-exclusive *or* exclusive] royalty-free licence, during the term of this agreement, for the whole world [optional in the alternative: for the Licensed Territory]; and
    b. a non-exclusive royalty-free licence, after the expiry or term of this agreement, for the whole world.

New goods

1. During the course of this agreement each Party shall notify the other Party promptly of New Goods and all technology and know-how relating thereto. Each party shall have the exclusive right to file a patent in relation to the New Goods developed or acquired by it.

Option A

2. The other Party shall have the right to use

> free of charge New Goods and all related technology and know-how [during the course of this agreement *or* during the course of this agreement and after this agreement expires or is terminated].
>
> *Option B*
> 2. For —— following receipt of the notice of availability of any such New Goods, the notified Party shall have the right to agree with the other Party on a mutually acceptable price for any New Goods and all of the applicable technology, know-how and technical information relating to the same. In default of such an agreement, the New Goods may be sold or licensed to a third party.

Confidentiality

> 1. The Principal agrees that all information made available to the Principal by the Licensee is confidential irrespective of the source of such information, including but not limited to information about the Licensee, its subsidiaries and associated corporations.
> 2. The Principal agrees that such information is made available to it solely for its use in accordance with the terms of this agreement.
> 3. The Principal shall keep confidential all such information and shall use such information only in connection with its activities under this agreement.
> 4. The Principal may provide all or some of the information to [its officers, directors, employees and advisors, agreed upon by the Parties and listed in Schedule —— *(option A) or* its officers, directors, employees and advisors, who require such information to execute the activities agreed upon under this agreement *(option B)*], once [these officers, directors, employees or advisors have agreed to be bound by the terms of this agreement *(option C) and/or* these officers, directors, employees or advisors have signed a confidentiality and non-exploitation agreement, on terms to be agreed upon by the Parties *(option D)*].
> 5. The Principal shall protect such information, to avoid unauthorised disclosure, with the same degree of care, no less than reasonable care, it employs in order to protect its own information of a similar nature.
> 6. The Principal shall not disclose such information to any third person(s) unless the same is expressly provided for in this agreement. 'Third person' in this context will be read to include a corporation, company, group, partnership, agency, or individual, including but not limited to corporations or companies in the same group as the one to which the Principal belongs, as well as any employees of the Principal not employed at the branch, office or local establishment in the Territory.
> 7. The Principal shall not use such information to compete with the Licensee at any time or provide such information to a third party to compete with the Licensee.
> 8. This provision shall survive the expiry or termination of this agreement.

As discussed above, the licensee is likely to request an obligation from the principal to keep proprietary information confidential. Furthermore in order to manage the risk of leakage, the licensee will also try to insist on the inclusion of one or more of the following provisions:

1. The principal ensures that those with access to the information agree to be bound by the terms of the agreement (option C).
2. Those with access to the information enter into confidentiality and non-exploitation agreements (option D).
3. The parties agree on who should have access to the information and those people are listed in a schedule (option A).

The confidentiality clause above is drafted widely enough to encompass those situations where the principal is part of a multinational and the licensee is looking to ringfence the information provided to the principal.

Warranties[189]

The Principal represents and warrants that
1. the Licensed Property constitutes all the patents, patent applications, specifications and rights that are needed in order to produce, have produced and use the Licensed Goods;
2. the Licensed Property is owned by the Principal or has been licensed exclusively to the Principal and the Principal has full rights and powers to disclose and license the same to the Licensee; and
3. no claims have been made, nor to the best of the knowledge of the Principal are any claims threatened or pending, based on an alleged infringement by the Principal of third party patents, trade marks or other industrial property rights in relation to the Licensed Property.

Indemnities

The Principal shall indemnify the Licensee for any expenses, loss or damage resulting from a claim by a third party that, as a result of or based upon the Licensee's use of the Licensed Property, there has been
a. an infringement of the third party's intellectual property rights; or
b. a wrongful use of the third party's proprietary information

Termination (grounds and consequences)[190]

Grounds for termination[191]

1. Either Party may terminate this agreement with immediate effect by notice given in writing in the following situations:
   a. The other Party commits any breach of any of the provisions of this agreement resulting in such detriment to the Party terminating so as to substantially deprive him of that which the Party terminating is entitled to expect under this agreement and, in the case of a breach capable of remedy, fails to remedy such a breach within ——— after receipt of written notice setting out the particulars of the breach

and requiring the breach to be rectified.
b. A receiver is appointed over any of the property or assets of the other Party.
c. The other Party enters into a voluntary arrangement with its creditors or becomes the subject of an administration order.
d. The other Party goes into liquidation.
e. Anything analogous to any of the aforementioned under the law of any jurisdiction occurs in relation to the other Party.
f. The other Party ceases or threatens to cease to carry on business.
g. There is at any time a material change in the management, ownership or control of the other Party.
h. The other Party is substantially prevented from performing its obligations under the agreement.
i. The other Party assigns or tries to assign the agreement without prior authorisation.
2. A breach shall be considered capable of remedy if the Party in breach is able to comply with the provision concerned in all respects other than as to time of performance, on the proviso that time of performance is not of the essence.
3. Any waiver by either Party of a breach of any provision of this agreement shall not constitute a waiver of any consequent breach of the same or any other provision thereof.
4. Any termination of this agreement shall be without prejudice to any rights or remedies of either Party in respect of the breach concerned (if any) or any other breach.

An agreement will run its full term (if the agreement is for a fixed term) unless there is a reason for a premature termination of the agreement. The termination clause lists the contingencies that permit the contracting parties to bring the agreement to a premature end before its final term. Such contingencies may include bankruptcy, takeover of the business and failure to comply with the obligations set out in the agreement.

On the part of the principal, a failure to comply with the obligations set out in the agreement may include a delay or failure to pay sums due under the agreement, a failure to meet sales targets and a breach of quality standards. On the part of the licensee, a failure to comply with the obligations set out in the agreement may include a failure to provide training and support promised in the agreement.

Consequences of termination

Upon termination of this agreement, for whatever reason, the Licensee shall
a. deliver to the Principal free of charge all materials supplied by the Principal and all materials used by and on behalf the Licensee or destroy all such materials if the Principal so decides in the presence of the Principal's authorised representative;
b. remain liable for and shall pay the Principal all royalties due on the sale of the Licensed Goods executed by the Licensee prior to this termination;
c. remain obliged to perform its obligations under clause [*insert the number*

> *of the confidentiality clause here*];
> and
> d. *(optional)* ensure the servicing of Licensed Goods sold by the Licensee in the Licensed Territory during the course of this agreement.

Such a provision will list the consequences for the contracting parties once the agreement comes to an end.

XXIV Boilerplate clauses[192]

Assignment[193]

In certain situations, the principal would be wise to reserve the right to assign without restrictions, so that it can for example sell its business on as a going concern or use the business or even the Licensed Property as collateral for a loan.

Once there is a licensing agreement in place the role of the principal may become largely passive. Take the example of an inventor of a new improved salad spinner who licences his device to the manufacturer of kitchenware; once the agreement is in place the inventor will probably assume a more passive role. It is the licensee who will be responsible for assuming an active role once the licensing agreement is in place. The licensee will be responsible inter alia for producing, promoting, ensuring quality control and providing after-sales service.

As the principal is reliant on the efforts of the licensee to generate revenue, to safeguard its licensed property and to enhance and preserve its brand image, it must take special care to scrutinise any prospective assignee before allowing the assignment to proceed.

Assignability of licence[194]

A licence may be assignable or non-assignable. Under an assignable licence, the licensee can choose whether or not to transfer the licence to another party, where the latter takes the place of the original licensee. In most licences, the licensee will usually have a right to assign on condition that he complies with strict prerequisites that are typically set out in the assignment clause.

It is not commonly a problem to assign a running royalty licence as the new licensee simply takes over the payment of the royalties on the basis found in the licensing agreement. However, in such a situation it is sensible for the principal to reserve the right to scrutinise the transfer before granting the authorisation needed for the transfer. It is particularly important that the principal examines the credentials of the proposed transferee before giving the authorisation for the transfer.

To prevent the transfer of the licence in the event of the licensee's bankruptcy to an unknown trustee in bankruptcy, the licensing agreement will usually include a provision permitting the principal to terminate the agreement. This contingency is provided for in the termination clause reviewed above.

XXV Back of the contract[195]

Schedules

The schedules accompanying a licensing agreement are likely to address amongst other matters licensed property, licensed goods, licensed territory, the list of officers, employees and advisors with access to confidential information, quality specifications for the licensed goods, licensed trade marks and licensed technology.

Summary

In this chapter we looked at various issues that concern international licensing agreements. Firstly, we reviewed the fundamental characteristics of intellectual property and the role of intellectual property law. Secondly, we considered a variety of different international licensing agreements. Thirdly, we discussed the key provisions that should be included in an international licensing agreement. In relation to each such provision, we considered its purpose and wording.

Useful links

http://www.ipo.gov.uk/ (UK Intellectual Property Office)
http://www.ipo.gov.uk/pro-types/pro-copy/c-law.htm (UK copyright law)
http://www.ipo.gov.uk/pro-types/pro-patent/p-law/p-legislation.htm (UK patent law)
http://www.ipo.gov.uk/pro-types/pro-tm.htm (UK trade mark law)
http://www.legislation.gov.uk/ukpga/1977/37 (Patents Act 1977)
http://www.wipo.int (World Intellectual Property Organization)
http://www.wipo.int/ipstats/en (intellectual property statistics)

Further reading

August, Ray, Mayer, Don and Bixby, Michael (2009), *International Business Law: Text, Cases and Readings*, 5th ed., Pearson Education.

Bainbridge, David and Howell, Claire (2009), *Intellectual Property Law*, Pearson Education (UK law).

Bortolotti, Fabio (2008), *Drafting and Negotiating International Commercial Agreements: A Practical Guide*, International Chamber of Commerce.

Bradgate, Robert (2000), *Commercial Law*, 3rd ed., Butterworths.

Christou, Richard (2003), *International Agency, Distribution and Licensing Agreements*, 4th ed., Sweet & Maxwell.

Fowlston, Brendan (1984), *Understanding Commercial and Industrial Licensing*, Waterlow.

Fox, William F. Jr (1992), *International Commercial Agreements: A Primer on Drafting, Negotiating and Resolving Disputes*, Kluwer Law and Taxation.

Konigsberg, Alex S. (1996), *International Franchising*, Juris.

Lopez, Victor D. (2011), *Intellectual Property Law: A Practical Guide to Copyrights, Patents, Trademarks and Trade Secrets*, Victor D. Lopez (US law).

Mendelsohn, Martin (1979), *The Guide to Franchising*, 2nd ed., Pergamon Press.

Mendelsohn, Martin (ed.) (1984), *International Franchising: An Overview*, Elsevier.

Mendelsohn, Martin (ed.) (1992), *Franchising in Europe*, Cassell.

Norman, Helen (2011), *Intellectual Property Law*, Oxford University Press (UK law).

Pollzien, Götz and Bronfen, George (eds) (1965), *International Licensing Agreements*, Bobbs-Merrill.

Poltorak, Alexander and Lerner, Paul (2004), *Essentials of Licensing Intellectual Property*, John Wiley.

Poole, Jill (2008), *Textbook on Contract Law*, Oxford University Press.

Sherman, Andrew (2011), *Franchising and Licensing: Two Powerful Ways to Grow Your Business in Any Economy*, 4th ed., American Management Association.

Shippey, Karla C. (1999), *A Short Course in International Contracts: Drafting the International Sales Contract for Attorneys and Non-attorneys*, World Trade Press.

Notes

1. Mendelsohn, Martin (ed.) (1992), *Franchising in Europe*, Cassell, 3.
2. Ibid.
3. August, Ray, Mayer, Don and Bixby, Michael (2009), *International Business Law: Text, Cases, and Readings*, 5th ed., Pearson Education, 510.
4. Gerhard, Frederick (1868), *Will the People of the United States Be Benefited by an International Copyright Law, or, Will Such a Law Be an Injury to Them?*, 6–8.
5. *Rockwell Graphics Sys., Inc.* v. *DEV Indus., Inc.*, 925 F.2d 174, 180 (7th Cir. 1991).
6. Siwek, Stephen (2004), *Copyright Industries in the U.S. Economy: The 2004 Report*, Economists Incorporated, available at http:/www.iipa.com/pdf/2004_SIWEK_FULL.pdf (last accessed 28 January 2013). International statistics available at http:/www.wipo.int/ipstats/en (last accessed 28 January 2013).
7. Reviewed below.
8. Norman, Helen (2011), *Intellectual Property Law*, Oxford University Press, 12–14.
9. Norman 2011, 13.
10. Norman 2011, 12.
11. Pollzien, Götz and Bronfen, George (eds) (1965), *International Licensing Agreements*, Bobbs-Merrill, 9–10.
12. Patent registration under US law is reviewed in Pressman, David (2008), *Patent it Yourself*, 13th ed., Nolo. Patents under US law and UK law are reviewed in the chapters dedicated to patents in the books listed in the further reading list at the end of this chapter.
13. Pollzien and Bronfen 1965: 10.
14. The full title is 'An Act to establish a new law of patents applicable to future patents and applications for patents; to amend the law of patents applicable to existing patents and applications for patents; to give effect to certain international conventions on patents; and for connected purposes' and it is available at http://www.legislation.gov.uk/ukpga/1977/37 (last accessed 28 January 2013). Later legislation has been introduced addressing patents including the Copyrights, Designs & Patents Act 1988 (CDPA) and the Patents Act 2004, which revised the 1977 Act.
15. §1 Patents Act 1977.
16. §1(3) Patents Act 1977.
17. §1(2) Patents Act 1977.

18. §1(5) Patents Act 1977.
19. Title 35 US Code, §101.
20. Ibid.
21. Title 35 US Code, §103.
22. Trade marks under US law and UK law are reviewed in the chapters dedicated to trade marks in the books listed in the further reading list at the end of this chapter.
23. Trade Marks Act 1994, available at http://www.legislation.gov.uk/ukpga/1994/26 (last accessed 28 January 2013). A registered trade mark is personal property (§22 Trade Marks Act 1994) that can be protected against infringement by the proprietor of the trade mark (§14(1)). Infringement proceedings are addressed in §§14–21 Trade Marks Act 1994. A registered trade mark is transmissible by for example assignment, either in connection with the goodwill of a business or independently (§24(1)). Any such assignment or other transmission of a registered trade mark may be partial so as to apply in relation to some but not all of the goods or services for which the trade mark is registered, or in relation to the use of the trade mark in a particular manner or a particular locality (§24(2)). An assignment of a registered trade mark is not effective unless it is written and signed by or on behalf of the assignor or a personal representative (§24(3)).
24. Title 15 US Code, §1127.
25. Trade Marks Act 1994.
26. §1(1) Trade Marks Act 1994.
27. *Blanchard Importing & Distrib. Co. v. Charles Gilman & Son, Inc.*, 353 F.2d 400, 401 (1st Cir.1965), cert. denied, 383 US 968, 86 S.Ct. 1273, 16 L.Ed.2d 308 (1966) (US).
28. *Keebler Co. v. Rovira Biscuit Corp.*, 624 F.2d 366, 372 (1st Cir. 1980) (US).
29. Copyrights under US law and UK law are reviewed in the chapters dedicated to copyrights in the books listed in the further reading list at the end of this chapter.
30. Title 17 US Code, §202m; *Salinger* v. *Random House Inc.* 811 F.2d Cir. 1987 (US).
31. Title 17 US Code, §201(d)(2).
32. De Wolf, Richard C. (1925), *An Outline of Copyright Law*, John W. Luce,
33. Ibid.
34. De Wolf 1925: 1–2.
35. Full text of the Statute of Anne accessible at http://avalon.law.yale.edu/18th_century/anne_1710.asp (last accessed 28 January 2013).
36. Preamble, Statute of Anne.
37. §1 Statute of Anne.
38. De Wolf 1925: 1.
39. Solberg, Thorvald (complier) (1906), *Copyright Enactments of the United States 1783–1906*, Government Printing Office (Washington, DC), available at http://archive.org/stream/copyrightenactm00statgoog (last accessed 28 January 2013).
40. Solberg 1906: 14.

41. Article 1, clause 8 US Constitution, available at http://constitutioncenter.org/constitution (last accessed 28 January 2013).
42. Copyright Act 1956 as amended by the Copyright (Computers Software) Amendments Act 1985 (UK); §117 Copyright Act 1976 was updated by the Computers Software Protection Act 1980 (US).
43. The full title of the CDPA 1988 is 'An Act to restate the law of copyright, with amendments; to make fresh provision as to the rights of performers and others in performances; to confer a design right in original designs; to amend the Registered Designs Act 1949; to make provision with respect to patent agents and trade mark agents; to confer patents and designs jurisdiction on certain county courts; to amend the law of patents; to make provision with respect to devices designed to circumvent copy-protection of works in electronic form; to make fresh provision penalising the fraudulent reception of transmissions; to make the fraudulent application or use of a trade mark an offence; to make provision for the benefit of the Hospital for Sick Children, Great Ormond Street, London; to enable financial assistance to be given to certain international bodies; and for connected purposes'. The Act is available at http://www.legislation.gov.uk/ukpga/1988/48 (last accessed 28 January 2013).
44. See §§3–8 CDPA 1988.
45. §90 CDPA 1988; such an assignment is not effective unless it is written and signed by or on behalf of the assignor.
46. §§2, 16 CDPA 1988.
47. §12(2) CDPA 1988. Durations for other types of work are listed in §§13A–15 CDPA 1988.
48. §16(2) CDPA 1988. The different forms of infringement are elaborated upon in Chapter 2 of the CDPA 1988.
49. Title 17 US Code, §102.
50. Title 17 US Code, §§102–3.
51. Title 17 US Code, §104.
52. Pollzien and Bronfen 1965: 4.
53. Entry structures are reviewed in Chapter 1.
54. Pollzien and Bronfen 1965: 4.
55. Pollzien and Bronfen. 1965: 7–9.
56. Ibid.
57. Ibid.
58. Poltorak, Alexander and Lerner, Paul (2004), *Essentials of Licensing Intellectual Property*, John Wiley, 17–19, 57–9.
59. Pollzien and Bronfen. 1965: 9–10.
60. Fowlston, Brendan (1984), *Understanding Commercial and Industrial Licensing*, Waterlow, 8–9.
61. Ibid.
62. Ibid.
63. Ibid.
64. Pollzien and Bronfen 1965: 9–10.
65. An exclusive licence is defined in §92 CDPA 1988 as 'a licence in writing signed by or on behalf of the copyright owner authorising the licensee to the

exclusion of all other persons, including the person granting the licence, to exercise a right which would otherwise be exercisable exclusively by the copyright owner'.
66. Pollzien and Bronfen 1965: 10.
67. Manufacturing licences are reviewed above in the section on licensing a patent.
68. Exclusivity is reviewed above in the section on licensing a patent.
69. Franchising is reviewed in the following textbooks: Mendelsohn, Martin (1979), *The Guide to Franchising*, 2nd ed., Pergamon Press; Mendelsohn, Martin (ed.) (1984), *International Franchising: An Overview*, Elsevier; Mendelsohn (1992); Konigsberg, Alex S. (1996), *International Franchising*, Juris; Mendelsohn, Martin (2004), *The Guide to Franchising*, 7th ed., Thomson Learning. In Mendelsohn (1979), Chapter 2 discusses the features offered by the franchisor to the franchisee, Chapter 3 addresses the advantages and disadvantages of franchising, Chapter 4 the subject-matter of a franchise arrangement, Chapter 5 the setting up of a franchise, Chapter 6 the sources of income for the franchisor, Chapters 7 and 8 the initial and ongoing support structures (respectively) offered by the franchisor and Chapter 9 the provisions in a franchise agreement. In Mendelsohn (1984), Chapter 1 (written by Lewis G. Rudnick) examines the history of franchising in the US, Chapter 2 (Iain Baillie) examines franchising of trade marks, Chapter 3 (Nicholas Fyfe) examines franchising of images, and Chapters 4–11 look at franchising in the US, Canada, Latin America, the Asia/Pacific region, the UK, Europe, France and Germany respectively. In Mendelsohn (1992), Chapter 2 (written by Martin Mendelsohn) looks at the European treatment of franchise arrangements, Chapter 3 (Martin Mendelsohn) looks at the international exploitation of franchising arrangements, Chapter 4 (Manzoor G. K. Ishani) looks at the tax concerns associated with franchising arrangements, and Chapters 5–16 address the treatment of such arrangements in the then member states of the European Union. Konigsberg (1996) looks at the law governing franchising arrangements (Chapters 3 & 4), the concerns associated with international franchising operations (Chapter 5) and the formats available for international expansion of a franchising operation (Chapters 6–12).
70. Barbe, Erwin (1975), 'Fraud in Connection with Franchise or Distributorship Relationship', *American Law Reports 3d* 64, 11; Martin Mendelsohn 2004, Chapter 1.
71. Mendelsohn 1992: 1.
72. Mendelsohn 2004: 16.
73. Ibid.
74. Mendelsohn 1992: 1–2.
75. Mendelsohn 2004, Chapter 1.
76. Mendelsohn 1992: 3.
77. Mendelsohn 2004: 48.
78. Mendelsohn 2004: 48–51.
79. Mendelsohn 2004: 40–2.

80. *Aaron E. Levine & Co.* v. *Calkraft Paper Co.*, 429 F. Supp. 1039 (E.D. Mich. 1976), 1050, citing *Rubinger* v. *Int'l Tel. & Tel. Corp.*, 310 F. 2d. 552 (2nd Cir. 1962) cert. denied, 375 US 820 (1962) (US).
81. Mendelsohn 2004: 1–2.
82. Mendelsohn 1979: 4.
83. Mendelsohn 1979: 12.
84. Mendelsohn 1979: 13.
85. For a full review of the features offered by the franchisor to the franchisee, see Mendelsohn (1979), Chapter 2.
86. Reviewed in Mendelsohn (2004: 3–5).
87. Mendelsohn 2004: 3.
88. Mendelsohn 1979: 3.
89. Mendelsohn 2004: 4–5.
90. Mendelsohn 2004: 4.
91. Mendelsohn 2004: 3–4.
92. Mendelsohn 2004: 4–5.
93. The DCFR is reviewed in Chapter 7.
94. Paragraph Intr. 7 DCFR.
95. Paragraph Intr. 8 DCFR.
96. Contained in DCFR, Chapters IV.E.–1 and IV.E.–2 respectively.
97. Paragraph IV.E.–1:101(1) DCFR (Book IV, Part E, Chapter 1, Section 1, subsection 1, paragraph 1).
98. Paragraph IV.E.–1:101(2) DCFR.
99. Subsection IV.E.–2:101 DCFR.
100. Ibid.
101. Subsection IV.E.–2:201 DCFR as supplemented by subsection IV.E.–4:103.
102. Subsection IV.E.–2:202 DCFR.
103. Paragraph IV.E.–2:203(1) DCFR.
104. Paragraph IV.E.–2:203(2) DCFR.
105. Subsection IV.E.–4:102 DCFR.
106. Subsection IV.E.–2:301 DCFR.
107. Subsection IV.E.–2:301 DCFR.
108. Ibid.
109. Paragraph IV.E.–2:302(1) DCFR.
110. Paragraph IV.E.–2:302(2) DCFR.
111. Ibid. Calculation of the length of a reasonable period is addressed in subsection IV.E.–2:302. Calculation of damages for termination with inadequate notice is addressed in subsection IV.E.–2:303.
112. Subsection IV.E.–2:402 DCFR.
113. Subsection IV.E.–4:101 DCFR.
114. Subsection IV.E.–4:201 DCFR.
115. Subsection IV.E.–4:203 DCFR.
116. Subsection IV.E–4:205 DCFR.
117. Paragraph IV.E.–4:204(1) DCFR.
118. Subsection IV.E.–4:301 DCFR.
119. Subsection IV.E.–4:302 DCFR.

120. Subsection IV.E.–4:302 DCFR.
121. Subsection IV.E.–4:303 DCFR.
122. Subsection IV.E.–4:304 DCFR.
123. Pollzien and Bronfen 1965: 4.
124. For a review of the impact of European competition law on vertical agreements, see Chapter 4.
125. A review of licensing regulations is provided in August et al. (2009), 493–517.
126. See also *Arnott* v. *American Oil Co.*, 609 F.2d 873, 1979-2 Trade Cases P 62,967 (8th Cir.(SD) Oct 24, 1979) (NO. 79-1150) (US).
127. *Mariniello* v. *Shell Oil Co.*, 511 F.2d 853, 185 USPQ 71 (3rd Cir.(NJ) Feb 14, 1975) (NO. 74-1385) (US).
128. Ibid., paragraphs 6 and 7.
129. Ibid., paragraph 4.
130. Title 15 US Code, §§105 et seq. (1963). This Act provides a national system for registration of trade marks used in interstate commerce and extends registered holders of trade marks the exclusive right to determine the use of their marks by other parties.
131. *Mariniello* v. *Shell Oil Co.*, 511 F.2d 853, 185 USPQ 71 (3rd Cir.(NJ) Feb 14, 1975) (NO. 74-1385) (US), paragraphs 5 and 6. The court referred to the Senate report accompanying the Lanham Act S. Rep. No. 1333, 79th Cong., 2d Sess. in 1946 US Code Cong. Serv. 1274 (US).
132. *Mariniello* v. *Shell Oil Co.*, 511 F.2d 853, 185 USPQ 71 (3rd Cir.(NJ) Feb 14, 1975) (NO. 74-1385) (US), paragraphs 7 and 8.
133. Article 6, clause 2 US Constitution reads: 'This Constitution, and the Laws of the United States which shall be made in Pursuance thereof; and all Treaties made, or which shall be made, under the Authority of the United States, shall be the supreme Law of the Land; and the Judges in every State shall be bound thereby, any Thing in the Constitution or Laws of any State to the Contrary notwithstanding.' Available at http://constitutioncenter.org/constitution (last accessed 28 January 2013).
134. *Hines* v. *Davidowitz*, 312 US 52, 67, 61 S.Ct. 399, 404, 85 L.Ed. 581 (1941), quoted in *Florida Lime & Avocado Growers, Inc.* v. *Paul*, 373 US 132, 83 S.Ct. 1210 (1963) (US).
135. *Mariniello* v. *Shell Oil Co.*, 1975, paragraph 21 (US).
136. Prior approval schemes and notification-registration schemes are reviewed in Schaffer, Richard, Agusti, Filiberto, Dhooge, Lucien and Earle, Beverley (2012), *International Business Law and Its Environment*, 8th ed., South-Western Cengage Learning, 556–8.
137. Schaffer et al. 2012: 557.
138. August et al. 2009: 493–517.
139. Available at http://eur-lex.europa.eu/LexUriServ/LexUriServ.do?uri=OJ:L:2008:177:0006:0006:en:PDF (last accessed 21 January 2013).
140. Available at http://eur-lex.europa.eu/LexUriServ/LexUriServ.do?u ri= CELEX:41980A0934:EN:HTML (last accessed 21 January 2013).

141. Where states have several territorial units each of which has its own rules of law in relation to contractual obligations then each territorial unit will be treated as a country for the purposes of identifying the law applicable under Rome I (Article 22.1 Rome I).
142. Article 3 Rome I.
143. Article 3.1 Rome I.
144. Ibid.
145. Article 4.1(d) Rome I.
146. The type of licensing agreement should be selected in the heading of the agreement by the parties.
147. More in Chapter 2.
148. More in Chapter 2.
149. More in Chapter 2.
150. Fowlston 1984: 8–9.
151. Poltorak and Lerner 2004: 17–19, 57–9.
152. Reviewed at the start of this chapter.
153. August et al. 2009: 503–4.
154. Reviewed below.
155. Reviewed in Chapter 4; Poltorak and Lerner (2004: 21, 62).
156. Regulation by EU law of agency arrangements is reviewed in Chapter 5.
157. Grounds for termination are reviewed below.
158. The use of certain provisions is regulated in various countries; for a review of the subject of regulation see August et al. (2009: 493–517).
159. At the start of this chapter in the section entitled 'Regulation of the licensing agreement'.
160. August et al. 2009: 493–517.
161. Reviewed below.
162. The use of grant-back provisions is regulated in certain countries; for a review of the subject of regulation see August et al. (2009: 510).
163. Pollzien and Bronfen 1965: 15; Poltorak and Lerner 2004, Chapter 9.
164. Poltorak and Lerner 2004: 99–100.
165. Pollzien and Bronfen 1965: 15; Poltorak and Lerner 2004: 99–100.
166. Poltorak and Lerner 2004: 99–100.
167. Poltorak and Lerner 2004: 101–2.
168. Ibid.
169. Pollzien and Bronfen 1965: 15.
170. Poltorak and Lerner 2004: 101–2.
171. Ibid.
172. Ibid.
173. Ibid.
174. See factors listed in *Georgia-pacific Corporation* v. *United States Plywood Corp.* 318 F Supp 116 [SDNY 1970] (US).
175. See factors listed ibid.
176. The factors detailed here are amongst those listed by the court when assessing the royalty rate in default of an agreement by the parties in *Georgia-pacific Corporation* v. *United States Plywood Corp.* 318 F Supp 116 [SDNY 1970] (US).

177. See also 'Principal's concerns' in this chapter. The use of such provisions is regulated in various countries; for a review of the subject of regulation see August et al. (2009: 493–517).
178. For a review of the subject of regulation see August et al. (2009; 506–7).
179. See also 'Principal's concerns' in this chapter.
180. See also 'Principal's concerns' in this chapter.
181. See also 'Principal's concerns' in this chapter.
182. See also 'Principal's concerns' in this chapter.
183. See also 'Principal's concerns' in this chapter.
184. See also 'Principal's concerns' in this chapter.
185. See also 'Principal's concerns' in this chapter.
186. See also 'Principal's concerns' in this chapter.
187. See also 'Principal's concerns' and subsection on territorial exclusivity in Section XXIII, 'Body of the contract', in this chapter.
188. See also subsection on the obligations of the licensee in Section XXIII, 'Body of the contract', in this chapter.
189. Poltorak and Lerner 2004: 20, 68.
190. Poltorak and Lerner 2004: 21, 62–3.
191. See also the corresponding section in Chapter 3.
192. See the corresponding section in Chapter 2.
193. Poltorak and Lerner 2004: 18–19. See also the corresponding section in Chapter 2.
194. Poltorak and Lerner 2004: 18–19.
195. See also the corresponding section in Chapter 2.

7
International Instruments Governing International Commercial Agreements

Contents
Overview 282
Glossary 282
I Introduction 283
II The UNIDROIT Principles and the Principles of European Contract Law (PECL) 286
III United Nations Convention on Contracts for the International Sale of Goods 1980 (CISG) 293
IV Draft Common Frame of Reference (DCFR) and Common European Sales Law (CESL) 299
Summary 301
Useful links 301
Further reading 301
Notes 302

Overview

This chapter looks at the key instruments introduced in the field of international contract law. It starts with a brief overview of the principal instruments formulated in the field of international contract law (Section I), before examining the Principles of International Commercial Contracts (UNIDROIT Principles) and the Principles of European Contract Law (PECL) (Section II), the United Nations Convention for the International Sales of Goods (CISG) (Section III) and the Draft Common Frame of Reference (DCFR) and Common European Sales Law (CESL) (Section IV).

By the end of the chapter the reader will have a better understanding of
- the instruments governing international contract law;
- the role of the UNIDROIT Principles;
- the role of the PECL;
- the key provisions of the UNIDROIT Principles, the PECL and the CISG; and
- the role and content of the DCFR.

Glossary

Breach of contract Without lawful excuse, a failure of or refusal by a contracting party to perform an obligation imposed on it under the contract. Alternatively a failure by a party to the contract to perform a contractual obligation to the requisite standard of performance required in relation to the said contractual obligation.[1]
Contracts that are enforceable in law See **legally enforceable contracts**.
Counteroffer A new offer made by the offeree to the original offeror.
Discharge by performance A contract is discharged by the performance of the contracting parties of all the primary

I INTRODUCTION

obligations owed by them under the contract.[2]
Express warranties Warranties that are set out in the contract.
Force majeure clause A contractual provision that suspends and excuses performance when an event arises which is beyond the control of the parties, until the event in question has passed.
Freedom of contract The notion that persons (natural or juristic) are free to choose whether or not they wish to enter into a given contract and to determine the terms of their contract.
Implied terms Terms that are read into the contract by law or by the arbiter of the case.
Implied warranties Warranties that are read into the contract by law.
Legally enforceable contracts (or **contracts that are enforceable in law**) Contracts recognised by law and the courts as binding on the parties to the agreement.

Non-conforming goods Goods supplied that fail to conform with warranties (express or implied).
Non-performance A failure to perform a contractual obligation.
Offeree Party receiving an offer.
Offeror Party making an offer.
Order for specific performance A court order requiring the defaulting party to do that which they are contracted to do.
Penalty clause A contractual provision imposing a penalty on the defaulting party for its failure to perform contractual obligations.
Right to cure An option, occasionally made available to a **non-performing** party, of remedying a **breach of contract**.
Warranties Contractual terms defining the design, performance characteristics, qualities and workmanship of the product being sold or service being supplied.

I Introduction[3]

Efforts have been made at the international level to find solutions to the question of which law to apply in the context of international commercial agreements. One such solution, uniform law, presents itself in a number of ways.[4] Firstly, it presents itself as international conventions prepared by international organisations, adopted at diplomatic conferences and afterwards hopefully ratified by a large number of States. Secondly, it presents itself as model laws prepared with the aim of being used by legislatures at the national level as well as the international level. Thirdly, it presents itself as legal guides intended for use by private as well as public operators in the domain of international trade. Fourthly, it presents itself as standard terms (or general conditions) prepared by organisations of business people or international intergovernmental organisations which only become law between the parties when the parties contracting elect to use these standard terms as the law governing their contract. The International Chamber of Commerce (ICC) has been instrumental in this context, producing a number of model contracts covering an array of international transactions (agency, distribution, sales and so on) for use by parties contracting in the international commercial context.[5] These model contracts include provisions that are intended to regulate the relationship between the parties as fully as possible.

Finally in the case of international organisations, unique structures may exist that permit the development of uniform law in specific domains. In the case of the European Union (EU), for example, uniform law has been developed through the introduction of directives, regulations and court decisions.

Bearing in mind the need to find solutions to the question of which law to apply in the context of international commercial agreements, certain entities have worked on the formulation of a body of uniform law specifically tailored to the needs of international commercial parties. Different entities have worked separately towards this same end. In certain cases one body of uniform law has been the inspiration for another body of law. For example the Hague Uniform Laws on International Sale of Goods served as a key source of inspiration for the CISG.[6]

The common objective of these different entities has been the formulation of a body of law that may be used in the context of commercial contracts of an international nature. The resulting bodies of law include the United Nations Convention on Contracts for the International Sale of Goods (CISG),[7] the Principles of European Contract Law (PECL), the UNIDROIT Principles[8] and the Draft Common Frame of Reference (DCFR).[9] These bodies of law may take the form of either binding instruments or non-binding instruments (the latter is also referred to as soft law).[10] Whilst the CISG is an example of a binding instrument, the UNIDROIT Principles, the PECL and the DCFR are examples of non-binding instruments.

These bodies of law are either general in their scope or specific. Whilst the CISG addresses sales agreement of an international nature, the UNIDROIT Principles, the PECL and the DCFR address international contracts more generally as they are wider in scope of application. For example the DCFR covers an array of agreements including international distribution agreements, international agency agreements and international franchise agreements. Unlike the CISG, both the PECL and the UNIDROIT Principles apply to all types of contract.

More topic-specific instruments exist addressing inter alia limitation periods in international sales agreements[11] and **penalty clauses** for non-performance.[12]

Instruments governing international commercial agreements

Non-binding instruments (soft law)

The organisations known as UNIDROIT (International Institute for the Unification of Private Law) and the Lando Committee (Commission on European Contract Law) have each separately drafted and issued principles designed for use in relation to international commercial agreements.[13] UNIDROIT has issued successive enlarged versions of the UNIDROIT Principles, whilst the Lando Committee has issued successive enlarged versions of the PECL. Both sets of principles were issued with the intention that they serve as a template for national and other international instruments.[14]

The principles issued by UNIDROIT and the PECL are intended to provide a useful reference point in situations where the system or the rules of law applicable do not provide a solution to an issue raised.[15] This could occur for example where domestic law is either vague or fails to provide a solution to a difficulty confronted by the arbiter in the context of an international commercial agreement. The UNIDROIT Principles or the PECL may be applied as if the parties contracting expressly elect to use these instruments as the governing law in their contract or where the contracting parties refer to the 'general principles of law', 'lex mercatoria' or the like as the governing law in their contract.[16] Alternatively, these instruments will apply where the contract is

I INTRODUCTION

deemed by the final arbiters to be governed by the 'general principles of law', 'lex mercatoria' or the like.[17]

The parties to an international commercial agreement may expressly opt to use either the PECL or the UNIDROIT Principles in their choice of law clause, either alone or alongside the CISG or the law of a specific jurisdiction. The parties contracting may for example want certain clauses in their contract to be dealt with by reference to either the PECL or the UNIDROIT Principles, whilst other clauses are dealt with by reference to the CISG or the law of a selected jurisdiction. Since the CISG is narrower in terms of the substantive matters that it covers, the UNIDROIT Principles and the PECL are useful for filling any gaps.[18]

UNIDROIT[19]

UNIDROIT was originally set up in 1926 as an auxiliary organ of the League of Nations with the objective of promoting the unification of private law. In 1940, it was re-established following the demise of the League of Nations on the basis of a multilateral agreement. UNIDROIT aims to look at the ways in which the private law of states and groups of states may be harmonised and coordinated and to prepare uniform rules of private law for adoption by the various states.[20]

The UNIDROIT Principles were issued by UNIDROIT after extensive comparative research into the different national systems of contract law. The UNIDROIT Principles are a set of rules designed for use in international commercial contracts throughout the world. These principles are drafted as articles and are accompanied by comments which include illustrations.

Due to their success, new and enlarged versions of the UNIDROIT Principles were released in 2004 and in 2010. These extended versions contain additional chapters and are adapted to electronic contracting. The UNIDROIT Principles are now available in more than twenty languages and are increasingly being used by national legislatures as a source of inspiration for local reform of the law, by lawyers as guidelines in the negotiation and drafting of contracts and by arbitrators as the legal basis for the resolution of commercial disputes.

Scope of application of UNIDROIT Principles The UNIDROIT Principles set out the general rules that are applicable to international commercial contracts. As such they are applicable to contracts that are both international and commercial.[21]

The principles themselves do not expressly lay down any specific criteria in relation to the term 'international'. However, there is an assumption that the term is broadly defined, so that ultimately the only situations excluded from the scope of the principles would be those where no international element at all is involved, for example contracts that are connected to one country alone.[22]. Though the principles are intended for use in international commercial transactions, there is nothing that prevents private parties from agreeing to use them in purely domestic contracts.[23]

In this context, the term 'commercial' is used in the widest sense of the word. It is taken to encompass not only commercial transactions involving the sale of goods, but also transactions involving the exchange of goods and the supply or exchange of services including the provision of investment and professional services.[24]

PECL[25]

The European Parliament's resolution of 6 May 1994 called on the Lando Committee to commence work on the harmonisation of contract law in the European Union. This resolution, called 'The Harmonization of

Certain Sectors of the Private Law of the Member States', concluded that harmonisation of the different sectors of private law was essential for the completion of the internal market.

The current version of the PECL comprises three successive parts that were published separately. Part I was published in 1995, Part II was published in 2000 as a consolidated version with Part I, and Part III was published in 2003.

Part I of the PECL contains the fundamental principles of contract law and the rules governing performance and remedies. Part II contains the rules governing formation of the contract, interpretation of the contract, the validity of the contract and the authority of agents. Part III of the PECL contains the rules governing inter alia the assignment of claims, illegality, set-offs and conditional contractual provisions.

Binding instruments

European Union law
European Union law governs the operations of businesses incorporated in the European Union, as well as the operations of businesses incorporated outside the European Union but operating in one or more of the EU member states.

United Nations Commission on International Trade Law (UNCITRAL)
Established on 17 December 1966 by United Nations General Assembly Resolution 2205 (XXI), UNCITRAL is entrusted with, amongst other tasks, that of harmonising and unifying the rules governing international trade, as it is recognised that disparities in national laws have resulted in the creation of barriers to the flow of trade. In a bid to harmonise and unify the rules governing international trade, UNCITRAL has been responsible for the creation of several key international instruments. These instruments include the 1974 Convention on the Limitation Period in the International Sale of Goods (as amended), the 1980 Convention on Contracts for the International Sale of Goods (CISG), the 1983 Uniform Rules on Contract Clauses for an Agreed Sum Due upon Failure of Performance, the 1996 Model Law on Electronic Commerce (as amended) and the 2001 Model Law on Electronic Signatures.

II The UNIDROIT Principles and the Principles of European Contract Law (PECL)

Contracts are agreements recognised by law and the courts as binding on the parties to the agreement. In other words such agreements are said to be **enforceable in law** or **legally enforceable**. Where an agreement is recognised as legally enforceable, the promises made in it will be treated as obligations or duties in law and if one of the provisions in the agreement is not met, the law will likely provide for remedies that can be enforced by the courts.

Contracts are governed by law – legislation and in certain jurisdictions by judge-made law – as well as by the particulars of the agreement reached by the parties (otherwise referred to as private law). Interestingly, private law may override many of the rules otherwise established by law (the principle of party autonomy) due to the importance placed on the intentions of the parties and the reluctance of the state to intervene in the private bargaining of the parties.

Parties to a contract may be individuals, business entities (such as corporations or partnerships), or governments. Contracts are typically made between two parties, but certain three-sided agreements also exist involving three distinct and different parties. Contracts may be concluded between businesses, between a business and a consumer and between a business and a government.

Persons are free to choose whether or not they wish to enter into a given contract. What is more, such persons are free to choose what the terms of their contract will be. This principle is referred to as the principle of **freedom of contract**[26] and can be found in national law and international law. Under international contract law, it can be found in the CISG (Article 6),[27] the UNIDROIT Principles (Article 1.1),[28] the PECL (Article 1:102)[29] and the DCFR.[30]

Formation of a contract[31]

In order for a binding contract to exist between the parties, an offer and acceptance should be established.

In certain jurisdictions there are a number of supplementary requirements, namely the presence of an intention to be bound, the existence of capacity on the part of the contracting parties to contract and the existence of either consideration or cause. The UNIDROIT Principles and the PECL have done away with consideration and cause[32] in order to encourage commerce and greater certainty and to reduce the need for litigation.[33] According to the UNIDROIT Principles, a contract may be concluded either through acceptance of an offer or through conduct of the parties that is sufficient to demonstrate agreement.[34] Pursuant to the PECL, a contract is concluded when two requirements are met: firstly the parties in question intend to be legally bound and secondly they reach a sufficient agreement without any further requirement.[35] In a simple business-to-consumer (B-to-C) transaction, the making of an offer and its acceptance is a straightforward affair and there is typically no room for negotiation of terms by the customer.

Box 7.1 B-to-C contract illustrated

When a customer enters a supermarket for biscuits, he chooses a packet of biscuits from the shelf (making note of the price displayed) and walks to the checkout to pay. When reaching the checkout, the customer does not usually proceed to negotiate the price of the packet of biscuits with the cashier. Instead he simply presents the biscuits to the cashier and pays the price marked on the packet.[36]

Business-to-business transactions are distinct from B-to-C transactions as they do usually involve a certain amount of ongoing negotiation of terms until the parties agree on a final version that is acceptable to both parties.

Offer[37]

A contract is based on an agreement, which arises when one party (the **offeror**) makes an offer to another party (the **offeree**). As the recipient of the offer, the offeree has the ultimate power to decide whether to accept, reject or even renegotiate the said offer.

The definitions of an offer in both the PECL and the UNIDROIT Principles are analogous.[38] Both the PECL and the UNIDROIT Principles in their definition of an offer refer firstly to the need for clarity of terms (terms that are referred to in both as 'sufficiently definite') and an intention on the part of the proposer to be bound in the event of acceptance.

When an offer becomes effective[39]

The concepts of offer and acceptance have traditionally been used to determine whether, and if so when, the parties have concluded an agreement. In commerce, contracts are often concluded after prolonged negotiations between the parties with no clear sequence of offer and acceptance. In such cases it is often hard to determine firstly, whether a contract has been concluded and secondly, where a contract is concluded, when the contract in question was concluded.

Both the PECL and the UNIDROIT Principles determine the point in time at which the offer becomes effective. Pursuant to both the PECL and the UNIDROIT Principles, an offer becomes effective when it reaches the addressee (in other words the offeree).[40]

Withdrawal of an offer

As noted above, an offer becomes effective under the PECL and the UNIDROIT Principles when it reaches the offeree. As such, it may be withdrawn (even if it is irrevocable) on the proviso that the withdrawal reaches the offeree before or at the same time as the offer.[41]

Under the PECL and the UNIDROIT Principles, an offer may be terminated either as a result of revocation by the offeror or due to its rejection by the offeree. Whilst the offeror is capable of revoking an offer,[42] his right to revoke is cut off once the offeree dispatches his acceptance.[43] Revocation must be actually communicated to be effective (in English law[44] as well as under the UNIDROIT Principles and PECL)[45] and as such the revocation must reach the offeree.

Rejection of the offer

Pursuant to the UNIDROIT Principles, an offer is terminated when a rejection (dispatched by the offeree) reaches the offeror.[46] Pursuant to the PECL, an offer will lapse when the rejection of the offer (dispatched by the offeree) reaches the offeror.[47] Under both the PECL and the UNIDROIT Principles, an offer may be terminated by the offeree in the event that the latter makes a new offer (a **counteroffer**). A counteroffer will effectively operate as a rejection of the original offer and a proposal of a new offer.[48]

Acceptance[49]

Under the UNIDROIT Principles and the PECL,[50] acceptance can take the form of a statement made by the offeree indicating assent to the offer, or conduct by the offeree similarly indicating assent. Such acceptance becomes effective when the indication of assent reaches the offeror.[51]

The time at which the contract is concluded

The concepts of offer and acceptance have traditionally been used to determine whether the parties have reached an agreement and, if they have reached such an agreement, when the agreement was reached. Pursuant to the UNIDROIT Principles, a contract may be concluded either through acceptance of an offer or through conduct of the parties that is sufficient to demonstrate agreement.[52] Under the PECL, the point in time when a contract is concluded will depend on the circumstances of the case.[53] In the event that acceptance is by means of a statement, the contract is concluded at the point in time when the acceptance (dispatched by the offeree) reaches the offeror.[54] In the case of acceptance through conduct, a contract is concluded when notice of such conduct reaches the offeror.[55]

Interpreting terms[56]

When negotiating the terms that govern the relationship between them, the contracting parties may overlook some of them, or they may agree on terms which are either vague or incomplete. In such circumstances, the courts are called upon to fill the gaps left in the contract and to determine the meaning of vague or incomplete terms through the process of construction.

Interpretation of terms is addressed in the UNIDROIT Principles and the PECL.[57] The point of departure in both the UNIDROIT Principles and the PECL is the parties' common intention.[58] In the event that the common intention of the parties cannot be established, then when interpreting the contract, reference should be made to the 'meaning that a reasonable person would give to it in the same circumstances'.[59]

Form[60]

It is a common misconception that contracts need to be written in order to have legal effect. If this were the case then each time we purchased a newspaper or a ticket for the bus, we would be expected to countersign an invoice, which would have the net result of making even the simplest and most mundane daily task time consuming, costly and burdensome. For this reason, as a general rule there is no requirement that contracts be written.

Pursuant to the UNIDROIT Principles and the PECL, a contract will be valid and enforceable irrespective of its form and even if it is not written or evidenced in writing.[61] The parties to a contract are of course free to choose whether or not they wish to record the terms agreed upon between them in writing. In commercial transactions, it is often sensible to do so, in order to ensure clarity and certainty in the event of difficulties further down the line.

Implied terms[62]

In many contracts, although the main provisions are contained in express terms, from time to time the contracting parties will not necessarily articulate all the obligations and rights that ensue under the contract or will not provide for every potential contingency that could arise in their dealings. Terms may be left out either intentionally or due to an oversight by the contracting parties, in which circumstances certain terms may be read into the contract. Such terms are referred to as **implied terms**.

The UNIDROIT Principles and the PECL acknowledge the fact that the contractual obligations of the contracting parties may be express or implied.[63] Pursuant to the UNIDROIT Principles and the PECL, implied obligations are capable of stemming from the nature and purpose of the contract[64] and from good faith and fair dealings.[65] In addition, such obligations are capable of stemming under the PECL from the intention of the parties[66] and under the UNIDROIT Principles[67] from reasonableness,[68] practices established between the parties and usages.[69]

The UNIDROIT Principles and PECL also supply specific key terms that operate by default. The UNIDROIT Principles incorporate terms for when the parties have failed to determine the quality of performance of a contractual obligation,[70] the price,[71] the time of performance,[72] the order of performance,[73] the place of performance[74] and the currency of payment.[75] PECL incorporates terms for when the parties have failed to determine the price,[76] the quality of performance of a contractual obligation,[77] the place of performance,[78] the time of performance[79] and the currency of payment.[80]

Discharge of a contract

A contract can be discharged by performance, frustration, breach or agreement.[81]

Discharge by performance[82]

More often than not a contract is discharged through performance by the parties (**discharge by performance**), in which case it is essential to establish the requisite standard of performance in relation to each contractual obligation, as a failure to perform to the requisite standard (**non-performance**) will amount to a **breach of contract**. Such a failure to perform will include a delay in performance and defective performance[83] and in the case of PECL a failure to cooperate in order to give full effect to the contract.[84]

Where the parties each perform their obligations under the contract in line with the terms agreed and recorded in the contract then there is no issue of breach under the contract.

Box 7.2 Discharge by performance illustrated

A contract is concluded for the delivery of 100 Christmas hampers on 30 November 2009. Under the contract, payment is due on 7 December 2009.

Where the hampers contracted for are delivered on time and the price due is paid on time then full performance by both parties is deemed to have taken place. Accordingly the contract is treated as having come to an end.

If the parties wish to contract for a further delivery of hampers then they will need to conclude another contract.

A failure to deliver the hampers on 30 November 2009 will constitute a breach of contract; this applies if the hampers are delivered prematurely as well as if they are delivered late. A breach of contract will also occur if the price due is not paid on time.

Discharge by breach[85]

A breach of contract will arise if a party to the contract refuses or fails to perform an obligation imposed on him in the contract, or he performs the obligation in a defective manner, or his performance of his contractual obligation is tardy.[86] In the case of the PECL, a failure to cooperate in order to give full effect to the contract is also classed as non-performance.[87]

Not all breaches will give rise to the right to treat the contract as terminated. Certain breaches may give rise only to a claim in damages. In the event that a breach does give rise to a right to treat the contract as terminated, the non-breaching party will have the option of either accepting the breach as terminating the contract (in which case, all the future obligations on the parties under the contract are discharged)[88] or affirming the contract (in which case the contract will remain operational and the parties to the contract will be expected to continue performing their obligations under it and to complete performance of any relevant obligations imposed on them by the contract).[89] The non-breaching party has no obligation in such circumstances to affirm the contract.

Right to cure the non-performance

A non-performing party may occasionally have the option available to him of remedying the non-performance or the defective performance (**the right to cure**).[90] Such an option will be available only if certain conditions are met.[91] In a bid to preserve the contract, this option allows the non-performing party to extend the period for performance for a brief period beyond the period stipulated in the contract, unless timely performance is a requirement in the contract or is required by the circumstances.[92]

This right to cure non-performance will arise if the non-performing party furnishes the aggrieved party with timely notice indicating the proposed manner and timing of the cure and the cure is executed promptly.[93] When a non-performing party opts for this option he will bear the cost of the rectification himself.[94]

Right to additional time for performance
The provision of further performance time is also permissible in certain circumstances.[95] Such a remedy is intended for use in circumstances where one party performs his contractual obligation late and the other party is willing to grant extra time for performance.[96] In such circumstances, the aggrieved party may by notice allow the non-performing party an additional time for performance.[97]

Anticipatory non-performance

If before the due time for performance by one of the contracting parties it is clear that there will be a fundamental non-performance by that party, the other party has the option if he so chooses to terminate the contract.[98] In the alternative, the aggrieved party may affirm the contract by extending the other party a further opportunity to perform its contractual obligations.

Box 7.3 Anticipatory non-performance illustrated
Anticipatory non-performance may arise when, for example, in the case of a contract for the supply of goods, the seller is on the brink of bankruptcy and the buyer is aware that the seller will not be able to supply the goods. In such a situation, the buyer has the option of either accepting the breach as terminating the contract or affirming the contract and awaiting the due date of performance by giving the other party a further opportunity to perform its contractual obligations.

Excuses for non-performance and force majeure clauses[99]

One of the problems that could arise in the context of performance is the occurrence of an external event that is beyond the control of the parties, which in turn prevents one of the parties from fulfilling his obligations under the contract, or diminishes his ability to perform these obligations, or delays his performance of these obligations. Such impediments include natural disasters, civil unrest, wars and so on. To address such contingencies, most of the time the parties will include in their contract a provision entitled a **force majeure clause**. Such a provision will suspend and excuse performance where such an event arises until such a time as the event in question passes. Both the UNIDROIT Principles and the PECL make provision for such situations.[100]

Remedies for non-performance[101]

If one of the parties has failed to perform his obligations under the contract and the other party has suffered a loss as a result, what can the aggrieved party do?

The contract will usually include within its provisions ones providing for remedies in relation to a breach intended for the benefit of the aggrieved party. The remedies available under the terms of the contract will typically depend on the severity of the breach. A more minor breach (for example non-conformity of some of the goods in a given batch) will probably permit the aggrieved party to demand compensation or replacement goods or to carry out repairs to the defective goods in the batch before requesting a refund of the sums dispensed on the repairs from the non-performing party. For a major breach (for example a failure to deliver a batch or a failure to pay) the aggrieved party is likely to have the right to terminate the agreement upon giving notice to the non-performing party.

The UNIDROIT Principles and the PECL address the remedies available in the event of non-performance. Where one of the parties to the contract fails to perform one of his obligations under the contract and non-performance is not excused[102] then the aggrieved party may resort to any one of the remedies for non-performance.[103] In the event of non-performance, the aggrieved party has the following remedies available to him under the UNIDROIT Principles and PECL. He may pursue

1. a right to performance;[104]
2. a right to withhold performance;[105]
3. a right to terminate;[106]
4. a right to a price reduction;[107] and/or
5. a right to claim damages and interest.[108]

A right to performance
An aggrieved party may seek performance of a monetary obligation[109] as well as a non-monetary one.[110] Where one of the contracting parties is obliged to pay money and does not do so, then the other party may require payment.[111] Where a contracting party who owes a non-monetary obligation fails to perform this obligation, the aggrieved party may demand specific performance of the non-monetary obligation by means of an application to court for an order to this effect (an **order for specific performance**).[112]

A right to withhold performance
A party obliged to perform simultaneously with the other party or after the other party is entitled to withhold performance until such a time as the other party has performed.

A right to terminate
The aggrieved party may terminate the contract by notice in the event that non-performance by the other party is fundamental.[113] Non-performance is likely to be fundamental under the UNIDROIT Principles and the PECL when the failure to perform substantially deprives the aggrieved party of what he was entitled to expect under the contract, unless the non-performing party did not foresee and could not have reasonably foreseen such a result.[114] Furthermore, non-performance is likely to be fundamental under the UNIDROIT Principles and the PECL when strict compliance with the obligation is of the essence under the contract.[115]

Notice must be given within a reasonable time by the aggrieved party in order for him to rely on his right to terminate.[116]

Termination of the contract will have the effect of releasing both contracting parties from their obligations to effect and to receive future performance under the contract.[117] Termination will not preclude a claim for compensation in relation to the non-performance.[118]

III United Nations Convention on Contracts for the International Sale of Goods 1980 (CISG)

Introduction

Formulated by UNCITRAL, the CISG is a convention that binds nations (contracting states). An list of countries that have ratified the CISG can be found on the UNCITRAL website.[119]

Matters dealt with by the CISG and issues excluded

The CISG is not meant to cover the whole range of contractual issues nor is it intended to cover the international sale of all types of goods. The issues covered by the CISG include formation of the contract as well as the rights and obligations of the parties to the contract, leaving other matters (such as validity of the contract, legal capacity of the contracting parties, fraud and misrepresentation) to be dealt with in conformity with either the applicable set of uniform rules or the applicable domestic law.[120] These issues were left out of the CISG to ensure a speedy conclusion.[121]

Contracts excluded from the CISG include those for the sale of consumer goods,[122] the supply of services,[123] the sale of stocks, securities and money,[124] the sale of ships and aircraft[125] and the supply of electricity,[126] as well as those where the contracting parties specifically agree to opt out of the CISG on the basis of Article 6. In the main, opting out of the CISG is only possible where the parties clearly express their intent to do so, as the following case illustrates.

Box 7.4 Express exclusion of the CISG illustrated[127]

The seller and buyer entered into a contract for the sale of goods (electronic components). The goods were allegedly defective as they failed to conform to certain designated technical specifications.

The choice of law clause of the seller adopted the law of the Canadian province of British Columbia. The choice of law clause of the buyer adopted the laws of the US state of California. The CISG is the law of British Columbia and under general California law, the CISG is applicable to contracts where the contracting parties are from different countries that have adopted the CISG.[128]

In this case the court held that the particular choice of law provisions made in the terms and conditions of both contracting parties were insufficient by themselves in order to result in an opt-out of the CISG. Though these selections made by the parties could be treated as an implied exclusion of the CISG, the court stated that in order to opt out of the CISG, the contracting parties should use clear language indicating that that is what they both intended to do.

Scope of applicability of the CISG

The CISG applies to international contracts for the sale of goods and governs the rights and obligations of the buyer and seller arising out of such a contract. It will apply to a contract if the following conditions are met:[129]

1. A contract for the sale of goods has been concluded
2. between commercial parties whose places of business are in different states (the nationality of the parties is not a determining factor) and
3. these states are contracting states or the rules of private international law

lead to the application of the law of a contracting state.[130]

Where one of the parties has more than one place of business, the place of business for the purposes of the CISG is that which has the closest relationship to the contract and its performance, having regard to the circumstances that are either known or taken into account by the parties at any time prior to the conclusion of the contract or at the conclusion of the contract.[131]

Mixed contracts comprising supply of goods and services or labour[132]

Pursuant to Article 3(2), the CISG will apply to mixed contracts involving the supply of labour or other services by the seller alongside the delivery of goods, on the proviso that the supply of labour or other services does not constitute a preponderant part of the seller's obligations. Though the phrase 'preponderant part' is not defined in Article 3(2) of the CISG, case law clarifies this concept. Where within the overall performance the provision of a service only plays a subordinate role, then the contract is capable of being governed by the CISG.[133]

Formation

Part II of the CISG, comprising Articles 14 to 24, sets out the rules that govern the formation of an international contract for the sale of goods. Articles 14 to 17 address the offer whilst Articles 18 to 22 address acceptance. Articles 23 and 24 address the question of when a contract is made and when a communication reaches the addressee respectively.

The offer

A proposal for concluding a contract which is addressed to one or more specific persons constitutes an offer if it is sufficiently definite and it indicates the intention of the offeror to be bound in the event of acceptance.[134] As such a communication between parties will amount to an offer under the CISG, if it meets the following three requirements.[135] Firstly, the communication must be a proposal for concluding a contract. Secondly, it must be sufficiently definite. Finally, it must indicate the intention of the party making the offer (the offeror) to be bound in the case of acceptance.

A proposal is sufficiently definite pursuant to the CISG if it indicates the goods and expressly or implicitly fixes or makes provision for determining the quantity and the price.[136]

Communication of an offer

The offer must be communicated to and accepted by the offeree in order for a contract to be formed.

Option of withdrawing or revoking the offer

The offeror has the right to change his mind. He may withdraw the offer until such a time as the offer becomes effective and once the offer is effective, he may revoke it. Withdrawal and revocation of an offer permit an offeror to change his mind or to respond to changes in market conditions.

The offer becomes effective when it reaches the offeree.[137] The offeror who changes his mind after dispatch may withdraw the offer, so long as the withdrawal reaches the offeree before or at the same time as the offer.[138] Once the offer becomes effective, the offeror may still cancel it by revoking it, but only if the offer is one that is capable of revocation (a revocable offer) and the offeror's revocation reaches the offeree, before the offeree has dispatched his acceptance.[139]

Once the offeree has dispatched his acceptance, the offeror loses his right to revoke the offer.[140]

Box 7.5 Revocation of an offer illustrated

A seller (whose place of business is based in Canada) makes an offer to sell a cargo of cocoa to a buyer (whose place of business is based in the United States).

Due to a change in market conditions, the price offered by the seller is no longer commercially viable. Accordingly, the seller (the offeror in this example) is considering his options and is looking into the possibility of revoking the offer he has made to the buyer (the offeree in this example). The seller will have a right to revoke the offer until a contract is concluded, so long as the revocation reaches the buyer before the buyer has dispatched his acceptance.[141]

The seller will not be able to revoke the offer made to the buyer if the offer indicates that it is irrevocable or if it was reasonable for the buyer to rely on it as being irrevocable and the buyer acted in reliance on the offer by for example contracting with others for the resale of the cocoa.[142].

An offer is terminated when a rejection reaches the offeror.[143] As such a rejection of the offer that is made by the offeree will be effective at the point in time when it reaches the offeror.[144] An offer is terminated when a rejection reaches the offeror even if the offer is irrevocable.[145]

Box 7.6 Termination of an offer illustrated[146]

On 1 May, the seller delivered to the buyer an offer, stating: 'I will hold the offer open until 1 June.' On 7 May, the buyer delivered the seller the following message: 'I cannot accept your offer as the price is too high.' On 10 May, the buyer delivered a further message to the seller in the following terms: 'I hereby accept your offer of 1 May.' The seller immediately informed the buyer that this 'acceptance' was not effective because of the earlier rejection. The buyer replied that this was not so, because the seller had promised to hold open the offer until 1 June.

Here the buyer's letter of 7 May effectively terminated the offer, even though the offer would have been binding until 1 June. Accordingly there is no contract here.

Acceptance of the offer[147]

If the buyer sends the seller an order form and a week later receives the goods, is there a contract?

A statement made by the offeree indicating assent to an offer can be acceptance ('I accept your offer'). Conduct of the offeree indicating assent to the offer can also be treated as acceptance. An offeree may accept by performing an act even if he does so without notifying the offeror but only if the act in question is performed within the time allocated for acceptance by the offeror or, if no such time is allocated, within a reasonable period of time *and* the act is one that is treated as acceptance by virtue of the following:

1. the terms of the offer deem it as such;
2. the parties have established a particular practice between them;[148]; or
3. such conduct is routinely treated as acceptance in that particular trade.[149]

Acceptance becomes effective
An acceptance of an offer becomes effective at the moment the indication of assent reaches the offeror.

Withdrawing acceptance
An acceptance may be withdrawn if the withdrawal reaches the offeror before or at same time as acceptance would have become effective.[150]

Time of conclusion of the contract
A contract is concluded at the moment when an acceptance of an offer becomes effective in accordance with the provisions of the CISG.[151]

Content of the acceptance[152]
If the buyer is willing to accept the terms and conditions of the other party subject to a change in the date of delivery or the quantity of goods, what effect will this have?

Under the CISG a reply containing further or different terms that do not materially alter the terms of the offer constitutes an acceptance, unless the offeror without undue delay objects orally to the discrepancy or dispatches a notice to this effect.[153] The terms of the resulting contract are the terms of the offer with the modifications contained in the acceptance, unless the offeror without undue delay objects orally or dispatches a notice to this effect.[154]

By way of comparison, where the reply of the offeree either states or implies additional or different terms that materially alter the terms of the offer, it will constitute a rejection of the original offer. This reply may also constitute a new offer (a counteroffer) if it meets the requirements that need to be met in order to be considered an offer in its own right.[155] In the latter case, no contract will ensue unless the original offeror accepts the terms of the counteroffer. Under the CISG, acceptance of a counteroffer may arise by assent or by performance.

In order to ascertain whether an element of the acceptance materially alters the terms of the corresponding offer, a list of items is provided in Article 19(3) of the CISG. Pursuant to this article, the additional terms that 'are considered'[156] to materially alter the terms of an offer include 'among other things'[157]

- price;
- payment terms;
- quality and quantity of the goods;
- place and time of delivery;
- extent of one party's liability to the other; and
- settlement of a dispute.

This list is illustrative, as can be inferred from the use of the expression 'among other things'.[158]

Formalities

Read subject to Article 12 of the CISG, Article 11 establishes the principle of freedom from form. As such a contract of sale need not be concluded or evidenced in writing and is not subject to any other requirement as to form. An upshot of this article and the principle of freedom from form is the idea that a contract may be modified or terminated by the mere agreement of the parties.[159]

Key obligations of the buyer

The buyer's principal obligations are as follows:[160]

- duty to inspect goods and notify seller of non-conformity;[161]
- duty to notify seller of a third party claim;[162] and
- duty to pay the price and to take delivery of the goods as required by the contract and by the provisions of the CISG.[163]

Duty to inspect goods and notify seller of non-conformity

The objective of this obligation is to give the seller sufficient information to remedy the lack of conformity.

The buyer must inspect the goods or make sure that they are inspected within the shortest period of time possible in the given circumstances.[164] If a defect is detected upon inspection, the buyer must notify the seller exactly why the goods are non-conforming. This notification must be provided within a reasonable period of time after the defect was detected or should have been detected.[165] Failure to give such notice to the seller will result in the buyer losing his right to rely on the said lack of conformity.[166]

Duty to notify the seller of a third party claim

A seller is obliged to furnish goods that are free from the rights or claims of third parties.[167] A buyer for his part will be able to pursue the seller for supplying goods that are not free from the rights or claims of others only if he notifies the seller of these claims within a reasonable period of time after he became aware or ought to have become aware of these rights or claims by other parties in relation to the goods supplied.[168]

Duty to pay the price and take delivery

The buyer is obliged to pay the seller and take delivery of the goods, complying with obligations agreed upon with the seller in relation to payment of the price and the taking over of the goods.[169] Even if the price payable for the goods, the place of payment and the time of payment have not been determined by the parties, the CISG helps the parties by inserting provisions into the contract that help the seller and the buyer determine the same.[170]

Key obligations of seller

The seller's principal obligations are as follows:[171]

- duty to deliver the goods, hand over any documents relating to the goods and transfer property in the goods;[172]
- duty to deliver conforming goods;[173] and
- duty to deliver goods which are free from third party claims or rights.[174]

Conforming goods should be delivered[175]

Warranties are terms in the contract that define the design, performance characteristics, qualities and workmanship of the product being sold. **Express warranties** are those set out in the contract, whilst **implied warranties** are those warranties that are read into the contract by the law. The seller is obliged to deliver goods which are of the quantity, quality and description set out in the contract and which are contained or packaged in the manner defined in the contract.[176]

Unless a buyer knew or could not have been unaware of a problem with the goods at the time of the conclusion of the contract[177] and subject to the right of the parties to disclaim these warranties,[178] a seller is obliged to deliver to the buyer goods which

- are fit for the purpose or purposes for which goods of the same description would ordinarily be used;
- are fit for any particular purpose expressly or implicitly made known to the seller at the time the contract was concluded;
- possess the qualities of goods which the seller held out to the buyer as a sample or model; and
- are contained or packaged in the manner usual for such goods or, where there is no such manner, in a manner that is adequate to preserve and protect them.[179]

In the event that the goods supplied by the seller to the buyer fail to conform with the express or implied warranties, they are said to be **non-conforming goods**.

Remedies

The remedies available under the CISG generally attempt to preserve the contractual relationship by keeping the parties engaged in the contract. Only as a last resort will the contract be treated as terminated.

Remedies available to both parties

- Right to modify or terminate the contract by mere agreement[180]
- Right to avoid the contract[181]
- Right to damages[182] and interest[183]
- Right to specific performance[184]
- Right to anticipatory breach.[185]

Remedies specific to the seller

- Right to cure[186]
- Right to additional time for performance of his contractual obligations[187]
- Right to fix additional time for performance by the buyer of his obligations.[188]

Remedies specific to the buyer

- Right to a price reduction[189]
- Right to fix additional time for performance by the seller of his obligations.[190]

Fundamental breach

A fundamental breach is the prerequisite for certain remedies available to the buyer and seller under the CISG, namely the right to terminate the contract and to demand specific performance.

A breach committed by one of the parties is deemed fundamental if it results in such a detriment to the other party as to substantially deprive him of what he is entitled to expect under the contract, unless the party in breach did not foresee such a result and a reasonable person of the same kind in the same circumstances would not have foreseen such a result.[191]

Remedies available to both parties

Right to modify or terminate the contract by mere agreement

The parties may agree to terminate the contract or to modify it.[192]

Right to avoid the contract

Avoidance of a contract is a remedy available to both parties.[193] Both the seller and the buyer may avoid the contract where there is a fundamental breach by the other party.[194] A declaration of avoidance is effective only if made by notice to the other party.[195] Such notice may be written or oral and can be transmitted by any means. Avoidance releases both parties of their obligations under the contract subject to any damages which may be due.[196]

Right to damages[197] and interest[198]
Damages for breach of contract will consist of a sum equal to the loss sustained by the aggrieved party including a claim for loss of profit.[199] Damages may not exceed the loss which the breaching party foresaw or ought to have foreseen as possibly resulting from the breach of contract at the time when the contract was concluded.[200]

The aggrieved party pursuing a claim based on a breach of contract is obliged to take steps that are reasonable bearing in mind the circumstances of the case to mitigate the loss resulting from the breach.[201] Where the aggrieved party fails to take such steps, the breaching party may claim a reduction in the damages equivalent to the sum by which the loss should have been mitigated.[202]

Right to specific performance
Where one of the contracting parties fails to perform an obligation, the other contracting party may require performance by the defaulting party[203] by means of an application to the court. The aggrieved party may in certain circumstances obtain an order requiring performance of a specific obligation by the defaulting party (an **order for specific performance**). Such an order is at the discretion of the court.[204] A court is not bound to enter a judgment for specific performance unless it would do so under its own law in relation to similar contracts of sale that are not governed by the CISG.[205]

Right to anticipatory breach[206]
A party may, if he so elects, suspend performance of his obligations under the contract upon the provision of notice of the suspension to the other party,[207] if at a point in time after conclusion of the contract it becomes apparent that the other party will not perform a substantial part of his obligations under the contract, due to a serious deficiency in his ability to perform or in his creditworthiness or as a result of his conduct in preparing to perform or in performing the contract.[208] The party looking to suspend performance must continue with performance if the other party provides adequate assurance of his performance.[209]

Remedies specific to the seller

In addition to the remedies common to both parties, the seller has the right to remedy before and after the due date for delivery. Before the due date for delivery, the seller has the right to make up a deficiency in the quantity of goods delivered or to deliver conforming goods in replacement for non-conforming goods.[210] After the due date for delivery, he has an additional right to perform if this can be done without unreasonable delay and without causing the buyer unreasonable inconvenience.[211] The seller has the option if he so chooses to fix an extra period of time of reasonable length for the buyer to perform his obligations.[212]

Remedies specific to the buyer

Beyond the remedies common to both seller and buyer, the buyer has the right to opt for a price reduction[213] and to provide the seller with additional time to perform his obligations.[214]

IV Draft Common Frame of Reference (DCFR) and Common European Sales Law (CESL)

Introduction to the DCFR

Work on the DCFR started in 1982 with the establishment of the Commission on European Contract Law (CECL). Work was furthered by the establishment of the Study Group on the European Civil Code (the Study Group) in 1998 and the Research Group on EC Private Law (the Acquis Group) in 2002. The DCFR is the culmination of the work of the Study Group, the Acquis Group and the CECL. The DCFR was presented to the European Commission in December 2008 and was published in 2009.[215]

In April 2010, the European Commission issued a decision[216] to set up a group made up of experts with competence in the field of contract law.[217] This group, known as the Expert Group on a Common Frame of Reference and chaired by the European Commission,[218] has been entrusted with assisting the European Commission in preparing its proposal for the Common Frame of Reference (CFR) using the DCFR as a point of departure.[219]

Common European Sales Law (CESL)

In October 2011, the European Commission issued a proposal for a regulation for a body of substantive law governing cross-border contracts concluded between businesses, as well as such contracts concluded between businesses and consumers.[220] This body of proposed law, which is annexed to this proposed regulation, is referred to within it as the Common European Sales Law (CESL).[221] The CESL, which is intended as a self-standing body of contract law,[222] will not replace national contract law in the various member states but rather will operate as a second regime of contract law intended for use by parties concluding cross-border contracts.[223] As such the member states will not be required to revise their pre-existing national law.[224]

Scope of application of the DCFR

The DCFR consists of ten books. The scope of application and the theme of each book are shown in Table 7.1.

Table 7.1 Books making up the DCFR

Book number	Scope and theme
I	General provisions
II	Contracts and other juridical acts
III	Obligations
IV	Specific contracts
V	Benevolent intervention in another's affairs
VI	Non-contractual liability arising out of damage caused to another
VII	Unjustified enrichment
VIII	Acquisition of goods and loss of ownership of goods
IX	Proprietary security in movable assets
X	Trust

Most of the books that make up the DCFR are subdivided into chapters, sections, subsections and articles. Save for Book I all the books contain chapters. Book IV is further subdivided into eight distinct parts. Each of these parts is dedicated to a different category of contract, as shown in Table 7.2.[225]

Table 7.2 List of parts in Book IV

Part number	Scope and theme
A	Sales contracts
B	Contracts involving leasing of goods
C	Contracts involving the supply of services
D	Mandate contracts
E	Commercial agency, franchise and distribution agreements
F	Loan agreements
G	Personal security agreements
H	Donations

Summary

In this chapter we examined the principal instruments formulated in the field of international contract law. Firstly, we reviewed the UNIDROIT Principles and the PECL and considered their respective scope and key provisions. Secondly, we examined the CISG and its key provision. Thirdly, we considered the DCFR and the CESL.

Useful links

http://www.cisgac.com/index.php (CISG Advisory Council general information)
http://www.cisgac.com/default.php?sid=128 (CISG Advisory Council opinions)
http://www.cisgac.com/default.php?ipkCat=132&sid=132 (CISG Advisory Council bibliography)

Further reading

Anderson, Ross Gilbert, Oliphant, Ken, Evans-Jones, Robin and Steven, Andrew (2011), 'Principles, Definitions and Model Rules of European Private Law: Draft Common Frame of Reference (DCFR), Full Edition', *Edinburgh Law Review* 15:2, 306.

Beale, Hugh, Fauvarque-Cosson, Bénédicte, Rutgers, Jacobien, Tallon, Dennis and Vogenauer, Stefan (2010), *Cases, Materials and Text on Contract Law*, 2nd ed., Hart.

Bonell, Michael (2000), 'The UNIDROIT Principles and Transnational Law', *Uniform Law Review* (new series) 2000:2, 199.

Bonell, Michael (2002), 'The UNIDROIT Principles of International Commercial Contracts and the Harmonisation of International Sales Law', *Revue Juridique Thémis* 36, 335.

Bonell, Michael (2004), 'Agency', in Hartkamp, Arthur and Hesselink, Martijn (eds), *Towards a European Civil Code*, 3rd ed., Kluwer Law International.

Commission on European Contract Law (2000), *The Principles of European Contract Law, Parts I & II*, Kluwer Law International.

Hesselink, M. W. and de Vries, G. J. P. (2001), *Principles of European Contract Law*, Kluwer Law International.

Honnold, John O. (1991), *Uniform Law for International Sales under the 1980 United Nations Convention*, Kluwer Law and Taxation.

Kronke, Herbert (2000), 'International Uniform Commercial Law Conventions: Advantages, Disadvantages, Criteria for Choice', *Uniform Law Review* (new series) 2000:1, 13.

Niglia, Leone (2003), *The Transformation of Contract in Europe*, Kluwer Law International.

Poole, Jill (2008), *Textbook on Contract Law*, Oxford University Press.

Principles of International Commercial Contracts (1994), UNIDROIT.

Study Group on a European Civil Code and Research Group on EC Private Law (Acquis Group) (eds) (2009), *Principles, Definitions and Model Rules of European*

Private Law: Draft Common Frame of Reference (DCFR) Outline Edition, Sellier European Law Publishers.

Viscasillas, Maria del Pilar Perales (1996), 'UNIDROIT Principles of International Commercial Contracts: Sphere of Application and General Provisions', *Arizona Journal of International and Comparative Law* 13:2, 381.

Viscasillas, Maria del Pilar Perales (2002), 'Battle of the Forms, Modification of Contract, Commercial Letters of Confirmation: Comparison of the United Nations Convention on Contracts for the International Sale of Goods (CISG) with the Principles of European Contract Law (PECL)', *Pace International Law Review* 14:1, 153.

Zweigert, Konrad and Kötz, Hein (1998), *An Introduction to Comparative Law*, 3rd ed., Clarendon Press.

Notes

1. Poole, Jill (2008), *Textbook on Contract Law*, Oxford University Press, 328.
2. Poole 2008: 324.
3. Professor Herbert Kronke, the former secretary general of UNIDROIT, discusses the advantages and disadvantages associated with international instruments, both binding and non-binding in Kronke, Herbert (2000), 'International Uniform Commercial Law Conventions: Advantages, Disadvantages, Criteria for Choice', *Uniform Law Review* (new series) 2000:1, 13.
4. Hartkamp, Arthur S. (2004), 'Principles of European Contract Law', in Hartkamp, Arthur and Hesselink, Martijn, *Towards a European Civil Code*, 3rd ed., Kluwer Law International, 125.
5. These model contracts are reviewed in Chapters 3 (in the context of international sales agreements) and 5 (in the context of international agency agreements).
6. Hartkamp 2004: 126.
7. A select bibliography relating to the CISG is available at http://www.cisg.law.pace.edu/cisg/biblio/full-biblio.html (last accessed 30 January 2013). The CISG Advisory Council has released several opinions that examine different aspects of the CISG. The CISG Advisory Council is a private initiative which has as its objective the promotion of 'a uniform interpretation of the CISG' and which intends to 'look beyond the cooking pot for ideas and for a more profound understanding of issues relating to CISG' (from the homepage of the CISG Advisory Council, (last accessed 30 January 2013)).
8. UNIDROIT (International Institute for the Unification of Private Law) presented the Principles of International Commercial Contracts (UPICC) in 1994. UPICC will be referred to as the UNIDROIT Principles. Documents and preparatory works are available at http://www.unidroit.org/english/principles/contracts/main.htm (last accessed 30 January 2013).
9. The DCFR is reviewed in Chapter 2 (general overview), Chapter 4 (DCFR and distribution agreements) and Chapter 5 (DCFR and agency agreements).
10. A review of various binding and non-binding instruments governing European contract law is provided in Beale, Hugh, Fauvarque-Cosson, Bénédicte,

Rutgers, Jacobien, Tallon, Dennis and Vogenauer, Stefan (2010), *Cases, Materials and Text on Contract Law*, 2nd ed., Hart.
11. UNCITRAL Convention on the Limitation Period in the International Sale of Goods 1974 as amended. Adopted on 12 June 1974, this convention establishes uniform rules governing the period of time within which legal proceedings relating to international sales contracts must be commenced. The list of contracting states can be viewed at http://www.uncitral.org/uncitral/en/uncitral_texts/sale_goods/1974Convention_status.html (last accessed 30 January 2013).
12. Penalty clauses in the context of international contracts for sales are addressed by UNCITRAL in the Uniform Rules on Contract Clauses for an Agreed Sum Due upon Failure of Performance 1983.
13. Limits were imposed on UNIDROIT's work in formulating the UNIDROIT Principles. UNIDROIT, 'like any other inter-governmental organisation, is not free in its choices in the way that an individual scholar or research institution may be. Any policy decision must start from the mandate formulated by the member states' (Kronke 2000: 13). Kronke states that whilst the mandate assigned is clear it is also 'undoubtedly too narrow' (Kronke 2000: 14). Nevertheless, he adds that the mandate also injects a measure of flexibility (ibid.).
14. Article 1:101 PECL; Preamble, UNIDROIT Principles 2010.
15. Ibid.
16. The UNIDROIT Principles will apply by the express agreement of the parties, as confirmed by the second paragraph of the Preamble to the Principles, which states that the Principles 'shall be applied when the parties have agreed that their contract be governed by them' (Viscasillas, Maria del Pilar Perales (1996), 'UNIDROIT Principles of International Commercial Contracts: Sphere of Application and General Provisions', *Arizona Journal of International and Comparative Law* 13:2, 396). Moreover these Principles may be applied to a contract as lex mercatoria 'when the parties have agreed that their contract be governed by "general principles of law", the "lex mercatoria" or the like'. (paragraph 3 of the Preamble to the Principles, cited in Viscasillas (1996: 396)). Professor Michael Bonell reviews a case in which the parties themselves expressly chose the UNIDROIT Principles as governing law and two further cases in which the UNIDROIT Principles were applied without the parties expressly choosing them (Bonell, Michael Joachim (2002), 'The UNIDROIT Principles of International Commercial Contracts and the Harmonisation of International Sales Law', *Revue Juridique Thémis* 36, 343–4).
17. Bonell looks at scenarios when the UNIDROIT Principles have been applied in the context of disputes involving contracts with state agencies or branches of the state (referred to as 'state contracts') (Bonell 2002: 344–6).
18. The scope of application of the CISG is reviewed later on in this Chapter.
19. The different roles of the UNIDROIT Principles in practice (present and future) are explored in Bonell (2002) and in the following articles, also by Professor Bonell: 'The UNIDROIT Initiative for the Progressive Codification

of International Trade Law', *International and Comparative Law Quarterly* 27, 413 (1978); Some Critical Reflections on the New UNCITRAL Draft Convention on International Sale, *Uniform Law Review* (old series) 1978:II, 2 (1978); 'A "Restatement" of Principles for International Commercial Contracts: An Academic Exercise or a Practical Need?', *International Business Law Journal* 1988, 873 (1988); 'Unification of Law by Non-legislative Means: The UNIDROIT Draft Principles for International Commercial Contracts', *American Journal of Comparative Law* 40, 625–33 (1992); 'The UNIDROIT Principles of International Commercial Contracts: Towards a New Lex Mercatoria', *International Business Law Journal* 1997, 145 (1997); 'Soft Law and Party Autonomy: The Case of the UNIDROIT Principles', *Loyola Law Review* 51, 229 (2005).

20. Article 1, Statute of UNIDROIT Incorporating the Amendment to Article 6(1) Which Entered into Force on 26 March 1993 (Statute of UNIDROIT), accessible at http://www.unidroit.org/english/presentation/statute.pdf (last accessed 30 January 2013).
21. A review of the scope of application of the UNIDROIT Principles is provided in Bonell (1992: 620–2).
22. Commentary accompanying Preamble UNIDROIT Principles (1994); Bonell 1992: 621.
23. Commentary accompanying Preamble UNIDROIT Principles (1994). Any agreement of a purely domestic nature even if governed by the UNIDROIT Principles would still be subject to applicable mandatory rules of national law (Viscasillas 1996: 392).
24. Commentary accompanying Preamble UNIDROIT Principles (1994); Viscasillas 1996: 395–6.
25. A review of the objectives of the PECL is provided in Commission on European Contract Law (2000), *The Principles of European Contract Law, Parts I & II*, Kluwer Law International, xxi–xxvii.
26. A review of the freedom of contract principle can be found in Williston, Samuel (1921), 'Freedom of Contract', *Cornell Law Quarterly* 6:4, 365; Kessler, Friedrich (1943), 'Contracts of Adhesion: Some Thoughts about Freedom of Contract', *Columbia Law Review* 43, 620; Kessler, Friedrich, and Fine, Edith (1964), 'Culpa in Contrahendo, Bargaining in Good Faith, and Freedom of Contract: A Comparative Study, *Harvard Law Review* 77:3, 401; Pettit, Mark Jr (1999), 'Freedom, Freedom of Contract, and the "Rise and Fall"', *Boston University Law Review* 79, 263; Movsesian, Mark (2002), 'Two Cheers for Freedom of Contract', *Cardozo Law Review* 23:4, 1529.
27. Article 6 CISG states: 'The parties may exclude the application of this Convention or, subject to Article 12, derogate from or vary the effect of any of its provisions.'
28. Article 1.1 UNIDROIT Principles states: 'The parties are free to enter into a contract and to determine its content.'
29. Article 1:102 PECL states: 'Parties are free to enter into a contract and to determine its contents . . . [and may] exclude the application of any of the Principles or derogate from or vary their effects.'

30. In the DCFR freedom of contract is contained within the principle of freedom, which is one of the four principles underlying the rules found in the DCFR.
31. A review of this topic under English law is provided in Poole, Jill (2008), *Textbook on Contract Law*, Oxford University Press, Chapters 2–5. A detailed review of this topic under the PECL is provided in Commission on European Contract Law (2000), xxx *ff.*
32. Article 3.1.2 UNIDROIT Principles; Commentary accompanying Article 3.2 UNIDROIT Principles (1994); Article 2:101(1) PECL.
33. Commentary accompanying Article 3.2 UNIDROIT Principles (1994).
34. Article 2.1.1 UNIDROIT Principles.
35. Article 2:101(1) PECL.
36. This example is used in Poole (2008), Chapter 2.
37. For a review of this topic under English law, see Poole (2008), Chapter 2.
38. Article 2.1.2 UNIDROIT Principles states: 'A proposal for concluding a contract constitutes an offer if it is sufficiently definite and indicates the intention of the offeror to be bound in the case of acceptance.' Article 2:201(1) PECL states: 'A proposal amounts to an offer if: (a) it is intended to result in a contract if the other party accepts it, and (b) it contains sufficiently definite terms to form a contract.'
39. This topic under English law is reviewed in Poole (2008), Chapter 2.
40. Article 2.1.3 UNIDROIT Principles; Article 1:303 PECL.
41. Ibid.
42. Article 2.1.4 UNIDROIT Principles; Article 2:202 PECL.
43. Ibid.
44. *Byrne & Co.* v. *Van Tienhoven & Co.* (1880) 5 CPD 344; *Henthorn* v. *Fraser* [1892] 2 Ch. 27.
45. Article 2.1.4 UNIDROIT Principles; Article 2:202 PECL.
46. Article 2.1.5 UNIDROIT Principles.
47. Article 2:203 PECL.
48. In line with Article 2.1.5 UNIDROIT Principles and Article 2:203 PECL.
49. This topic is reviewed under English law in Poole (2008), Chapter 2.
50. Article 2.1.6 UNIDROIT Principles; Article 2:204 PECL. A comparison of the treatment of modified acceptance under both the CISG and PECL can be found in Viscasillas, Maria del Pilar Perales (2002), 'Battle of the Forms, Modification of Contract, Commercial Letters of Confirmation: Comparison of the United Nations Convention on Contracts for the International Sale of Goods (CISG) with the Principles of European Contract Law (PECL)', *Pace International Law Review* 14:1, 153.
51. Article 2.1.6(2) UNIDROIT Principles; Articles 1:303(2) and 1:303(6) PECL.
52. Article 2.1.1 UNIDROIT Principles.
53. Article 2:205 PECL.
54. Ibid.
55. Ibid.
56. A review of the content of a contract under the PECL is provided in Commission on European Contract Law (2000), xxxv–xxxvii.

57. Chapter 5 PECL.
58. Article 4.1 UNIDROIT Principles; Article 5:101(1) PECL.
59. Article 4.1(2) UNIDROIT Principles; Article 5:101(3) PECL. The test is phrased somewhat differently under UNIDROIT and the PECL. Pursuant to Article 4.1(2) UNIDROIT Principles the meaning should be the one that a reasonable person of the same kind as the *other party* would give to it in the same circumstances. In contrast, pursuant to Article 5:101(3) PECL, reference is made to the meaning that reasonable persons of the same kind as the *parties* would give to it in the same circumstances. The test under the PECL is arguably wider than that provided under UNIDROIT as it concerns the contracting party, not simply one of the parties. This is especially so in an international setting.
60. Formality requirements under English law are reviewed in Poole (2008: 176–88); a comparative view of this topic is provided in Zweigert, Konrad and Kötz, Hein (1998), *An Introduction to Comparative Law*, 3rd ed., Clarendon Press.
61. Article 1.2 UNIDROIT Principles states: 'Nothing in these Principles requires a contract, statement or any other act to be made in or evidenced by a particular form. It may be proved by any means, including witnesses.' Article 2:101 PECL states: 'A contract need not be concluded or evidenced in writing nor is it subject to any other requirement as to form. The contract may be proved by any means including witnesses.'
62. Implied terms in English law are reviewed in Poole (2008: 229–40).
63. Article 5.1.1 UNIDROIT Principles; Article 6:102 PECL.
64. Article 5.1.2 UNIDROIT Principles; Article 6:102 PECL.
65. Article 1.7 UNIDROIT Principles. The concepts of good faith and fair dealings are reviewed in Berger, Klaus Peter (2000), 'The Relationship between the UNIDROIT Principles of International Commercial Contracts and the New Lex Mercatoria', *Uniform Law Review* (new series) 2000:1, 153. In this article, Professor Berger characterises these twin concepts as 'the Magna Charta of international commercial law'. (Berger 2000: 159).
66. Article 6:102 PECL.
67. Article 5.1.2 UNIDROIT Principles.
68. Professor Berger states (2000: 160) that 'whilst the concept of reasonableness plays a dominant and recurrent role in almost all the UPICC provisions ... [unlike PECL] the UPICC do not contain a blanket clause defining the notion as such'. He refers to the fact that 'the reasonableness test is of particular relevance to all those provisions which require flexible interpretation and application in individual cases. These include provisions relating to: the application of usages and practices (Article 1.8(2)); the time of acceptance in cases where none has been fixed by the offeror (Article 2.7); the interpretation of the contract in cases where no common intention of the parties can be determined (Article 4.1(2)); the determination of the quality of performance which is neither fixed by, nor determinable from, the contract (Article 5.6); the determination of the contract price where the contract does not fix or make provision for determining the price (Article 5.7); the determination of

the time of performance absent an agreement by the parties (Article 6.1.1(c)); "hardship" (Article 6.2.2) and "force majeure" (Article 7.17). In the context of these provisions, the standard of reasonableness frequently takes the place of party agreements, thereby reflecting the drafters' attitude to the existence of a general standard of conduct in transnational contract law' (Berger 2000: 161).

69. Article 1.9 UNIDROIT Principles.
70. Article 5.1.6 UNIDROIT Principles.
71. Article 5.1.7 UNIDROIT Principles.
72. Article 6.1.1 UNIDROIT Principles.
73. Article 6.1.4 UNIDROIT Principles.
74. Article 6.1.6 UNIDROIT Principles.
75. Article 6.1.10 UNIDROIT Principles.
76. Article 6:104 PECL.
77. Article 6:108 PECL.
78. Article 7:101 PECL.
79. Article 7:102(3) PECL.
80. Article 7:108 PECL.
81. Discharge by performance, agreement and breach in English law are reviewed in Poole (2008), Chapter 8.
82. Reviewed in Poole (2008), Chapter 8; Commission on European Contract Law (2000: xxxv–xxxvii).
83. Article 7.1.1 UNIDROIT Principles; Article 1:301 PECL.
84. Article 1:301 PECL.
85. Reviewed in Poole (2008), Chapter 8.
86. Article 7.1.1 UNIDROIT Principles; Article 1:301 PECL (fundamental non-performance is defined in Article 8:103 PECL).
87. Article 1:301 PECL.
88. Article 9:305(1) PECL confirms that termination of the contract has the effect of releasing both parties from their obligation to effect and to receive future performance.
89. In English law, *Decro-wall International SA* v. *Practitioners in Marketing Ltd* [1971].
90. Article 7.1.4 UNIDROIT Principles; Article 8:104 PECL.
91. Ibid.
92. Commentary accompanying Article 7.1.4 UNIDROIT Principles (1994).
93. Article 7.1.4 UNIDROIT Principles.
94. Ibid.
95. Article 7.1.5 UNIDROIT Principles; Article 8:106 PECL.
96. Commentary accompanying Article 7.1.5 UNIDROIT Principles (1994).
97. Article 7.1.5 UNIDROIT Principles; Article 8:106 PECL.
98. Article 7.3.3 UNIDROIT Principles; Article 9:304 PECL.
99. Force majeure clauses are reviewed at Murray, Carole, Holloway, David and Timson-Hunt, Daren (2007), *Schmitthoff's Export Trade: The Law and Practice of International Trade*, 11th ed., Sweet & Maxwell, 6-017–6-021.
100. Article 7.1.7 UNIDROIT Principles; Article 8:108 PECL.

101. Remedies for non-performance under English law are reviewed in Poole (2008), Chapters 9 and 10.
102. Excuse for non-performance is addressed in Article 7.1.7 UNIDROIT Principles and Article 8:108 PECL.
103. The remedies for non-performance are set out in Chapter 7 UNIDROIT Principles and Chapter 9 PECL.
104. Right to performance is addressed in Chapter 7, Section 2 UNIDROIT Principles and Chapter 9, Section 1 PECL.
105. Right to withhold performance is addressed in Article 7.1.3 UNIDROIT Principles as supplemented by Article 6.1.4 UNIDROIT Principles (addressing the order of performance) and Chapter 9, Section 2 PECL.
106. Right to terminate is addressed in Chapter 7, Section 3 UNIDROIT Principles and Chapter 9, Section 3 PECL.
107. Right to a price reduction is addressed in Chapter 9, Section 4 PECL.
108. Right to damages and interest is addressed in Chapter 7, Section 4 UNIDROIT Principles and Chapter 9, Section 5 PECL.
109. Article 7.2.1 UNIDROIT Principles; Article 9:101 PECL.
110. Article 7.2.2 UNIDROIT Principles; Article 9:102 PECL.
111. Article 7.2.1 UNIDROIT Principles; Article 9:101 PECL.
112. Article 7.2.2 UNIDROIT Principles; Article 9:102 PECL.
113. Article 7.3.1(1) UNIDROIT Principles; Article 9:301(1) PECL. Fundamental non-performance is addressed in Article 7.3.1 UNIDROIT Principles and Article 8:103 PECL.
114. Article 7.3.1(2) UNIDROIT Principles; Article 8:103 PECL.
115. Ibid.
116. Article 7.3.2 UNIDROIT Principles; Article 9:303 PECL.
117. Article 7.3.5 UNIDROIT Principles; Article 9:305(1) PECL.
118. Article 7.3.5(2) UNIDROIT Principles.
119. http://www.uncitral.org/uncitral/en/uncitral_texts/sale_goods/1980CISG_status.html (last accessed 17 January 2013).
120. Article 4 CISG states that the CISG governs only the formation of the contract of sale and the rights and obligations of the seller and buyer arising from the contract other matters fall outside the remit of the CISG amongst them validity.
121. *Report of the Working Group on the International Sale of Goods on the Work of Its Ninth Session (Geneva, 19–30 September 1977)* (A/CN.9/142), reproduced in *United Nations Commission on International Trade Law Yearbook 1978*, United Nations (1981), 61, paragraphs 48–51, 66, 69.
122. Article 2 CISG.
123. Article 3(2) CISG.
124. Article 2 CISG.
125. Ibid.
126. Ibid.
127. *Asante Technologies, Inc. v. PMC-Sierra, Inc.*, US District Court [California] 27 July 2001, available online at http://cisgw3.law.pace.edu/cases/010727u1.html (last accessed 31 January 2013).

128. 'California is bound by the Supremacy Clause to the treaties of the United States. U.S. Const. art. VI, cl. 2 ("This Constitution, and the laws of the United States which shall be made in pursuance thereof; and all treaties made, or which shall be made, under the authority of the United States, shall be the supreme law of the land.")' (Ibid., Section IV.A).
129. CLOUT case No. 482 (France Cour de Cassation (Supreme Court) 5 January 1999), available at http://cisgw3.law.pace.edu/cases/990105f1.html (last accessed 31 January 2013).
130. Article 1 CISG.
131. Article 10(a) CISG, as illustrated in *Asante Technologies, Inc. v. PMC-Sierra, Inc.*, US District Court [California] 27 July 2001.
132. Article 3(2) CISG.
133. CLOUT case No. 196 (Switzerland Handelsgericht (Commercial Court) Zurich 26 April 1995), available online at http://cisgw3.law.pace.edu/cases/950426s1.html (last accessed 31 January 2013).
134. Article 14 CISG.
135. Ibid.
136. Article 14(1) CISG.
137. Article. 15(1) CISG.
138. Article 15(2) CISG.
139. Article 16 CISG.
140. Article 16(1) CISG.
141. Ibid.
142. Article 16(2) CISG.
143. Article 17 CISG.
144. Article 17 CISG.
145. Ibid.
146. Example given in Honnold, John O. (1991), *Uniform Law for International Sales under the 1980 United Nations Convention*, Kluwer Law and Taxation, 169–171.
147. Article 18 CISG.
148. Where implied Article 8 CISG may be used to interpret the parties' intention.
149. Article 18.3 CISG.
150. Article 22 CISG.
151. Article 23 CISG.
152. Viscasillas 2002.
153. Article 19(2) CISG.
154. Ibid.
155. Viscasillas 2002: 154.
156. Wording used in Article 19(3) CISG.
157. Wording used in Article 19(3) CISG.
158. Viscasillas 2002: 154.
159. Article 29(1) CISG.
160. These obligations are subject to such derogations or variations introduced in accordance with Article 6 CISG and subject to Article 12 CISG.

161. Articles 38 and 39 CISG.
162. Article 43 CISG.
163. Articles 53–60 CISG.
164. Article 38(1) CISG.
165. Article 39(1) CISG.
166. Ibid.
167. Article 41 CISG.
168. Article 43(1) CISG.
169. Articles 53–60 CISG.
170. Article 55 CISG (determination of price due); Article 57(1) CISG (determination of place of payment); Article 58(1) CISG (determination of time of payment).
171. These obligations are subject to such derogations or variations introduced in accordance with Article 6 CISG and subject to Article 12 CISG.
172. Articles 30–4 CISG.
173. Articles 35–7 and 40 CISG.
174. Articles 41 and 42 CISG.
175. Article 35 CISG.
176. Article 35(1) CISG.
177. Article 35(3) CISG.
178. Article 35(2) CISG.
179. Ibid.
180. Article 29(1) CISG.
181. Article 49 CISG (buyer's right); Article 64 CISG (seller's right).
182. Articles 74–6 CISG.
183. Article 78 CISG.
184. Article 46 CISG (buyer's right); Article 62 CISG (seller's right).
185. Articles 71–73 CISG.
186. Article 37 CISG.
187. Article 48 CISG.
188. Article 63 CISG.
189. Article 50 CISG.
190. Article 47 CISG.
191. Article 25 CISG.
192. Article 29(1) CISG.
193. Article 49 CISG (buyer's right); Article 64 CISG (seller's right).
194. Article 49(1)a CISG (failure by the seller to perform any of his obligations amounts to a fundamental breach of contract); Article 64(1)a CISG (failure by the buyer to perform any of his obligations amounts to a fundamental breach of contract).
195. Article 26 CISG.
196. Article 81(1) CISG.
197. Articles 74–6 CISG.
198. Article 78 CISG.
199. Article 74 CISG.
200. Ibid.

201. Article 77 CISG.
202. Article 77 CISG.
203. Article 46 CISG (buyer's right); Article 62 CISG (seller's right).
204. Article 28 CISG.
205. Ibid.
206. Articles 71–3 CISG.
207. Article 71(3) CISG.
208. Article 71 CISG.
209. Article 71(3) CISG.
210. Article 37 CISG.
211. Article 48 CISG.
212. Article 63 CISG.
213. Article 50 CISG.
214. Article 47 CISG.
215. Beale et al. (2010), Chapter 1.
216. 'Commission Decision of 26 April 2010 Setting Up the Expert Group on a Common Frame of Reference in the Area of European Contract Law' (2010:233/EU OJ L105/109) (Commission Decision), available at http://eur-lex.europa.eu/LexUriServ/LexUriServ.do?uri=OJ:L:2010:105:0109:0111:en:PDF (last accessed 31 January 2013).
217. A review of the composition of this body is provided in Beale et al. (2010), Chapter 1.
218. Article 5 Commission Decision.
219. Preamble, Commission Decision.
220. *Proposal for a Regulation of the European Parliament and of the Council on a Common European Sales Law* (COM(2011) 635 final) (Proposed Regulation), 4.
221. Annex I to the Proposed Regulation contains the CESL.
222. Proposed Regulation, 4.
223. Proposed Regulation, 4, 8.
224. Proposed Regulation, 8.
225. Book E is reviewed in the context of distribution agreements, agency agreements and franchise agreements, in Chapters 4, 5 and 6 respectively of this book.

Index

acceptance
 CISG, 295–6
 content, 296
 effect, 3, 288–9, 296
 UNIDROIT/PECL, 288
 withdrawal, 296
 see also offers
Acquis Group, 300
ad valorem duty, 1, 6
adaptation of contracts
 flexible price terms, 10–11
 force majeure clauses, 10
 modification clauses, 57, 58
 open price terms, 11
 overview, 10–11
 severance clauses, 2, 11, 36, 55, 58
advances, 231, 238
advertising *see* marketing
agency agreements
 acceptance of orders, 205–6
 accounts, 184, 191
 agents and principals, 165
 agents' assumption of responsibility, 167
 agents' concerns, 180, 183–4
 agents' liabilities, 183
 agents' non-contractual activities, 183
 agents' obligations, 183–4, 191, 197–203
 apparent authority, 172, 177–8
 appointment of agents, 171, 176, 187, 193–4
 authority of agents, 170, 172, 175–8, 182, 185, 200–1
 authority restrictions, 200–1, 202, 205
 back of contracts, 192, 215–16
 bank accounts, 201
 body of contracts, 192, 193–215
 boilerplate clauses, 192, 215
 bribery and, 181–2, 184
 brokers, 165, 167–8
 checklist, 191–2
 choice of law, 169–70, 188
 civil v common law, 180
 commercial agents, 165, 168, 186, 190–1
 commission agents, 165, 168
 commissions, 191, 202, 206–8, 215–16
 commodity exchanges, 186
 common types of agents, 167–8
 company officers and, 186
 competition law, 115, 124, 128, 130
 complaint transmission, 197, 198
 confidentiality, 184, 199–200
 conflicts of interests, 184
 consent, 174
 contractual relationships, 124

control over customer base, 122–3
control over goods, 122
control over operations, 121–2
control over pricing, 123
creation of relationship, 171–3
credit risks, 124
Crown Agents for the Overseas Governments and Administrations, 186
currency, 201, 216
DCFR, 125, 189–91
death of agents, 214
definitions, 113, 165, 190–1
definitions clauses, 193
del credere agents, 113, 123, 165, 168, 203, 216
del credere guarantees, 203
designated customers, 216
designated transactions, 216
direct and indirect agency, 180
disclosed agencies, 165, 179, 181
distribution or agency, 120–4
documentation, 187, 204
emergencies, 171–2
employers liability, 24, 174–5
English law, 183
estoppel and, 172
EU law, 169–70, 184–7, 196, 197, 203–15
examples, 167
exclusive agreements, 205
expenses refunds, 205
express appointments, 171, 176
factors, 165, 167–8
fiduciary relationship, 174
financial control, 123–4
financial risk, 124, 130
fixed terms, 190, 195, 196
force majeure, 214, 215
formalities, 186–7
front of contracts, 192–3
general obligations, 196–7
good faith duty, 187, 196, 197, 199, 203–4
implied authority, 171, 176–7
implied clauses, 183
indefinite terms, 190, 195–6
indemnification, 174, 183
independence of agents, 191
indirect transactions, 208
information obligations, 204
initial periods, 195, 196
insolvency of agents, 174, 201
insolvency practitioners and, 186
intellectual property rights, 210–11, 216
international law, 187–91

INDEX

introductory clauses, 193
land transactions, 186
liens, 183, 190
local law compliance, 183, 199
marketing, 181, 198, 209
mercantile agents, 165, 167–8
mixed contracts, 186
monitoring performance of agents, 123
named principals, 179
necessity, 171–2
non-compete clauses, 202
notarisation, 171
notice periods, 195, 196, 214
ostensible authority, 172, 177–8
parties, 4
partners and, 186
payments collection, 201
principals, 165, 166
principals' concerns, 180–3
principals' liability to third parties, 175–8
principals' obligations, 191, 203–10
privity of contract, 120, 121
profits, 124, 184
proper facilities, 197, 198
ratification after the fact, 171, 178
reasons for, 166
recitals, 193
regular market updates, 197, 198
remuneration, 183, 206–8
rights and obligations, 173–4
sale of goods, 186, 200–1
sales forecasts, 209
sales targets, 209–10, 216
samples supply, 204
scenarios, 172–3
schedules, 215–16
secret profits, 184
sources of law, 168–9
standard conditions of sale, 216
statements of terms, 190
term of agreements, 190, 195–6
termination, 124, 175, 208, 211–15
territory, 193, 194, 216
third parties, 165, 166
third parties' concerns, 184
third parties' creditworthiness, 203
three-sided relationship, 166–7
titles of agreements, 192
undisclosed agencies, 165, 179–80, 181
unnamed principals, 179
unpaid agents, 186
vertical integration and, 115
alphabetical-numeration systems, 35, 54–5
alternative dispute resolution (ADR)
 conflict of laws, 38–9
 drafting clauses, 37–8, 55, 60
 forms, 14
 meaning, 2
 obligation to use before litigation, 17
 sample clause, 60
anti-competitive agreements, 128–30
anticipatory breaches, 291, 298, 299
arbitration
 advantages and disadvantages, 15
 appointment of arbiters, 16
 awards, 17
 binding decisions, 15
 challenging awards, 17

choice of law, 41–2
 clauses, 15, 16
 conduct of tribunals, 16–17
 costs, 15
 enforcement of awards, 17
 expert evidence, 17
 hearings, 16
 interim measures, 16
 meaning of arbiter, 35
 numbers of arbiters, 16
 overview, 15–17
 planning, 14
 privacy, 15
 procedures, 15–16
 termination of proceedings, 17
arms, 8
artificial persons, 165
assignment
 assignees, 35
 assignors, 35
 clauses, 56–7
 copyright, 236
 licensing agreements, 272
 meaning, 35, 55
 prohibition and restrictions, 56
 scenarios, 55–6
attachments, 62
auditing
 agency agreements, 215
 distribution agreements, 133, 152
 licensing agreements, 259
avoiding contracts, 298

back of contracts
 agency agreements, 192, 215–16
 distribution agreements, 135, 154
 licensing agreements, 272
 overview, 60–2
 sales agreements, 82, 102
bankruptcy see insolvency
bearer bills of lading, 68, 87
Berne Convention, 235
bilateral trade agreements, 1, 8
bills of lading, 68–9, 86–7
block exemptions, 113, 129–30
body of contracts
 agency agreements, 192, 193–215
 articles and sections, 53–5
 distribution agreements, 134–5, 136–54
 form, 53–5
 licensing agreements, 254–72
 numbering systems, 53–5
 sales agreements, 82, 83–102
boilerplate clauses
 agency agreements, 192, 215
 distribution agreements, 135, 154
 licensing agreements, 272
 meaning, 36, 55
 overview, 55–60
 sales agreements, 82, 102
Bradgate, Robert, 86
branches/subsidiaries
 distribution arrangements, 116
 entry strategy, 25–6
 franchises and, 243
 habitual residence, 42, 169–70
 non-tariff barriers and, 8
brand image, 4, 15, 133–4, 242, 272

313

breach of contract, meaning, 282
bribery, 181–2, 184
Bridge, Michael, 87
brokers, 165, 167–8
Bronfen, George, 246
business, definition, 74

capacity to contract, 4, 5, 36
carriage of goods, allocation of risk, 9
chattels, 69, 71
checklists
　agency agreements, 191–2
　contract clauses, 46–7
　distribution agreements, 134–5
　licensing agreements, 252–3
　sales agreements, 82
chemicals, 142
choice of court
　ADR and, 39
　boilerplate clauses, 55
　drafting clauses, 38, 59
　example, 59
　issue, 13
　meaning, 1
　no express choice, 18, 59–60
choice of law
　absence of choice, 42, 127–8, 169–70, 252
　ADR and, 38–9
　agency agreements, 169–70, 188
　boilerplate clauses, 55
　conflict of law rules, 41–2
　considerations, 13, 18
　distribution agreements, 42, 127–8
　domestic contracts, 39
　EU and non-EU parties, 40
　EU parties, 39–40
　EU rules, 169–70, 251–2
　express choice, 39, 41–2
　freedom to choose, 41–2, 127, 169, 252
　hybrid clauses, 36, 40, 41
　licensing agreements, 251–2
　local law and, 41, 69
　meaning, 2
　mixed contracts, 40
　opting out of CISG, 42–3
　planning, 38, 39–43
　sales agreements, 69–70
Cicero, 235
CIF (cost insurance freight) contracts, 78–81
CISG
　additional time for performance, 298, 299
　allocation of risk, 9
　anticipatory breaches, 298, 299
　avoiding contracts, 298
　binding instrument, 70, 284
　buyers' obligations, 296–7
　counteroffers, 296
　damages, 298, 299
　delivery, 93, 297
　form of contracts, 296
　formation of contracts, 294–6
　freedom of contract, 287
　implied warranties, 9, 37, 95, 297–8
　importance, 37, 187
　mixed contracts, 294
　non-conforming goods, 297
　offers, 294
　open price terms, 11

　opting out of, 42–3, 60, 293
　origins, 284, 293
　overview, 293–9
　packaging, 298
　payment obligations, 297
　price reduction, 298, 299
　ratifications, 293
　remedies, 298–9
　right to cure, 298
　right to performance, 299
　risk transfer, 81
　scope, 40, 41, 70, 284, 285, 293–4
　sellers' obligations, 297–8
　specific performance, 298, 299
　termination of contracts, 298
　third party claims, 297
　United Kingdom and, 70
claimants, meaning, 2
class actions, 2, 19
commercial agents *see* agency
commercial organisations, meaning, 181
commission agents, 113, 120–1, 165, 168
Commission on European Contract Law (Lando
　　Committee), 284, 285, 299–300
commissions, agency agreements, 191, 202, 206–8, 215–16
Common Custom Tariffs, 2, 6
Common European Sales Law (CESL), 300
common nouns, 36, 52
compensatory damages, meaning, 2, 20
competition law
　anti-competitive agreements, 128–30
　block exemptions, 113, 129–30
　commercial agents and, 115, 124, 128
　distribution agreements and, 120, 124, 128–30, 149
　licensing agreements and, 248, 250, 257–8, 262
　price fixing, 128, 149, 251, 257
　vertical integration and, 114
conciliation, 14–15, 18
concluding clauses, 60
confidentiality
　agency agreements, 184, 199–200
　distribution agreements, 125, 132, 154
　licensing agreements, 248, 258, 263–4, 269–70
　sales agreements, 102
conflict of laws
　drafting clauses, 38–43
　EU rules, 41–2
　meaning, 36, 68
　sales agreements, 69–70
　see also choice of court; choice of law
conflicts of interests, 184, 232
construction industry, 10
consultations, 10
cooling-off period, 37
copyright
　assignment, 236
　Berne Convention, 235
　development, 235–6
　duration, 236
　economic importance, 232
　English law, 235, 236
　exclusive rights, 236
　infringement, 236
　licensing agreements, 241
　ownership of objects and, 235
　US law, 236, 237
corporations
　agency scenarios, 172–3

INDEX

authority to contract, 4
habitual residence, 42, 127–8, 252
juristic persons, 165
names in front of contracts, 51–2
as parties, 4
signatures, 61
cost insurance freight (CIF) contracts, 78–81
counteroffers, 282, 288, 296
countries of export, 2
countries of importation, 2
cover sheets, 47
criminal offences
    corporate liability, 24
    cybercrime, 21
    illegal contracts and, 4
    torts and, 20–1
crops, 69, 71
Crown Agents for the Overseas Governments and Administrations, 186
cultural artefacts, 8
cure, right to, 283, 290–1, 298
currency
    agency agreements, 201, 216
    distribution agreements, 139
    export controls, 8
    licensing agreements, 260
    politics, 5
    sales agreements, 83, 84, 85, 88
    UNIDROIT/PECL, 289–90
customs duties *see* tariffs
customs formalities, 7, 91, 148
cybercrime, 21

damages
    agency agreements, 212–15
    categories, 20
    CISG, 298, 299
    compensatory damages, 2, 20
    meaning, 2
    non-performance, 292
dates of agreements, 49–50
dates of delivery, 90
DCFR *see* Draft Common Frame of Reference
death/personal injuries
    dangerous driving, 20
    distribution agreements, 141
    meaning, 74
    negligence liability, 73, 95
    product liability, 22, 24
    tort claims, 19
defendants, meaning, 2
definitions clauses
    advantages, 43–4
    agency agreements, 193
    clarity, 51–2
    distribution agreements, 136
    example, 44
    flagging, 44, 51
    importance, 55
    inclusive and exclusive definitions, 44
    indexes, 48
    licensing agreements, 254
    open and closed definitions, 44
    sales agreements, 83
del credere agents, 113, 123, 165, 168, 203, 216
delivery
    CISG, 93, 297
    dates, 90

    delay, 93–4
    distribution agreements, 140
    location, 90
    non-delivery, 93
    sales agreements, 90, 93–4
description of goods, 72, 84, 136
directors
    agents, 167, 171, 172–3, 177
    authority to contract, 4
    criminal liability, 24
discharge of contracts
    breaches, 290
    discharge by performance, 282–3, 290
    non-performance, 290–2
    UNIDROIT/PECL, 290–2
discretion, 45–6
dispute resolution
    considerations, 9–10, 37–9
    devices, 14
    issues, 13
    overview, 12–18
distribution agreements
    accounts, 152–3
    after-sale services, 132
    assignment scenarios, 56
    back of contracts, 135, 154
    block exemptions, 113, 129–30
    body of contracts, 134–5, 136–54
    boilerplate clauses, 135, 154
    branches/subsidiaries, 116
    brand image, 133–4, 146
    checklist of clauses, 134–5
    choice of law, 42, 127–8
    commission on sales, 133
    competition law and, 113, 120, 124, 128–30, 149
    confidentiality, 125, 132, 154
    contingencies, 154
    contractual relationships, 124
    control over customer base, 122–3
    control over goods, 122
    control over operations, 121–2
    control over pricing, 123
    copying prohibition, 148–9
    costs and charges, 140, 145
    credit risks, 124
    customs charges, 141
    customs formalities, 148
    DCFR, 125–7, 189–90
    definite terms, 125–6
    definitions clauses, 136
    delivery, 140, 149
    description of goods, 136
    direct and indirect channels, 116
    distribution or agency, 120–4
    distribution or sales agreements, 119–20
    distributors' concerns, 130–1
    distributors' obligations, 145–9
    divisibility of orders, 139–40
    documentation, 152
    due diligence, 145, 147
    English law, 124
    financial control, 123–4
    fixed or indefinite periods, 139
    force majeure, 154
    franchises or distribution, 119
    front of contracts, 134, 135–6
    full line forcing, 147
    hybrid system, 116

distribution agreements (*continued*)
  improvement of goods, 150
  indefinite terms, 127, 139
  indemnities, 141, 145, 149
  independence of parties, 120–2
  initial fixed sums, 133
  initial periods, 138, 139
  intellectual property rights, 120, 127, 133–4, 140, 143–4
  introductory clauses, 135, 136
  invoicing, 140
  liabilities, 141, 145
  licensing of IPRs, 143–4
  liens, 126
  local law compliance, 132, 142, 145, 146, 147
  marketing, 117, 131, 133, 145, 150–2, 154
  modification of goods, 150
  monitoring performance, 123
  non-compete clauses, 146, 148
  packaging, 145
  parallel imports, 132
  parties' relationship, 137–8
  payment, 133, 139
  performance, 140
  permissions and consents, 141–2
  policies, 153
  preface, 134
  price of goods, 136
  principal/distributor relationship, 115–16, 118–20
  principals' concerns, 131–4
  principals' obligations, 149–50
  privity of contract and, 120, 121
  profits, 124
  quality control, 133–4
  quantity of goods, 136
  re-export restrictions, 140
  recitals, 135, 136
  registration, 142
  retail pricing, 149
  retail units, 146–7
  sales agreements and, 118–19, 134
  schedules, 154
  single channels, 116
  sole suppliers, 149
  statements of terms, 126
  stocking obligations, 131, 145, 147
  storing arrangements, 145, 148
  strategic alliances, 116
  strategies, 116–18
  targets, 145, 148
  term of agreements, 120, 125–6, 127, 138–9
  termination, 117–18, 124, 133, 134, 142, 153–4
  territory, 120, 131, 133, 136, 137, 148
  title to goods, 122
  titles, 135, 136
  trade marks, 133–4, 140, 143–4, 145, 146
  training, 117, 119, 120, 131, 133, 151
  transfer of risk, 118
  verification, 152–3
  vertical integration, 113–15
  warranties, 140–1
documents
  against payment, 68, 85–7
  agency agreements, 187, 204
  customs, 91
  distribution agreements, 152
  sales agreements, 85–7, 91, 93
domestic law *see* local law
doorstep selling, 36–7

Draft Common Frame of Reference (DCFR)
  agency agreements, 189–91
  choice of law, 39
  commercial agents, 125
  confidential information, 125
  contents, 125, 189, 300
  definite terms, 125–6
  distribution agreements, 125, 126–7, 189–90
  duties of parties, 125
  franchises, 125, 189–90, 244–5
  freedom of contract, 287
  general provisions, 125, 189–90
  indefinite terms, 126
  liens, 126, 190
  origins, 189, 299–300
  overview, 125–7
  PECL and, 189
  scope, 125, 189, 300
  soft law, 284
drafting contracts, meaning, 2

electrical goods, 142, 242
electrical industry, 240
electrical standards, 7
electricity, 24, 293
emblements, 69, 71
emergencies, 171–2
employers liability, 24, 174–5
encumbrances, 71
endangered species, 8
enforcement proceedings, 2, 13, 17, 38
entire agreement clauses, 36, 57
entry strategies, 25–6
environmental protection, 5, 7
estate agents, 167
estoppel, 165, 172
European companies *(societas Europaea)*, 116
European economic interest groupings (EEIGs), 116
European Union
  agency agreements, 169–70, 184–7, 196, 197, 203–15
  anti-competitive agreements, 113, 129–30
  block exemptions, 113, 129–30
  Common Custom Tariffs, 2, 6
  conflict of laws rules, 39–42, 69, 127–8, 169–70, 251–2
  Draft Common Frame of Reference (DCFR), 39, 125–7
  harmonisation of laws, 283–4
  international commercial agreements and, 286
  notices, meaning, 113, 130
  notices on vertical agreements, 130
  packaging, 142
  product liability, 23–4
ex-works contracts (EXW), 76
execution in counterparts, 55, 59
exhibits, 62
expert evidence, 17, 20
Expert Group on a Common Frame of Reference, 300
export barriers, 2, 5, 8
export controls, 8
extra-judicial parties, 2
extrinsic evidence, 57

factors, 165, 167–8
false statements, 21
fast food chains, 115, 243
fiduciary relationships, 121, 174
financial control, agents and distributors, 123–4
financial risk
  allocation of risk, CISG, 9

INDEX   317

anti-competitive agreements and, 130
carriage of goods, 9
credit risks, 124
definition, 130
transfer of risk, 75–8, 80–1, 92–3, 118
fitness for purpose, 71, 72
flexible price terms, 2, 10–11, 11
FOB (free on board) contracts, 76–8
force majeure, 2, 10, 101–2, 154, 214, 215, 283, 291
foreign investment, 25, 26
foreign judgments, enforcement, 38
formation of contracts
 CISG, 294–6
 offer and acceptance, 3–4, 287–8
 time, 288–9, 296
 UNIDROIT/PECL, 287–9
forum shopping, 18
France, 184, 235
franchises
 accounts, 245
 branches and, 243
 categories, 242
 characteristics, 242–3
 choice of law, 42
 DCFR, 125, 189–90, 244–5
 distribution franchises, 115
 distribution or franchises, 119
 fixed-terms, 245
 franchisees, meaning, 231
 franchisors, meaning, 231, 242
 indefinite terms, 245
 intellectual property rights, 114–15, 242, 245
 meaning, 231, 241
 origins, 241–2
 overview, 241–5
 production franchises, 114–15
 regulation, 242, 250–1
 royalties, 243, 244
 statements of terms, 245
 total business franchises, 243–4
 trade marks, 114–15, 242
 training, 115, 242, 243, 244, 245
free on board (FOB) contracts, 76–8
free trade, 8
freedom of contract
 41–2, 127, 169, 252, 8
 international law, 287
 meaning, 36–7, 283
 restrictions, 36–7, 286
front of contracts
 agency agreements, 192–3
 date of agreements, 49–50
 defined terms, 51–2
 distribution agreements, 134, 135–6
 introductory clauses, 48, 49–50
 licensing agreements, 253–4
 overview, 48–53
 parties, 49, 50–2
 recitals, 48, 52–3
 sales agreements, 82, 83
 titles, 48, 49
full line forcing, 147

GATS, 8
GATT, 6, 8
Gerhard, Frederick, 231
Germany, 184, 235
good faith

agency agreements, 168, 187, 196, 197, 199, 203–4
estoppel and, 172
implied terms and, 289
meetings, 10, 11, 12, 101
Goode, R. M., 86
governing law see choice of law
grant-back clauses, 231, 257, 258, 266
grey market see parallel imports

habitual residence, 42, 127–8, 169–70, 252
Hague Uniform Laws on International Sale of Goods, 105n, 284
Hellenic law, 180
horizontal agreements, 113, 128

ICC
 Incoterms, 70, 75, 92
 model contracts, 70, 283
 Model International Sale Contract, 94, 95–6, 188, 191, 210
 UCP, 88
illegal contracts, 4, 11, 37
implied terms
 agency agreements, 183
 CISG, 9, 37, 95, 297–8
 exclusion, 37, 72–3
 meaning, 8, 69, 283
 overview, 8–9
 PECL, 8, 289–90
 sale of goods, 9, 37, 71–2, 289–90, 297–8
 UNIDROIT Principles, 8, 289–90
 warranties, 9, 37, 95, 140, 141, 283, 297
import barriers, 2, 5, 6
Incoterms, 70, 75, 92
indexes, 47, 48
individuals see natural persons
industrial diseases, 24
insolvency
 agency and insolvency officials, 186
 agents' insolvency, 174, 201
 anticipatory non-performance, 291, 299
 conciliation, 14–15
 licensing agreements, 271, 272
 sales agreements, 98
 termination of contracts, 54, 98, 211, 271, 272
insurance, 91, 92
integration clauses, 36, 57
intellectual property rights
 actors' concerns, 232–3
 agency agreements, 210–11
 categories, 233–7
 characteristics, 233
 consumers' concerns, 233
 copyright see copyright
 definition, 231–2
 distribution agreements and, 120, 127, 140, 143–4
 divisibility, 233
 dynamism, 233
 franchises, 114–15, 242, 245
 geographical boundaries, 233
 independent categories, 233
 inventors' concerns, 232
 licensing see licensing agreements
 patents see patents
 producers' concerns, 232
 role, 232
 sales agreements, 96–7
 trade marks see trade marks

INDEX

intentional torts, 2, 21
International Chamber of Commerce *see* ICC
international distribution agreements *see* distribution agreements
international law
  agency, 187–91
  binding instruments, 286
  harmonising contract law, 37, 283–4
  model laws, 283
  private international law *see* conflict of laws
  sales agreements, 70
  soft law, 284–92
  see also European Union
international licensing agreements *see* licensing agreements
international sales agreements *see* sales agreements
interpretation of terms, UNIDROIT/PECL, 289
introductory clauses
  agency agreements, 193
  distribution agreements, 135, 136
  drafting, 48, 49–50
  licensing agreements, 253, 254
  sales agreements, 83
invoicing
  distribution agreements, 140
  sales agreements, 94
Ireland, 184
irrevocable letters of credit, 69, 87, 88
Italy, 184
ivory, 8

John of Speyer, 235
Johnson, Howard, 242
jurisdiction, meaning, 2
juristic persons, meaning, 165, 166

land transactions, 186
Lando Committee (Commission on European Contract Law), 284, 285, 299–300
language of contracts
  active voice, 44, 45
  consistency, 44
  discretion, 45–6
  language clauses, 55, 58–9
  obligations, 45
  overview, 44–6
  passive voice, 45
  performance, 44–5
  plain English, 44
  present tense, 44, 45
  prohibitions, 46
League of Nations, 285
legalese, 44
legally enforceable contracts, 283, 286
letters of credit
  fees, 88
  irrevocable, 69, 87, 88
  meaning, 69, 87–8
  method of payment, 85
  payment method, 87–8
  revocable, 69, 88
  Uniform Customs and Practice for Documentary Credits (UCP), 88
lex mercatoria, 284
licensing agreements
  accounts, 260
  advances, 238
  agency agreements and licensing, 210–11
  artistic licensing, 239

assignment, 272
back of contracts, 272
body of contracts, 254–72
boilerplate clauses, 272
capital, 246, 251
categories, 239
checklist of clauses, 252–3
choice of law, 251–2
commercial licensing, 239
competition law and, 248, 250, 257–8, 262
confidentiality clauses, 248, 258, 263–4, 269–70
consideration, 238–9
copyright *see* copyright
definitions clauses, 254
distribution agreements and licensing, 143–4
entry strategy, 25, 26
export restrictions, 257
finding licensees, 238
fixed terms, 257
format, 238–9
franchises *see* franchises
front of contracts, 253–4
grant-back clauses, 257, 258
grants, 254–5
guaranteed annual minimum payments, 261–2
improvements, 265–6, 267, 268
indefinite terms, 256–7
indemnities, 270
initial sums, 259
introductory clauses, 253, 254
IPR restrictions, 251
licensees' benefits, 246–7
licensees' concerns, 251
licensees' obligations, 257–66
licensors' concerns, 237–8
maintenance of licensed property, 265
marketing, 247–8
monetary consideration, 238–9
new goods, 266, 267, 268–9
non-compete clauses, 248, 257–8, 262, 266–7
non-monetary consideration, 238
parallel imports, 248
patents, 233, 239–40
payments, 258–62
principals' benefits, 246
principals' concerns, 247–51
principals' obligations, 266–70
protection of IPRs, 249
quality control, 249, 258, 264
recitals, 253, 254
regulation, 250–1, 257–8
relationship of parties, 257
restrictions on use of licensed property, 265
retention of title, 264
role, 237–8
royalties, 231, 232, 239, 258, 259, 260–1
sales agreements and licensing, 96–7
samples, 249, 258, 264
schedules, 272
sublicensing, 249, 262
support services, 267–8
technical licensing, 239
term of agreements, 238, 256–7
termination, 270–2
territory, 247, 248, 255–6, 258
titles, 253
trade marks *see* trade marks
training, 241, 242, 246, 247, 249, 254, 267, 268, 271

transfer of technology, 237, 239, 241, 253, 254, 259, 266, 272
unauthorised use of licensed property, 248–9
vertical integration and, 115
warranties, 270
liens, 126, 183, 190
liquidation *see* insolvency
liquidators, 186
litigation
  advantages, 18
  choice, 14
  clauses, 18
  drafting clauses, 38
  enforcement proceedings, 3, 13, 17, 38
  last resort, 17–18
  obligation to use out-of court settlement clauses before, 17
  overview, 17–18
  pre-empting potential disputes, 38–9
Llewellyn, Karl, 79
local law
  agency and, 183, 199
  applicability, 26
  choice of law and, 41, 69
  distribution agreements and, 132, 142, 145, 146, 147
  researching, 18–25, 37
  torts, 19–22
  trade marks, 144

marketing
  agency agreements, 181, 198, 209
  distribution agreements, 117, 131, 133, 150–2, 154
  franchises, 115
  licensing agreements, 247–8
marketing consultants, 114
mediation, 14, 18, 60
mental health, capacity to contract, 5
mercantile agents, 165, 167–8
merger clauses, 36, 55, 57
minors, capacity to contract, 5
missing terms, 43
mixed charges, meaning, 2, 6
mixed contracts, 40, 186, 294
modification clauses, 57, 58
multilateral trade agreements, 2, 8
multiple-numeration systems, 36, 53–5

NAFTA, 8
names of parties, 51–2
natural persons
  agency, 166
  habitual residence, 42, 128, 252
  meaning, 165
  as parties, 4
  signatures, 61
negligence
  agency agreements, 200
  distribution agreements, 141, 145
  examples, 22
  meaning, 2, 21, 74
  medical negligence, 20
  negligent advice, 20
  torts, 19, 21–2
  unfair contract terms and, 73, 74
non-compete clauses
  agency agreements, 202
  distribution agreements, 146
  licensing agreements, 248, 257–8, 262, 266–7
non-conforming goods, 69, 95–6, 283, 297

non-performance *see* performance
non-tariff barriers, 2, 3, 6, 7–8
notarisation, 36, 62, 165, 171, 186
notice clauses
  agency agreements, 195, 196, 214
  drafitng, 55, 59
  UNIDROIT/PECL, 292
nuclear material, 8
numbering terms, 53–5

offers
  becoming effective, 288
  CISG, 294–5
  example, 4
  formation of contracts, 3–4
  offerees, 283, 288
  offerors, 283
  rejection, 288
  UNIDROIT/PECL, 287–8
  withdrawal, 288, 294–5
  see also acceptance
oil prices, 11
open price terms, 2, 11
order bills of lading, 69, 87
out-of-court settlements *see* alternative dispute resolution

packaging, 93, 142, 298
parallel imports, 113, 132, 248
Parsons, Theophilus, 218n
parties
  authority to contract, 4
  capacity, 4, 5, 36
  categories, 4
  defined terms, 51–2
  front of contracts, 49, 50–2
  legal entities, 4, 50–1
  names, 51–2
  PECL/UNIDROIT, 286–7
patents, 233, 234, 239–40
payment
  agents' commissions, 191, 201, 202, 206–8, 215–16
  CISG, 297
  costs and charges, 89–90, 140
  currency *see* currency
  distribution agreements, 139–40
  documents against payment, 68, 85–7
  letters of credit, 69, 85, 87–8
  licensing agreements, 258–62
  methods, 85–9
  sales agreements, 85–90, 100
PECL *see* Principles of European Contract Law
penalty clauses, 283, 284
performance
  additional time, 291, 298, 299
  anticipatory non-performance, 291, 299
  CISG, 298–9
  distribution agreements, 140
  language, 44–5
  non-performance, 290–2
  remedies for non-performance, 291–2
  right to performance, 292
  right to withhold, 292
  sales agreements, 97
  specific performance, 283, 292, 298, 299
  time of the essence, 97
  UNIDROIT/PECL, 290–2
personal chattels, 69, 71
personal injuries *see* death/personal injuries

pharmaceuticals, 15, 142, 242
photocopying services, 115
Plain English, 44
plaintiffs, meaning, 2
Pliny, 235
Pollzien, Götz, 246
powers of attorney, 171
price fixing, 128, 149, 251, 257
price of goods, 84
price reduction, 292, 298, 299
principals, meaning, 113, 165, 166
Principles of European Contract Law (PECL)
   agency agreements, 188
   breach of contract, 290
   DCFR and, 189
   discharge of contracts, 290–2
   force majeure, 291
   form of contracts, 289
   formation of contracts, 287–9
   freedom of contract, 287
   harmonising contract law, 37
   implied terms, 8, 289–90
   interpretation of terms, 289
   objectives, 284–5
   open price terms, 11
   origins, 285–6
   overview, 286–92
   parties, 286–7
   remedies, 291–2
   scope, 284, 286
   soft law, 70, 127, 188, 251–2, 284
printing services, 115
private international law *see* conflict of laws
privity of contract, 113, 120, 121, 165, 168, 173
procurement policies, 7
product disparagement, 21
product liability, 22–4, 121
products, definition, 125
prohibitions, language, 46
promoting *see* marketing
public morality and order, 36
punitive damages, 2, 20

quantitative restrictions, 2, 7
quantity of goods, 84
quotas, 7

re-export restrictions, 94, 140
receivers, 54, 98, 186, 211
recitals
   agency agreements, 193
   distribution agreements, 135, 136
   drafting, 36, 48, 52–3
   licensing agreements, 253, 254
   sales agreements, 82, 83
regional trade agreements, 8
registered user agreements, 96, 143, 144, 231, 241
renegotiation of terms, 11–12
requirement of writing, 3, 289
Research Group on EC Private Law (Acquis Group), 300
retention of title, 89, 264
revocable letters of credit, 69, 88
right to cure, 283, 290–1, 298
risk *see* financial risk; transfer of risk
Roman law, 180
royalties
   franchises, 243, 244
   inventors' concerns, 232

licensing agreements, 239, 258, 259, 260–1
meaning, 231

sales agreements
   1979 Act, 71–3
   agency agreements and, 186, 200–1
   backs of contracts, 102
   body of contracts, 83–102
   boilerplate clauses, 82, 102
   checklist of clauses, 82
   choice of law, 69–70
   CISG *see* CISG
   confidentiality, 102
   conflict of laws, 42, 69–70
   contingencies, 101
   costs and charges, 89–90
   definitions clauses, 83
   delayed delivery, 93–4
   delivery arrangements, 90–4
   description of goods, 72, 84
   distribution agreements and, 118–20, 134
   documents against payments, 68, 86–7
   English law, 70–4
   exclusion of implied terms, 72–4
   fitness for purpose, 72, 298
   force majeure, 101
   front of contracts, 82, 83
   implied terms, 9, 37, 71–2, 289–90, 297–8
   indemnities, 96
   insurance, 91, 92
   intellectual property rights, 96–7
   international law, 70
   introductory clauses, 83
   invoicing, 94
   licensing, 96–7
   mixed contracts, 40, 294
   non-conforming goods, 95–6
   non-delivery, 93–4
   packaging, 93
   payment, 85–9
   performance, 97
   price of goods, 84
   quantity of goods, 84
   re-export restrictions, 94
   retention of title, 89
   satisfactory quality, 72, 298
   termination, 97–102
   time of the essence, 97
   title to goods, 71, 73, 92
   titles, 83
   trade terms, 75–81, 90, 91, 92
   transfer of risk, 76–8, 80–1, 92–3
   transfer of title, 92–3
   unfair contract terms, 73–4
   warnings on goods, 24
   warranties, 94–5
sanitary measures, 7
schedules
   agency agreements, 215–16
   distribution agreements, 154
   drafting, 62
   licensing agreements, 272
   sales agreements, 102
Scotland
   things in action, 71
   unfair contract terms, 74
services, choice of law, 42
severance clauses, 2, 11, 36, 55, 58

INDEX

shipping terms, 69, 75
showrooms, 114
signature blocks, 60–2
Singer Sewing Machine Company, 242
societas Europaea (European companies), 116
soft law, 284–92
specific duties, meaning, 2, 6
specific performance, 283, 292, 298, 299
straight bills of lading, 69, 86–7
strict liability, 3, 19, 22–3
structure of contracts, 47–8
Study Group on the European Civil Code, 125, 189, 244, 300
subject matter, 4
sublicensing, licensing agreements, 249, 262
subsections, 53–4
successor liability, 24
supply of services, choice of law, 42

table of contents, 47
tariffs, 2, 3, 6, 141
taxation, 25, 85, 90, 141, 215, 216, 265
technical regulations, 7
term of agreements
 agency agreements, 190, 195–6
 DCFR, 125–6
 distribution agreements, 120, 125–6, 138–9
 franchises, 245
 licensing agreements, 238, 256–7
 meaning, 36
termination of contracts
 agency agreements, 124, 175, 208, 211–15
 agents v distributors, 124
 CISG, 298
 contingencies, 101–2
 distribution agreements, 117–18, 124, 133, 134, 142, 153–4
 force majeure, 2, 10, 101–2, 154, 214, 215, 283, 291
 licensing agreements, 270–2
 non-performance, 117–18, 292
 notices, 55, 59, 195, 196, 214, 292
 right to terminate, 292
 sales agreements, 97–102
 UNIDROIT/PECL, 292
territory
 agency agreements, 193, 194, 216
 distribution agreements, 120, 131, 133, 136, 137, 148
 licensing agreements, 247, 248, 255–6, 258
things in action, 69, 71
time
 additional time for performance, 291, 298, 299
 formation of contracts, 288–9, 296
 time of the essence, 97
 see also term of agreements
title to goods
 distribution agreements, 122
 licensing agreements, 270
 sales agreements, 71, 73, 92
 transfer of title, 92–3
titles of agreements
 agency agreements, 192
 distribution agreements, 135, 136
 drafting, 48, 49
 licensing agreements, 253
 sales agreements, 83
tortfeasors, 3, 19
torts, 3, 19–22
trade barriers, 2, 3, 5–8

trade in goods *see* sales agreements
trade liberalisation, 8
trade marks
 agency agreements, 210–11, 216
 benefits of licensing, 247
 definition, 234–5
 distribution agreements, 133–4, 140, 143–4, 145, 146
 English law, 235
 franchises, 114–15, 242
 licensing agreements, 240–1, 264, 265
 registered user agreements, 96, 143, 144, 231, 241
 registration, 144, 235
 sales agreements, 96–7
 schedules, 216
 US law, 234–5
 user agreements, 231, 241
 warranties, 94, 140
trade terms
 CIF contracts, 78–81
 clauses, 90, 91, 92
 English law, 76–81
 ex-works contracts (EXW), 76
 FOB contracts, 76–8
 Incoterms, 70, 75, 92
 sales agreements, 75–81
 standard terms, 75
training
 distribution agreements, 117, 119, 120, 131, 133, 151
 franchises, 115, 242, 243, 244, 245
 licensing agreements, 241, 242, 246, 247, 249, 254, 267, 268, 271
transfer of risk
 distribution agreements, 118
 sales agreements, 75–8, 80–1, 92–3
transfer of technology, 237, 239, 241, 253, 254, 259, 266, 272
transfer of title, 92–3
transport, sales agreements, 91
trespass on land, 19, 21
trustees in bankruptcy, 186, 272

UNCITRAL
 CISG *see* CISG
 harmonising contract law, 26, 37, 70
 model rules, 16
 objective, 286, 303n
 origins, 286
 penalty clauses, 303n
unfair contract terms, 73–4
UNIDROIT Principles
 agency agreements, 188, 189
 breach of contract, 290
 discharge of contracts, 290–2
 force majeure, 291
 form of contracts, 289
 formation of contracts, 287–9
 freedom of contract, 287
 harmonising contract law, 37
 implied terms, 8, 289–90
 interpretation of terms, 289
 objectives, 284–5
 open price terms, 11
 overview, 286–92
 parties, 286–7
 remedies, 291–2
 scope, 284, 285
 soft law, 70, 188, 284
 success, 285

Uniform Customs and Practice for Documentary Credits (UCP), 88
United Nations Convention for the International Sale of Goods *see* CISG
United States
  agency law, 183
  copyright, 232, 236, 237
  franchises, 241–2, 242–3
  licensing, 246
  open price terms, 11
  patents, 234
  product liability, 23
  trade marks, 234–5
  trade terms, 75
user agreements, 231, 241

vague terms, 43, 52
Venice, 235
vertical agreements
  anti-competitive agreements, 128
  block exemptions, 129–30
  meaning, 113, 160n
vertical integration
  benefits, 113–14
  competition law and, 114
  disadvantages, 114
  distribution, 113–15
  economies, 113–14
  expertise, 114
  supply chain levels, 114–15
void contracts
  anti-competitive agreements, 128–9, 130
  meaning, 3
voidable contracts, 3, 5
volume discounts, 116–17

warehousing, 131
warnings on goods, 24
warranties
  CISG, 9, 37, 95, 297–8
  distribution agreements, 140–1
  express warranties, 283, 297
  implied warranties, 9, 37, 95, 140, 141, 283, 297
  licensing agreements, 270
  meaning, 283
  sales agreements, 94–5
  trade marks, 94, 140
witnesses, signature blocks, 60, 62
World Trade Organization (WTO), 6, 8, 26
written contracts, 3, 289
wrongful interference with contracts, 21

zipper clauses, 36, 57